Writing Paragraphs and Essays

FIRST CANADIAN EDITION

Joy Wingersky

Jan Boerner

Diana Holguin-Balogh

Enid Gossin

Susan Stancer

Nelson Canada

I⊤P An International Thomson Publishing Company

Toronto • Albany • Bonn • Boston • Cincinnati • Detroit • London • Madrid • Melbourne
Mexico City • New York • Pacific Grove • Paris • San Francisco • Singapore • Tokyo • Washington

I(T)P⁻
International Thomson Publishing
The ITP logo is a trademark under licence

© Nelson Canada
A division of Thomson Canada Limited, 1995

Published in 1995 by
Nelson Canada
A division of Thomson Canada Limited
1120 Birchmount Road
Scarborough, Ontario M1K 5G4

Canadian Cataloguing in Publication Data
Main entry under title:
    Writing Paragraphs and Essays

1st Canadian Edition
Includes index.
ISBN 0-17-604848-0

1. English language – Rhetoric. 2. English language – Grammar. 3. College readers.
I. Wingersky, Joy.

PE1408.W75 1995   808'.042   C94-932874-X

Acquisitions Editor   Andrew Livingston
Developmental Editor   Joanne Scattolon
Art Director   Liz Harasymczuk
Cover and Interior Design   Kevin Connolly
Composition Analyst   Frank Zsigo
Input Operators   Elaine Andrews and Michelle Volk
Senior Production Coordinator   Sheryl Emery

Printed and bound in Canada

1 2 3 4 (WC) 99 98 97 96

The pages in this book open easily and lie flat, a result of the Otabind bookbinding process. Otabind combines advanced adhesive technology and a free-floating cover to achieve books that last longer and are bound to stay open.

Bound to stay open

Table of Contents

Unit 7   Making Ideas Flow Clearly

Unit 8   Composing with Effective Alternate Patterns   289

Preface to the Instructor

In *Writing Paragraphs and Essays*, we integrate reading, writing, and grammar skills to teach students to write well. We use reading to help students generate ideas and to serve as strong models for their writing. We use extensive writing instruction with many suggested writing assignments. The section titled "Something to Think About, Something to Write About" in Units 2–8 includes writing assignments that are based on the reading in each of these sections. We also include material on the grammar skills necessary for students to write effective paragraphs and essays. Students learn to integrate this material and to generate effective paragraphs and essays.

We have written a simple yet challenging text that students can understand and can assimilate with the guidance of their instructors. We separate each step of the writing process into thinking skills needed by students as they work toward becoming successful writers. In this way, students gain confidence because they find success in doing simple steps correctly, and ultimately they have a better chance of succeeding in more complex writing assignments.

At the same time, the book is thorough because we do not wish to present a developmental book with too little information that leaves a gap between the material covered in a lower-level course and the material covered in a college-level composition book. Instead, we bridge the gap for developing writers by presenting all of the skills necessary for mastering both paragraphs and short essays complete with effective introductions, support paragraphs, and strong conclusions. We then show the students how they can apply these skills to more complicated essays.

Our motivation in writing this book was to provide students and teachers with a text that

- integrates reading, writing, and grammar skills

- is self-contained because it
  explains the writing process clearly yet simply
  includes grammatical concepts aimed at improving writing skills
  includes writing by students and professionals to illustrate the concepts taught throughout the book

- contains selections by professionals for generating ideas for writing

- discusses rhetorical modes

We have found the book to be understandable and appealing to students with diverse backgrounds. We wrote with simple diction so that students coming from diverse backgrounds can understand the concepts presented in the text. Likewise, we used explanations that are intended to be encouraging and motivating. The text has been extensively class tested and revised to make it as advantageous for instruction as possible.

Each unit, particularly in the writing section, models the thinking processes that students must practise to accomplish particular tasks. Each unit also provides exercises that require the students to think through and master the concepts taught in that unit.

Features of the Book

Self-Contained Text

Students can buy only one textbook and still have access to the writing, reading, and grammar concepts normally found in a combination of texts. Instructors have access to a full range of teaching concepts and may choose to use whichever they feel are most important for their own course needs.

The logical progression of the text facilitates instruction in an integrated approach. The book starts with simple writing, reading, and grammar concepts and progresses to more sophisticated modes of writing.

Step-by-Step Approach

The information on writing process is presented in a clear step-by-step approach that builds confidence as students see how the individual writing steps fit together to create a coherent paragraph or essay. This text focuses on the development of the paragraph and short essay by helping students generate and support one main idea. Students concentrate on topic sentences with support and on thesis sentences with support so that they can transfer these skills to more sophisticated strategies, either in this developmental course or in other college-level composition courses.

In addition, this text reduces instructor and student frustration by setting up realistic goals for developing writers. The text is divided into eight units. Units 2 through 7 are divided into four parts: writing instruction, reading to generate thinking, examples for analysis written by students and professionals, and a grammar concept. Units 2 through 8 have two sets of writing suggestions with special emphasis on the skills covered in that unit.

Unit 9 contains nine readings, nonfiction and fiction, by Canadian writers. Each piece is followed by questions for discussion and analysis.

Explanation and Modelling of the Writing Process

Part 1 of Units 2 through 8 focuses, one at a time, on steps of the writing process. Part 1 in these Units begins with a list of skills that are covered in that part. After these skills are explained and modelled, the students are asked to apply them by working through exercises that reflect the kind of thinking that student writers have to do in composing, revising, and editing.

Reading Selections by Professionals for Generating Ideas for Writing

Part 2 of each unit contains a "Something to Think About, Something to Write About" section that includes a high-interest article written by a professional. These articles are used to generate ideas that students can use for their writing assignments. These selections cover a range of topics.

Examples of Writing by Students and Professionals

In Part 3 of each unit, writing examples by both students and professionals are provided for illustration, discussion, and/or analysis. The writing examples included in the text illustrate the concepts taught in that unit. The authors of these selections have a range of writing experience and come from diverse backgrounds, and thus their writing appeals to students of different ages, both sexes, and a variety of ethnic backgrounds.

Grammar Exercises Aimed at Improving Writing

The exercises in the grammar section of each unit (Part 4) go beyond drill and practice to include thinking exercises such as sentence combining and paragraph editing. Many exercises for in-class and out-of-class work are provided. Half of the answers are provided in Appendix D. As a result, teachers can have the students check their own exercises, or they can be used as homework and handed in to be graded by the instructor.

Unit on Rhetorical Modes

The unit on rhetorical modes is self-contained and includes fully developed essays illustrating how one topic can be developed into many different types of essays by using different modes. The text begins with illustration, a strategy with which students are familiar, and progresses through comparison/contrast, classification, definition, cause/effect analysis, process, and argument.

Unit 9: The Readings

We include a separate unit of readings because we believe that students learning to write should encounter good writing. Reading and discussing literature throughout a composition course encourage students to read not only to understand, but also to evaluate; that is, to think. Reading and discussing literature encourage students to make connections: between their lives and those of the writers; between their ideas and those expressed; between content and form.

These essays and short stories present thought-provoking ideas and experiences as well as they exemplify the use of form and language in the service of this content. Reading provides new worlds to discover; writing is an important tool with which we document our discoveries for ourselves and others.

The Canadian focus not only highlights good writing by Canadians but also gives students insight into the diversity of our Canadian culture and Canadian ideas. Featuring Canadian writers serves to engender pride in our Canadian literary tradition and to familiarize newcomers, especially, with this tradition's experience.

The questions for discussion and analysis following each selection are intended for oral and/or written responses.

Teaching Aids

We have prepared materials to aid the teaching process. These aids appear in the Instructor's Resource Package.

Content Designed to Prepare Students for Proficiency Testing

Writing Paragraphs and Essays provides instruction that will prepare students to perform well on proficiency tests. For example, it covers basic grammar and usage: subject-verb agreement; consistent verb tense; fragments, run-on sentences, and comma splices; consistent point of view; and a thorough review of punctuation. The text encourages development of revision skills needed by students to pass proficiency tests. In addition, an appendix includes commonly confused words, such as *their*, *there*, and *they're*.

Writing Paragraphs and Essays provides practice in the skills students need in varied writing situations, including writing and revising essays for proficiency tests. In addition, students draft, revise, and edit both paragraphs and multiparagraph essays. Because variety in sentence structure is one of the major criteria used to evaluate student essays, *Writing Paragraphs and Essays* also includes instruction in sentence combining to achieve sentence variety. Furthermore, the book includes a unit on rhetorical modes, which provides the skills students need when they are asked on a proficiency test to write an essay using a specific mode.

Joy Wingersky, Glendale Community College, Arizona
Jan Boerner, Glendale Community College, Arizona
Diana Holguin-Balogh, Front Range Community College, Colorado
Enid Gossin, Seneca College, Ontario
Susan Stancer, Seneca College, Ontario

Acknowledgments

In adapting this text to fill the needs of Canadian students, we have applied our classroom experience. Working together has been a joy; we are grateful for having had this opportunity.

Special thanks to the usual suspects.

We would also like to thank those people at Nelson Canada who worked on this book, especially Andrew Livingston, Acquisitions Editor; Joanne Scattolon, Developmental Editor; and Cecilia Chan and Tracy Bordian, Production Editors. Thanks must also go to the reviewers: Chris Frank (Georgian College), John Lucas (Dawson College), and Margo Bath-Bartlett (Durham College of Applied Arts), and other reviewers from George Brown College, Humber College, Red Deer College, Seneca College, and Sir Sandford Fleming College.

Enid Gossin and Susan Stancer
Seneca College

Unit One

Introduction to Writing

ABOUT WRITING

Writing is a way of gaining control over your ideas and getting them down on paper. There is nothing mysterious about this process. You can learn to write effectively and feel confident about your writing if you are willing to put in the time and effort.

Many people find it necessary to write at one particular place or with a certain colour of ink or a special type of keyboard. It is true that having these things may help you to write, but more important than these external aids is the ability to concentrate. Sometimes it will be necessary to tune out everyone and everything in order to reflect and recreate incidents that you have read or heard about, experienced, or observed. With total concentration, you can "replay" these incidents and share them with your reader. For instance, if you want to remember that first day of school long ago when you were six years of age, all you have to do is close your eyes until a mental picture enters your mind. That room, that teacher, that moment of fear, happiness, or excitement can be a video played in your mind. And from your "mind's video" you can write your thoughts on paper to share with your reader.

Ways to Help Yourself Become a Better Writer

What experiences have you had with writing? Have you had good experiences or bad experiences? How do you feel about yourself as a writer? How important is writing to you? If your feelings and experiences about writing have been negative, the best thing you can do for yourself is to try to put those impressions behind you. You need to be willing to take a risk, be receptive, and be yourself.

Be Willing to Take a Risk

Being willing to take a risk might be the most difficult task you have ever had to do. Even though writing is often a personal experience, you can improve your writing if you relax and concentrate on what you have to say, rather than worrying about what your instructor or classmates will think.

Be Receptive

Along with being willing to take a risk, try to be receptive to your instructor's suggestions for improving your writing. As your instructor works with you on your paper or as you work in peer editing groups, keep an open mind about their comments. These comments are not intended to offend you; rather, they are directed toward helping you achieve your writing goals.

Be Genuine

Being genuine means being your real self. When you write, it is not necessary to try to impress anyone with an artificial vocabulary. On the other hand, you do want to write on a level that is appropriate for the particular purpose you have for each writing situation. The goal of writing should be to communicate with the reader simply and sincerely.

Benefits of Becoming a Better Writer

Maybe you are asking yourself questions like these: "Why is becoming a better writer so important?" "How can writing help me?" "Will improving my writing skills bring me money, self-worth, opportunities, or friends?" If you spend time on this valuable skill, your writing can improve. Writing well will bring many rewards your way.

You can become more successful in school, whether you write essays, do research papers, or take essay exams.

You can become more competent in your job.

You can help others with their schoolwork.

You can satisfy yourself by writing a personal journal or letters to friends.

You can write to companies, or organizations or government departments for a variety of purposes, including praising someone's good work or defending yourself if you feel you have been treated unjustly.

You can make writing a professional career.

THE WRITING PROCESS

Writing is a process through which you discover, organize, and write your thoughts to communicate with a reader. When you speak, you have tone of voice and facial expressions to help you get your point across. You also have the chance to clarify miscommunications quickly. When you write, you have only words and punctuation to form your message, but you do have the opportunity to organize your thoughts and words until you are happy with the finished product. The writing process gives you a chance to compose, draft, rethink, and redraft to control the outcome of your writing.

The general steps in the writing process include prewriting, organizing ideas, drafting, revising, editing, and making a final draft. If you use these steps when you have a writing assignment, you will give yourself an opportunity to make the most of your time and get your best ideas on paper. At times, you may repeat a particular step. When you become more comfortable with the writing process and become a more experienced writer, you may be able to do some steps in your mind; however, skipping important steps is not advisable when you are learning the writing process.

Each step has different activities that will help you get the ideas from your mind onto the paper in an organized fashion. **Prewriting** is a way of generating ideas, narrowing a topic, or finding a direction. **Organizing** involves sorting ideas in a logical manner to prepare to write a draft. **Drafting** is the part of the writing process in which you compose sentences in paragraph form to produce the first copy of your essay. **Revising**, one of the most important steps in writing a paper, involves smoothing out your writing, adding more detail, and making other changes that will help you say what you want to say most effectively. **Editing** includes checking for mechanical problems and correcting them. **Making a final draft** and deciding it's ready for your intended audience is a step that takes patience and judgment. Being patient gives you a chance to take a sincere look at your paper and decide if the essay is in its best form. If not, you need to revise it even further.

Each of the steps of the writing process will be illustrated, beginning with prewriting.

Prewriting

Prewriting is the first major step in the writing process. As the following chart shows, prewriting can be accomplished in several ways.

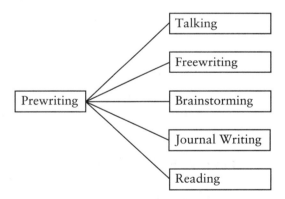

The prewriting chart lists some useful activities to help you begin a writing project. Five activities are offered, and you may find some of them more useful than others. All the prewriting approaches are designed to help you get started because, at times, starting can seem difficult. Starting a writing project means becoming actively involved in one or more of the activities listed above. The objectives are the same for each activity; however, each offers a different approach. You may want to try all of them to find out which ones work best for you.

Talking

One simple way to relieve anxiety and start the writing process is to talk about a subject with fellow students, instructors, family members, and knowledgeable people who can provide the inspiration you need to begin writing. Talking assists you in expressing ideas that you can later put onto paper. You might want to begin jotting down ideas that occur to you as you talk to others.

Talking to Find a Topic   The following conversation could very well be an actual dialogue between two students who are using talking to begin an assignment.

"What are you writing about?"

"I'm not sure. The teacher wants a pet peeve or a pleasure. I'm not sure what a pet peeve is, so I guess I'll do pleasure."

"A pet peeve is something that constantly irritates you, like not being able to do what you would like to do."

"If that's what it is, I have lots of those, like never having any free time."

"Well, why don't you spend less time with your girlfriend then?"

"It's more than just my girlfriend. I have to rush to work right after class. And then I work so many hours that I don't have much time to do my homework or see my girlfriend."

"Well, why don't you write about that problem—not having enough time to get everything done?"

"Maybe I will. That's it! That's what I'm going to write about—too many things to do and not enough time to get them done. At least this gives me a start on something to write about."

Keep in mind that it is not advisable to use only the talking approach as a prewriting activity. Talking, unlike freewriting or brainstorming, is not on paper, and ideas can be lost unless you take notes as you go along. But talking is a good starting point. In the preceding dialogue, the student decided that he could write about the impact of his heavy workload on college and his personal life. Now that a subject for the writing assignment has begun to take shape, the student could talk to someone else to gather even more ideas.

Talking with Direction: The Informal Interview   The student wanted to talk to someone who had graduated from college and who, he thought, had had a similar experience. After deciding on interviewing one of his instructors, he wrote out questions he felt would be useful for giving him some ideas for his paper. Here are some of the questions he prepared. Other questions that came to mind during the interview are also included.

"You have graduated from college. Did you work while you were going to college?"
   1.   "No, I didn't have to work."

"Did you have plenty of time to do your homework?"

   2. "Yes, I did. I rode the bus, so I was able to do my homework on the bus."

"Did you have to ride the bus because you didn't have a car?"

   3. "You're right. I had to do without some things, and a car was one of those luxuries."

"Even though you had to do without things, why do you think it's better not to work?"

   4. "I wouldn't have gotten through in four years. My sister did, though. She worked for two years before she started college so she could have enough money to get through college."

"Did she make more money after she graduated than she did before she went to college?"

   5. "Oh yes, and she loved her job after she graduated."

"Would you do it differently?"

   6. "No, because I wanted to make good grades. I appreciated the time I had to do my schoolwork."

This informal interview gave the student a different point of view, one that he might not have considered before. After the informal interview the student needed to analyze the information to see what could be used for a paper. Here's how the student analyzed the responses he got.

Ideas Gathered from Talking	Possible Use of Ideas
1. "No, I didn't have to work."	gives a new perspective of not working while going to school
2. "Yes, I did. I rode the bus, so I was able to do my homework on the bus."	provides an advantage for new perspective of not working
3. "You're right. I had to do without some things, and a car was one of those luxuries."	offers support for a new slant
4. "I wouldn't have gotten through in four years. My sister did, though. She worked for two years before she started college so she could have enough money to get through college."	shows a different view; could be another paragraph
5. "Oh yes, and she loved her job after she graduated."	offers additional support for the new idea
6. "No, because I wanted to make good grades. I appreciated the time I had to do my schoolwork."	shows a good reason for not working

Once you have enough information after interviewing one or more people, you might go on to the next step: organizing. If you do not have enough information to write a paper, you will need to interview more people or go on to freewriting, brainstorming, journal writing, or reading to generate information that can be used for writing. Next, let's examine freewriting.

Freewriting

Like other prewriting strategies, freewriting is intended to help you generate ideas. **Freewriting** is writing anything that comes to mind about your topic. It is writing without stopping to correct spelling or other mechanical errors. If you can't think of anything to write, just start with anything on your mind at that moment, even if it's just repeating the assignment. Ideally one idea leads to another, and soon your page will be filled with many different ideas. You are not expected to stay with any one idea; as a matter of fact, freewriting should bring out many different thoughts. This prewriting technique can be used when you are trying to find something to write about or are trying to get more ideas about a chosen topic.

Freewriting involves writing ideas in sentence form. Freewriting has three basic steps:

1. freewriting for a topic and direction

2. deciding on a topic

3. freewriting with direction

Examine these steps more closely.

Freewriting for a Topic and Direction   Look at the following example of freewriting by a student who did not have a topic for a paper and who did not use talking as a prewriting aid. The freewriting that he did was done without regard to correct mechanics and spelling.

> Well, I have to write for ten minutes on anything that I can think about. I'm not sure what I am interested in. I wish the other people in this room weren't writing so much. I wonder what they are writing about. I need to get my work done so I can get to work. I didn't get all of my work finished last night. I left the place in a mess. I hope my boss didn't notice. He is pretty nice most of the time. (1) <u>Sometimes that place gets to me</u>. I don't have enough time to get my schoolwork done. Maybe dad was right. (2) <u>I should try to cut down on my work hours so I can spend more time on school</u>. (3) <u>At this rate I won't ever get through</u>. Rob is almost ready to graduate and I only have one year behind me. If I could just take more courses I could get through and get the job I really want. But then I wouldn't have money to take my girlfriend out. (4) <u>She is a pretty nice girl</u>. Maybe she would understand if I quit my job. If she broke up with me over that I guess she wouldn't be a very good girlfriend anyhow. (5) <u>There are lots of things we could do that don't cost a lot of money</u>. There is always something going on at school. (6) <u>Her brother is a lot of fun</u>. We enjoy playing racquetball with him and his sister. I bet we could find lots of things to do. (7) <u>I could get through school faster</u>. Let's see, what should I write about? I wonder if anyone will think that what I wrote is dumb. I hope we don't have to read this

in class. I guess if I have to I will. Cheee, that guy next to me has a whole page filled up. I wonder if he is going to stop pretty soon. Oh well, I guess I will just have to keep writing.

Much of the content in this freewriting probably will not be used, but it has served the purpose of warming up. After you finish freewriting, go back and see if there is anything that looks interesting enough to write about. With close reading, you can find ideas that can be turned into possible topics for further development. Here is an example of one way to analyze this freewriting to find a topic and direction.

Freewriting Idea	Possible Topic and Direction
1. "Sometimes that place gets to me."	negative aspects of my job
2. "I should try to cut down on my work hours…"	educational benefits of cutting back on work hours
3. "At this rate I won't ever get through."	obstacles I face in finishing college
4. "She is a pretty nice girl."	neat traits of my girlfriend
5. "There are lots of things we could do that don't cost a lot of money."	enjoyable, low-cost recreational activities my girlfriend and I could do
6. "Her brother is a lot of fun."	her brother's personality
7. "I could get through school faster."	benefits of completing college as soon as possible

Deciding on a Topic   After you have finished freewriting, sort through your ideas. Decide which idea seems the most interesting, which you know the most about, and which you could write about most easily. The idea you choose may also suggest the direction for you to take.

Freewriting with Direction   After you have decided on the topic and direction, you need to freewrite again, this time with direction. This writing is generally easier because it concentrates on one topic. Usually most of the information that comes out in this freewriting is usable because a focus has been established, and this information can become support for a main idea. In the example, the one idea that the student has chosen to freewrite with direction is "What would happen if I cut down on my work hours?" His next step was to freewrite with direction on that idea. Here is what he wrote:

What would happen if I cut down on my work hours? I would have (1) more time to go see my girlfriend, but I would have to do without money. That means I (2) would have to give up some things that are important to me like my car. That would be rough. I wonder if my girl would find a new boyfriend. If she did, I guess she wouldn't care about our future. I (3) could study in the afternoons without having to worry about getting to work on time. (4) At night I wouldn't be too tired to go out, but then I wouldn't have any money to go out. Of course, (5) if I graduated from college, I could get a good job that I like and that pays well. (6) Dad would like that. He would be unhappy now because he is tired of supporting me. (7) My boss is going to be unhappy because he is counting on me to work forty hours a week and he is going to have to hire another employee. Of course he only pays me minimum wage. He might even fire me, but I have to decide what is most important for me. If I just cut down on my work hours, dad would be happy because I was still making some money and I would be happy because I could take more courses.

Once you have completed your freewriting with direction, reread it and find any information that can be used in writing your paper. Here is how the student analyzed this freewriting:

Results of Cutting Work Hours	Interpretation of Results
1. "More time to see my girl-friend…"	helps my social life
2. "Would have to give up some things…"	may mean a sacrifice
3. "Could study in the after-noons…"	allows time to study
4. "At night I wouldn't be too tired to go out…"	increases energy but not money
5. "If I graduated from college…"	could get better job later
6. "Dad would like that."	pleases dad
7. "My boss is going to be unhappy…"	not too important

This list shows many writing options for the student writer. The student may choose to write on the advantages of cutting work hours, the disadvantages of cutting work hours, or just the results of cutting work hours.

If you feel you have enough information to write a paper, go on to the part of the writing process called organizing. If not, you might need to freewrite further or try brainstorming. If you were to write a longer paper, your next step would be to group together the ideas that would make separate paragraphs. (This is covered in detail in Unit 4, "Organizing Ideas and Writing Them Clearly.")

Brainstorming

Brainstorming is writing words or phrases that occur to you spontaneously. This free association can be done individually or in a group. Brainstorming and freewriting are similar in that they both produce ideas. If your teacher gives you a topic, you can begin by brainstorming to get some direction. If not, you will need to brainstorm to find a topic. You may find it easier to brainstorm for a topic than to freewrite, but others may find freewriting easier. When you are brainstorming for a topic, you will probably create a list of very general words that interest you.

Brainstorming to Find a Topic When a student who did not have a topic was asked to brainstorm to find a topic, he responded with this list:

music	school	politics
fears	cities	family
sports	homes	vacation

As this list illustrates, the topics generated can be very broad. Because of this, it is necessary to brainstorm again, this time for direction.

Brainstorming for Direction The student decided on "school" as a topic and brainstormed again. Here is what he wrote this time:

Topic: School

1. fun—social activities
2. not enough time to get work done
3. hate English and writing
4. tired and confused
5. enjoy school when there
6. money—where to get it
7. want to spend time with friends
8. still a first-year student
9. why working hours should be cut
10. finish in four years or two years

The list shows some alternative topics for writing a paragraph. The possible topics in the list above are still general, so you need to decide which one seems the most interesting and brainstorm again. When you brainstorm again on the chosen topic, a new list of more focused topics will result.

Brainstorming with Direction The student looked at the list of topics and decided that "why working hours should be cut" would be a good topic for him to select because it was important to him. He decided to find out what all the results would be if he cut his work hours. Here is the list he produced while brainstorming on this more focused topic:

more time to read assignments

making decisions is frustrating

boss will be unhappy

more time to study

more time to get help

less spending money for weekends

less money to spend on my girlfriend

can spend time with friends without worrying about studying

would miss the feel of money in my pocket

hate bad grades

could take more classes and graduate from college sooner

dad will be unhappy

At this point, if you have enough information to write a paragraph, move on to the section on organizing. If not, try talking, freewriting, or brainstorming again—or you could begin keeping a journal for ideas.

Journal Writing

Journal writing is recording in a notebook information on your daily inner thoughts, inspirations, and emotions. This is usually done in a relaxed writing atmosphere. Writing in this manner can provide you with an opportunity to connect with important thoughts, analyze your life environment, relieve writing anxiety, and practise spontaneous writing. Journal writing can provide ideas that you might be able to use in later writing assignments, and it can even help you find a starting place for new writing assignments.

The following brief excerpt is taken from two pages of a journal in which the student wrote about the frustrations he was feeling. This segment shows his frustration at working and going to school at the same time. He found this part when he was skimming through material he remembered writing about his job. (Journal entries are written for content, so they often contain spelling and grammar errors. This is permissible.)

> I am tired. I don't think I can every keep this up. There is so much to worry about. Sometimes I wish I didn't have to grow up. Maybe I could just quit school for a little while and get a job. I don't want to work at a hamburger dump. Dad thinks I should work as a plumber, but I'm sick of working in the ditch. Last year I could tell the time of day by the flow of the sewer. I always knew it was noon because everyone was flushing toilets and the stuff began to flow fast and furious. No way—I want to get through with school. Maybe dad wouldn't bitch too much if I could just hurry up and get through school. One semester I took three courses and got through ok. *If I quit work I could take even more courses and then get a good job.* [emphasis added]

Sometimes you will want to look through your journal to find a topic and a direction; other times you will already have them and will simply be looking for ideas already expressed about your topic.

Much of this excerpt of journal writing is not appropriate for a paragraph, but the student found one sentence that would support his idea, and he also realized that because he had spent so much time writing about this subject, it must be important enough to write about.

Reading

Reading in magazines or newspapers can also help you get started with your writing. For instance, browsing through a magazine like *Time* or *Macleans*, whether you are in the library, at home, or at the doctor's office, can spark an idea for a topic. After that, additional reading will help you become more informed about your topic so that you can write intelligently about it.

Reading can also help you find ideas to support your paragraph or essay. This might be necessary if you do not have enough firsthand information about your topic. Some papers, especially those concerning political issues or social problems, require reading for factual information that can be used in your writing. Unit 8, "Composing with Effective Alternate Patterns," illustrates how additional reading can give you the information you need.

Summary of Ways to Get Started Writing

Talking: informal conversation about a subject or topic

Freewriting: writing (in sentences) anything that comes to mind without stopping

Brainstorming: listing words or phrases as they come to mind

Journal writing: recording your own thoughts in a notebook

Reading: browsing through materials that might be used for writing

---

Organizing

Organizing is the second major step in the writing process. After you have completed one or more of the prewriting activities, it's time to think about organizing these ideas into a rough outline that includes a main idea and supporting ideas.

Before you actually start using the ideas from your prewriting to compose your paragraph or essay, you should decide which details support the main idea and in what order these ideas need to be presented. As you sort these details into groups, you are organizing your information. This step in the writing process is called grouping. Logic and a sense for putting together similar ideas can help you do this quickly and easily. Grouping is one of the most important steps in the writing process and is covered again in detail in Unit 2, "Writing Sentences and Paragraphs," and in Unit 4, "Organizing Ideas and Writing Them Clearly." Here is how grouping can help you organize ideas for writing.

Grouping

Here is the list generated by the student who brainstormed his topic "school" with respect to "cutting work hours":

more time to read assignments

making decisions is frustrating

boss will be unhappy

more time to study

more time to get help

less spending money for weekends

less money to spend on my girlfriend

can spend time with friends without worrying about studying

would miss the feel of money in my pocket

hate bad grades

could take more classes and graduate from college sooner

dad will be unhappy

The task now is to organize the list into meaningful groups of related ideas, which will eventually become paragraphs. Grouping related ideas is easy if you stop and ask yourself the following very specific questions. These questions are intended to help you see how certain material can be put together to form one paragraph.

1. What phrases are similar or seem to be about the same idea?
    Group 1
    more time to read assignments
    more time to study
    more time to get help
    could take more classes and graduate from college sooner
    Group 2
    boss will be unhappy
    less spending money for weekends
    less money to spend on my girlfriend
    dad will be unhappy
    would miss the feel of money in my pocket

2. In what way is each group alike?
    The first grouping shows the *advantages* of cutting work hours.
    The second grouping shows the *disadvantages* of cutting work hours.

3. What ideas don't seem to fit anywhere?
    making decisions is frustrating
    hate bad grades
    can spend time with friends without worrying about studying

4. What general word or phrase could be used that would represent each group?
    The general phrase for Group 1 could be "educational advantages."
    The general word for Group 2 could be "disadvantages."

5. Are there other general words or phrases that would group the items differently?

financial matters
>   less spending money for weekends
>   less money to spend on my girlfriend
>   would miss the feel of money in my pocket

social aspects
>   less spending money for weekends
>   can spend time with friends without worrying about studying

personal considerations
>   making decisions is frustrating
>   boss will be unhappy
>   hate bad grades
>   dad will be unhappy

Remember, each group represents one paragraph. If a group has only two ideas, you may want to brainstorm again for additional ideas.

Outlining

Outlining involves identifying a word or phrase that represents a group of related ideas and then arranging these words or phrases in the order in which you want to discuss them. Notice that in answering questions 4 and 5 earlier, you have already grouped related ideas and found a general word or phrase that represents all of the ideas in the group. Using this process, you have made a rough outline that can be followed in writing your paragraph.

The student chose the group on "educational advantages." Here is one outline he could make:

>   Educational advantages
>   more time to read assignments
>   more time to study
>   more time to get help
>   could take more classes and graduate from college sooner
>   bring up my grade point average*
>   more time to use the library*

The general word or words will be made into a topic sentence, and each idea listed under these general words will become a support sentence.

Drafting

After you have organized your ideas in the form of an outline, you are prepared to write a first draft. **Drafting** involves taking the information that you have generated and organized and patiently writing a paragraph or an essay in which you consciously start with the main ideas and add supporting ideas that flow smoothly. You can feel confident about starting your draft because

---

*These are new ideas that occurred to him as he studied the group.

you have laid the foundation through prewriting and organizing your information. Try to write the ideas without worrying about spelling or other mechanical errors. In the first draft, you are simply interested in communicating content or meaning to the reader.

If you are writing a paragraph, look at the general word or phrase that represents the ideas in that group. Begin your draft with a sentence that includes this general word or phrase or a variation of it. Using the grouping done earlier, "educational advantages," the student wrote the following first draft of a paragraph. (Note that this and future "topic sentences" have been highlighted for you by using bold type.)

If I cut down at work I could have more time to spend on my education. By having more time to spend on school I could bring up my grade point average. Plus, I could probably have more time to do my work. I could spend as much time as I needed to get my assignments done and still have time to spend with my girlfriend. I could go to class and study in the afternoons without having to worry about getting to work on time. At night I wouldn't be too tired to go out. Tutering is offered free of charge at school and I would have time to get a tutor. I could take more classes and still do well in all of them. I often have to go to the library but really don't have the extra time. It takes even more time to go to work and then have to drive back to campus on Saterdays to do my research. My car is not running right and this adds to my problems. Just as I am getting the material that I need it is time for the library to close or I begin to get tired.

After you finish your first draft, put it away for a while, if possible, so that when you come back to it, you will be able to see it from a fresh point of view. This new perspective will help you revise the draft.

Revising

Revising means making changes to clarify wording and organization. Revise several times until you are satisfied that you have done your best. It is all right, even recommended, that you let other people read your paper and make suggestions for change. It is not all right, however, to have other people actually make the changes for you. Your major objective is not to produce just one excellent paper but to have the ability to write many excellent papers, even when you may not have anyone to help. Here are some possible questions to ask yourself when you are revising:

1. Is the general word or phrase (or a similar one) from the group in the first sentence?

2. Are there words, phrases, or sentences that are not related to the main idea in the first sentence?

3. Does the paragraph make sense to you and to someone else?

4. Have you covered all ideas in the group?

5. Can some words be changed for clarity?

6. Are any words excessively repeated?

7. Does the last sentence give a sense of closure to the paragraph?

As you begin to learn how to revise, it is easier to read for one or two kinds of changes at a time. Notice in the following examples that only two or three questions are asked and that only those revisions are made in the next draft.

First Revision

The first revision is based on questions 1 and 2:

1. Is the general word or phrase (or a similar one) from the group in the first sentence?

2. Are there words, phrases, or sentences that are not related to the main idea in the first sentence?

If I cut down at work I could have more time to spend on my **education**. By having more time to spend on school I could bring up my grade point average. Plus, I could probably have more time to do my work. I could spend as much time as I needed to get my assignments done ~~and still have time to spend with my girlfriend~~. I could go to class and study in the afternoons without having to worry about getting to work on time. ~~At night I wouldn't be too tired to go out~~. Tutering is offered free of charge at school and I would have time to get a tutor. I could take more classes and still do well in all of them. I often have to go to the library ~~but really don't have the extra time~~. It takes even more time to go to work and then have to drive back to campus on Saterdays to do my research. ~~My car is not running right, and this adds to my problems. Just as I am getting the material that I need it is time for the library to close or I begin to get tired~~.

Second Revision

The second revision is based on questions 3 and 4:

3. Does the paragraph make sense to you and to someone else?

4. Have you covered all ideas in the group?

If I cut down at work I could have more time to spend on my education. By having more time to spend on school I could bring up my grade point average. Plus, *I would have more time to do my homework because* ~~I could probably have more time to do my work~~.

I could spend as much time as I needed to get my assignments done. I could go to class and study in the afternoons without having to worry about get-*every day* ting to work ~~on time~~. Tutering is offered free of charge at school and I *wouold have time to day get a tutor. I could take more classes and still do well in all of them. I often have to go to the library. It takes even more time to go to work and then have to drive back to campus on Saterdays to do my research.* If I could take five courses instead of three I could finish college almost twice as fast. I bet I would be more interested in it because that is all I would have on my mind.

Notice that script type has been used to indicate new ideas added to the draft.

Third Revision

The third revision is based on questions 5, 6, and 7:

5. Can some words be changed for clarity?

6. Are any words excessively repeated?

7. Does the last sentence give a sense of closure to the paragraph?

If I cut down at work I could have more time to spend on my education. By having more time to spend on school I could bring up my grade point average. ~~Plus,~~ *Also,* I would have more time to do my homework because I could spend as much time as I needed to get my assignments done. ~~I could go to class and study~~ *After class I could concentrate on studying* in the afternoons without having to worry about getting to work every day. Tutering is offered free of charge at school and I wouold have time to ~~get a tutor.I could take more classes and~~ *work with someone.* ~~still do well in all of them.~~ I often have to go to the library ~~It takes even~~ *but really don't have enough time. If I cut down at work, I would have time to go to the library* ~~more time to go to work and then have to drive back to campus on~~ *after class as well as on* Saterdays ~~to do my research.~~ ~~If~~ *Also, if* I could take five courses instead of three I could finish college almost twice as fast. ~~I bet I would be more interested in~~ *Cutting my working hours would give me more time to concentrate on my studies.* ~~it because that is all I would have on my mind.~~

Here is how the revised draft would look before editing:

If I cut down at work I could have more time to spend on my education. By having more time to spend on school I could bring up my grade point average. Also, I would have more time to do my schoolwork because I could spend as much time as I needed to get my assignments done. After class I could concentrate on studying in the afternoons without having to worry about getting to work every day. Tutering is offered free of charge at school and I wouold have time to work with someone. I often have to go to the library but really don't have enough time. If I cut down at work, I would have time to go to the library after class as well as on Saterdays. Also, if I could take five courses instead of three I could finish college almost twice as fast. Cutting my working hours would give me more time to concentrate on my studies.

Editing

Before you consider your paper finished, check for any problems in mechanics. When you are learning the writing process, content comes before mechanics and grammar, but correct mechanics and grammar will be expected as you master the writing process. The following list contains some of the items you want to find and check.

spelling

punctuation

capitalization

grammar usage

errors in sentence structure

consistency in verb tense

consistent point of view

abbreviations and numbers

You will not be expected to have all of these editing skills at first. But you will acquire these skills through writing your paragraphs and essays. To make this mechanical review easier, you might want to learn to use a good word processing program that includes a spell-check feature and other writing aids. This is also a good time for peer editing groups to help in polishing drafts.

The student took the time to make one final check before turning in the paper. Here is how the latest draft looked after editing:

If I cut down at ~~work I~~ could have more time to spend on my _work, I_

education. By having more time to spend on ~~school I~~ could bring up my _school, I_

grade point average. Also, I would have more time to do my homework

because I could spend as much time as I needed to get my assignments

done. After ~~class I~~ could concentrate on studying in the afternoons without _class, I_

having to worry about getting to work every day. ~~Tutering~~ is offered free of _Tutoring_

charge at ~~school and I wouold~~ have time to work with someone. I often _school and I would_

have to go to the library but really don't have enough time. If I cut down at

work, I would have time to go to the library after class as well as on
Saturdays
~~Saterdays~~. Also, if I could take five courses instead of ~~three I~~ three, I could finish col-

lege almost twice as fast. Cutting my working hours would give me more

time to concentrate on my studies.

Here is how the edited draft that is ready to be turned in would look:

> **If I cut down at work, I could have more time to spend on my education.** By having more time to spend on school, I could bring up my grade point average. Also, I would have more time to do my schoolwork because I could spend as much time as I needed to get my assignments done. After class, I could concentrate on studying in the afternoons without having to worry about getting to work every day. Tutoring is offered free of charge at school, and I would have time to work with someone. I often have to go to the library but really don't have enough time. If I cut down at work, I would have time to go to the library after class as well as on Saturdays. Also, if I could take five courses instead of three, I could finish college almost twice as fast. Cutting my working hours would give me more time to concentrate on my studies.

Now that you have seen a finished paragraph produced, review the major steps in the writing process.

Steps in the Writing Process

Prewriting: gathering ideas

Organizing: grouping and ordering details

Drafting: writing the first copy of a paragraph or essay

Revising: changing wording and organization

Editing: making mechanical changes

The writing process can prove to be a challenging but fulfilling venture, just as learning to ride a bicycle was when you were a child. The first time you tried to ride a bike, you had to take a risk that you would look silly as you wobbled down the street, or that you would fall and get hurt, or that you would get upset because others were moving faster than you were. However, you had more to lose by not trying, and if you had never taken that risk, you would never have learned to ride.

Learning the writing process is a similar experience. But writing is also a skill that requires many thinking activities, and you must use them all to produce an effective piece of writing. Just as you didn't give up when learning to ride a bicycle, don't give up on the writing process, and you will experience a new pride and confidence whenever you face a writing task.

Unit Two

Writing Sentences and Paragraphs

PART 1 | **Parts to Whole: Topic Sentences and Paragraphs**

OBJECTIVES

The Topic Sentence

- Recognize the parts of a topic sentence.
- Expand topics into topic sentence ideas.
- Recognize suitable topic sentences.
- Recognize the topic sentence within a group of related sentences.

The Paragraph

- Identify the parts of a paragraph: topic sentence, support sentences, and concluding sentence.
- Practise the steps in the process of writing a paragraph:

    Prewrite to generate ideas.

    Group ideas to find a direction and a focus for developing a topic sentence.

    Name a general word that describes the group.

    Outline (list from the group) the topic sentence and the support sentences that will go into the paragraph.

    Add to the list a concluding sentence to finalize the main idea.

- Recognize the four elements of a good paragraph: completeness, logical order, unity, and coherence.
- Write a paragraph that demonstrates completeness, logical order, unity, and coherence.

When you can write clear sentences, you can make yourself understood by others. You can express any idea, feeling, opinion, or belief that you desire. No matter how long, short, simple, or complicated your subject may be, you must write your ideas in sentences. The sentence, then, is the basis for almost all writing.

Most of your college writing, of course, involves not just one sentence, but several, because you probably will have to explain or discuss many details to make your meaning clear. The person reading your ideas, however, will not be able to understand the overall meaning of your sentences unless you group them in a logical way. This group of logically related sentences is called a paragraph.

Following specific steps is necessary for writing good paragraphs. Before you study this step-by-step process in depth, it is important for you to recognize and understand the parts of a well-written paragraph.

The Topic Sentence

Parts of a Topic Sentence

A good paragraph contains several related sentences that support *one main idea*, which is limited to and focused in one sentence. This sentence helps guide your reader through the related sentences in the paragraph. This vital sentence serves as a commitment for the writer to provide an explanation or illustration of this main idea. The term used to identify this main idea is **topic sentence**.

A topic sentence has two parts:

1. **a topic** (key word or phrase)

2. **a direction or general word**, which may be a conclusion, opinion, or statement *about* the topic

For example, the following sentences could be topic sentences:

> Doing housework can be very boring.
>
> Browsing in a library is an exciting experience.
>
> My trip to the botanical garden taught me a lot.

You could use each one of these sentences as a topic sentence because each main idea is limited to and focused into two essential parts: a **topic** (key word or phrase) and a **general direction** (conclusion or opinion) about the topic:

Topic	Direction or General Word
Doing housework	can be very boring.
Browsing in a library	is an exciting experience.
My trip to the botanical garden	taught me a lot.

The following exercise will help you practise recognizing the parts of topic sentences.

EXERCISE 1

In each sentence below, identify the topic *(key word or phrase) and the* direction *or general word (the conclusion or opinion) about the topic.*

Example:

Taking a young child to lunch requires patience.

Topic: <u>Taking a young child to lunch</u>   *Direction:* <u>requires patience</u>

1. Enrolling in college can be a surprising experience.

Topic: _____ *Direction:* _____

2. Trying to buy a house is sometimes frustrating.

Topic: _____ *Direction:* _____

3. That movie has a lot of action.

Topic: _____ *Direction:* _____

4. The party was fun.

Topic: _____ *Direction:* _____

5. Planting a tree is hard work.

Topic: _____ *Direction:* _____

6. Successful students have good attitudes in school.

Topic: _____ *Direction:* _____

7. Owning a car can be expensive.

Topic: _____ *Direction:* _____

8. An aerobics class can be fun.

Topic: _____ *Direction:* _____

9. Walking to school in the spring saves money.

Topic: _____ *Direction:* _____

10. My family enjoys summer fishing trips.

    Topic: _____   *Direction:* _____

11. Going out to eat can be a cultural experience.

    Topic: _____   *Direction:* _____

12. Riding a bicycle takes coordination.

    Topic: _____   *Direction:* _____

13. Some people find doing cross-stitch pictures relaxing.

    Topic: _____   *Direction:* _____

14. A healthy body can be achieved through exercise.

    Topic: _____   *Direction:* _____

15. Character can be built through studying karate.

    Topic: _____   *Direction:* _____

16. Doing well in college requires organization.

    Topic: _____   *Direction:* _____

17. Figure skaters give graceful performances.

    Topic: _____   *Direction:* _____

18. Airline attendants have demanding jobs.

    Topic: _____   *Direction:* _____

19. A remodelled kitchen brings pleasure.

    Topic: _____   *Direction:* _____

20. Looking at an old picture album brings fond memories.

    Topic: _____   *Direction:* _____

To help you become more familiar with the parts of topic sentences, do the following exercise for expanding simple topics into full topic sentences.

EXERCISE 2

Complete each topic below by writing a **statement** *(conclusion or opinion) about it. You will be focusing the topic by adding a* **direction** *(your opinion or conclusion).*

Example:

Whistler is a good place for skiing.

1. Riding a bike _____

2. Working on my car _____

3. The stories in the book _____

4. The pizza restaurant _____

5. My sister _____

6. Jeeps _____

7. I discovered that cheerleading _____

8. To go to college _____

9. Maria _____

10. Pine trees _____

11. Reading the newspaper _____

12. I saved my money to _____

13. A family reunion _____

14. The football game _____

15. A trip to Cape Breton Island _____

16. Keeping a garden _____

17. Relatives _____

18. Making a quilt _____

19. Rebuilding an engine _____

20. Crossword puzzles _____

As you can see, a topic sentence is limited to or focused on one main idea. At the same time, a topic sentence is *general* in nature because it sums up the information or details that you will present to make your writing believable for your reader. Thus, even though a topic sentence is limited, it is the most general statement in the paragraph.

Distinguishing Topic Sentences from Statements of Simple Fact

Because the *topic sentence* is general, it cannot be just a simple fact. The following sentences would *not* be suitable topic sentences:

Susan paid $24.95 for her new blouse.

The living room contains a Canadiana desk.

Two of my friends went on Star Tours four times.

Study the following pairs of sentences. The first sentence in each pair is a simple fact that could not be developed into a paragraph. The second sentence in each pair shows how the simple fact has been changed into a more general idea that could be used as a topic sentence for a paragraph.

Fact:	Susan paid $24.95 for her new blouse.
Topic sentence:	Susan loves to shop for bargains.
Fact:	The living room contains a Canadiana desk.
Topic sentence:	The living room is furnished in authentic early Canadiana style.
Fact:	Two of my friends went on Star Tours four times.
Topic sentence:	My friends and I had an exciting day in Disneyland.

The second sentence in each pair would be a suitable topic sentence because each contains a *general* word or phrase—the **direction** for the topic:

loves to shop for bargains

is furnished in authentic Canadiana style

had an exciting day in Disneyland

Each of these broader statements would suggest details that you could name—examples of bargains, examples of Canadiana furniture, and examples of activities and events in Disneyland. It is important to understand that the topic sentence in a paragraph is a general idea that is also focused in one direction or on one opinion. However, it is just as important to keep the topic sentence from being so general that it cannot be developed in one paragraph. For example, it would take much more than one paragraph to fully develop the idea in a sentence like this: "The causes of war are many."

Just remember that a topic sentence must be more than a statement of simple fact because that type of statement cannot be expanded into a fully developed paragraph.

The following exercise will help you identify sentences that could be used as topic sentences.

EXERCISE 3

Study each sentence below and decide if it is a statement of simple fact (fact), too broad to be developed in one paragraph (broad), or a more general but focused statement that could be used for a topic sentence (TS).

Examples:

fact   **The birds ate all of the figs on the tree.**

TS   **The birds are enjoyable to watch.**

broad   **The evolution of birds is complex.**

_____ 1. Yard work can be fun.

_____ 2. My math book is on the floor.

_____ 3. The causes of world hunger are complicated.

_____ 4. My den is a mess.

_____ 5. The historical events that have affected our English language are many.

_____ 6. A small fan is running in the living room.

_____ 7. Our spring weather was unusual this year.

_____ 8. Children are a mystery.

_____ 9. Pollution causes many environmental problems.

_____ 10. Abortion is a complicated moral issue.

_____ 11. Blue Rodeo will appear at 9:00 next Saturday night.

_____ 12. Our neighbours expect us to be good citizens.

_____ 13. Howard drove his Jeep to the garage.

_____ 14. Howard found it hard to save money for car repairs.

_____ 15. Listing the people who have died of AIDS is heartbreaking.

_____ 16. Many desert plants begin to bloom in March.

_____ 17. Native Canadian cultures are varied.

_____ 18. The cocker spaniel rushed into the room.

_____ 19. The English computer lab is open twelve hours a day.

_____ 20. Dogs often provide protection for their owners.

Additional practice in thinking about how sentences relate to each other will help you write better topic sentences. The following exercises will help you distinguish general sentences from more specific, factual statements.

EXERCISE 4

Study each group of related sentences. Underline the most general statement that could be a topic sentence.

Example:

The red oleanders have finally started to bloom.

The daisies have filled the side yard with white.

The peach trees are covered with pink blossoms.

<u>Many beautiful flowers have begun to bloom this spring.</u>

The path to the back door is edged with blue alyssum.

1. Small cars are easy to park.

   Many advantages result from owning and operating small cars.

   Small cars usually run on twelve or sixteen litres of gas per week, depending on the kilometres driven.

   Cleaning small cars does not take much time.

   Small cars are easier to drive in traffic.

2. Making a list of clothing to take on a vacation is useful.

   Figuring out where to go on a vacation avoids wasting time.

   Packing suitcases carefully avoids wrinkled clothing.

   Making reservations early helps.

   Having somebody to check your house while you're gone is a good idea.

   Careful planning helps ensure a good vacation.

   Stopping the mail and the newspaper delivery is helpful.

3. Buying lottery tickets is not a good idea. Opening a savings account is necessary.
   Putting money out of each paycheque into savings should be done regularly.
   Eating at home is better than eating out.
   Walking to school (if it's possible) might save some money.
   Saving money may not be as hard as you think.

4. Richard really likes Peter Robinson.
   Wednesday's Child is one of his favourites.
   Richard enjoys Canadian and British detective fiction.
   He has read several of Agatha Christie's books.
   Of current writers, he enjoys P. D. James and Eric Wright.
   He especially likes Howard Engel's detective stories.

5. "Call waiting" lets a person talking on the phone know there is an incoming call.
   Telephones have become sophisticated home appliances.
   Answering machines can record messages so that calls are never missed.
   People can use mobile phones to communicate while travelling to and from work.
   Cordless phones allow people to walk around the house and still talk on the phone.

6. Some people fear flying.
   Phobias are varied.
   Acrophobes get nervous when they are looking down from great heights.
   Agoraphobia causes people to withdraw and remain indoors for years.
   People who feel anxiety in closed spaces are claustrophobic.

7. Fans can be installed.
   Some shade screens reduce the sun's glare by 20 percent.
   Large trees on the west side shield a house from the afternoon heat.
   Insulation in attics helps keep a house cool in the summer.
   Tips for keeping a home cooler in the summer heat are helpful.

8. Journal entries must be turned in.
   Five short papers are assigned.
   The class has many requirements.
   Five long papers are assigned.
   Ten grammar tests must be passed.

9. Dogs need to be trained by their owners.
   Dog food must be nutritious and balanced for the size of the dog.
   People should groom their pets.
   A good pet owner has several responsibilities to meet.
   The owner must provide a clean and comfortable place for the pet to sleep.

10. Oil tankers were moving fast in the centre lane.

    Slow-moving cars filled the right lane.

    One or two reckless drivers were cutting back and forth across all the lanes.

    Traffic on the highway was heavy.

    Other cars and trucks were booming along in the left lane.

11. A large, comfortable van was near the west door.

    Several sedans were next to the window.

    Two chrome-trimmed sports models, their hoods up, were at either side of the large room.

    The showroom presented a carefully arranged collection of automobiles.

    A gleaming red truck was near the east door.

12. People from throughout the province will come to see the games.

    Hundreds of people connected to the team will need to buy or rent homes or apartments in the new location.

    When a professional basketball team moves to a new city, the city gains much revenue.

    Souvenirs, such as T-shirts, will be sold in thousands of stores.

    Many concession stand owners selling beverages and food at the games will pay taxes to the city.

13. Canoes can be rented at the lagoons.

    Many kilometres of quiet paths are reserved for walking or jogging.

    Tennis players can use the lighted courts for a few coins in the meter.

    In one corner of the park is an Olympic-sized swimming and diving pool.

    The beautiful public park offers many inexpensive outdoor activities for the city.

The Paragraph

Parts of a Paragraph

Now that you have learned about topic sentences, you are ready to study the full paragraph. Becoming familiar with the parts of strong paragraphs will help you when you begin to write your own paragraphs.

A paragraph has three parts:

1. **a topic sentence**

2. **support sentences**

3. **a conclusion**

Read the following example of a paragraph.

My blind date last night was a disaster. I got wet because just as I stopped to pick up my date, it started raining, and she borrowed my rain-coat. At dinner, she ate so much that I had to use my next day's lunch money to pay for her meal. I had a terrible time because she could not dance. To make matters worse, I had a cut on my lip that hurt when I kissed her. **That's the last blind date I will ever have.**

The topic sentence (main idea) and the conclusion are in bold type so that you can easily identify them. All the other sentences, which contain details that explain why the blind date was a disaster, are support sentences. All parts of the paragraph work together to express the main idea clearly so that the reader can understand and appreciate the writer's disappointing blind date.

The Paragraph Writing Process

Now that you can identify and develop topic sentences, it's time for you to practise writing so that you can improve your ability to express your ideas in an organized way. There is no one correct way to write a paragraph, but if you learn the process one step at a time, you will eventually find writing to be simple and rewarding. In this part you will see the writing process illustrated again so you can practise prewriting, organizing, and drafting. An example of the step-by-step process as done by a student is given so that you can see how it works. Getting enough ideas and information to put into a paragraph is not something that just happens, and you may need some patience with yourself during each step of the process. You begin by choosing a topic.

Choose a Topic   Choose a simple topic. (Choose from what your instructor suggests for topics, or follow the directions your instructor gives you for choosing a topic. You might choose a topic listed in Exercises 1 or 2 in this chapter.) Suppose the student selected "recreation" from a list provided by the teacher.

Prewrite   Use one or more of the prewriting activities explained in Unit 1: **talking, freewriting,** or **brainstorming.** Don't worry about spelling or grammar or having complete ideas. Just let your mind produce ideas that have some connection with your topic.

A sample brainstormed list for the topic "recreation" might look something like this:

Recreation

jet skiing on weekends	fishing
reading mysteries	needlepoint
make quilts	good fishing spots
fishing equipment	cooking light meals
aerobics for fitness	stamp collecting

The student now has more specific topics from which to find direction for one main idea. The student chose "fishing" for the topic.

Brainstorm for Direction   Brainstorm to generate more ideas that can be grouped into details that seem to have something in common. As you might recall, this group of related ideas will suggest your focus or direction for the paragraph. You probably will have more than one group from which to choose. Here is what the student's brainstorming produced:

Fishing

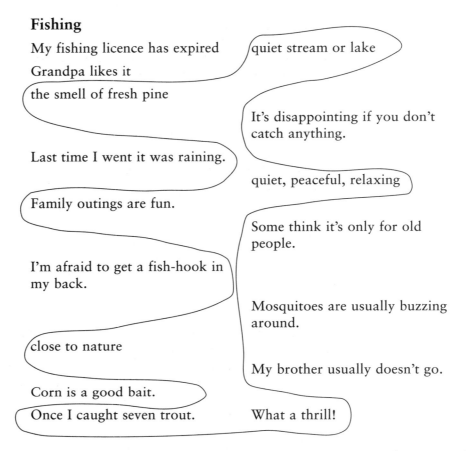

My fishing licence has expired

Grandpa likes it

the smell of fresh pine

quiet stream or lake

It's disappointing if you don't catch anything.

Last time I went it was raining.

quiet, peaceful, relaxing

Family outings are fun.

Some think it's only for old people.

I'm afraid to get a fish-hook in my back.

Mosquitoes are usually buzzing around.

close to nature

My brother usually doesn't go.

Corn is a good bait.

Once I caught seven trout.

What a thrill!

Name General Words to Describe the Group of Ideas Notice that some ideas in the brainstorming about "fishing" are positive aspects of fishing. A **general word** that represents the ideas in this group might be "enjoyment." This grouping of details that have something in common has been marked in the above example. It is helpful to list them separately (and possibly add more).

quiet stream or lake

the smell of fresh pine

Family outings are fun.

close to nature

Once I caught seven trout.

quiet, peaceful, relaxing

What a thrill!

Some of the ideas have something negative in common. These could form another group that might be described by other general words: the "hazards" or "frustrations" of fishing.

I'm afraid of getting a fish-hook in my back.

Last time I went it was raining.

It's disappointing if you don't catch anything.

Mosquitoes are usually buzzing around.

This group could be developed into a separate paragraph.

Finally, some of the items in the list introduce different ideas that might not fit anywhere.

Grandpa likes it.

My licence is expired.

My brother usually doesn't go.

Some think it's only for old people.

Corn is good bait.

Choose Direction for the Topic Sentence To find your focus and to be able to write your topic sentence, select the general word you want to use to represent your group: "enjoyment" or "frustration." The student decided to focus on the "enjoyment of fishing."

Think about the Topic Sentence Your next step is to develop your topic sentence. Remember that it must have two parts: a topic and a statement about the topic that includes a general word to represent your group. The topic sentence should also be broad enough to include all of the items in the group you have selected as the direction of your topic.

Here are some *unacceptable* topic sentences for this group:

It is fun to tie flies.

Fishing is peaceful.

These two topic sentences do not contain the general word "enjoyment," and "It is fun to tie flies" is not broad enough to include all of the details in the group. "Fishing is peaceful" would make a good topic sentence, but not for this group of ideas.

Write the Topic Sentence The next step is to write the topic sentence. You might say, "Fishing is enjoyable," "Fishing is an enjoyable activity," or "Fishing is an enjoyable leisure-time activity." Choose the version of the topic sentence that works best for you.

Outline the Paragraph After you have written your topic sentence, it is time to list the supporting details and include a concluding (or summary) thought for the end of the paragraph. Put all the sentences into an outline form, just as the student did in the following example. (If more support details occur to you as you make the outline, include them.)

Topic sentence	Fishing is an enjoyable leisure-time activity.
Support idea	quiet stream or lake
Support idea	I love the smell of fresh pine.
Support idea	Family outings are fun.
Support idea	close to nature
Support idea	Once I caught seven trout. What a thrill!
Support idea	quiet, peaceful, relaxing
Concluding idea	Fishing will always be a positive experience for me.

All the supporting ideas are the "proof" given to the reader for the topic sentence. You will be able to write a strong paragraph if you develop a rough outline similar to this one.

Draft the Paragraph   The next step is to write the first version or draft of your paragraph. If new, *related* details occur to you, include them because they may help you clarify your main idea. You may want to put the ideas into a different order when you draft your paragraph. As you draft, add whatever is needed to make the sentences flow smoothly and help the reader understand the experience.

Here is the student's draft, with the topic and concluding sentences in bold type:

> **Although I have several hobbies, fishing is my most enjoyable leisure-time activity.** When I am fishing, this is the time I feel closest to the natural elements. The sunrise, the quiet stream or lake, the green pine scent, and the one-on-one experience with nature relax me more than any other activity. In this peaceful scene, there is also the thrill of conquering a bit of the wilderness. For years, I will remember the seven big trout I caught on a fishing trip several years ago. It was one of the greatest experiences I have ever had. **I am convinced that fishing will always be a positive experience for me.**

Notice that the supporting ideas have been expanded in the drafting process and give a clear and convincing picture of the main idea suggested by the topic sentence. They also clarify the idea of being "close to nature." The sunrise, the stream or lake, and the green pine scent all help complete the "picture."

The following exercises will help you practise the steps in prewriting, organizing, and drafting. Even though you have improved these three skills in this unit, they are not the only important parts of the writing process. Revising and editing, which were introduced in Unit 1, are also important parts of the writing process.

EXERCISE 5

Brainstorm either the topic "television" or the topic "school." Find your direction.

Topic: _____

Brainstorm for direction:

_____

_____

_____

_____

_____

State the direction you have chosen:

_____

_____

Brainstorm with direction:

_____

_____

_____

_____

_____

_____

Make a new list of all the ideas that support the direction you have chosen:

_____

_____

_____

_____

_____

_____

_____

Write a general word that represents the group you have chosen: _____

Write a possible topic sentence: _____

_____

_____

Write another possible topic sentence:

_____

_____

Select one of the topic sentences. Using your new list of ideas that support the direction of this topic sentence, list each idea in a rough outline. Add a concluding thought.

Topic sentence: _____

_____

Support idea: _____

Support idea: _____

Support idea: _____

Support idea: _____

Support idea: _____

Concluding idea: _____

You now have ideas that can be used in a first version of a paragraph about your chosen topic.

EXERCISE 6

Using the information you have generated about your chosen topic, write a paragraph for practice.

_____

_____

_____

_____

_____

_____

_____

_____

_____

_____

Elements of a Strong Paragraph

You have learned to recognize the topic sentence, the support sentences, and the conclusion in a paragraph. You have also learned to generate the ideas that you need to write a paragraph. Now you are ready to study the four elements of strong paragraphs:

completeness

logical or sensible order

unity

coherence

All these elements work together to make the paragraph clear and effective. Study each of these and learn how to master them in your writing.

Completeness A paragraph must have enough information in it to give the reader a clear picture or a full discussion of its main idea (the topic sentence). Without details or examples, a paragraph will be vague and unconvincing. When a paragraph does not have enough information, it is called **incomplete** or **undeveloped**.

The following first version of a paragraph about dancing has a main idea but very little specific information. This draft is an incomplete or undeveloped paragraph, and, therefore, it needs more specific details that can be generated through talking, freewriting, brainstorming, looking through journal, or reading. Then another draft can be composed.

> **Dancing can be good exercise.** It can be entertaining. It can be lots of fun as well. **Dancing can be very beneficial for everyone.**

This paragraph has a topic sentence and a conclusion, but it includes only two very general statements about dancing. In fact, the "support" statements are neither details nor examples. The sentence "It can be lots of fun as well" could even be another main idea. What does "good exercise" really mean? Specific answers to this question are not in the paragraph. You can see, then, that this paragraph needs more information to explain what "good exercise" means. The reader could only guess at the meaning suggested by the topic sentence.

Here is a revised draft of this paragraph about dancing that contains more information:

> **Dancing can be good exercise.** The constant arm and leg movements are like aerobics. They can be a really good workout if the dance lasts long enough. If the dance requires lots of quick movements, many calories can be used up, and more fat will be burned. Some dances require movements that are like stretching, so flexibility and muscle tone will be increased. **Dancing can help maintain weight and can be beneficial exercise for everyone.**

There is no "correct length" for an effective paragraph, but four to eight support sentences can make a strong paragraph if they contain supporting details. When you are judging the completeness of a paragraph, look for details and examples that make the topic sentence clear.

EXERCISE 7

Revise the following paragraphs for completeness. Underline the topic sentence and the conclusion in each paragraph. Then add two or more sentences that support the topic sentence.

Example:

Hawaii is fun to visit on a vacation. I can sample fresh pineapples served by friendly Hawaiians. I can scuba dive for coral in the ocean. Having the chance to enjoy different activities in Hawaii could mean a great vacation.

> Each island offers different
> sights and activities.

<u>Hawaii is fun to visit on a vacation.</u> ⋀ I can sample fresh pineapples

Close by, I can browse in a
variety of interesting shops.

served by friendly Hawaiians. ∧ **I can scuba dive for coral in the**
I can join in native Hawaiian dances.
ocean. ∧ <u>**Having the chance to enjoy different activities in Hawaii**</u>
<u>**could mean a great vacation.**</u>

Paragraph 1

Some parents try to buy their children's love by giving them presents. They think that giving a child a new doll or a new toy car every month or so will make up for not paying much attention to the child. Children probably need fewer material objects and more affection and real communication if parents want their love returned.

Paragraph 2

Becoming a parent for the first time changed my life. I was no longer free to come and go whenever I wanted. I had to think of my child first before I could make any decisions. I guess all first-time parents have their lives changed like this.

Paragraph 3

Planning a vacation to Japan means that you have to have money saved. Airfare and hotel rooms, for example, require a lot of money. You have to decide if you can do without some things to save money for that special vacation to Japan.

Paragraph 4

If you want to change the landscaping around your house, you might need expert advice in order to avoid making mistakes. Someone at the nursery could help you decide what kinds of trees and shrubs would be best for your area. The experts can help you avoid disappointment while you improve your yard.

Paragraph 5

Parents are usually concerned with how their children act because they hate to be embarrassed by their children. They want them to be polite and respectful toward others. Parents have definite ideas about how their children should act both at home and in public.

Logical Order You have learned that all the sentences in a strong paragraph relate to one main idea and that there should be enough supporting details to make the main idea clear. A second element that strong paragraphs have is **logical or sensible order.**

All the support sentences of a good paragraph should be in clear, logical order so that the reader does not miss the main point of the paragraph. For example, read the following sentences. Notice how they relate to each other but are *out* of logical order.

> I opened the front door of my house and went inside.
>
> I walked up the front steps to my front door.

These sentences are out of logical order because the person would have to walk to the door before it could be opened. This example shows what "logical" or "sensible" order is. The sentences should be in this order:

> I walked up the steps to my front door.
>
> I opened the front door of my house and went inside.

Here is another example of illogical order:

> Marie washed the mud off her dog.
>
> Marie made sure she put warm water in the big tub.
>
> She dried the dog with a towel.

These sentences are not in logical or sensible order because they are not *in the order in which the actions would be done*. Here is the logical order:

> Marie made sure she put warm water in the big tub.
>
> Marie washed off the mud.
>
> She dried the dog with a towel.

Here is another example of logical order:

> At noon today, the engineers met at a special luncheon.
>
> The luncheon ended at two o'clock.

These sentences are in logical order because of the *time signal* in each sentence. "Noon" comes before "two o'clock."

Another kind of order exists in describing a place, such as a room in a house. The details are described or "seen" in the order in which they really exist in the room.

> When you enter the living room, you see a couch on the left and a chair and table next to that. Walking straight ahead into the room, you see at the end of the dining room a fairly large table and four chairs. To the right of this large table is the door into the kitchen.

When several details flow together in a paragraph, it is important for the reader to be able to follow the ideas in a clear order. Sometimes—as in the previous example—the natural physical movement from one place to another will determine the order of the sentences.

One final example might help clarify this idea of order in a strong paragraph. In the following paragraph about sea turtles, the support sentences are in a clear, logical order. The ideas in bold type should not be rearranged because they show a logical order of what the scientists did.

> Scientists are working hard to gather facts about sea turtles called leatherbacks. **The observers work**, no matter what the weather is like—on clear days or in pouring rain. **They count the turtles** as they come ashore. When the turtles lay their eggs, **the scientists walk up and down** the beaches for many hours at a time. They count the eggs in the sand. Then, later, they count the eggs that hatch. These biologists know that they are collecting information that will someday be important to other scientists.

The actions are described in the normal, natural order in which they occur.

Note Another way of clarifying the logical order in a paragraph is by the use of coherence, which will be explained later.

The following exercise will help you practise arranging sentences in logical order.

EXERCISE 8

Study the following sets of sentences and decide what their logical order would be in a paragraph. Number the sentences in the order in which they should logically appear.

Example:

____2____ Diana went to Quebec.

____1____ She packed her suitcases.

1. _____ Charlie planted the lettuce seed in early spring.

   _____ He spaded his garden carefully and worked in fertilizer.

2. _____ We looked up the address in the phone book.

   _____ We took the car to the shop.

3. _____ Ruth attended classes.

   _____ Ruth paid her registration fees for two classes in the fall.

   _____ Ruth took a hundred dollars from savings for her fees.

4. _____ Sammy put the food down for his puppies at three o'clock.

   _____ Sammy got the food ready with his mom's help.

   _____ Sammy and his mother bought dog food at the store.

5. _____ Kenita turned in her essay at the beginning of class.

   _____ Kenita wrote her name carefully at the top of the essay.

   _____ Kenita typed her assignment on the computer.

6. _____ Lou Ann walks to the bus stop at 7:00.

   _____ Lou Ann eats breakfast at 6:15.

   _____ The bus ride lasts about thirty minutes. Lou Ann gets on the bus at 7:10.

7. _____ Harry deposited his paycheque in the bank.

   _____ Harry walked to the personnel office to pick up his paycheque.

   _____ Harry filled out the deposit slip on the way to the bank.

8. _____ Sharon shovelled the snow from the front walk in the morning.

   _____ Snow fell most of the night.

   _____ Sharon sprinkled rock salt from her front door to the street.

   _____ Sharon opened the bag of rock salt.

   _____ Sharon got out the snow shovel and bag of rock salt.

9. _____ Paula filled out the application for the mechanic's job.

   _____ Paula checked the jobs advertised in the local paper.

   _____ Paula waited patiently to be called for an interview.

   _____ Paula went to Robinson Motor Company the next morning.

   _____ Robinson Motor Company was advertising for a mechanic.

10. _____ Once home, Bert and Larry decided to wax their mom's car.

    _____ Bert and Larry got home from school at 4:00.

    _____ Bert and Larry finished their homework and left the school library at 3:30.

_____ Bert and Larry drove to the discount store to buy the car wax.

_____ Bert and Larry carefully read the directions for putting on the wax.

Unity All sentences in a good paragraph relate to the topic sentence (main idea). When any idea doesn't relate specifically to the topic sentence, then that paragraph lacks unity. Look again at the paragraph about giant sea turtles. This draft has one main idea and several support sentences that help to explain the general word(s) expressed in the topic sentence.

> **Scientists are working hard to gather facts about sea turtles called leatherbacks.** The observers work, no matter what the weather is like—on clear days or in pouring rain. They count the turtles as they come ashore. When the turtles lay their eggs, the scientists walk up and down the beaches for many hours at a time. They count the eggs in the sand. Then, later, they count the eggs that hatch. **These biologists know that they are collecting information that will someday be important to other scientists.**

This paragraph shows the three parts of a good paragraph—topic sentence, support sentences, and concluding sentence (or conclusion). Now check to see if the paragraph has the important element of unity.

To check for unity, first separate the topic sentence into its two parts:

Topic:	Scientists
Direction or general word(s):	are working hard to gather facts about sea turtles called leatherbacks.

Second, check each support sentence against the topic sentence. Each supporting idea is a specific fact or detail that explains what the scientists actually do to work hard to gather information. In this case, each sentence after the topic sentence explains how the scientists are working hard to gather facts about sea turtles.

Topic Sentence
Scientists are working hard to gather facts about sea turtles called leatherbacks.

Support Sentences
The **observers work, no matter what the weather is like**—on clear days or in pouring rain.

They count the turtles as they come ashore

...the **scientists walk up and down the beaches for many hours** at a time.

They count the eggs in the sand.

Then, later, **they count the eggs that hatch**.

Notice that the bold words in each support sentence make reference to the main idea in the topic sentence. The fact that all the information in the support statements clearly and directly relate to the general idea in the topic sentence gives this paragraph **unity**.

All you have to do to check a paragraph's unity is to see if each sentence gives details that explain the main idea in the topic sentence. Similarly, the best way to write good, unified paragraphs is to make all the sentences between your topic sentence and the conclusion explain your main idea.

Now read the following draft of the preceding paragraph. Look for the sentence that does not explain the topic sentence. This sentence breaks the unity of the paragraph.

> Scientists are working hard to gather facts about sea turtles called leatherbacks. The observers work, no matter what the weather is like—on clear days or in pouring rain. The leatherback is the only kind of turtle that can live in the cold North Atlantic Ocean. They count the turtles as they come ashore. When the turtles lay their eggs, the scientists walk up and down the beaches for many hours at a time. They count the eggs in the sand. Then, later, they count the eggs that hatch. These biologists know that they are collecting information that will someday be important to other scientists.

The sentence that breaks the unity is "The leatherback is the only kind of turtle that can live in the cold North Atlantic Ocean." This sentence tells about the turtles; it does not directly relate to how the observers work to get their information. Consequently, this sentence spoils the paragraph's unity.

The following exercise will help you identify sentences that do not support a topic sentence. Being able to identify such unrelated sentences will help you preserve the unity in the paragraphs you are writing.

EXERCISE 9

Study each group of sentences. Identify the sentences as follows:
1 = a possible topic sentence
2 = a factual support sentence (a detail or example)
3 = an unrelated sentence

Example:

_____1_____ Elderly people enjoy outdoor activities.

_____3_____ Children swim in the pool next to the shuffleboard court.

_____2_____ Elderly people play shuffleboard.

1. _____ George bought a Ford.

    _____ George admires North American cars.

    _____ He needs a new lawn mower.

2. _____ The puppies loved to play running games in the house.

    _____ Chokka dashed headlong under the bed.

    _____ The puppies ate a lot.

3. _____ The science teacher started a chemistry class for nurses.

    _____ The English department needed computers.

    _____ The school planned new math and science courses.

4. _____ The football training program is strenuous.

    _____ The coach makes less money than the quarterback.

    _____ The runningbacks have to run many wind sprints.

5. _____ The librarian ordered fifteen new Canadian novels.

    _____ The library has an extensive collection of Canadian literature.

    _____ The library's art collection is outstanding.

6. _____ The scout troop learned three outdoor skills.

    _____ Jackie enjoyed the needlecraft.

    _____ The scouts learned the safe way to build a campfire.

7. _____ Going to college and having a job may leave little time for recreation.

    _____ Gerald forgot to do his math homework.

    _____ Gerald could not go to the movies last weekend.

8. _____ John wrote a research paper for Biology 101.

    _____ The biology class required several lab and writing assignments.

    _____ John missed two biology lectures.

9. _____ The rose quartz was one of the best pieces displayed.

   _____ Kim liked to go rock hunting on weekends.

   _____ The school library had a special rock and gem collection.

10. _____ A monkey can turn pages of a book for the owner.

    _____ Monkeys are often brown.

    _____ A monkey can aid handicapped people.

11. _____ Children need a lot of attention.

    _____ Susan loves to be read to before bedtime.

    _____ Susan ate all the ice cream.

12. _____ Passengers can look out the window.

    _____ A train ride can bring pleasure.

    _____ Working overtime can be stressful.

13. _____ The dishes need to be done.

    _____ I finally hired a gardener to do the yard work.

    _____ Housekeeping can be a never-ending job.

14. _____ Swimming is good physical therapy.

    _____ Many of my neighbours wonder why I swim at 6:00 a.m. every day.

    _____ Paraplegics increase muscle tone in the swimming pool at Saint Luke's Hospital.

EXERCISE 10

Check the following drafts for **unity.** *Underline any sentences that do not support or explain the main idea in the topic sentence.*

Paragraph 1

People from other countries have different reasons for wanting to come to live in Canada. For example, some might want higher-paying jobs than they can get in their own countries. Some want the freedom to change jobs or professions. Some might want the chance to get more education for themselves and their families. Church groups often sponsor people coming to Canada. Perhaps one of the most important reasons would be the desire to own and operate a business. Many people wait a long time for the chance to live in Canada. Every year, regardless of the reasons, many more people come to live in Canada.

Paragraph 2

Going back to school in the fall requires some advanced planning because registration fees and books will take a lot of money. Students generally like to spend their savings on recreational activities. Thinking ahead would mean that money from a summer job should have been saved to pay for these necessary items. Also, the boss should be told ahead of time that a change in working hours will be needed. Perhaps going back to school will mean that fewer hours can be spent on the job, and expenses like gas and car repairs may have to be taken out of money usually set aside for fun and recreation. Registering for the fall semester can be a positive experience. With enough planning, financial problems can be avoided.

Coherence One of the most important considerations in writing a paragraph is **coherence**—which means that all the sentences should be clearly connected to each other. Without connecting words or phrases, supporting ideas may be hard to follow and sometimes may even seem to be unrelated to the topic sentence and to each other. In those cases, the sentences sound like a list.

The following paragraph has the coherence it needs:

When Sue was a child, she learned from her dad how to be a hard worker. For example, she always helped in the yard. Many times they mowed the lawn together. Sue emptied the grass catcher (which her dad did not overfill), and he did the heavy part by lifting the barrels full of grass. Working together, they did not quit until the job was done. She and her dad worked even after the sun was gone, making sure that the edges of the lawn were neat. In this way, Sue learned to stay with a job until she had done it well and could feel proud of her effort.

This paragraph shows **coherence** because *at least one* of the key words or phrases—or variations of them—is repeated either directly or indirectly *in each sentence.*

Key Words or Phrases	Variations of Key Words
Sue	she
learned	learned
her dad	he
Sue and her dad	they, together
hard worker	job, helped in the yard, did the heavy part, lifting, work, working, didn't quit until the job was done, making sure, stay with a job, effort

Each sentence in the paragraph is *clearly* connected to the one before it by a clear pronoun or a clear example of a key word. Other words or phrases also help set the scene or provide time signals in order to clarify the experience for the reader:

Other Words or Phrases That Provide Coherence

always

many times

even after

A very important signal to the reader—"for example"—occurs near the beginning of the paragraph. This phrase tells the reader to watch for specific details that will clarify the topic sentence. It helps to signal to the reader where the support sentences begin.

At the end of the paragraph, the most important connecting words "in this way" introduce the concluding sentence. This phrase points back to all the examples that help make the main point clear.

Making clear connections between two consecutive sentences is very important. Do not assume that your readers know what you are talking about. Try to emphasize the relationship between sentences. The extra effort is well worth it. (You will learn more about coherence in Unit 7.)

The following exercise will help you understand and practise giving paragraphs coherence.

EXERCISE 11

Read each paragraph below. Underline the topic sentence. Circle the key words or phrases in the topic sentence that could be used to add coherence. Revise each paragraph below and put in connecting words and phrases to show clearly how sentences relate to each other and to the topic sentence. Use the key words or variations of them. Put in "time signal" words like "then" or "next" or "later." Use "for example" to introduce specific examples. You may combine ideas if necessary to make each paragraph flow more smoothly. Finally, make sure that the concluding sentence clearly refers to the main idea in the topic sentence.

Example:

When they went in, they

(Carol and Bev) had a (good time) at the (movie.) Carol and Bev decided to sit

so   They liked the movie because the
in the back where they could relax and have lots of room. The music was

exciting and the   During the show, they
exciting. The story was suspenseful. They ate popcorn and drank a soft

The best part of all was watching the   in front of them. All of these
drink. There were lots of good-looking guys there. They enjoyed

things added up to an enjoyable
their afternoon at the movies.

Paragraph 1

Newspaper reporters write stories about unusual people. Reporters meet many kinds of people. Reporters write about business people and sports stars. They may interview a balloon pilot. They might know someone with a huge collection of old fountain pens. Senior citizens have hobbies and leisure activities. Some reporters want to entertain their readers.

Paragraph 2

Jason enjoys card games. He learned to play when he was a child. He likes solitaire. He likes gin rummy. He plays fifty-two-pickup with his four-year-old brother. Jason does not like to gamble. He would rather play for fun and relaxation.

Paragraph 3

My favourite birthday present was a trip through the zoo. I was ten years old. Three friends and I were taken by my mom to the zoo. My sister went, too. We made a lot of noise when we saw the snakes. My mom said she liked tigers. We saw birds and monkeys at the zoo. I took pictures of everybody with a new camera. We had a picnic lunch. They gave me presents. We had hot dogs, ice cream, and pop. We had a great time at the zoo.

PART 2 | # Something to Think About, Something to Write About

Sometimes reading a scholarly article can make you stop and think about the world in which you live. Articles of this type can be about political or social issues that directly affect you. They could also make you think about your past or future. By reading these articles, you can get information about the world as well as ideas that you can use in your writing. They may trigger something in your memory that you can put into your writing.

The following article may make you reflect upon events that happened early in your life or events that are going on right now as a result of your past. These events, then, can become a valuable resource for your writing.

Read the following article and then work through one or more of the suggested writing assignments that require memory of past events. If you cannot remember your past, then maybe you could focus on something that you have experienced recently.

Childhood

Adapted from the original by **Dr. Linda Coble**, *therapist and psychologist*

1   Do you remember what you were doing and how you were feeling in the first grade? Who was your teacher in kindergarten? Can you remember what you were doing before starting school? How far back can you reach into your past? Can you recollect your first experience of emotional awareness? What was it? fear? security? warmth? The answers to these questions can be extremely valuable to therapists working with their clients. Some people may think pulling out long-past, ancient detail is impossible, but Adlerian therapists and clients are doing it every day. In fact, a very important aspect of many psychotherapy approaches is to gather details from clients about their early history, for these early experiences may have an important impact on the clients' personality development.

2   Adlerian theory, a popular counselling approach, calls these events "early recollections." Clients are asked to recall incidents from as far back as they are able. Experiences can be both positive and negative. Therapists gather these memories. As they sort the information, they pay attention to the age of the person at the time of the recollection, the specific details of the occurrence, and the feelings the client experienced. The therapist, upon gathering several of these recollections, will use them in analyzing the client's goals and attitudes.

3   Birth order is also considered by Adlerian therapists to be an important influence on personality development. Our first interaction with people is within our family structure, and the position in the family may have set up certain expectations from significant family members. Children, in their effort to achieve a sense

of belonging, will take on roles in the family. Commonly, the oldest children adopt the role of being responsible, serious, and dependable. The middle child is in the uncomfortable position of following the first-born and will often experience pressure in her/his attempt to catch up with the older sibling(s). If the second-born feels a struggle, she or he may develop opposite traits from those of the older brother or sister. The youngest child is often a charmer who struggles with being taken seriously. Of course, these are generalizations, and many combinations of the family structure can be more accurately analyzed by a qualified therapist. No doubt, however, this position in the family, as well as an understanding of how the child interpreted early family situations, provides valuable insight for the therapist.

4   In some extreme cases, a therapist may find that a client has had an unusually traumatic experience. Perhaps a serious fire, a prolonged illness of a family member, a death of a parent, or an early encounter with alcoholism may have affected a child's perception of family life, consequently affecting the child's view of the world. In this case, the therapist tries to help the client to explore the event. A therapist may use simulated drama, dialogue, simulated confrontation with conflicting family members, or writing to shed the negative feelings and "clean the slate" for the client. By re-exposing the details of negative occurrences and accepting the help of a therapist to put the events to rest, so to speak, the client experiences a cathartic relief and can have a healthier, more positive outlook.

5   Early recollections and birth order are effective beginning places for therapists; however, what is done with the information once it is obtained is equally important. Even though such beginnings provide an insight into what may be the cause of the problem, the strategies for new directions or solutions provided by therapists are what make the total therapeutic process worthwhile for the client.

Something to Write About
Now that you have read the article, write a paragraph that addresses one of the following topics:
  1. How did it feel to be the oldest child? middle child? youngest child? only child?
  2. Describe a place that gave you a feeling of warmth or security as a child.
  3. Describe the most negative or ugly place you remember as a child.
  4. Describe the most beautiful object you remember seeing.
  5. What responsibilities did you have while growing up?
  6. What qualities should a good parent possess?
  7. Which people influence a child the most?
  8. What types of problems do working parents encounter?
  9. What are the advantages of being a working parent?
 10. How can parents minimize conflicts in a family?

After you draft your paragraph, do each of the following:
Revise it so it has a clear topic sentence.
Include four to six supporting sentences.
Include a closing sentence.
Check for unity and a smooth flow of ideas.

PART 3 | Paragraphs for Discussion and Analysis

My Grandmother and Grandfather's House

Michael Gaspar, *student*

The corner of my grandmother and grandfather's house is not an ordinary corner of a house but a very special place to me. As a young child, I could feel the warmth of the blankets and the sound of gas seeping out of the burner keeping me warm. The floor was so soft, and my brother's back against mine was reassurance that nothing could harm me. I could gaze up at the ceiling and watch the candle's reflection dancing as if to entertain me. Most of all, I could hear a very subtle breathing sound as if it were singing to me. The love in that place made me get the chills if not a slight tear to my eye. I go back once in a while to see this place, and you know, it is still the same, and I miss it dearly.

Questions on Content
1. What made the author get the chills?
2. Where was the special place?
3. What danced on the ceiling?

Questions on Form
1. What is the topic sentence?
2. Does the paragraph stay with the main idea?
3. What details can you name?

Concentration Camp

Jan-Georg Roesch, *student*

My visit to the concentration camp was a frightful and thoughtful experience. In the 1930s and 1940s under the regime of Adolf Hitler, this place ended many innocent people's lives. The building looked as unwelcoming as a graveyard by night. The heavy iron door, which slowly gave way to the pulling force, creaked as it was opened. Each footstep echoed through the chamber as each individual slowly pondered and walked from one end of the room to the other. Every unconscious mumble could be heard clearly. The smell was so sharp and distinct, yet I could not identify it with anything explicable. The glaring light which lit the room was unbearable, and for many it was the last sight of daylight before entering the execution room. The major impact this place had on me was that even the most negative thought could not describe the coldness of this place.

Questions on Content
1. When was this concentration camp used?
2. What does the author compare this place to?
3. What was the overall feeling the author experienced at this place?

Questions on Form
1. Which senses does the author use?
2. What makes the topic sentence effective?
3. State the concluding sentence.

Visiting a New City

Jason Beezley, *student*

I enjoy visiting different cities because of all the places there are to see and all the interesting things there are to do. If I go to Los Angeles, for example, I do not want to see the museums. Rather, I go to the beach and the cool shops. But if I go to a place like Leningrad, USSR, I would go to the museums, government buildings, and places like that. The last time I went to Los Angeles, all I did was skateboard, walk along the beach, and go to the cool shops. That was one of the best times I have ever had in California. However, when I was in Russia over the summer, I visited the most beautiful museums I have ever seen. I also went to an old Russian circus. Now that was quite an experience. Even though I did not understand a word they said, I had lots of fun. No matter what city I visit, I am sure I will find worthwhile places to go.

Questions on Content
1. What two cities did he visit?
2. What did he do in Russia?
3. What did he do in Los Angeles?

Questions on Form
1. In what way do the examples support the topic sentence idea?
2. Could the student use more specific examples?
3. Is there a conclusion? If so, what is it?

An Eyewitness Account of the San Francisco Earthquake

Excerpt from article in *Collier's* (1906) by **Jack London**

On Wednesday morning at a quarter past five came the earthquake. A minute later the flames were leaping upward. In a dozen different quarters south of Market Street, in the working-class ghetto, and in the factories, fires started. There was no opposing the flames. There was no organization, no communication. All the cunning adjustments of a twentieth-century city had been smashed by the earthquake. The streets were humped into ridges and depressions and piled with debris of fallen walls. The steel rails were twisted into perpendicular and horizontal angles. The telephone and telegraph systems were disrupted. And the great water mains had burst. All the shrewd contrivances and safeguards of man had been thrown out of gear by thirty seconds' twitching of the earth-crust.

Questions on Content
1. What could be done about the earthquake?
2. What damage did the earthquake do?
3. At what time did the fire start?

Questions on Form
1. Do all the examples support the topic idea?
2. How is the topic idea stated?
3. Does the concluding sentence echo the topic idea?

....

Martin Luther King

Excerpt from *Martin Luther King* by **Rae Bains**

In Atlanta and other parts of the South, blacks were not treated the same as whites. For example, a white person who wanted to ride a bus simply got on, paid the fare, and took a seat. But a black person got on, paid the fare, got off again, walked to the rear door of the bus and got on there. Blacks could only sit in the back of the bus. If all the seats became filled, the blacks had to give up their seats to white people who got on.

Questions on Content
1. Where did blacks sit on a bus?
2. What did blacks do when the bus was full and a white person got on?
3. What part of the country is the author talking about?

Questions on Form
1. Does the idea of blacks sitting in the back support the topic sentence?
2. Where is the topic sentence stated?
3. How is the topic sentence supported?

....

Subway Station

Excerpt from *Talents and Geniuses* by **Gilbert Highet**

Standing in a subway station, I began to appreciate the place—almost to enjoy it. First of all, I looked at the lighting: a row of meager electric bulbs, unscreened, yellow, and coated with filth, stretched toward the black mouth of the tunnel, as though it were a bolt hole in an abandoned coal mine. Then I lingered, with zest, on the walls and ceiling: lavatory tiles which had been white about fifty years ago, and were now encrusted with soot, coated with the remains of a dirty liquid which might be either atmospheric humidity mingled with smog or the result of a perfunctory attempt to clean them with cold water; and, above them, gloomy vaulting from which dingy paint was peeling off like scabs from an old wound, sick black paint leaving a leprous white undersurface. Beneath my feet, the floor was a nauseating dark brown with black stains upon it which might be stale oil or dry chewing gum or some worse defilement; it looked like the hallway of a condemned slum building. Then my eye traveled to the tracks, where two lines of glittering steel—the only positively clean object in the whole place—ran out of darkness into darkness about an unspeakable mass of congealed oil, puddles of dubious liquid, and a mishmash of old cigarette packets, mutilated and filthy newspapers, and the debris that filtered down from the street above through a barrel grating in the roof. As I looked up toward the sunlight, I could see more debris sifting slowly downward, and making an abominable pattern in the slanting beam of dirt-laden sunlight. I was going on to relish more features of this unique scene: such as the advertisement posters on the walls—here a text from the Bible, there a half-naked girl, here a woman wearing a hat consisting of a hen sitting on a nest full of eggs, and there a pair of girl's legs walking up the keys of a cash register—all scribbled over with unknown names and well-known obscenities in black crayon and red lipstick; but then my train came in at last, I boarded it, and began to read. The experience was over for the time.

Questions on Content

1. What did the author enjoy at first?
2. In spite of the negative details, what was his reaction as he stood and looked at the place?
3. What was the only "positively clean object in the whole place"?

Questions on Form

1. State the topic sentence.
2. What makes the paragraph effective?
3. How does the paragraph conclude?

| PART 4 | The Writer's Tools: Basic Sentence Skills |

OBJECTIVES

....

- Identify prepositional phrases to avoid confusing them with subjects.
- Identify subjects and verbs in sentences.
- Recognize sentence structure errors.
- Maintain subject-verb agreement in sentences.
- Maintain constant verb tense in paragraphs or essays.

Having a paragraph that focuses on one idea and stays with that one idea is the most important part of writing. Sometimes, however, the effectiveness of a paragraph is diminished because of simple grammatical errors. These grammatical problems distract the reader from the ideas in the paragraph.

After writing your paragraph and making sure that all the information supports the topic sentence, you will need to do some editing. In order to help you in your editing, this section reviews prepositional phrases, subjects, and verbs. It also reviews basic sentence structure errors. Emphasis is then placed on identifying subjects and verbs within a paragraph to make sure that they are both singular or both plural (subject-verb agreement). Emphasis is also placed on how to check the verbs in a paragraph to see if they are all in the present or all in the past (consistent verb tense).

Before you can edit your paragraph for sentence structure errors, subject-verb agreement, and consistent verb tense, you must be able to identify subjects and verbs in sentences. Subjects are words that function as nouns or pronouns. Sometimes the nouns or pronouns in prepositional phrases are mistaken for the subject of a sentence. One of the most common errors students make in finding the subject of a sentence is to mistake an object of a preposition for the subject of the sentence. Because this is true and because prepositional phrases are easy to identify, you will find it easier to locate subjects if you identify prepositional phrases first.

Finding Prepositional Phrases

Generally, prepositional phrases are phrases that begin with a preposition and end with a noun or pronoun. The noun or pronoun that ends the phrase is called the **object** and can never be the subject of a sentence. The object of a preposition can be identified by asking a question consisting of the preposition and "what":

prep.   obj.
by the rider   (by what?)

prep.   *obj.*
with careful training   (with what?)

prep. *obj.*
into water   (into what?)

prep. *obj.*
to the other   (to what?)

- **A prepositional phrase may show location.**
  The mother bird quickly hopped *from one baby to the other*.
  ("From one baby" and "to the other" show the location of the mother.)

- **A prepositional phrase may show exclusion.**
  The baby birds had nothing on their minds *except food*.
  ("Except food" shows that all other thoughts were excluded.)

- **A prepositional phrase may show ownership or identification.**
  This spring a mother sparrow *with her two young sparrows* ventured forth.
  ("With her two young sparrows" shows that the young sparrows belong to the mother.)

- **A prepositional phrase may show time.**
  The mother sparrow and her babies ventured out *for the first time*.
  ("For the first time" shows when they ventured out.)

- **A prepositional phrase may have more than one object.**
  The mother sparrow and her babies searched for food and water.

The best way to learn to identify a prepositional phrase is to look for a pattern that always includes the preposition and its object. It also includes any word(s) that come between the preposition and its object.

prep   *obj.* (noun)
in high esteem

prep *obj.* (pronoun)
by no one

prep   *obj.* (noun)
of the young boys

prep   *obj.* (pronoun)
to the pretty one

prep *obj.* (noun) *obj.* (noun)
for his bow and arrow

Now, refer to the following list of prepositions until they become easy to recognize.

Prepositions

aboard	between	out off
about	beyond	outside
above	but	over
across	by	since
after	down	through
against	during	throughout
along	except	to
along with	for	toward
among	from	under
around	in	underneath
at	into	until
because of	like	unto
before	of	up
behind	off	with
below	on	within
beneath	on account of	without
beside	onto	
besides	out	

To check your ability to identify prepositional phrases, work through the following exercises. In the first exercise, the sentences are isolated so that you can identify the prepositional phrases more easily. In the second exercise, paragraphs are used to help you see how prepositional phrases are a natural part of writing.

EXERCISE 1

Identify the prepositional phrases in the following sentences by placing parentheses ( ) around each phrase.

Example:

Baskets (of all sizes and shapes) covered the shelves.

1. Jill went home early because of the rain.

2. The mother of those twins left without a moment's hesitation.

3. During the winter we enjoy travelling to a warmer climate.

4. Everyone except the little boy went to the beach.

5. The peaches on the table are ripe.

6. The information concerning his job is on top of the file.

7. Beside the lake is a wonderful place.

8. Jim leaned against the table for support.

9. We floated down the river on an inner tube.

10. The six puppies ran beyond the little child's reach.

11. I appreciate working with people like her.

12. Without a second thought Jenny donated blood every four months.

13. One of my favourite sights is the Vancouver sunset.

14. They walked around the track for two hours.

15. The child behind the tree is looking for her kitten.

16. In spite of the rain, they drove their Jeep off the main road onto a side road.

17. They will be back within an hour or two.

18. I need a litre of paint in the kitchen.

19. The participant in the Iron Man contest continued beyond human limits.

20. I like the butterflies on display.

EXERCISE 2

Identify the prepositional phrases in the following paragraphs by placing parentheses ( ) around each phrase.

Paragraph 1

A person who wants to earn a living by crabbing must learn about crabs and their varying market value. A Jimmy or male bull crab sells for the most money. It is large and provides a generous supply of sweet, white meat. A sook or full-grown female crab is next in size to the Jimmy. She sheds her shell, becomes soft, mates, and rehardens. She then becomes a mature crab. At this point, she is a fairly large crab, but she cannot compete with the bull crab for equal market value because she is a bit smaller. A young female crab also lacks the size needed for the market. Crabbing can be a profitable business if a person learns about crabs, especially from a good crabber.

Paragraph 2

High jumping is a challenging sports event. The athletes compete against other athletes, but more importantly, they compete against themselves. Every time a height is reached, a new, greater height is facing them. Consequently, the sport is a constant process in which a person sets a goal, reaches it, and sets a new one. Determination and perseverance are needed to succeed in this demanding competition. Another difficult trial present in high jumping is a test of psyche or stressed mindset. As the jumpers see the pole getting higher and higher, they might panic and think they cannot jump over the bar. The cool, confident competitor is usually the one who can fly over the bar. For those athletes who can meet these challenges, high jumping can bring a genuine "peak" experience.

Finding Subjects and Verbs

Once you are skilled at finding prepositional phrases, it is easier to identify subjects and verbs. Learning to edit for certain grammar problems is usually easier if you are able to identify subjects and verbs.

Subjects

A subject is the word that answers "who" or "what" to the main verb in the sentence. Some sentences have a simple subject, and other sentences have a compound subject. Only a word that functions as a noun or a pronoun (except the noun or pronoun in a prepositional phrase) may be the subject of a sentence.

- **A simple subject is a word that functions as a noun or pronoun and is what the sentence is about.**

  Here are two sentences in which a noun is the subject:

  Ron gave me a great idea. (Who gave me a great idea?)
  The **flowers** in the vase fell on the floor. (What fell on the floor?)

  Here are two sentences in which a pronoun is the subject:

  He gave me a great idea. (Who gave me a great idea?)
  Others were planted yesterday. (What was planted yesterday?)

- **The compound subject is two or more words that the sentence is about.**

  Trisha and Sam are late. (Who are late?)

  Ron and **Carrie** gave me a great surprise. (Who gave me a great surprise?)

- **All sentences *must* have a main subject and a verb. However, when a command is used, the subject is understood to be "you."**

         V

  Close the door.

         S   V

  (You) close the door.

 V
Water the plants.

 S V
(You) water the plants.

 V   V
Come in and sit down

 S V   V
(You) come in and sit down

- **"Here" and "there" can never be the subject of a sentence.**

 V   S
Here are the books.

 V   S
There are five pages to complete.

To check your ability to identify subjects and prepositional phrases, do the following exercises. In the first exercise, the sentences are isolated so that you can identify the prepositional phrases more easily. Then paragraphs are used for further practice.

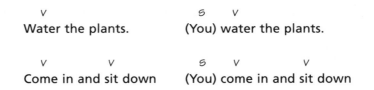

EXERCISE 3

In each of the following sentences, enclose all prepositional phrases in parentheses. Then underline the subject(s) once. Some sentences will have simple subjects, and others will have compound subjects.

Example:

<u>Women</u>, <u>children</u>, and <u>men</u> (of all ages) enjoy holidays.

1. There are many jobs left to be completed.

2. The man in the blue Levis is leaving.

3. Jana was late for the meeting.

4. The children are leaving for Black Creek Pioneer Village.

5. The dog and the cat are playing together.

6. Please close the door.

7. The water in the swimming pool is clear and blue.

8. Two of my friends left for vacation at the same time.

9. Here are the books for you.

10. The dog stood on two legs and barked twice.

11. The members of the committee left at 6:00 in the evening.

12. Josh is the smartest person in the world.

13. Pick the books up off the floor and do your homework.

14. The students in the classroom brought paper and pencils to class.

15. Ting and Li shopped and shopped for clothes.

16. The bananas with brown spots taste sweet.

17. The wedding took much planning and work.

18. The bride and groom had a wonderful day.

19. Turn the water off, please.

20. During the movie, the man and his daughter ate popcorn and drank pop.

EXERCISE 4

Identify prepositional phrases in the following paragraphs by enclosing them in parentheses. Underline the subject of each sentence.

Paragraph 1

This spring a mother sparrow with her two young sparrows ventured out of their nest in search of food and water for the first time. As the trio bounced along, it was easy to pick out the baby birds from the mother because the young sparrows fluttered their wings and opened their beaks. Then the mother sparrow inserted a crumb of bread or a little bug into the tiny gaping beaks. In her effort to feed both babies, she quickly hopped from one to the other, attending to both of them. She then slowly drank from a small rain puddle. The babies, however, had nothing on their minds except food. It was a pleasant sight to see.

Paragraph 2

The time is June, and the cicadas in larval form make their way from the ground to nearby trees. They begin to emerge from their final stage of metamorphosis. In their final form, they are insects with antennae, large eyes, and large wings. However, they are best known for the loud buzzing sound they continually make. At night, during early June, thousands of them shed their cases and are transformed into adult cicadas. Within a month, they mate and die. Before death, however, the females lay as many as six hundred eggs in trees. In six weeks, wingless nymphs hatch, drop to the ground, and work their way into the soil. There during their next stage, they feed on tree sap constantly as they mature into the larval stage to begin the process all over again.

Verbs

A verb is what the subject of the sentence does. The verb may show action—"run" or "hit"; it may be a form of "be"—"is" or "am"; or it may be "state of being"—"appears" or "sounds."

Action: Ralph **ran** through the woods.
Sara **hit** the car broadside.

Nonaction: form of "be"
Ralph **is** in the woods.
Sara **was** in her car.

state of being
Ralph **appears** cool and strong.
Sara **sounds** confident and impressive.
The ice tea **tastes** good.

- **The verb may consist of one word or several words.**

The simple verb is one action verb or nonaction verb that tells what the subject does. The simple verb may be this one action or nonaction word alone or may be combined with a helping verb.

Here are some helping verbs:

be (all forms)	does	might
can	had	shall
could	has	should
did	have	will
do	may	would

Action: Todd blew his horn. (action verb)
Todd did blow his horn. (action verb + helping verb)

Nonaction: form of "be"
Todd **is** my brother. (nonaction verb)
Todd **has been** my brother.
(nonaction verb + helping verb)

state of being
Todd **appears** happy. (nonaction verb)
Todd **does appear** happy.
(nonaction verb + helping verb)

Sometimes forms of *do (do, does, did)* and *have (have, has, had)* are the main verb in a sentence; other times these forms are used with another main verb to form the simple verb.

Main verb: Todd **did** his homework.

Helping verb: Todd **did finish** his homework.

- Compound verbs are two or more verbs that tell what the subject does.

   The man **looked** down and **found** a diamond ring.

   The camel **ate** the apple and then **snorted**.

Recognizing Sentence Structure Errors

Learning to identify subjects and verbs in a sentence is a skill that can help you edit your writing. For example, you can find and revise sentence problems so that your ideas are expressed in clear and complete sentences. Examine the following sentence structure errors: sentence fragments, comma splices, and run-on sentences.

Sentence Fragments

To be complete, a sentence needs a subject and a main verb that together form a completed idea. If one or more of these parts are missing, then the sentence is a **fragment**. Consider the following example of a complete sentence:

People with loyalty for their country voted.

However, if you left out the verb, you would not have a complete sentence:

People with loyalty for their country.

Leaving out "voted" makes the idea a fragment. In all honesty, your readers could get some meaning, but they would not know the completed thought you wanted to express.

Likewise, if you left out the subject, "people," you would again have a fragment instead of a complete sentence:

With loyalty for their country voted.

Here are other examples of incomplete thoughts that would not work as sentences because one or more parts are missing:

Being honest and being loyal to each other.

Without these qualities for a friendship.

To make complete sentences out of these ideas, you could revise so that each idea has a subject and a verb and, therefore, is a completed thought.

Being honest and being loyal to each other are necessary for two people to be close friends.

Without these qualities for a friendship, two people might not be close friends.

Here is another kind of sentence fragment that would have to be recognized and revised:

When we first met in high school.

People who are loyal to their country.

"When we first met in high school" may sound all right because it has a subject and a verb, but the idea is still a fragment because "when" leaves the thought incomplete. The reader expects an explanation of what happened "when we first met in high school." Revised and completed, the thought might sound like this:

When we first met in high school, we did not think of each other as friends.

In the second sentence, "who" makes the sentence a fragment because the reader wants to know what happens when "people are loyal to their country." The completed thought could sound like this:

People who are loyal to their country probably vote.

Note This is a quick discussion of sentence fragments. Unit 4 provides more detailed help, including exercises.

There are also two other kinds of sentence problems that need to be eliminated: comma splices and run-on sentences.

Comma Splices

Comma splices occur when two complete sentences are separated with only a comma marking the end of one sentence and the beginning of the next.

The speed skater raced across the frozen lake, he ignored the thin ice.

Revised to indicate the end of the first sentence and the beginning of the next, the separated sentences would look like one of these:

The speed skater raced across the frozen lake. He ignored the thin ice.

The speed skater raced across the frozen lake, and he ignored the thin ice.

Note Unit 4 provides additional help and exercises to eliminate comma splices.

Run-On Sentences

Run-on sentences occur when two or more complete ideas are expressed with no punctuation or connecting words to mark the end of one sentence and the beginning of the next one.

The speed skater raced across the frozen lake he ignored the thin ice.

To eliminate the confusion of two ideas that run together, you could mark the end of the first sentence with a comma and a connecting word, or you could use a period and start a new sentence with a capital letter. You might also use a semicolon if you are familiar with its use.

The speed skater raced across the frozen lake, and he ignored the thin ice.

The speed skater raced across the frozen lake. He ignored the thin ice.

The speed skater raced across the frozen lake; he ignored the thin ice.

Note Unit 4 provides additional help and exercises to eliminate run-on sentences.

These three kinds of sentence problems will cause confusion for your reader. Sometimes they are hard to find in your own writing, but reading aloud or getting some feedback from another reader will help you identify and eliminate these confusing sentence structure errors.

Maintaining Subject-Verb Agreement

In addition to revising to eliminate sentence structure problems, you will need to check for subject-verb agreement errors. All sentences must have both a subject and a verb that agree in number. In other words, they must both be singular (one) or must both be plural (more than one).

For example, consider the following sentences:

S   V
The dog likes to play in the sprinkler.

S   V
The dogs like to play in the sprinkler.

In the first sentence, "dog" (which is singular) agrees with "likes" (which is also singular). In the second sentence, "dogs" (which is plural) agrees with "like" (which is also plural).

Forming Plural Nouns

Most nouns are made plural by adding an -s. When in doubt about how to make a word plural, check your dictionary.

Singular	Plural
dog	dogs
book	books
car	cars
rock	rocks
plate	plates

Forming Plural Verbs

Adding -s to a noun makes it plural; however, adding -s to a verb makes it singular. Singular verbs should be used when the subject is a singular noun or one of the pronouns she, he, or it.

Incorrect: The **book** **seem** interesting.

Correct: The **books** **seem** interesting.

Correct: The **book** **seems** interesting.

Correct: **It** **seems** interesting.

EXERCISE 5

In the following sentences, put parentheses ( ) around the prepositional phrases. Then underline the subject once and fill in the blank with the verb that agrees in number with the subject.

Example:

The <u>lions</u> (at the zoo) _____*sleep*_____ **peacefully (sleep, sleeps)**

1. Mike _____ putting chrome on his Jeep. (enjoy, enjoys)

2. The leader of the group _____ the answers. (know, knows)

3. He _____ me of my brother. (remind, reminds)

4. The leader of the group _____ at 7:00 tonight. (speak, speaks)

5. The parents of young children _____ many responsibilities. (have, has)

6. Vegetable soup _____ an inviting aroma. (have, has)

7. There _____ many tasks to complete today. (is, are)

8. My new watch _____ perfect time. (keep, keeps)

9. The bags of groceries _____ to be put away. (need, needs)

10. The circus _____ enjoyment to all. (bring, brings)

11. The blue book on the shelf _____ many home projects. (illustrate, illustrates)

12. Many desert plants _____ here. (grow, grows)

13. The telephone _____ many times each day. (ring, rings)

14. The kittens in the box _____ all day long. (sleep, sleeps)

15. The puppies _____ with each other. (play, plays)

16. The student fine arts magazine often _____ many awards. (receive, receives)

17. All phases of production _____ by the students. (is done, are done)

18. The dean of students _____ the students. (enjoy, enjoys)

19. The flowers in the vase _____ water. (need, needs)

20. The red and white striped shirt _____ to Regina. (belong, belongs)

EXERCISE 6

Put all prepositional phrases in parentheses ( ). Underline the subject once and the verb twice. Then change both the subject and the verb from singular to plural form.

Example:

     geese   *bring*
The ~~goose~~ (with golden feathers) ~~brings~~ him fortune.

1. The box on the top of the table weighs five kilograms.

2. The child puts the paper by the door.

3. The deer at the zoo is very tame.

4. The bush looks healthy.

5. The leaf falls from the tree onto the sidewalk.

6. The woman on the bus leaves packages behind.

7. The church needs a new paint job.

8. Lunch at the park is a lot of fun.

9. My cat likes to climb on the roof.

10. The man at the counter donates many extra hours of work.

11. A pair of scissors needs to be sharpened.

12. The car appears to be out of gas.

13. The doctor works on cars in the evenings.

14. The recycling box is full of newspapers.

15. The child on the bicycle likes to play tag.

16. The sheep grazes in the meadow.

17. A good thesis is important in an essay.

18. A mouse lives in the basement.

19. A goose lives at the park.

20. My tax seems high.

Checking for Subject-Verb Agreement

1. **Identify all prepositional phrases**; place them in parentheses.

2. **Identify the subject and verb** of each sentence; underline the subject once and the verb twice.

3. **Check whether the verb agrees in number with its subject.**

4. **If not, change the verb** to agree in number with the subject.

Recognizing Singular and Plural Pronouns

Because pronouns can be the subject of a sentence, it is helpful to know which pronouns are singular, which are plural, and which can be either singular or plural.

- **Some indefinite pronouns are always singular, even though we often think of them as plural.**

anybody	everybody	no one
anyone	everyone	nothing

anything	everything	somebody
each	neither	someone
each one	nobody	something
either		

     s   v   v

Everything is working out quite well.

     s   v

No one wants to work late.

       v   s

There is something on the table for you.

- **When "each," "every," and "any" modify the subject, the verb is singular.**

       n   v   v

  Each person is asked to contribute to the United Way.

       n   v

  Any carpenter knows the answer

- **Some pronouns are always plural.**

  few

  many

       s   v

  A few of my friends are happy about the decision.

       s   v

  Many are willing to work.

- **Some pronouns may be singular or plural. When these pronouns are immediately preceded by a prepositional phrase, the verb agrees with the prepositional phrase.**

all	most
any	part
half	some

       s   v

  Some (of the books) are very old

       s   v

  Some (of the candy) is on the table.

     S   V V

Most (of my homework) is finished

     S   V

Most (of the boys) live in the dorm.

    S   V V

All (of the work) is completed.

    S   V V

All (of the assignments) are completed.

Noun:	name of a person, place, or thing
Pronoun:	word that takes the place of a noun
Verb:	word that tells what the subject of a sentence does
Subject:	word that tells who or what to the main verb in the sentence

EXERCISE 7

In the following sentences, put parentheses ( ) around the prepositional phrases. Then underline the subject once and fill in the blank with the verb that agrees in number with the subject.

Example:

<u>Someone</u> **(in the stands) always** _____*sees*_____ **the mistake. (see, sees)**

1. All of the players _____ the rules. (know, knows)

2. Each of the batters _____ to hit the ball. (try, tries)

3. Neither batter _____ the balls. (see, sees)

4. Someone in the stands _____ at the pitcher. (yell yells)

5. Few of the fans _____ the pressure players are under. (realize, realizes)

6. Most of the players _____ many hours each day. (practise, practises)

7. Nobody _____ to lose a ball game. (like, likes)

8. Some of the outfielders _____ a large area. (cover, covers)

9. Each one of the players _____ hard to play well. (try, tries)

10. Everybody _____ a lot of weight in each game. (carry, carries)

11. Each play _____ a difference in the outcome of the game. (make, makes)

12. Nothing _____ a team happier than winning. (make, makes)

13. There _____ something special about this team. (is, are)

14. Many of the players _____ paid well for their work. (is, are)

15. Each person on the team _____ expected to perform well. (is, are)

16. Few of the fans _____ hostility toward the players. (feel, feels)

17. Some of the players actually _____ underpaid. (feel, feels)

18. People _____ baseball whether at the ballpark or at home in front of the television set. (enjoy, enjoys)

19. Baseball _____ to a wide range of people. (appeal, appeals)

20. Every Canadian probably _____ some kind of baseball game during the year. (watch, watches)

EXERCISE 8

Put all prepositional phrases in parentheses ( ). Underline each subject once. Then find the verb in each sentence and, if necessary, correct it to agree in number with the subject. Write "C" to the left of the number if there is no error.

Example:

wants
Each person ~~want~~ the best (for her child).

1. Everybody need to take time to enjoy the little things in life.

2. Half of the people in Canada puts a lot of emphasis on money.

3. Some even likes money more than time with their children.

4. Many spends more hours working than sleeping or eating.

5. Some of the people finds time for themselves.

6. Everybody need to find time for family and friends.

7. Any diversion from routine activities are rewarding.

8. All of my friends enjoys a picnic with their families.

9. Others enjoys playing soccer.

10. A few prefers the opera.

11. Children often enjoys camping.

12. Everyone hope to find some way to relax.

13. Nobody enjoy working all the time.

14. Everyone needs to spend time enjoying life.

15. Everyone want to be around friends.

16. All of the planning needs to be done early.

17. Each of the drivers need more practice.

18. Everything from that factory is made of oak.

19. Without a doubt, someone think of a good solution.

20. Nothing behind the fence are worth keeping.

EXERCISE 9

Edit the following paragraphs for subject-verb agreement. Underline the subject(s) in each sentence once and the verb(s) twice. Then find any incorrect verb forms and correct them to agree in number with the subject.

Paragraph 1

College years is more than just a time when students can achieve knowledge. These years are also a time when students acquires lifetime friends that are never forgotten. Years later a person hear of the new president of a company and say, "I know him. We went to college together." A student have the opportunity to date others on her or his own intellectual level and enjoy the same activities. Students meet friends, and they become professional contacts many years later. They also finds others with the same personal feeling as they moves into the residences or apartments and, subsequently, into an independent lifestyle. In college, as friends share the same political and social beliefs, they comes together and strives to help humanity. The friendships in college is as important as any other aspect of a student's education.

Paragraph 2

When Americans visit Canada, they is surprised to learn the many differences in the way people speak. Canadians do not use the word "porch." Instead they uses "verandah." Canadians say the word "chesterfield" rather than "sofa." They says "zed" for "zee." What Americans call "soda," Canadians call "pop." Tourists may be identified by their speech.

Maintaining Consistent Verb Tense

Once you can identify subjects and verbs, another important skill you can master is keeping verbs consistent in your writing. What does "consistent" mean in this case? Keeping two or more verbs in a sentence or paragraph consistent means keeping them in the same time or "tense"—most of the time, either in the **present tense** or the **past tense**.

Read the following sentences and note the time (tense) of each of the verbs.

> The old man **fished** in the lake every day. Even on rainy days, he **walks** to the lake and **throws** out his line at the same spot. He seldom **caught** a fish, but he never **stopped** going until he **broke** his fishing pole.

The description begins in the past tense ("fished") because all the events happened in the past. The last sentence clearly indicates this. The verbs in the second sentence, though, shift to the present tense ("walks" and "throws"). The present tense suggests to the reader that these events are still going on. The last sentence then moves back to the past tense. All the verbs should be in the past tense, so "walks" and "throws" would have to be changed to "walked" and "threw." All the sentences would then be a description of events in the past. Present-tense verbs would not be appropriate in this description because the man stopped going fishing when he broke his pole. These events are *not* happening now.

Here is the easiest revision to make to eliminate the verb shift:

> The old man **fished** in the lake every day. Even on rainy days, he **walked** to the lake and **threw** out his line at the same spot. He seldom **caught** a fish, but he never **stopped** going until he **broke** his pole.

Because all the verbs are now in the past tense, they are *consistent*.

Present-tense verbs are used to describe something that is still true in the present. For example, one way to show activities that are still going on regularly would be to use the present tense consistently to describe these events. If the old man *had not broken* his pole, he might still be fishing *regularly*.

> The old man **fishes** in the lake every day. Even on rainy days, he **walks** to the lake and **throws** out his line at the same spot. He seldom **catches** a fish, but he never **stops** going.

Using the present tense *consistently* in this way is appropriate. Your writing will be clearer and will convey your ideas more accurately if you make an effort to use the right time signals for your reader. One such signal is consistent verb tense that is appropriate for your intended meaning.

Checking Consistent Verb Tense

1. **Find the first verb in a paragraph**, and determine whether it is in the **present tense or the past tense**.

2. **Check whether all other verbs in the paragraph are in the same tense as the first verb.**

3. **If not, change the verbs** so that they are all in the same tense.

Note A list of irregular verbs can be found in Appendix C.

EXERCISE 10

Identify the tense of the verb in the first sentence as either present or past, and then make the remaining sentences match that tense.

Paragraph 1

Tense: _____

Our favourite vacation spot was Disneyland. We enjoy the many sights and activities in this famous park. We look forward to seeing the Disney characters at the entrance. We know that we would enjoy the walk down Main Street again. We always see eager children who ride in strollers or run and skip beside their parents. As we walked down Main Street, we all probably think of the first attractions that we want to ride. Disneyland never loses its ability to enchant us.

Paragraph 2

Tense: _____

A large city like Toronto offers visitors many kinds of exciting activities. If someone wanted to attend sporting events, a large city usually has college and university basketball and hockey teams as well as professional basketball and hockey teams. If visitors did not care for sports, perhaps museums filled the bill. A large city usually has art museums as well as historical and scientific museums. For the visitor who liked shopping, the large city provided a range of stores from small specialty shops to large department stores. Since Toronto is near Lake Ontario, it offered a harbour cruise, windsurfing, and other waterfront activities. Theatres and nightclubs also gave visitors a chance to experience evening entertainment they did not have at home. A large city usually gives an out-of-town visitor a wide range of activities for excitement and fun.

Paragraph 3

Tense: _____

Senior citizens receive many recreational opportunities by living in retirement communities. Retired men and women attended craft classes that range from needlecraft to woodwork. Community members frequented one or more recreational halls that are usually equipped with pool tables and shuffleboard courts. In the evenings, they stayed busy attending dances or parties. They received exercise in indoor or outdoor swimming pools, depending on the specific region of the country. Fervent golfers teed off on well-manicured greens or played tennis on clean courts any time of the day. No matter what activity people enjoy, they find many others who enjoyed doing the same type of things.

When you edit and revise your writing, do not try to eliminate all the problems at the same time. Read for one kind of difficulty at a time.

To check for verb consistency in your own writing, read the first sentence in your paragraph. What tense is the verb? Are you describing or discussing an event that happened in the past? Are you talking about something in the future or the present? Make the verbs in the rest of the paragraph consistent with the time established in that first sentence.

Concentrate on the time signals as you read from sentence to sentence. Add other appropriate "time" words ("yesterday" or "last week" or "ten years ago" or "tomorrow" or "now" or "currently") that will clarify meaning for the reader. The extra **time** spent on **tense** will pay off!

WRITING ASSIGNMENT

Freewrite or brainstorm on one of the following activities that you have done. In one paragraph, explain what you like or dislike *about:*

1. Going to a concert
2. Visiting a relative
3. Walking through a cemetery
4. Watching a fireworks display
5. Shopping at the mall
6. Riding a bus
7. Driving a car
8. Eating at home
9. Eating out
10. Playing a musical instrument

Note *Do not narrate a story or explain how to do this activity. Rather, relate what you like or dislike about the activity.*

After you draft your paragraph, revise for content and edit for mechanics.

Content

Revise it so it has a clear topic sentence.

Include four to six supporting sentences.

Include a closing sentence.

Mechanics

Check for subject-verb agreement.

Check for consistent verbs.

Unit Three

Being a Sensitive Writer

PART 1

Parts to Whole: Interaction of Topic, Purpose, Audience, and Voice

OBJECTIVES

....

- Understand the interaction of topic, purpose, audience, and voice.

- Identify topic, purpose, audience, and voice in a given situation.

- Identify changes in wording needed when writing for different audiences.

- Compose paragraphs with predetermined topic, purpose, audience, and voice.

- Revise a paragraph when one of the four elements has been changed.

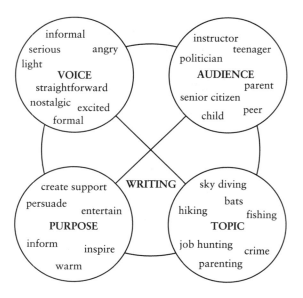

The diagram labelled "writing" shows the interaction of topic, purpose, voice, and audience within your writing. **Topic** is the subject or focus of your paper and helps to establish your **purpose**, which is essentially your reason for writing the paper. The purpose for writing your paper and your **audience**, the intended reader, determine what voice you use. **Voice** is the way the author "sounds" to the reader. If any one of these is ignored, miscommunication occurs, and the message can be misunderstood.

The following example shows how this miscommunication can occur. Dr. Wilson Riles, a well-known California educator, quoted a father who received the following note from his son's principal:

> Our schools' cross-graded, multi-ethnic, individualized learning program is designed to enhance the concept of an open-ended learning program with emphasis on a continuum of multi-ethnic, academically enriched learning, using the identified intellectually gifted child as the agent or director of his own learning.

According to Riles, the father replied with his own note:

> I have a college degree, speak two foreign languages and four Indian dialects, have been to a number of county fairs and three goat ropings, but I haven't the faintest idea as to what the hell you are talking about. Do you?

The principal had a purpose and topic but ignored his voice and his audience. Consequently, misunderstanding and anger occurred. The father also had a topic and purpose, but he considered his voice and audience. He used a straightforward, clear, yet angry voice to achieve his purpose—communicating the principal's failure to explain clearly what his message was.

The note written by the principal seems pretentious and written with the purpose of impressing the father rather than communicating with him. The father, on the other hand, responds simply and honestly, and his son's principal probably got the message.

How do you want your reader to respond to what you have to say? If your purpose for writing is to entertain, then you want your reader to react lightheartedly. If your purpose is to inform, you want your reader to take you seriously and to have a clear understanding of your message. If your purpose is to persuade, you may want your reader to take some action or to acknowledge a problem.

To review, then, here are the four elements of writing:

Topic: focus of the paper

Purpose: reason for writing the paper

Audience: intended reader

Voice: way writing "sounds" to the reader

The following situations show how topic, purpose, audience, and voice work together.

Situation 1

Mr. Latham has worked hard at his job as a newspaper editor for six years. He has demonstrated creativity and journalistic talent. In those years, he has received favourable evaluations but not a significant raise. He is writing a memo to his boss to convince him that he deserves a raise.

Topic: Mr. Latham's raise

Purpose: inform and persuade boss to give him a raise

Audience: Mr. Latham's boss

Voice: formal, polite, respectful, yet forceful

Situation 2

Mary Jones is a nurse in an elementary school. Recently a measles epidemic has swept through the community. Ms. Jones is responsible for the health and well-being of the children. Therefore, she is writing a notice to be taken home to explain to the children and their parents why the children must be vaccinated and why it is important not to be afraid to have this done.

Topic: measles vaccination

Purpose: inform them of the facts; persuade them to participate

Audience: children and parents

Voice: simple but serious, knowledgeable

Situation 3

Tessie's friend has just had a skiing accident that has kept her from trying out for the Winter Olympics. Tessie is going to write her friend a note to let her know what has happened at school while she was gone.

Topic: school activities

Purpose: entertain with funny happenings to cheer her up

Audience: Tessie's friend

Voice: humorous, light, sincere, informal

Each of these situations is going to require clear, effective communication to make the writing accomplish the desired purpose. To get the message to the audience, consider how topic, purpose, audience, and voice interact. Try working through the following exercise with this interaction in mind.

EXERCISE 1

Read the following situations and then identify the topic, purpose, audience, and voice. If you wish, use the diagram at the beginning of the chapter for types of words you can use.

Situation 1

Marie bought a television from a department store. The set worked for two weeks before it broke. She took it to an authorized repair shop; however, it wasn't repaired for five months because the television parts distributor would not send the needed parts. She called the parts distributor several times but decided to write to the president of the company that manufactured the television to get her money back.

Topic: _____

Purpose: _____

Audience: _____

Voice: _____

Situation 2

A college student living in residence has failed one class during her first semester. She has to write a note to her parents because she knows her transcript is being mailed home.

Topic: _____

Purpose: _____

Audience: _____

Voice: _____

Situation 3

Noriko has just learned that her friend recently lost her mother. She sits down to write her a note.

Topic: _____

Purpose: _____

Audience: _____

Voice: _____

Situation 4

Anna received a ticket for not stopping at a stop sign. Because she lived out of the province, she could not conveniently keep the court date, so she wrote to the judge to see if she could settle the matter through correspondence.

Topic: _____

Purpose: _____

Audience: _____

Voice: _____

Situation 5

Benjamin is applying for a job as a cashier at a computer store and on the application is asked to write a paragraph about himself.

Topic: _____

Purpose: _____

Audience: _____

Voice: _____

As you become a more experienced writer, you will become more aware of how you can adjust your writing to suit topic, purpose, audience, and voice. You will be more aware of how these elements all work together to convey ideas effectively.

Topic and Purpose Influence Voice

Often a **topic** may be given to you, or you may find one by brainstorming or freewriting. In that case, you might know right away how you want your **voice** to sound to your audience. For example, it would be difficult to write a humorous paper about cancer or AIDS. You would probably want to sound serious so your reader would take you seriously. On the other hand, if you were writing about dieting, you might want to sound lighthearted rather than serious.

Sometimes topic and **purpose** for writing may come to you almost simultaneously. If your topic were cancer, for instance, you might soon discover that you wanted to persuade your audience to have annual physical checkups. To be *persuasive*, you would certainly want your writing voice to sound knowledgeable and convincing. If you wanted to *inform* your reader about facts concerning AIDS, you would want to sound honest and informed. If you were writing about dieting, you might want to *inform and entertain* the reader at the same time. Then your writing voice could be informative as well as humorous. As you gain experience in writing, you will learn to choose a writing voice that is appropriate for the topic and purpose you have identified.

Purpose and Audience Influence Voice

Frequently, purpose and audience seem to interact and become major influences on voice. After you have chosen a topic and have identified a purpose, you should ask yourself, "Who is my audience?" If you wanted to persuade children to do something, you would use words that children could understand. If you wanted to entertain your peers, you would choose words that would be appropriate for this situation. If you were writing to someone in authority over you because you needed that person to do something for you, you most certainly would choose your words carefully so that your purpose could be accomplished.

Read the following notes, each written to a different person and with a different audience in mind. In the first note, the topic for the writer is permission to take a make-up test. The audience is the instructor, so the purpose is to persuade the instructor to allow the student to take a make-up test. Consequently, the student's voice is polite, somewhat formal, and respectful. In the student's note to the instructor, the italicized words show how words were chosen that sounded appropriate for the situation.

Note to Teacher

Ms. Mathews:

Please accept my apology for being absent on Friday, November 8. I stayed up very late the night before doing *some homework* that I was having *a hard time understanding. Consequently,* I overslept the next morning. *Please allow me* to make up the test that was given. *I will try* to catch up with the class by *borrowing the notes* from someone in the class.
Thank you.

In a second note, the purpose is the same—to persuade someone to do something. However, because the topic and the audience are different, the voice has changed to match the situation. The topic is missed lecture notes, and the audience is a fellow student. So the voice is informal, friendly, and honest. In the student's note to a friend, the italicized words show how words were chosen to sound informal—simpler phrasing throughout sounds less formal and more appropriate for the fellow student.

Note to Friend

Carla, I *missed math* yesterday because I overslept. Bill came over, and after he left, I still had to do my biology homework. The *stuff* was so hard I had a hard time reading it, and I stayed up until 2:00 this morning studying.

I left a note on Ms. Mathews's door *asking her to let me make up the test we had. Anyhow*, I told Ms. Mathews I would borrow the notes from someone in the class, *so can you let me borrow yours?*

Word Choice Alters Voice

The preceding two notes show how word choice changed when the audience changed. The note to the student also shows how changing the words made the voice sound very different. Word choice will probably determine whether or not you get your message across. Making poor word choices and not writing for the appropriate audience can distract the reader so much that the message you intended to convey is missed. Recall the earlier situation:

Mr. Latham has worked hard at his job as a newspaper editor for six years. He has demonstrated creativity and journalistic talent. In those years, he has received favourable evaluations but not a significant raise. He is writing a memo to his boss to convince him that he deserves a raise.

Consider the following two memos written by Mr. Latham to his boss. The words used in each memo will affect the boss in very different ways, even though both are written for the same purpose of requesting a raise. The words in italics show how the voice sounds to Mr. Latham's boss.

Memo 1 to Boss

Dear Mr. Stevens,

As you well know, I have worked for this company for six years as a newspaper editor. Obviously you haven't *seemed to notice* that *you owe me a raise. You can't help but notice* that I have received favourable evaluations, and it is *long past time to give me a raise.* I have gotten awards, but these awards don't *help me pay my bills any easier. I am sick and tired* of watching other people get raises instead of me. Everyone else thinks that I am doing a good job, so *what is wrong with you*?

In this first memo, Mr. Latham uses words like "obviously" and "you owe me a raise" that distract his boss from hearing a fair request for a raise. Instead, Mr. Stevens is going to feel angry and upset that one of his employees has the nerve to use a condescending, demanding voice. Now read the second memo.

Memo 2 to Boss

Dear Mr. Stevens,

I have worked for this company for six years as an *effective newspaper editor* and have devoted these years to quality work. In this time, I have watched the circulation of this newspaper grow tremendously. I have never missed a deadline, and during the time that I have been here, I have received two awards, one of which was authorized by you. My evaluations reflect a *hardworking, serious employee.* I plan to continue with the same dedicated performance. At the same time, I hope that you will *seriously consider my request for a raise in pay.*

In this memo, Mr. Latham has changed his voice by putting in different information. He has used more factual information about his job and about the newspaper. This second memo is directed toward ideas that highlight his own ability or performance. In the first memo, the emphasis was on accusing the boss of wrongdoing. In the second memo, however, word choices like "effective newspaper editor" and "hardworking, serious employee" emphasize Mr. Latham's performance and enhance his image. His voice, then, is polite rather than arrogant.

Which memo do you think is more likely to accomplish its purpose? Clearly, the second memo is more appropriate for the purpose intended by the writer. It is also important to know that words cannot only create negative feelings but can also create negative images. For instance, if you describe a chair as being a "dull, drab green," the chair may be perceived as being ugly. On the other hand, if you describe the chair as being "bright, leaf-green," the chair is probably perceived as being attractive. These word choices are very important because the negative words result in a negative voice, whereas the positive words result in a positive voice.

A positive voice (like Mr. Latham's in memo 2) is more apt to get the message across because the reader is not distracted by negative or offensive words. Making word changes to suit the purpose and audience is an important goal of revision.

Now it is time to practise creating different voices—whether angry, humorous, sad, or informative.

EXERCISE 2

Read the following sentences and then write words to describe the voice or voices reflected by each statement.

Example:

a. **Shawn was so perceptive that he understood what I was saying.**

Voice/s: <u>positive, praising</u>

b. **Shawn weaseled the information from me.**

Voice/s: <u>angry, resentful</u>

c. **Shawn obtained the information from me.**

Voice/s: <u>formal, neutral</u>

1. a. That shirt is yellow.

   Voice/s: _____

   b. That shirt is a bright, sunny colour.

   Voice/s: _____

   c. That shirt is a drab off-yellow.

   Voice/s: _____

2. a. The deep growl rumbled from the dog's throat as he looked at the shadow in the yard.

   Voice/s: _____

   b. As the dog turned toward me, he growled deep in his throat.

   Voice/s: _____

   c. My dog eagerly wagged her tail as I came in the door.

   Voice/s: _____

   d. My dog perked up her ears and followed me with her eyes as I came closer to her.

   Voice/s: _____

3. a. Joe was hired for the job.

   Voice/s: _____

   b. Joe's sharp thinking during the interview got him the job.

   Voice/s: _____

   c. Joe got the job in spite of his muddled answers during the interview.

   Voice/s: _____

4. a. I often think of the kindness that woman extended to me as a child.

   Voice/s: _____

   b. That woman took me, a poor child, to her store and helped me select any new clothes I wanted as an Easter gift.

   Voice/s: _____

c. When I was a child, the women's organization dumped used, outdated clothes on me.

Voice/s: _____

d. On Easter morning, I admired my new clothes in the mirror and then skipped lightly down the hall.

Voice/s: _____

5. a. The middle-aged woman smiled appreciatively when the award was bestowed upon her.

Voice/s: _____

b. The dumpy-looking woman in her late thirties smiled secretively as she grabbed the award.

Voice/s: _____

c. The austere woman tried hard to keep her composure when she realized she had been selected for such a prestigious award.

Voice/s: _____

6. a. The young people wolfed down their food as though they had not eaten in a week.

Voice/s: _____

b. The young people ate heartily, enjoying everything that had been prepared.

Voice/s: _____

c. The young people savoured the food that had been prepared.

Voice/s: _____

d. The young people had the food thrown at them as if they were animals.

Voice/s: _____

7. a. It is very important that we finish the job today.

Voice/s: _____

b. Maybe we could try to finish the job today.

Voice/s: _____

c. When I was a boy, we could finish the entire job in one day.

Voice/s: _____

d. Wow! We can finish the job today.

   Voice/s: _____

e. Today, we must finish.

   Voice/s: _____

f. We would be finished, except that guy kept making stupid mistakes.

   Voice/s: _____

8. a. Robert, stop that nonsense and report to the manager's office immediately.

   Voice/s: _____

   b. Robert, when you finish what you are doing, will you please come to the manager's office?

   Voice/s: _____

   c. The crowded, stuffy manager's office reminded me of my basement.

   Voice/s: _____

   d. The bright, cheery posters on the wall of the manager's office reflect a warm atmosphere.

   Voice/s: _____

EXERCISE 3

Read the following sentences and then revise them to reflect the new voice given.

Example:

The building was tan. *(neutral)*

<u>The building was painted in earth-tones.</u>
(positive)

<u>The building was painted a boring tan.</u>
(negative)

 1. Turn on the light! (angry)

_____

(polite)

(frightened)

2. I remember the long, graceful skirts my grandmother wore. *(nostalgic)*

(negative)

(excited)

3. The future of Canada depends upon the integrity of every citizen. *(formal, serious)*

(angry)

(informal)

4. The circus is enjoyed by many people. *(informative, neutral)*

(angry)

(humorous)

(nostalgic)

5. My back throbbed as I finished shovelling the snow that the plow left in my yard. *(angry)*

(positive)

(informal)

6. The food served at that restaurant was moldy and unappetizing. *(negative)*

(excited)

(positive)

7. The multicoloured Easter basket was filled with delicious treats. *(enthusiastic)*

(angry)

(negative)

_____

8. The blue car had been in the parking lot for three days. *(neutral, informative)*

_____

(nostalgic)

_____

(polite)

_____

9. The ecstatic players on the hockey team jumped up and down, celebrating victory. *(enthusiastic)*

_____

(angry)

_____

(negative)

_____

10. The little boy was covered with gooey chocolate. *(nostalgic, humorous)*

_____

(angry)

_____

(positive)

Maintaining the *same voice* within a paragraph or an entire essay is also an important goal of revision. To help you extend your ability to create and keep a consistent voice, try working through the following exercises to see how all of these elements work together to form a paragraph that will accomplish its purpose.

EXERCISE 4

Read the following paragraphs and identify the topic, audience, and voice. The purpose for each is given.

Paragraph 1

Purpose: to share information about himself and his present conflict

I often wonder what my future life will be. I live on the reservation near Brantford, where my little brother and I spend time in the summer taking care of the animals and the small field of corn that my family owns. In the wintertime, I go to school away from the reservation, and when I am at Fanshawe Community College, I still think of the quiet hours we spend watching the cows eat the little sprigs of grass and weeds. As we work in the corn, we talk about what will happen when I get out of school. He will still be at home and thinks that living in the city all the time will not be good for me. We would have no peaceful times together anymore. We couldn't walk down the corn rows and feel the earth. I wish I could live in the city and still have my animals and a field of corn.

Topic: _____

Audience: _____

Voice: _____

Paragraph 2

Purpose: to inform and encourage people not to go to Crestview Mall

For the first time in my life, I feel that writing a letter to a newspaper is necessary. Yesterday I was walking through Crestview Shopping Mall and saw the traditional bell-ringer from the Salvation Army. As I approached, a man suddenly stopped by the woman ringing the bell and told her she would have to leave the mall because no solicitors were allowed there. What is this country coming to when a volunteer seeking help for the less fortunate in our city is not allowed to stand by a store? The bell-ringer represents the spirit of giving that, from my point of view, has just about disappeared from the holiday season. The merchants want all the dollars they can get from us, but they have forgotten the original meaning of Christmas. I for one will not patronize Crestview Mall to buy presents for my family!

Topic: _____

Audience: _____

Voice: _____

Paragraph 3

Purpose: to thank someone and to identify a change to be implemented

Rick, thanks for having Bill, Sam, and me out to your factory. I am impressed with the energy level of your people and with the pride shown in the product. Your products are certainly not simple to manufacture at this point, and I can see that it takes a team effort to make things happen on schedule. Bill and I agreed that the most opportune time for us to begin looking at the engineering issues is after Bill has had some time to get familiar with his responsibilities. For the short term, you should consider sending one or more of your AutoCAD users to an advanced training program, including training in applications programming. It is easy to look at AutoCAD as primarily a drafting tool when in reality it is a fairly powerful design and communications tool. A lot of the manual process, like Bills of Operations and Bills of Material, could be simply automated. Again, thanks for having us out. I look forward to working with you.

Topic: _____

Audience: _____

Voice: _____

Paragraph 4

Purpose: to get people to do bodybuilding

As you people know, the name of the game is to make your muscles big so the girls and guys will turn their heads to look at your beautiful body as you walk past. Just yesterday I was at the grocery store and some oversized, flabby guy said to some poor skinny lady, "Get out of my way." And all I could think of was if that lady would pump iron and drink protein shakes and mega-carbohydrate drinks, she could have decked that guy and taught him some manners. Could this skinny person be you? If so, why don't you change history by investing in your body and seeing if you can take charge of the way other people treat you? Decide now. Do you want people to admire your body and respect your strength or push you around like a forty-kilogram weakling?

Topic: _____

Audience: _____

Voice: _____

Paragraph 5

Purpose: to inform and persuade the fire department to admit Shawn Stevens to its training academy

To Whom It May Concern:

Everyone realizes the extreme importance of the qualities a firefighter must possess. On behalf of Shawn Stevens, I would like to make you aware of his ability to do the job of a firefighter. His strongest asset is his dedication. He has shown an ability to commit himself with great self-discipline. For example, five years ago Shawn decided to build his body and has put in the time and energy on a routine basis to achieve that goal. Also, Shawn has experienced panic situations and has remained clear-headed. As a lifeguard for the City of Hamilton, he rescued four near-drowning victims. He knows how to administer CPR and how to react in an emergency. Finally, Shawn has demonstrated leadership. As a swim instructor, he taught approximately two hundred youths to swim, and as a swim coach he directed and inspired several youths on his team to work hard and achieve their swimming goals. Dedication, calmness in an emergency, and leadership are three qualities I imagine you would like your firefighters to possess. I recommend Shawn Stevens because he has proven he has all these characteristics.

Sincerely,

Rebecca Ivans, English Instructor and Counsellor

Topic: _____

Audience: _____

Voice: _____

Now that you have thought about all the factors needed to get your point across to someone, you are ready to practise writing paragraphs that require thought about topic, purpose, audience, and voice.

EXERCISE 5

Using the topic, purpose, audience, and voice described below, draft a paragraph that reflects the four elements in either A or B. Revise each paragraph to create the most effective voice for the intended purpose. (You may wish to prewrite on other paper first.)

Paragraph 1

Audience:

A.

    Topic: smoking in offices

  Purpose: to eliminate smoking at work

Audience: supervisors

    Voice: straightforward, angry

B.

    Topic: smoking in offices

  Purpose: to eliminate smoking at work

Audience: fellow employees

    Voice: witty and sarcastic

_____

_____

_____

_____

_____

_____

Paragraph 2

Audience:

A.

    Topic: circus

  Purpose: to describe treatment of animals at a circus

Audience: animal-rights organization

    Voice: thoughtful

B.

    Topic: circus

  Purpose: to describe events at a circus

Audience: children

    Voice: excited

_____

_____

_____

_____

_____

_____

_____

Now, as you continue writing, you can be more conscious of and sensitive to your audience so that you can achieve the purpose of your writing. Because voice often determines what kind of attitude the reader has while reading the paper, you can communicate more effectively by selecting the right words.

P A R T   2 | **Something to Think About, Something to Write About**

Getting Off the Roller Coaster

Adapted from the original by **Jerry L. Palmer**, *former Utility Worker First-Class, Palo Verde Nuclear Generating Station, presently studying to be a rehabilitation counsellor for alcoholics*

1   "Hi, my name is Jerry, and I'm an alcoholic." I'll never forget the day I stood up and said that. It was not easy after twenty years of being an alcoholic to change my life around, yet there I stood at Bronson Rehabilitation Hospital saying those words to Group Ten, the support group of twelve people who helped me understand what alcohol did to me. These people, along with the doctor, helped me, a very depressed and insecure person, take the first step on the road back to recovery. However, in order to recover, I had to turn my life completely around emotionally, physically, mentally, and socially.

2   Emotionally, life as an alcoholic is a roller coaster ride. The only problem is the ride never ends. When I was high, I felt more confident, more relaxed, and happier. I could make everyone laugh, and I was always the life of the party. I would never think of going to a party unless I was high on something. But, when I was down, I was very shy, very insecure, and very depressed. I was afraid of life, responsibility, and most people. I needed a crutch in life, and I found it in alcohol. I kept that crutch for twenty years or more. Then on Sunday, April 10, 1986, I found my world closing in around me. I was very unhappy and totally confused about my life. I didn't know which way to turn or whom to turn to. I told my wife I was going to check out of this world and today was just as good as any other day. It was very clear to my wife that I was headed toward a nervous breakdown. The next day my wife had me admitted into Bronson Rehab Hospital. Bronson was different from the usual twenty-eight-day rehab hospital. At Bronson I had to stay until the doctors said I could go home. I didn't know it then, but my life was about to change.

3   When I entered the hospital ward at Bronson, the first rule I was taught was that to make the mind healthy, I must first make the body healthy. That meant that before I could start their program and be physically able to handle all the pressure, all the alcohol in my body had to be removed. I spent eight agonizing days in that dreadful hospital ward while my body became accustomed to functioning without alcohol in it. I went through terrible withdrawal (because of the drugs inside me) the first three days, and though I tried, I just could not keep anything down. The fourth day the sweating and shaking stopped, and I had lost eleven pounds. Still I wouldn't eat. All I wanted was a drink of alcohol. I knew without alcohol or drugs in my system I could not function. The doctors told me that alcohol and drugs were the reason that my family put me in there, and if I didn't start eating, they would have no other choice but to force-feed me. I was really determined to get out of that hospital, but at last I realized that no matter what I did or said I wasn't going anywhere. So on the eighth day I stopped fighting them and started eating. I had taken my first step.

4   When I went through detoxification and had all the alcohol and drugs removed from my body, it was like waking up from a twenty-year sleep. Even though the alcohol and drugs were out of my system, mentally I was still sick. When I tried to remember things about my life, I found out I couldn't. I didn't realize that while I was under the influence of alcohol, I was just existing in this world. Sure, I knew a lot of things, but I didn't know anything about me as a person. When I had started drinking alcohol, I had stopped thinking about myself. All I thought about was getting that next drink; mentally I had stopped growing. I was so thankful that the doctors and the people of Group Ten were there to help me when reality set in and I had that nervous breakdown. Without them, I would have never made it, emotionally or mentally, through one of the hardest times of my life. They helped me turn my life completely around by showing me how to get off and stay off that roller coaster ride, how to believe in myself as a person, how to deal with the pressure when I become nervous and shy around people, and how being myself is more fulfilling than trying to be someone I am not. It took a lot of tears, argument, and hard work to pull me through, but I made it. I was the only black person in that hospital; therefore, I was called "The Soul Survivor." They used a lot of tricks on me that kept me emotionally and mentally strong. They really cared about me, and I knew it.

5   Except for a two-hour visit each Saturday from my family, for seven months the people at Bronson were the only people I came in contact with. They told me that changing socially would be very difficult, especially toward family and friends. Socially all my friends were alcoholics. If they didn't drink, I didn't want to hang around them. I have four brothers who are all alcoholics. I knew that if I wanted to stay sober, I had to get away from all of them. It really hurt me to say good-bye to everyone, but I did, and I moved my family out to Victoria, B.C. Out here in Victoria, I have a new start in life, and my family has adjusted very well to the changes that they had to make. Though I travel back east once a year at Christmas time to visit Harvey, my only friend back home who doesn't drink, I still don't have the confidence in myself to be around my brothers and other friends when they are drinking. So, I sneak in and out of town without anyone knowing I am there. For now, even though it hurts me deep down inside, I know for me to stay sober things must stay this way. Some day, one day, I hope to be able to go home for a visit.

6   Every day I continue to fight a disease that took twenty years out of my life the same way someone would take a bite out of an apple. It is a disease that a lot of people know about, but only a few really understand. I must live with the fact that this disease will never die inside me until the day I die. This disease is called alcoholism. "Hi, my name is Jerry, and I'm an alcoholic, but I've been sober for three years."

Something to Write About
Write a paragraph on one of the following topics. Before you draft your paragraph, however, have your purpose clearly in mind. Also, be sure you have identified your audience and considered the voice that will be appropriate for your purpose.
1. In what way has someone you know changed in the last few years?
2. In what way does the author of this essay deserve respect from others?
3. How has your family influenced you positively or negatively?

4. How have your friends influenced you positively or negatively?
5. In what way do people need support from their friends?
6. What kinds of help and support are available to help someone overcome a problem like this?
7. Why is it difficult for people to change?
8. What are the reasons people get involved in drinking?

After you draft your paragraph, do each of the following:
Revise it so it has a clear topic sentence.
Include four to six supporting sentences.
Include a closing sentence.
Check to be sure your voice is appropriate for your purpose and audience.

Then,
Check for unity and a smooth flow of ideas.
Check for subject-verb agreement.
Check for consistent verb tense.

PART 3 | Paragraphs and Essays for Discussion and Analysis

Subways

Adapted from the original by **Muriel Gray,** *student*

When I visited New York City, travelling on the New York subway system to and from my hotel was sheer torture for me. I was sure that every insane perverted drunk in the world travelled only by train. It seemed that I would run into one each time. Some would threaten me with bodily harm while others would hound me until I would give them money. Whenever the train entered a tunnel, the hair stood up all over my body. The lights in each car went completely out, and I was sure that the weirdo in this car had staked me out for this precise moment. My heart pounded wildly until I reached my stop. The torments of the subway system are still vivid in my mind today.

Questions on Content
1. In what city did these incidents take place?
2. What does the author dislike about the subways?
3. What happened when the train entered a tunnel?

Questions on Form
1. What is the author's purpose? How well does she accomplish her purpose?
2. The author has successfully captured a distinct voice in this paragraph. How would you describe it?
3. Why is this experience so easy for the reader to relate to? What phrases or support sentences make this experience believable?
4. Who could be an appropriate audience for this paragraph?

The Journey Back

Lyn Leavens, *student*

1   When I was six, my mother decided that she needed a drastic change. She was 48 years old and until that point, her life had been a series of tragedies. She felt that if she was ever going to make a change, it had to be then. Besides, from the way life was going, it was clear that God had more important jobs than spreading a little happiness her way. So she left the small Ontario community she lived in and moved to Montreal. She and I, that is.

2   Montreal was different from any place we'd known, and we both reacted strongly. My mother, quite simply, was rejuvenated. She thrived on this new world of language and culture and anonymity. It was exactly what the doctor ordered

(or would have, had chronic fed-up-edness been a legitimate illness, with escape being the cure). My reaction would stay with me for the next thirty years. I resisted.

3   I didn't want to be surrounded by gray concrete, I didn't want to go to a school taught by nuns, and I especially did not want to begin the monumental task of trying to make friends with little girls whose language I didn't understand. Above all, there was a strong feeling that there was an important part of me that was left behind.

4   The kids that I eventually did meet used to call me "la p'tite Americaine" (the little American). An understandable misconception really, considering that I was an English-speaking person in their French-speaking world. It didn't bother me much, but for the life of me, I couldn't see why they found it so hard to believe that I was who I said I was. As it turned out, this was symptomatic of an identity problem that would challenge me for a very long time.

5   A few years went by and I had adapted to the Big City. I got used to the noise and the cement and the traffic. I spoke French haltingly, and enjoyed it. Yes, Montreal was kind of a fun place to live and when I was old enough to move back home, I would tell everyone about the great time I had in Montreal.

6   When I was twelve, something happened. I was watching one of those old westerns on T.V. and it occurred to me that the Indians were always the bad guys. I had noticed this before, but for some reason it really struck me this time. Memories were triggered, the place where my mother lived as a child and where I spent my summers, my bronze-coloured grandfather, the herbal cures for little ailments; and always, the wondering about what it was that I left behind. These random thoughts irritated me because there was no connection between them, plus I had missed about half an hour of the show.

7   But a door was opened, and whether I liked it or not I would have to walk through it one day.

8   At the age of fifteen, my mother dropped a bomb on me. At least, that was the way I saw it. The fact is, this bomb was nestled deep within her ever since I was born, and she lived all those years with the fear that it would explode. I was old enough by then to know that my life was not going right. I spent hours upon hours sitting at my bedroom window looking out, wondering if I was ever going to get back home. This desire was the one constant in my life, because I could just never shake the feeling that I didn't belong in this place.

9   This need for belonging grew on a steady basis and I had reached the point where I knew that I had to start getting some answers. So one day, as the bomb lay dormant, I lit the fuse. I asked my mother why my name was not the same as my father's. In my quest to know about myself, I had placed myself solidly into my mother's terrain of privacy, and yanked her out. The result was devastating.

10   For the first time in my life, I saw my mother cry. That in itself was shocking, because even though we clashed many times over the years, I considered this woman to be nothing less than Strength itself. I was afraid of what she was going to say. Then she spoke. I was born to her when she was 42 years old. I did not have the same name as my father because they were never married. My father, fifteen years her junior, denied his involvement.

11   "Is that why we left home?"

12   "No. We left because everywhere I looked reminded me of something that I wanted to forget. We left because you were my last child and I wanted to have a

chance to do it right this time. We left because I hoped that you were young enough to forget where you came from."

13   "There's something else, isn't there?"

14   "No. Well...yes."

15   "It's about who we are, isn't it?"

16   Her face took on a strange look. It was anger, fear, and pride all at the same time. She spoke and told me about how we are Indians and how being an Indian was not something that you wanted to shout from the rooftops in the town from which we came. She told me that she never spoke of it because when we moved away, she was running away from her past and she was running away from people who had hurt her and who could hurt me.

17   It took another 21 years for the full impact of what she had said that day to set in. I'm back home now with my husband and children, and I've got a lot of work to do. I have to continue my journey to the beginning and in doing so I have to cut a well-worn path for my children to follow.

Questions on Content

1. Why did the author's mother move to Montreal?

2. Recount the author's childhood memories.

3. What does the author mean by a "need for belonging"?

Questions on Form

1. How old do you think the author was when she wrote this article? Why is this perspective effective?

2. How would you describe the tone of this essay?

3. In what way is this essay forceful for different audiences?

4. For what purpose do you think this essay was written?

Dear Dad

Excerpt from *Dear Dad* by **Louie Anderson,** *comedian and actor*

God, what I would have given to hear and see you play. I never did, you know. I've never even seen a photo of you playing the horn. I remember a few times when there was a trumpet resting beside the platform rocker in the living room. But you didn't play it. I wonder, though, if when you performed it was the same as when I'm on stage? You're up there in front of the crowd and every moment is very real. Your heart seems connected to a light, and the truer you are to your heart, the brighter the light gets and the stronger your heart feels, and your eyes see the world spinning at its absolute clearest.

Questions on Comment

1. What was Louie Anderson's dad's profession?

2. What did the author wonder about?

Questions on Form

1. How would you describe the voice of the author?

2. What comparison does Louie Anderson make?

3. Who is Louie Anderson's audience?

PART 4 | The Writer's Tools: Consistent Point of View

OBJECTIVES

- Understand point of view.
- Identify shifts in point of view.
- Make point of view consistent in a paragraph or essay.

Point of view is the way you as the writer present ideas in a paragraph or an essay. You can talk from your own experience, can speak directly to the reader (such as giving directions), or can relate someone else's experience.

When you talk from your own experience, you can use the pronouns *I* or *we*. When you speak directly to the reader, use *you* for either singular or plural. When you relate someone else's experience, use *she*, *he*, *it*, or *they*.

When you use *I* or *we*, you are using **first person**. When you use *you*, you are using **second person**. When you use *she*, *he*, *it*, or *they*, you are using **third person**.

Person	Singular	Plural
First person	I	we
Second person	you	you
Third person	she, he, it	they

In other words, you can write information from different **points of view**. The first person point of view ("I," "we") allows the author to write it as if the experience has directly happened to her or him.

I will take Psychology 201 next semester.

We will take Psychology 201 next semester.

The second person point of view ("you") gives directions to the reader or allows the author to speak directly to the reader.

You will take Psychology 201 next semester.

You will enjoy Psychology 201 next semester.

The third person point of view ("she, he, it, they") allows the reader to be less personal and to discuss someone else's experience.

She will take Psychology 201 next semester.

He will take Psychology 201 next semester.

Helen will take Psychology 201 next semester.

They will take Psychology 201 next semester.

They will take **it** next semester.

Determining Point of View

Determining person or point of view is very simple. All you have to do is locate the main subject in a sentence and then decide which pronoun you will use in place of this subject.

For example, in the sentence "Bob and his stereo go everywhere together," the subject is "Bob" and "stereo." The pronoun, therefore, that you use to replace this subject must be "they," so the point of view is third person plural.

In the sentence "Janet and I often go hiking," the subject is "Janet" and "I." The pronoun used to replace this subject must be "we," so the point of view is first person plural.

In the sentence "The manager of the company hired new employees," the subject of the sentence is "manager." The pronoun needed to replace this subject must be either "she" or "he," so the point of view is third person singular.

In the sentence "For a high school graduate, summer work in a large city is generally easy to find," the subject of the sentence is "work." The pronoun needed to replace this subject must be "it," so the point of view is third person singular.

In the sentence "Bill needs to go on a vacation," the subject is "Bill," and if you were speaking directly to Bill, you would use the pronoun "you" instead of "Bill." "You" is second person singular.

Now try identifying the point of view in the following exercise by choosing the correct "person" for the pronoun.

EXERCISE 1

Underline the subject, and then above the word, write the correct pronoun.

Example:

                 They
~~The children~~ **walked home from school every day.**

1. Sam is doing well in calculus this semester.

2. The staff members need to use the attached form to request a new bookcase.

3. Mary returns to Prince Edward Island for vacation every summer.

4. Students believe they should have a campus day next spring.

5. Roger, Stephanie, and I watched the Santa Claus Parade, and we enjoyed it.

6. The faculty appreciated the new telephone system and used it often.

7. Real friends are always ready to help.

8. Quarrelling is not going to help anyone on the committee.

9. Maintaining a consistent point of view is really quite simple.

10. Phillip played a difficult role in the school production.

Maintaining Consistent Point of View

Maintaining a consistent point of view means that you establish the person (first person, second person, or third person) in the first sentence of your paragraph and then continue to use that same person throughout the paragraph unless there is a logical reason to change. For instance, if you say, "Parents often are surprised by the many unpredictable games their children play," you would establish the person as third person plural because the subject is "parents" (they). You would continue to use nouns that could be substituted for by third person pronouns (she, he, it, or they) or any of these pronouns throughout the remainder of the paragraph. As you read through the following paragraph, pay close attention to the bold type. Notice that the person of the pronouns is consistent throughout.

Parents (they) often are surprised by the many unpredictable games **their** children play. **Their** children often imitate activities that **they** have seen grown-ups do, or **they** simply want to be helpful. **Ann and her sister (they)** did just this when **they** decided to improve the neighbour's lawn chairs by covering them in a nice coating of mud. Not only did the **neighbour (she)** get a grand surprise, but so did the girls' **father (he)** when **he** found out that **they** had used his new paint brush. Another time their **brother Bobby (he)** set up a candy shop in the basement where **he** made a fresh batch of meringue with his **mother's (her)** laundry soap. Working hard to be a great chef, he whipped the mixture into a smooth consistency with his mother's egg beater. Their **mother (she)** was the one who was upset this time when **she** went to wash **her** clothes and found that the detergent box was empty. The **children (they)** decided to make lemonade one afternoon but used lemon detergent as the base. Fortunately, **their** effort to help was discovered before anybody drank any of this sparkling drink. Though **parents (they)** can be upset and frustrated when the **children (they)** are so helpful, **they** can also appreciate **their** efforts to be grown up.

Occasionally, you might have a logical reason to shift the point of view in your paragraph. However, if you were to change the first sentence in the previous paragraph to "Parents often are surprised by the many unpredictable games *your* children play," you are implying that the readers' children, not the parents' children, are unpredictable. That is probably not what you intended to say in the sentence.

Note Perhaps the most common writing difficulty you may run into is a shift from first or third person to second person. Therefore, be certain that when you use "you," you are really addressing the reader and not just shifting your point of view.

Use the following table to help you examine the preceding paragraph for consistent point of view of each sentence. Then do the following exercise. It will help you change point of view so that you can find and correct point-of-view shifts in your own paragraphs.

Person	Singular			Plural		
	SUBJ.	OBJ.	POSSESSIVE	SUBJ.	OBJ.	POSSESSIVE
First person	I	me	my, mine	we	us	our, ours
Second person	you	you	your, yours	you	you	your, yours
Third person	she	her	her, hers	they	them	their, theirs
	he	him	his			
	it	it	its			

EXERCISE 2

Underline the subject and then replace it with a pronoun in a different person or point of view as shown. Refer to the table if necessary. (Be sure to change any pronouns that might follow in the sentence.)

Example:

Change to second person.

Your

your

~~Charlene's~~ **assignments are always typed on ~~her~~ computer.**

1. *Change to second person.*

   Robert should consider the detrimental consequences as well as the advantages.

2. *Change to first person.*

   Mavis Gallant manipulates her point of view to conform to various purposes.

3. *Change to third person.*

   My friend and I have always tried to edit our papers carefully.

4. *Change to second person.*

   Our family went on a picnic.

5. *Change to second person.*

Mr. Jones is the most challenging math professor on campus.

6. *Change to first person.*

Lance plays football for his college team.

7. *Change to third person.*

Henry, listen to your conscience when decisions need to be made.

8. *Change to first person.*

Christina often volunteers at the school for handicapped adults.

9. *Change to second person.*

Some students have learned excellent time-management skills this semester.

10. *Change to first person.*

Others have procrastinated until the last minute.

Revising Inconsistent Point of View

In the following paragraph, the point of view shifts several times in a confusing way. Read the paragraph. Then study the sentence-by-sentence analysis that follows so that you can understand how and why the point of view should be revised throughout.

UPS

(1) The hardest job is working at United Parcel Service. (2) They pay well, but it is hard work. (3) You have to be able to lift seventy pounds into a truck. (4) They require that you load up to nine hundred packages an hour. (5) The hours I work are weird, and that makes it difficult, too. (6) I work third shift, which is three to nine in the morning. (7) There are no breaks. (8) You work until all the work is done. (9) I have four trucks to load. (10) I have to run and grab as many packages as I can off the slide and load them into the truck. (11) I am running constantly. (12) If it weren't for the money, there is no way I would work that hard.

Sentence 1: The hardest **job** is working at United Parcel Service.

The subject in the first sentence is "job." The correct subject pronoun to use in place of "job" would be "it." By looking at the table, you can find "it" listed as third person singular. Third person singular sets the point of view for this sentence and, consequently, for the entire paragraph. In using this point of view, the writer is speaking *about* something.

Sentence 2: **They** pay well, but **it** is hard work.

The second sentence has used the subject pronoun "they" rather than a noun for a subject, so to determine the point of view for this sentence, you simply have to find the subject pronoun "they" in the table. As you see from the table, "they" is third person, but because it is *plural*, it does not refer to "job" in sentence 1. To clear up the vague reference, "the company" might be used instead because it is more specific.

Revision: The company pays well.

Sentence 3: **You** have to be able to lift seventy pounds into a truck.

In the third sentence, the writer has shifted to the subject pronoun "you." As the table indicates, a major shift has occurred to second person. Now the writer is speaking directly to the reader.

Revision: Jobs require lifting up to seventy pounds into a truck.

Sentences 4 and 5: **They** require that you load up to nine hundred packages an hour.
The **hours** I work are weird, and that makes it difficult, too.

The fourth and fifth sentences have shifted back to third person plural. The writer is speaking *about* something.

Revision: Employees are required to load...The work hours are at odd times, too.

Sentence 6: **I** work third shift, which is three to nine in the morning.

In the sixth sentence, because the subject is "I," the writer has shifted to first person and is speaking from a personal perspective.

Revision: The third shift works three to nine

Sentence 7: There are no **breaks**.

In the seventh sentence, the writer has shifted to the third person *plural* point of view.

Revision: Third shift has no breaks.

Sentence 8: **You** work until all the work is done.

In the eighth sentence the writer has shifted back to "you" and addresses the reader directly again.

Revision: Employees are expected to stay until all the work is done.

Sentences 9–12: **I** have four trucks to load.
I have to run and grab as many packages as I can off the slide and load them into the truck.
I am running constantly.
If **it** weren't for the money, there is no way I would work that hard.

In the remainder of the paragraph the writer has shifted again to "I." The writer shifts the experience from second person (you), which directs the reader, to first person ("I"), which indicates that the writer is sharing his/her own personal experience.

> *Revision:* It is not unusual for employees to load four trucks. They have to run and grab...They are running constantly...

The shifting of point of view in the UPS paragraph makes it difficult for the reader to follow. At times, the reader may lose sight of who is doing the speaking and to whom the writer is speaking. The paragraph, in effect, loses an extremely important component—total coherence. Now read a thorough revision of this paragraph and compare it to the first draft.

Consistent Third Person Point of View

UPS

Working at United Parcel Service is strenuous, demanding work. The **company** pays well, but the work is hard. First of all, entry-level **jobs** require lifting up to seventy pounds into the bed of a truck. Furthermore, **employees** are required to load nine hundred packages an hour. The work **hours** are at odd times, too. The third **shift** works three to nine in the morning with no breaks. In addition, **employees** are expected to stay until all the work is done. It is not unusual for **employees** to load four trucks in one day. **They** have to run and grab as many packages as **they** can off the slide and load them into the truck. If the **money** weren't good, **United Parcel Service** wouldn't be able to find **people** to do this type of demanding work.

By keeping a consistent third person point of view ("she," "he," "it," "they"), the writer was able to use a variety of nouns as well as the four subject pronouns. Also, the voice now sounds more objective and more convincing.

As a contrast to third person point of view, first person ("I") point of view allows the writer to personalize his or her experience and make the tone of the writing more informal. Read the following paragraph and notice how the first person ("I") point of view helps the reader identify with the writer's experience.

Consistent First Person Point of View

UPS

The hardest job **I** ever had was working at United Parcel Service. **I** was pleased with my salary, but **I** thought it was hard work. First of all, **I** had to be able to lift seventy pounds into a truck and load up to nine hundred packages an hour. In addition, **I** had a difficult schedule. **I** worked the third shift, which was from three to nine in the morning, with no breaks. At times **I** had to stay longer until all the work was done. Often, **I** had four trucks to load, and **I** would have to run and grab as many packages as **I** could off the conveyor and load them onto the transporting truck. **I** was running constantly. **I** believe that if **I** hadn't been getting good money, there is no way **I** would ever have worked that hard.

This paragraph has maintained first person point of view. It allows the writer to identify all the experiences as his or her own. However, note that the "I" is repeated quite often, which may sound monotonous in a longer essay.

Now read the same paragraph written in the "you" point of view. Generally, the "you" point of view is found in papers that give instructions to a reader or in an explanation or discussion (like this textbook) that speaks directly to the reader. Notice how the second person point of view affects the tone of voice of the paragraph.

Consistent Second Person Point of View

UPS

If **you** enjoy hard work, **you** might like working at United Parcel Service. **You** will enjoy the salary because it pays well, but the work will probably be demanding for **you**. First of all, **you** have to be able to lift seventy pounds into the bed of a truck, as well as load nine hundred packages an hour. **You** will also discover that the work hours are at very odd times. If **you** are on the third shift, **you** have to come in at three to nine o'clock in the morning with no breaks. In addition, **you** have to stay until all the trucks are loaded. **You** often load four trucks in one day. **You** have to run and grab as many packages as **you** can off the conveyor and load them into the truck. However, the pay is good. If this job sounds appealing to **you**, apply at the United Parcel Service.

The preceding paragraph has a consistent second person point of view. Unless you are giving instructions to someone or are speaking directly to your audience, you may want to choose another point of view. Keep in mind that different points of view create different impressions on your reader. Because you can learn to control point of view, you have one more way of controlling how you sound in your own writing. As a result, you can feel more confident about how your reader will react.

Maintaining consistent point of view helps keep your paragraph focused on one main idea and brings your many sentences together as one piece of writing. For longer writing, consistent point of view is essential for clarity. Consequently, you should edit carefully for a consistent point of view that is appropriate for your topic, purpose, and audience.

As a writer, you must decide what your writing purpose is and conform your point of view to that purpose. Do you want to sound more authoritative or more personal? Do you want to inform or entertain? Do you want to remain distant or get close to your reader? Do you want to sound more formal or informal? Answering these questions will determine your point of view and give you greater control over a writing situation.

EXERCISE 3

Read the following paragraphs and identify the shifts in point of view. The first sentence establishes the point of view that should be maintained. Any deviation from the first sentence should be changed to an appropriate subject pronoun or noun that conforms to the point of view of the first sentence. Revise the following paragraphs by making the point of view consistent. When you have finished revising each paragraph, identify the purpose, voice, and audience.

Paragraph 1

Playing golf is a rewarding experience. It can be a time for relaxing and enjoying a beautiful day. Because many golf courses are located throughout the city, finding an available tee time is also easy and convenient. When you play eighteen holes, you walk approximately six kilometres and get your day's exercise. Furthermore, I believe that golf is challenging. I used to think that golf was an easy game that did not require any ability, but it does require precision, patience, and skill. In addition, unlike other high-endurance sports that only younger players can participate in, golf is a lifelong activity. You can enjoy it at just about any age. Consequently, golf is a sport everybody should consider playing.

Purpose: _____

Voice: _____

Audience: _____

Paragraph 2

I will never never forget not getting to go to my high school prom. I planned for weeks what I was going to wear, how I was going to fix my hair, and what accessories I was going to use. My only problem was who was going to take me. I had hoped that Tony Ricci, a popular football athlete, would ask me. He was about 5′10″ and had a warm smile, even though he was shy. He was also the Student Council president, which meant that he would be involved in setting up the decorations. He always seemed anxious and excited about the upcoming event, but he never mentioned his date. He finally invited me; however, he had bad luck because he was injured in a football game before the week of the prom and ended up staying home. We were both disappointed because we could not go to the dance.

Purpose: _____

Voice: _____

Audience: _____

Paragraph 3

The high-tech computer lab at our college is an efficient room. Over one hundred computers are laid out so that maximum room is obtained for traffic flow, comfort, and usability. Students can choose from a variety of hardware, and technicians are available to give help or to answer questions. In addition, you can easily check out the software you desire and sign in on the computer at the entrance to the room. One advantage that I have found in my experience in the high-tech centre is that I can get copies of my work quickly because all stations are hooked up to printers. You might say that the high-tech centre is a perfect place for computer business and pleasure.

Purpose: _____

Voice: _____

Audience: _____

WRITING ASSIGNMENT

Using the steps in the writing process, draft a paragraph about one of the following ideas. Decide on a purpose and an audience, and then choose the appropriate voice.

1. The best pet I ever had...
2. A senior citizen taught me...
3. The best neighbour I ever had...
4. Visiting a famous monument or building or a provincial park...
5. My brother's/sister's best trait is/was...
6. Something I appreciate most about my mother/father...
7. Something I dislike most about my mother/father...

After you draft your paragraph, revise for content and edit for mechanics.

Content

Revise it so it has a clear topic sentence.

Include four to six supporting sentences.

Include a closing sentence.

Check to see that the voice is appropriate for purpose and audience.

Mechanics

Check for subject-verb agreement.

Check for consistent verbs.

Check for a consistent point of view.

Unit Four

Organizing Ideas and Writing Them Clearly

PART 1 | Parts to Whole: The Thesis Sentence

OBJECTIVES

....

- Write a thesis sentence that states the direction of the paper.

- Brainstorm to generate ideas.

- Group related ideas.

- Identify and write the paragraphs in sequential order.

- Make sure the topic sentence of each support paragraph relates to the thesis.

Just as the paragraph depends on a topic sentence to restrict and control the paragraph, so the longer paper depends on a thesis sentence to restrict and control the longer paper. You have just learned that the most general statement in the paragraph is the topic sentence. The most general statement in the longer paper, similarly, is the **thesis sentence** which directs and determines the topic sentences that will be used to support it. For example, if you say that "learning disabilities can create problems for students in school," you can use supporting details to develop a paragraph. Read the following sample paragraph.

> Learning disabilities can create problems for students. *Often academic problems arise when learning-disabled students have a difficult time reading the textbook because they are reading two or more years below grade level. Also, the students may have trouble putting into writing what they know well. *This difficulty can lead to social problems because students

*Notice that the sentences in this sample paragraph that are marked with an asterisk could be developed into separate paragraphs for a longer paper.

with learning disabilities often spend two or three times longer doing their homework than other students do, leaving no time to spend with others. *Personal problems may emerge because they feel inferior to other students who can spell every word right the first time. *The least noticeable of all may be physical problems like coordination or balance that the average person will not even notice. Though these learning disabilities are difficult for others to detect, they certainly can make life difficult for otherwise bright students.

If you wish to expand this paragraph into a longer paper, you must develop the specific ways in which learning disabilities can create problems for students. A thesis sentence helps you organize your discussion.

You may write the thesis sentence in two ways: one that clearly states the direction for the longer paper or one that states the direction and specifies the points to be covered in the paper.

Thesis Sentence That States the Direction

The thesis sentence of the sample paragraph can still be "**Learning disabilities can create problems for students.**" However, you should discuss specific problems in a logical, organized manner. Brainstorming can give you these points. You may use the four main kinds of problems included in the sample paragraph (academic, social, personal, and physical) and develop each idea in one (or more) support paragraphs. Each support paragraph will need a strong topic sentence clarifying the point being discussed.

Look at the following list of topic sentences for each of the four support paragraphs. Each topic sentence will be the most general statement in the paragraph.

Students with learning disabilities may encounter many academic problems.

Likewise, students with learning disabilities also encounter many social problems.

Other problems that learning-disabled students experience are personal problems.

The least noticeable problems of all may be physical problems.

Thesis Sentence That States the Direction and Previews Main Points of the Paper

If you preview the main points to be covered in the paper, your thesis sentence might read:

                                                      #1   #2   #3   #4

Learning disabilities create academic, social, personal, and physical problems for the student.

(Again, the thesis sentence will be the most general statement in the paper.)

From the points previewed in this thesis sentence, you will be able to write a topic sentence for each support paragraph. You may use the same topic sentences presented in the previous list in this paper as well.

Support paragraph 1: **Students with learning disabilities may encounter many academic problems.**

Support paragraph 2: **Likewise, students with learning disabilities also encounter many social problems.**

Support paragraph 3: **Other problems that learning-disabled students experience are personal problems.**

Support paragraph 4: **The least noticeable problems of all may be physical problems.**

Coordinate and Subordinate Ideas in Thesis Sentences

Whether or not you preview the supporting ideas in the thesis sentence, you need to organize your paper logically with supporting ideas that are **coordinate**; that is, the two or more points in the paper must be of equal value. This degree of equality is determined by the restriction and direction of the thesis statement. If in one paper you are writing about working in the yard, having a party, sleeping late, and doing homework, your readers may wonder what these activities have in common. However, if you write

"I enjoy spring break because I enjoy

working in the yard

having a party,

sleeping late, and

doing homework,"

the reader is then aware that these activities are what you enjoy doing when school is in recess. They are all equal, even though you may enjoy one activity more than the others.

On the other hand, if you write

"I enjoy spring break because I enjoy

working in the yard and

pulling weeds,"

then your thesis statement is faulty because pulling weeds is not equal to working in the yard. Rather, it is one of the activities you may do when you work in the yard. Furthermore, if you write

"During my spring break, I enjoyed

my personal life,

my social life,

my spiritual life, and

picking flowers,"

it is easy to see that "picking flowers" is too restricted and narrow and, therefore, is not coordinate with the other ideas in the group.

Also, all of these points must be **subordinate** to one main idea. In this case they must all be activities you enjoy doing during spring break. These activities may be different for different people. For example, someone else might say, "But I do not enjoy doing homework." Then that person could substitute "working on a car" or "cooking gourmet meals" or "going on a trip." It really doesn't matter as long as all the points are *coordinate* (equal) and *subordinate* to (under) the main idea of the paper. Whether or not you preview the points in your thesis sentence, you need to decide on your supporting ideas before writing your paper.

The following exercises will help you determine which ideas are equal and will also help you realize that these coordinate ideas must be subordinate to a more general statement. These exercises will help you think about how ideas fit together into a paper whether or not they are included in the actual thesis statement.

EXERCISE 1

Read the following words or phrases that you might generate through brainstorming. First, determine which word or phrase is the most general. Second, decide which words or phrases are coordinate or equal to one another. Finally, decide which words or phrases are unrelated or part of another group.

Example:

a. **playing tennis**

b. **hitting the ball with the racquet**   ____*a*____ **is the most general word or statement.**

c. **volleying back and forth**   ____*b, c, d*____ **are equal to one another.**

d. **hitting the net**   ____*e*____ **is unrelated or part of another group.**

e. **drinking water**

1. a. roses

    b. flowers   _____ is the most general word or statement.

    c. plants   _____ are equal to one another.

    d. trees   _____ is unrelated or part of another group.

    e. bushes

2. a. working in a garden

    b. planting carrots   _____ is the most general word or statement.

    c. washing hands   _____ are equal to one another.

    d. hoeing weeds   _____ is unrelated or part of another group.

    e. thinning radishes

3. a. branch

    b. leaf   _____ is the most general word or statement.

    c. grass   _____ are equal to one another.

    d. tree   _____ is unrelated or part of another group.

    e. trunk

4. a. vehicle

    b. car   _____ is the most general word or statement.

    c. tire   _____ are equal to one another.

    d. truck   _____ is unrelated or part of another group.

    e. Jeep

5. a. types of pollution

    b. water   _____ is the most general word or statement.

    c. land   _____ are equal to one another.

    d. animal   _____ is unrelated or part of another group.

    e. air

6. a. cooking

   b. baking   _____ is the most general word or statement.

   c. doing dishes   _____ are equal to one another.

   d. frying   _____ is unrelated or part of another group.

   e. grilling

7. a. bird

   b. insect   _____ is the most general word or statement.

   c. beetle   _____ are equal to one another.

   d. cockroach   _____ is unrelated or part of another group.

   e. ant

8. a. pop

   b. drink   _____ is the most general word or statement.

   c. coffee   _____ are equal to one another.

   d. tea   _____ is unrelated or part of another group.

   e. sugar

9. a. chewing bubble gum

   b. fielding   _____ is the most general word or statement.

   c. playing baseball   _____ are equal to one another.

   d. batting   _____ is unrelated or part of another group.

   e. catching

10. a. sleeping in a tent

   b. camping   _____ is the most general word or statement.

   c. roasting marshmallows   _____ are equal to one another.

   d. cooking over an open fire   _____ is unrelated or part of another group.

   e. buying gas

EXERCISE 2

Study the following sentences. First, identify the most general idea in each sentence. Then identify which words are coordinate.

Example:

The mountains are beautiful in the spring because of the new growth, the rains, and the animal life.

<u>mountains are beautiful in the spring</u>
(most general idea)

<u>new growth, rains, animal life</u>
(words that are coordinate)

1. The children enjoyed the pictures that were large, simple, and colourful.

_____

(most general idea)

_____

(words that are coordinate)

2. Shopping is mentally, physically, and financially draining.

_____

(most general idea)

_____

(words that are coordinate)

3. Having surgery is difficult because it is expensive, painful, frightening, and depressing.

_____

(most general idea)

_____

(words that are coordinate)

4. Ice-sailing on frozen lakes can be dangerous yet exciting.

_____

(most general idea)

_____

(words that are coordinate)

5. Location, price, and size are important when a consumer buys a home.

_____

(most general idea)

_____

(words that are coordinate)

6. At fall fairs, the rides, games, food, and exhibits bring enjoyment to children.

_____

(most general idea)

_____

(words that are coordinate)

7. Appetizers, main courses, salads, and desserts are specialties of the cooking school.

_____

(most general idea)

_____

(words that are coordinate)

8. Swim teams help students develop confidence, coordination, and physical strength.

_____

(most general idea)

_____

(words that are coordinate)

9. As trees grow, they develop root systems, thick trunks, and full branches.

_____

(most general idea)

_____

(words that are coordinate)

10. Desks, chairs, and tables are furniture often found in classrooms.

_____

(most general idea)

_____

(words that are coordinate)

11. Pets aid the elderly by providing security, companionship, and self-esteem.

_____

(*most general idea*)

_____

(*words that are coordinate*)

12. Necklaces, earrings, and bracelets are jewellery that women often enjoy wearing.

_____

(*most general idea*)

_____

(*words that are coordinate*)

Parallel Grammatical Form in Thesis Sentences

If your thesis sentence previews the points to be covered in your paper, be sure that each point is written using the same grammatical form. This similar grammatical structure is called **parallel form**. You may choose whatever grammatical structure you like, such as nouns, verbs, phrases, or clauses. Study the following list to help you understand parallel form.

- **If you use an "-ing" verb form, all points must be in an "-ing" form.**

For the elderly, having a pet means receiving companionship, getting exercise, having protection, and feeling useful.

> receiving companionship
>
> getting exercise
>
> having protection
>
> feeling useful

- **If you use the present tense of the verb, all points must be in the present tense.**

Elderly people with pets receive companionship, get exercise, have protection, and feel useful.

> receive companionship
>
> get exercise
>
> have protection
>
> feel useful

- **If you use a noun, all points must be nouns.**

Having a pet can provide companionship, exercise, protection, and usefulness to the elderly.

> companionship
>
> exercise
>
> protection
>
> usefulness

- **If you use "to" before the verb, all points must have "to" written or understood before the verb.**

Elderly people often own a pet to receive companionship, get exercise, have protection, and feel useful.

> to receive companionship
>
> to get exercise
>
> to have protection
>
> to feel useful

- **If you use a prepositional phrase, all points must be prepositional phrases.** (If the same preposition is used, it does not need to be repeated.)

Elderly people often own pets for companionship, exercise, protection, and a sense of usefulness.

> for companionship
>
> for exercise
>
> for protection
>
> for a sense of usefulness

Whichever form you use, the thesis sentence will flow smoothly when all points are grammatically equal.

EXERCISE 3

In each group below, some ideas are not in parallel form. Revise the wording in each group to make the parts parallel. Try more than one parallel pattern. You may also change the order of the items within each group.

Example:

a. **to eat pie**   a. _to eat pie, to drink milk, to read a book_

b. **drinking milk**   b. _eating pie, drinking milk, reading a book_

c. **read a book**   c. _ate pie, drank milk, read a book_

1. a. to write memos

   b. making phone calls

   c. filed materials

2. a. live near mountain streams

   b. owning several horses

   c. enjoyed the outdoors

   d. hikes in the nearby mountains

3. a. to be happy

   b. was outgoing

   c. is helpful

4. a. typing on a computer

   b. corrected the mistakes

   c. writes his paper well

5. a. to practise long hours

   b. read the directions

   c. talking to experts

6. a. reads

   b. studied

   c. take the test

7. a. convenience

   b. to be fair

   c. of its variety

8. a. to get an education

   b. meeting new friends

   c. prepares for a job

    d. improved self-esteem   d. _____

9. a. growing wheat   a. _____

    b. canned wild blackberries   b. _____

    c. raises chickens   c. _____

10. a. size   a. _____

    b. colours   b. _____

    c. of the style   c. _____

    d. shaped   d. _____

EXERCISE 4

Revise the following thesis sentences so that the points previewed are parallel.

Example:

The flower garden provides a colourful sidewalk border, fresh table arrangements,

and gifts for my neighbours.
~~and my neighbours enjoy receiving them as gifts.~~

1. My summer spent in Muskoka brings pleasant memories of socializing with friends, extra money, and of buying my first car.

2. The students in my English class wrote many essays, passed all the grammar tests, and journals.

3. I enjoy going to that restaurant because the prices are reasonable, the food is excellent, and good service.

4. Mr. Edmonds was the best speaker I have ever heard because he spoke precisely, made clear points, and a serious speaker.

5. Many homeless people exist in Canada because of mental illness, being physically ill, and to lack ambition.

6. Some of the things we take into consideration when planning a vacation are how much money to take, interesting places to visit, and are we going to have time.

7. For safe driving, one must drive under control, obeying the speed limit, and never to drive under the influence of alcohol.

8. The Member of Parliament was impeached because he caused anger, embarrassed his province, and insensitive to minority cultures.

9. When you go river rafting, you must know how to pack the gear, manoeuvring a raft, and to judge the rapids.

10. Some Canadians seem to close their eyes to the problems of not having enough money, not providing enough jobs, and of not caring enough to help one another.

11. Before going to college, consider how much money you have to spend, time, and attitude.

12. Before quitting college, students must examine their academic goals, their obligations to themselves, and if they can financially make more money with their present educational level.

13. Leaving home was very difficult for me because I had to say goodbye to my family, I have to leave my friends, and I had to break up with my girlfriend.

14. The first month she was away from home, my daughter encountered problems involving responsibilities, finances, and with her roommate.

If you do not preview the subtopics in the thesis sentence, be sure that your subtopics are coordinate and identified clearly in your prewriting before drafting the paper.

Generating a Thesis Sentence

Now that you know what a thesis sentence is, you need to learn how to generate ideas that you can use to formulate this thesis sentence. The following steps can help you generate a thesis sentence.

1. **State your topic.**

2. **Brainstorm to find a direction.** Type or write anything that comes to mind. Brainstorming is like a game of free association. Continue to jot down ideas as rapidly as you think of them. Remember, now is the time to use your resources. Generate ideas that come from your personal experiences, including your feelings. These ideas and feelings may be positive or negative, as long as they reflect what you have seen or felt.

3. **Find a direction.** Because it is impossible to write everything you know about a subject, it is important to find the direction you want to take. As soon as you are aware of a direction in your brainstorming, write it down. If your topic were "divorce," you might write the following entries:

   a. My divorce has left me with many problems.

   b. My divorce was the best thing that ever happened to me.

   c. My divorce changed my life.

   d. My parents' divorce created many problems for me.

   e. My parents' divorce solved many of my problems.

   f. My parents' divorce changed my life.

   The direction you choose may be either positive (b,e), negative (a,d), or a combination of both (c,f).

4. **Brainstorm with direction.** Once again, jot down everything that comes to mind; however, this time your entries will be more specific because you already have a direction. Continue to brainstorm until you have ten to twelve entries.

5. **Group entries that fit together.** Carefully look over all entries you made while brainstorming. Combine these entries into groups until you have two to five separate areas that support the focused topic. **The key word and direction with two to five support groups form the thesis sentence.** Even if you do not preview the points of the paper in the thesis sentence, you still have coordinate groups of ideas to guide the paper.

6. **Formulate the thesis sentence.** Write it with a clear direction, or write it with a clear direction and previewed subtopics.

Carefully examine the following examples of stating the topic, finding the direction, brainstorming with direction, and sorting related ideas into groups.

Example 1

Topic: Divorce

Brainstorm to find direction:

my divorce   parents divorced

Being divorced has caused me many problems.

divorce is widespread   sister divorced

Direction: Being divorced has caused me many problems.

Brainstorm with direction:

no one to talk to	#2	feel uncomfortable around others
lonely		less time to talk to children
have to make all decisions concerning children	#3	
no one to take son to banquet		responsible for discipline
less money for clothes	#1	less extra money

Groups (topic outline):

1. money problems (financial)

2. personal problems (emotional)

3. responsibilities of son (parental)

Thesis sentence with clear direction:

Being divorced has caused me many problems that I did not face when I was married.

Thesis sentence with clear direction and previewed subtopics:

Being divorced has caused me financial, emotional, and parental problems that I did not face when I was married.

Note The groups can serve as a topic outline or as part of the thesis sentence.

Example 2

Topic: pets

Brainstorm to find direction:

dogs   fun for children

needs love   good for old people

Direction: beneficial to old people

Brainstorm with direction:

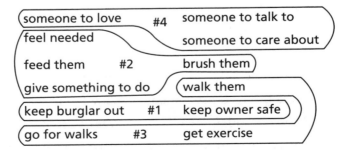

Groups (topic outline):

1. provide protection

2. make them feel needed

3. get exercise

4. have companionship

Thesis sentence with clear direction:

For the elderly, having a pet can be very beneficial.

Thesis sentence with clear direction and previewed subtopics:

For the elderly, having a pet means receiving companionship, getting exercise, having protection, and feeling useful.

Note The groups can serve as a topic outline or as part of the thesis sentence.

EXERCISE 5

Follow the same process as shown in Examples 1 and 2 in this section to develop a thesis statement for three of the following subjects:

tour of the college campus	*flowers*	*a particular restaurant*
rafting	*weight room*	
tour of your city	*hockey game*	

1. *Topic:* _____

Brainstorm to find direction:

_____

_____

_____

_____

_____

Direction:

_____

_____

Brainstorm with direction:

_____

_____

_____

_____

_____

_____

_____

Groups (topic outline):

_____

_____

_____

_____

Thesis sentence:

_____

_____

_____

2. *Topic:* _____

Brainstorm to find direction:

_____

_____

_____

_____

_____

Direction:

_____

_____

Brainstorm with direction:

_____

_____

_____

_____

_____

_____

Groups (topic outline):

_____

_____

_____

_____

Thesis sentence:

_____

_____

_____

3. *Topic:* _____

Brainstorm to find direction:

_____

_____

_____

_____

_____

Direction:

_____

_____

Brainstorm with direction:

_____

_____

_____

_____

_____

_____

Groups (topic outline):

_____

_____

_____

_____

Thesis sentence:

_____

_____

_____

Arranging the Order of Points or Subtopics

One last item you need to consider before writing your thesis sentence is the order in which you present your coordinate ideas. Sometimes there is more than one way to arrange the points in a paper, so use your best judgment to decide which order is most effective for the overall development of your essay. Even while drafting, you may discover that you need to rearrange the order of the subtopics. When the thesis sentence does not preview the points to be covered in the paper, the points generated through prewriting can serve as a rough outline. Remember, though, **you must present the points in some logical order.** Here are some possible arrangements for subtopics.

1. Place the points in the order of *increasing importance*, as *you* see them. Put the most important last.

   Example: Before buying a used car, a person must consider special features desired, type of car needed, cost, and condition of the car.
   Before buying a used car, a person must consider several factors.

   1. special features desired

   2. type of car needed

   3. cost

   4. condition of the car

2. Place the points in the order of *decreasing importance*, as you see them. Put the most important first.

   Example: Before buying a used car, a person must consider condition of the car, cost, type of car needed, and special features desired.
   Before buying a used car, a person must consider several important factors.

   1. condition of the car

   2. cost

   3. type of car needed

   4. special features desired

3. Place the second most important point first and the most important last, as *you* see them. Arrange the weaker points in the middle. This order begins and ends on a strong note.

   Example: A nurse must care for patients, fill out charts, and talk to family members.

   A nurse has many duties.

   1. care for patients

   2. fill out charts

   3. talk to family members

4. Place in the order of increasing interest, as *you* see them.

   Example: Being divorced has caused financial, emotional, and parenting problems.
   Being divorced has caused many problems.

    1. financial

    2. emotional

    3. parenting

5. Place in *chronological order*. This is similar to historical progression.

    Example: Transportation has progressed from trains to cars to jet planes.

    Transportation has progressed rapidly.

    1. trains

    2. cars

    3. jet planes

6. Place in *sequential* progression (one idea naturally follows the other).

    Example: To produce good essays, writers brainstorm, sort related ideas into groups, and formulate a thesis sentence.

    To produce good essays, writers use an organized process.

    1. brainstorm

    2. group

    3. formulate a thesis sentence

All of these steps will become automatic as you write more and more papers. No one method is used by all writers, and at times some steps come more easily than others. Just continue to work hard and have confidence in yourself.

PART 2 | **Something to Think About, Something to Write About**

The Business of Being a Good Citizen

by Margaret Wente

1   What can businesses do about the troubles of Canadian families?

2   So far, the response from business has mostly been denial, blame-laying, and helpless bafflement. It's not hard to understand why. Every week brings us another overwrought study on the family in crisis, usually from an interest group with much to gain. It's easy to dismiss this soft-headed stuff. It's also easy to blame our lousy schools, our materialistic society and our deadbeat dads.

3   It's easy for business executives to duck. After all, there's been a recession on. When you're fighting to keep your company alive, what CEO can afford to worry about the child-care difficulties of his work force?

4   The short answer is no CEO can afford not to. Amid all the alarmism is plenty of evidence that Canada's social deficits are mounting, and that they threaten our future every bit as much as fiscal deficits do. Once they are incurred, social deficits, like the other kind, dig for us a bottomless hole that is almost impossible to climb out of. Today's problem kids become tomorrow's social nightmare. And businesses everywhere will eventually have to pick up the tab for workers who are barely literate, poorly socialized and hard to train.

5   At risk is Canada's chief competitive advantage: our reputation as a peaceable nation in which to live and work.

6   What can businesses do about the crisis of the family? Plenty, I think, that is quite practical and not costly.

7   First, they can ask their own work force what would make a difference. Forget things like on-site day-care centres; that's the wrong business for businesses to be in. Family-friendly practices such as flextime, part-time work and time off to care for sick kids or parents are a good start and have a track record. Businesses could also offer parenting classes during lunch hour, to help people think through the way they are doing their other jobs.

8   It's also time to acknowledge that new mothers are not men. We can't expect them to magically reappear after a few months of maternity leave, primed for action and as if nothing had happened and their baby did not exist.

9   New mothers themselves often try hard to pretend that this is the case, because they don't want to be penalized in the workplace or because they genuinely don't want special treatment. Like it or not, companies have a stake in these babies, and sometimes they ought to make special arrangements to ease the transition back to work.

10   Much has been made of the sufferings of career-oriented women who are in danger of being sidelined to mommy tracks. These women are highly articulate about their problems, and also have the best means to cope with them. Companies need to pay more attention to the other 80 percent of the female work force—the ones who have jobs, not careers; who are least likely to com-

plain, and have the toughest juggling act. It's the legal secretaries, not the lawyers, who need help the most.

11   If I were CEO, I'd spend the company's charitable dollars to support small-scale, non-government, social experiments in helping and educating children. I would look for projects to sponsor that are efficient, cheap and measurable. This work is far too important to be left to the central planners, the bureaucrats and the policy entrepreneurs.

12   I would find a public school and have my company adopt it. That's a good way to start knitting up the strands of community.

13   I would donate employee time to community projects. This is a fine old tradition at senior levels, where vice-presidents are expected to do their bit for the hospital or the symphony. I'd give all the employees some paid time off to pitch in at their kids' school, or to mentor other kids.

14   I'd ask the fathers in the company to forget about coaching their sons hockey team—there are probably plenty of other dads to do that—and go coach the team where there aren't enough dads to go around. Adolescent boys need to know what being a man is all about—that it is about responsibility and caring, not about violence.

15   All this is no more than what Peter Drucker, that grand old man of management philosophers, has been saying for years. He argues that the only way to attack the ills of post-capitalist society is to rebuild a sense of citizenship through the social sector. He also argues that we won't survive unless we do. Businesses are under a heavy obligation to ask how they can be good citizens in their own communities, and to help their employees be good citizens too.

Something to Write About
Using one of the assignments listed below, develop a thesis sentence that either states a clear direction or previews the points to be covered in the paper. Then draft your essay.

1. In your view, what factors are responsible for "the troubles of Canadian families"?
2. Describe a business in which you have been employed that Wente would consider "a good citizen."
3. Describe a company you have worked for which disregards the concerns of families.
4. Disagree with Wente's thesis that businesses should involve themselves in the troubles of families.
5. Explain the difference between a job and a career.
6. What evidence is there that "Canada's social deficits are mounting"?
7. Argue the case for a "nonfamily person" employed by Wente's ideal company.
8. What contributions has Peter Drucker made to the philosophy of business management?
9. If you were CEO of a large company, what projects would you sponsor in your community?
10. Critique Wente's essay (tone, choice of language, organization, use of evidence).

After you draft your essay, revise for content and edit for mechanics.

Content

Revise it so it has a clear thesis sentence.

Be sure that each support paragraph has a strong topic sentence and ample support sentences.

Mechanics

Check for subject-verb agreement.

Check for consistent verbs.

Check for consistent point of view.

PART 3 | Essays for Discussion and Analysis

Being a Student

YoungMi Dauer, *Student*

1   "I'm so tired of high heels and business suits! I wish I could go back to school," I often grumbled in a cushy chair in my office. My wish came true, and today I once again wear blue jeans and T-shirts, carry a backpack, and hold heavy text-books in my arms as I had dreamed. But being an older student is not so much fun; financially, socially, and psychologically I am a handicapped person.

2   I used to enjoy the rainy campus in a school cafeteria, hang out with class-mates between and after classes, and go backpacking for a long summer break, experiences that are not available for me any more. Studying time eats most of my day! My social life is zero since I have become a student again. My important assets such as invitations from friends for a party, a potluck, bowling, and camp-ing are now a liability. I can't gladly greet a relative who calls me on the phone to tell me in a bright voice that she will visit me for a week during final exams!!! I murmur for God's mercy on me.

3   I am definitely not ready to be a social butterfly, and I am also limping finan-cially, which is humbling me quite a bit. Without my contribution to the budget, I'm just another item on the expense account. My tuition, expensive books, and other expenses have put my home economy in a recession. Even though I have restrained my personal spending on entertainment, clothing, and gifts for friends, my eyes still flash red lights as chunks of cash fly out for me to buy things. I pre-fer to be a contributor over being a dependent number on a tax form.

4   An older student isn't a healthy person psychologically; stress, anxiety, confu-sion, and nervousness are the words that surround my daily life. I can't be just a student as I had dreamed; consequently, my emotions are responsibilities that are divided between family and student life. Yes, I have things to be faced as a wife at home; I get a headache when thinking about buying a house, dealing with my husband on his bad days, and making a decision on starting a family. On my stu-dent side, pressures are not less. Reading the books for each class, meeting the due day for my computer program, doing math homework, and taking the tests make my days pretty rough.

5   School life as an older student isn't as romantic as it was in my old days. Too many responsibilities, pressures, and different priorities are interrupting my con-centration just on school work. Maybe I'd rather wear my high heels and business suits than blue jeans and T-shirts.

Questions on Content
1. How has the author cut down on spending?
2. What pressures does she refer to?
3. What new expenses does she have?

Questions on Form
1. Where is the thesis sentence located?
2. How does the author support the thesis sentence?
3. What makes this essay enjoyable to read?

Golf

Kathy Babgy, *student*

1   "I can't believe anyone would even want to try to hit a dumb little golf ball with one of those skinny little sticks, much less chase it all around a golf course." These were the exact words I had used before the summer I decided to take golf lessons. My daughter was playing on the junior golf team, and I thought it would be nice if we could play together. Much to my surprise and delight, after the first lesson I was hooked! I learned golf can be a terrific challenge, a very humbling game, and, most of all, a great family sport.

2   First of all, I learned that in playing golf, it is me against the course and Mother Nature. Naturally, it's great fun to play the game with friends; however, the real challenge comes when I tee off. I must tackle a fairway covered with innumerable obstacles such as hills, sand traps, rough grassy areas, and ponds. To make matters worse, I usually have only three or four chances to "plunk" the ball into a hole on the green if I want to make par. Then, of course, there is the weather. On a windy day my ball can be thrown in an off-direction or slowed down. Then there are the sandstorms that blind me or perhaps the up-and-coming rainstorm that I'm trying desperately to beat as I race to the ninth hole. It seems the challenges are never-ending, making the game so addictive.

3   Next, golf is a humbling game! I'll never forget the time I set up to tee off. I took my practice swing, stepped up, took form, felt confident, brought down my swing, and hit the ball, only to watch it go a foot! My face was as red as the ball I had just hit. Another example of humility came the day I was playing the front nine at the Bellair Golf Course. I had just birdied my first hole. It was hole seven. I must have jumped ten feet in the air. I let everyone near and far know what I had done! I was ready for the pro circuit now! Then came the ninth hole with a long, tough par 4. "A cinch for this old pro," I thought to myself as I stepped up to tee off—1st stroke, 2nd stroke, 3rd stroke, etc., etc., etc. With ten strokes on my card and my head between my knees, I headed for the ninth hole. In addition to these kinds of things, I've had my humbling moments at the water hole. I hit one ball after another, trying any way possible to get over or around the water, only to end up in it. I have definitely eaten a few pieces of humble pie playing this game!

4   The most important part of golf, however, is the pleasurable time I'm able to spend with my family playing together. As an example, we have found it is a great time to share our thoughts and ideas with each other as we walk the course. We will sometimes laugh, tell jokes, or just tease each other. My nine-year-old son loves to show off to his dad just how far he can hit the ball with his custom-made club. My husband and I enjoy moments of closeness as we just walk together quietly. Watching the beautiful grace and form with which my daughter plays swells up a pride within me. Playing together has really helped knit a special closeness in our family.

5   In conclusion, I have found playing golf to be a very positive and rewarding experience. It has taught me many things, such as patience, humility, and perseverance. To anyone who has never given the game a fair chance, I say, "Don't knock it until you try it!"

Questions on Content

1. What do sandstorms do to the player?
2. At Bellair Golf Course, how did the author do on hole seven? on hole nine?
3. How old is her son?
4. Does it appear as if the writer is a beginning golfer or an experienced player?
5. What does the author mean when she writes, "With ten strokes on my card and my head between my knees, I headed for the ninth hole"?

Questions on Form

1. This essay on golf is well written. However, of the three parts of the essay—introduction, support, and conclusion—which part could use a bit more development? What would you suggest to the writer?
2. Does the essay have a distinct thesis sentence? What makes it effective?

PART 4 | ## The Writer's Tools: Eliminating Fragments, Run-On Sentences, and Comma Splices

OBJECTIVES

....

- Recognize and correct fragments.

- Recognize and correct run-on sentences.

- Recognize and correct comma splices.

To be clearly understood, writing is organized into sentences. Each sentence must be complete; that is, it must contain at least a main subject and a main verb. If a sentence does not have these basic parts, it is a **fragment.**

Sentences must also be separated from one another with clear punctuation. Otherwise, you can create **run-on sentences** and **comma splices.** These sentence problems can confuse and distract the reader from the content of your writing.

Fragments, run-on sentences, and comma splices are major sentence structure problems that you can learn to eliminate from your writing. Following are explanations, examples, and exercises to help you identify and revise your own writing so that you can write clearly for your college classes and professionally.

Fragments

A sentence is a group of words that has a main subject and a main verb and states a complete thought. If a group of words lacks one of these parts, it is a **fragment.**

Types of Fragments

1. fragments that contain no subject

2. fragments that have no verb

3. fragments with verb forms that cannot be the main verb
   "-ing" form of the verb used alone
   "to" before a verb

4. fragments that have both a subject and a verb but are preceded by a subordinator

Fragments That Contain No Subject

Examples: Runs two miles every morning. (fragment)

Ate all of the pizza herself. (fragment)

To add clarity, you can change the fragment to a sentence simply by *adding a subject* —someone who "runs" or someone who "ate."

Steve runs two miles every morning. (sentence)

Theresa ate all of the pizza herself. (sentence)

Note A command is a sentence, not a fragment, although the subject "you" is not stated.

(You) close the door, please. (sentence)

EXERCISE 1

Change the following fragments to sentences by adding a subject.

Example:

> hand, Ellen often
> **On the other ~~hand, often~~ waited for class to begin.**

1. Perhaps even gave them a new perspective on life.

2. Then left the car in the middle of the road.

3. Suddenly and frantically searched for his girlfriend.

4. Furthermore, seems like a good idea.

5. Also gave us a new perspective on life.

Fragments That Have No Verb

Some fragments have no verb and can often be thought of as "tag-ons" or "after thoughts."

Examples: The soft, furry kitten. (fragment)

The soft, furry kitten in the basket. (fragment)

To correct these fragments, you can **add a verb** (and other words, if needed).

The soft, furry kitten in the basket **cried**.

The soft, furry kitten **was** in the basket.

Very often when you are writing, these fragments without a main verb become "tag-on" thoughts that belong with another sentence. The words in bold type in the following examples are fragments which you can easily add to the previous sentence.

He did not give us a number. **An exact number.**

The child looked longingly at the kitten. **The kitten in the basket.**

Rusty opened a store. **Her own store.**

The best way to correct these fragmented "tag-on" thoughts is to **combine the fragment with a complete sentence** (usually the one before or after it).

He did not give us **an exact number.**

The child looked longingly at the soft, furry **kitten in the basket.**

Rusty opened **her own store.**

Note Eliminating these fragments also eliminates a kind of wordiness that distracts from your writing.

EXERCISE 2

Revise the "tag-on" thoughts in the following paragraphs by combining them with another sentence.

Paragraph 1

Richard was looking for something in the refrigerator. Something to fix for lunch. He found luncheon meat and cheese. Mozzarella cheese. Red juicy tomatoes and sweet white onions. He looked further for lettuce. Crisp lettuce. Underneath the lettuce, he found a package. A package of bacon. If he could find the mayonnaise, he could make a sandwich. A "house special" sandwich.

Paragraph 2

I felt excited as I entered my spot. My favourite spot. I plucked ripe blackberries. Blackberries from the heavy vines. Nearby, I heard a stream flowing. Overhead, clouds comforted me as they appeared in the sky. White, billowy clouds. Oak trees and pine trees provided shade as I sat on the soft pine needles. Needles on the gently sloping ground. I ate the blackberries still in my hands, and as I ate them, I saw the stains. Stains left by the purple, juicy berries. But I didn't care, for I was surrounded by the freshness. The freshness of nature.

Fragments with Verb Forms That Cannot Be the Main Verb

Some verb forms cannot be used as main verbs in a sentence. If you use them as main verbs, you will create fragments.

Verb Forms That Cannot Be Main Verbs

1. the "-ing" form of a verb used alone

2. "to" before a verb

- The "-ing" form of the verb used alone cannot be the main verb in a sentence.

    Bill going to the gym after school. (fragment)

    Going to the ice-cream store. (fragment)

To be used as a main verb, this "-ing" form must be linked to some "be" verb.

"Be" Verbs			
is	are	were	has been
am	was	had been	have been

For example, if you convert the fragment "Bill going to the gym after school" to "Bill is going to the gym after school," you have a complete sentence, and the fragment has been eliminated.

You can correct these fragmented sentences in a variety of ways. The choice of how to revise them depends on the meaning you would like to communicate in your sentence. Here are some ways to correct the fragment "Going to the ice-cream store."

First, you could **add a subject and some form of the verb "be."**

Bill is going to the ice-cream store.

You can **make the fragment the subject and add a main verb.** (You may want to add other words to make the meaning clear.)

Going to the ice-cream store makes the children happy.

Or you could **add a complete sentence (subject and a verb) after the "-ing" verb phrase.**

Going to the ice-cream store, **Bill met his girlfriend**.

Note In the above example, the "-ing" verb form must refer to the subject in the sentence that it is linked to.

EXERCISE 3

Revise the following fragments using these same patterns.

Example:

Walking to the bus stop.

Lori is walking to the bus stop.
Add a subject and some form of the verb "be."

Walking to the bus stop invigorates me.
Make the fragment the subject and add a main verb. (Add other words if needed.)

Walking to the bus stop, I counted six rabbits.
Add a sentence (subject and a verb) after the fragment.

1. Playing chess.

_____

Add a subject and some form of the verb "be."

_____

Make the fragment the subject and add a main verb. (Add other words if needed.)

_____

Add a sentence (subject and a verb) after the fragment.

2. Collecting aluminum cans.

_____

Add a subject and some form of the verb "be."

_____

Make the fragment the subject and add a main verb. (Add other words if needed.)

_____

Add a sentence (subject and a verb) after the fragment.

3. Welcoming his friends.

_____

Add a subject and some form of the verb "be."

_____

Make the fragment the subject and add a main verb. (Add other words if needed.)

_____

Add a sentence (subject and a verb) after the fragment.

4. Running for political office.

_____

Add a subject and some form of the verb "be."

_____

Make the fragment the subject and add a main verb. (Add other words if needed.)

_____

Add a sentence (subject and a verb) after the fragment.

5. Typing a research paper.

_____

Add a subject and some form of the verb "be."

_____

Make the fragment the subject and add a main verb. (Add other words if needed.)

_____

Add a sentence (subject and a verb) after the fragment.

6. Writing my name.

_____

Add a subject and some form of the verb "be."

_____

Make the fragment the subject and add a main verb. (Add other words if needed.)

_____

Add a sentence (subject and a verb) after the fragment.

- **"To" plus a verb cannot be the main verb in a sentence.**

  To fish at the lake. (fragment)

Based on your sentence meaning, you may revise these types of fragments in any of the following ways.
First, you could **link the fragment to a complete sentence.**

  To fish at the lake, **Rene bought a fishing licence**.

You could add both a subject and a verb.

  Bill likes to fish at the lake.

Or you could make the fragment the subject and add a verb. Be sure to add any other needed words.

  To fish at the lake is relaxing.

EXERCISE 4

Revise the following fragments using these same patterns.

Example:

To get the work done.

To get the work done, Ralph hired new men.
Link the fragment to a complete sentence.

Ralph wanted to get the work done.
Add both a subject and a verb.

To get the work done cost a lot of money.
Make the fragment the subject and add a verb. (Add other words if needed.)

1. To say a kind word.

_____

Link the fragment to a complete sentence.

_____

Add both a subject and a verb.

_____

Make the fragment the subject and add a verb. (Add other words if needed.)

2. To get all of my work done.

_____

Link the fragment to a complete sentence.

_____

Add both a subject and a verb.

_____

Make the fragment the subject and add a verb. (Add other words if needed.)

3. To win the lottery.

_____

Link the fragment to a complete sentence.

_____

Add both a subject and a verb. (Add other words if needed.)

_____

Make the fragment the subject and add a verb. (Add other words if needed.)

4. To master the keyboard.

_____

Link the fragment to a complete sentence.

_____

Add both a subject and a verb.

_____

Make the fragment the subject and add a verb. (Add other words if needed.)

5. To play hockey.

_____

Link the fragment to a complete sentence.

_____

Add both a subject and a verb.

_____

Make the fragment the subject and add a verb. (Add other words if needed.)

6. To sleep late in the mornings.

_____

Link the fragment to a complete sentence.

_____

Add both a subject and a verb.

_____

Make the fragment the subject and add a verb. (Add other words if needed.)

Fragments That Have Both a Subject and Verb but Are Preceded by a Subordinator

Some fragments have both a subject and a verb but are preceded by a subordinator.

Example: **When** I get my paycheque. (fragment)

This fragment does not state a complete thought. For example, if you walked into a room and said to a friend, "When I get my paycheque," the person you are speaking to would expect to know "what about 'when I get my paycheque'?"

However, if you complete this thought by adding a sentence, your meaning will be clear.

When I get my paycheque, **we will go shopping**. or

We will go shopping when I get my paycheque.

("We will go shopping" is a complete sentence that can stand alone.)

In these fragments, the subordinator makes the thought incomplete. (You will learn more about subordinators later in this unit.) Here is a list of subordinators that change a complete sentence into a fragment:

Subordinators

after	in order that	whether
although	since	which
as	so that	whichever
as if	that	who
as long as	though	whoever
as soon as	till	whom
as though	unless	whomever
because	until	whose
before	what	whosoever
even though	whatever	why
how	when	
if	where	

EXERCISE 5

Revise the following fragments by linking them to a complete sentence.

Example:

When the work is done, *we will celebrate.* _____

1. As soon as I finish my homework, _____

2. Unless I can fix my car, _____

3. Even though his birthday is on Saturday, _____

4. So that I can go to the movies, _____

5. Before the day is over, _____

6. After I learn to cook, _____

7. If Ranjit will send us the information, _____

8. Until you buy insurance for your car, _____

9. If the price is right, _____

10. Even though the movie was long, _____

The best practice for revising fragments is to work on your own paragraphs. However, you can practise by correcting the following sample paragraphs and then applying the practice to your own paragraphs.

For the following sample paragraphs, do one or more of the following: (1) add a subject, a verb, or both a subject and a verb, or (2) combine the fragment with a sentence before it or with a sentence after it.

Paragraph 1

I found that setting up an aquarium is expensive. After buying the tank, light, filter, and heater. I had other initial expenses. I needed to purchase chemicals. Chemicals to eliminate chlorine and to reduce the acidity. I made the tank attractive. Adding coloured gravel and plants. Adding ceramic figures. Placing a nice background behind the glass. To test the water and to keep the tank water at the right temperature. Adding a variety of fish with beautiful colours. When everything was set up. I had fun. The aquarium can provide a centre of enjoyment.

Paragraph 2

Putting on a play takes a lot of work from everyone. Actors must learn their lines. In addition, they must "become" the person they are portraying. Also, building and painting flats. Takes the crew many hours. They must also make sure all of the sound effects are realistically delivered. Delivered on time. If there are many people in the cast. Everybody must work long hours sewing the costumes. However, when everyone works hard. The finished product is rewarding. Very rewarding.

Run-On Sentences

A second type of sentence-structure problem is the **run-on sentence**. The term "run-on" explains the mistake; two sentences have been run together. In other words, no punctuation mark separates the independent thoughts.

The assignment was easy it took only a couple of hours to complete. (run-on sentence)

In this run-on sentence there are two independent thoughts about the assignment. One is that it was easy, and the other is that it took only a couple of hours to complete. Two sentences have been written as one sentence. Here is one way to express these two thoughts:

The assignment was easy. It took only a couple of hours to complete.

One misunderstanding that some writers have is that if ideas are related to each other, they should be written as one sentence. Look at the following ideas.

My cousin is coming to Alberta she wants to visit the Rockies. (run-on sentence)

These two ideas (coming to Alberta and visiting the Rockies) are related, but they should be two separate sentences. Each idea has a subject and a verb and is an independent thought:

My cousin is coming to Alberta. She wants to visit the Rockies.

Another misunderstanding writers have concerning run-on sentences is that if the idea is short, it cannot be two sentences. However, sentences are determined by whether or not they have a subject and a verb, not by length.

If you say "We should hurry we are late," you have two sentences. "We should hurry" is one sentence with its own subject and verb. "We are late" is another sentence with its own subject and verb.

We should hurry. We are late.

It is important that your writing is free of run-on sentences because if you have not identified where one sentence ends and another begins, your reader may misinterpret your thoughts. You may revise these run-on sentences in several ways.

Ways to Revise Run-On Sentences

Add a period at the end of each complete thought.

Use a comma and a connecting word called a coordinate conjunction.

Use a semicolon.

Use a semicolon, a connecting word called a conjunctive adverb, and a comma.

Use a subordinator.

Note A list of conjunctive adverbs precedes Exercise 10, and a list of subordinators precedes Exercise 5.

Adding a Period at the End of Each Complete Thought

The simplest way of dealing with this problem is to add a period at the end of each complete thought. For practice, complete the following exercise.

EXERCISE 7

Identify the place where the first sentence ends and the second sentence begins. Then revise each run-on sentence by adding a period after the first sentence and by beginning the second sentence with a capital letter.

Example:

                          chores. They
The girls chose their ~~chores they~~ **did them rapidly.**

1. He wanted to ride his bike she wanted to walk.

2. We don't want to wait we want to rent a boat.

3. I feel sorry for Claude he had his tonsils out.

4. The phone rang it was in the other room.

5. Michelle sang in the talent show she danced, also.

6. The computers in the lab were all working the ones in the middle worked the best.

7. My cat had kittens we had to find homes for them.

8. We went to the store we bought bread.

9. Sam came over we played football.

10. Father came home we watched television.

Using a Comma and a Coordinate Conjunction

Another way of revising run-on sentences is to connect them with a comma and an appropriate coordinate conjunction.

Coordinate Conjunctions

for	but
and	or
nor	yet
	so

I enjoy my job the rewards are great. (run-on sentence)

I enjoy my job, **and** the rewards are great. (correct)

Note The first letters of the coordinate conjunctions spell "fan boys."

EXERCISE 8

Revise each of the following sentences by finding the place where the sentences should be separated. Then add a comma and a coordinate conjunction between the two sentences.

Example:

                    lunch, and they
The boys ate pizza for ~~lunch they~~ enjoyed it.

1. Let's applaud him he is a jolly good fellow.

2. The track team travelled to the conference meet they won second place.

3. The men placed third overall the women placed second overall.

4. You can stay you can go.

5. A frost came in May many flowers didn't blossom.

6. Classes are over for the day we can go home.

7. Jack walked to the library he forgot his library card.

8. We can go to the football game we can go to the school play.

9. Hank found a lost kitten he wanted to keep it.

10. We won the contest we could not keep the prize.

Using a Semicolon (;)

You may also revise run-on sentences by separating the complete thoughts with a semicolon.

I enjoy my job the rewards are great. (run-on sentence)

I enjoy my job; the rewards are great. (correct)

EXERCISE 9

Revise each of the following sentences by finding the place where the sentences should be separated. Then add a semicolon to separate the sentences.

Example:

                      me; I

Seven cars were in front of ~~me I~~ needed to turn left.

1. Airplanes are convenient for long-distance travel much time can be saved.

2. It is good I will try some.

3. Football players have employment benefits their jobs can be very exciting, too.

4. Airplane travel is safer than automobile travel air accidents are just more publicized.

5. I got plenty of sleep on the weekend it was nice.

6. Planning a vacation takes time you want to be sure you do not forget anything.

7. I bought a new computer now I need a printer.

8. His class is very interesting I am learning a lot.

9. The bus arrived on time I was waiting to get on.

10. Working after school is hard I need to do my homework.

Using a Semicolon, a Conjunctive Adverb, and a Comma

Run-on sentences may also be revised by joining the two complete thoughts with a semicolon, a conjunctive adverb, and a comma.

Most Frequently Used Conjunctive Adverbs

moreover	consequently
furthermore	however
in fact	moreover
nevertheless	otherwise
therefore	thus

I enjoy my job the rewards are great. (run-on sentence)

I enjoy my job; **moreover**, the rewards are great. (correct)

EXERCISE 10

Revise each of the following sentences by finding the place where the sentences should be separated. Then add a semicolon, a conjunctive adverb, and a comma between the two sentences.

Example:

delicious; in fact, it
The spaghetti was ~~delicious it~~ was homemade.

1. Eating well can help keep the body healthy exercising can also help keep the body healthy.

2. We took our boat to the lake we forgot our life jackets.

3. The road was winding it was several lanes wide.

4. Justine hiked through the woods she picked many colourful flowers.

5. Owning a new car can be exciting driving a new car can be expensive.

6. Nursing can be a rewarding profession it can also be stressful.

7. Keeping rivers clean should be a priority children can get involved.

8. Peanuts are high in protein they are high in calories.

9. Working is good for teenagers they learn responsibility.

10. Drugs can destroy a person's life resisting them is hard for some people.

Using a Subordinator

Another way to revise run-on sentences is to join them by using a subordinator. You can easily achieve sentence variety in this way.

I enjoy my job the rewards are great. (run-on sentence)

I enjoy my job **when** the rewards are great. (correct)

EXERCISE 11

Revise each of the following sentences by finding the place where the sentences should be separated. Then add a subordinator from the list that precedes Exercise 5 of this unit (page 144). (Use a comma when needed.)

Example:

store because I
I want to go to the ~~store I~~ just got paid.

1. I need to go on a vacation I am tired.

2. We ate the fruit it was sour.

3. I will be there on time I have a lot of work to do.

4. The children played on the swings they were called into dinner.

5. The bananas turned black we had put them in the refrigerator.

6. I finished all my homework I could go to the movies.

7. The occupational therapist put in long hours he had seen everyone.

8. The dog knocked over the lamp he ran into the room.

9. Playing chess can improve a person's mind most moves are based on strategy.

10. I enjoy fishing it is relaxing.

Comma Splices

Another sentence structure problem similar to the run-on sentence is the **comma splice.**

> We spent the day at the beach, we came home sunburned. (comma splice)

In this case, the writer has separated two sentences with a comma. Using only a comma, however, is *not* an acceptable way to divide two independent thoughts. The easiest way is to substitute a period for the comma and begin the next word with a capital letter.

> We spent the day at the beach. We came home sunburned. (correct)

Sometimes this method creates too many short sentences in a row. In such cases, other kinds of revision can help your sentences flowbetter. To correct comma splices and still retain sentence variety, do the following:

- **Use a comma and a coordinate conjunction.**

  > We spent the day at the beach, and we came home sunburned. (correct)

- **Use a semicolon.**

  > We spent the day at the beach; we came home sunburned. (correct)

- **Use a semicolon and a conjunctive adverb.** (See the list that precedes Exercise 10 in this unit.)

    We spent the day at the beach; **as a result**, we came home sunburned. (correct)

- **Use a subordinator that logically links the two sentences.**

    Because we spent the day at the beach, we came home sunburned. (correct)

Note   When the subordinator is added to the first sentence, this introductory idea is separated from the rest of the sentence with a comma. For more detailed explanation, see Unit 6, Part 4.

EXERCISE 12

Revise the following comma splices. Try using several of the methods explained in the text.

Example:

cats. Then

cats, and then

The old lady often took in hungry, stray ~~cats, then~~ she tried to find homes for them.

1. The young lady was hungry after work, she stopped at the grocery store.

2. In the springtime, the trees were covered with green leaves, the flowers were covered with lavender blossoms.

3. Fishing, kayaking, and rafting require skill, these activities can be exciting.

4. The children ended the school year with a swim party, they had a wonderful time.

5. Teenagers need a lot of sleep, they especially enjoy sleeping in the mornings.

6. While we were on the beach, we collected shells, then we built a sand castle.

7. Inside the registration building, students made out their schedules for next year, they checked the computers to see which classes were open.

8. The turtle hibernated for many months, he emerged famished and began to eat his way through the garden.

9. When we arrived at the beach, we headed for the water, then we took off our shoes and waded in the surf.

10. After cooking a big meal, everyone sat down to eat, no one wanted to clean up.

11. Harry read the three articles about drug abuse in the newspaper, he took notes for his history paper, yet he had more work to do.

> If you want further practice on these types of combinations, review the materials in Units 5 and 6, Part 4.

EXERCISE 13

Revise the fragments, run-on sentences, and comma splices in the following paragraphs. Be creative by using as many different methods as possible.

Paragraph 1

Because pizza is so versatile. It is no wonder that it is one of Canada's favourite foods. Pizza is available frozen at the grocery store or piping hot from a variety of pizza restaurants. It can be bought with thin crust or thick crust, it can be sandwiched between two crusts. Plain pizza crust can be bought frozen or already baked in packages much like bread, or mixed at home. Almost every person's individual taste can be satisfied because of the variety of toppings. Toppings spread on the sauce. Pepperoni leads the list for favourites, but jalapeño, anchovies, olives, and sausages are some of the other options, even sausage comes in different types. For a real "like-home" Italian taste. The pizza can be topped with garlic bits and a little Parmesan cheese without the sauce. Since pizza can be varied, almost everyone can be satisfied.

Paragraph 2

Owning cats can be a frustrating experience. Sometimes they want to be affectionate and even sit in their owner's lap, other times, they treat their owner like a second-class citizen and turn away. Turn away saucily. A person who does not know cats may be frustrated by their cautiousness. And mistake it for a lack of affection. For example, a lazy-looking cat gazing out the window may really be a lonesome pet, he may really be eagerly waiting for the owner to come home. When the owner does come home. The cat probably will not immediately jump down like a dog and run to greet the owner the cat may cautiously turn his head and look the other way. He is not ignoring his owner but just showing caution in case the owner may ignore him. This is the kind of lukewarm "hello" that frustrates people who do not understand. Understand cats.

Paragraph 3

Being able to save money is a valuable skill for teenagers to have. If they learn to save money from their jobs. They may be able to purchase expensive items like stereos, video recorders, or cars. Which their parents cannot afford. Saving money also gives them a big boost, they are able to go to college later to prepare for a career. Their parents may not be able to pay for their college tuition, books, and spending money while they are in college. Without saving money, the teenagers might have to spend the rest of their lives flipping hamburgers. Flipping hamburgers at minimum wage. Having saved for attending college would show maturity young people would have learned the valuable skill of putting aside money for something important for their future lives.

It is easy to identify fragments, run-ons, and comma splices when the sentences have been isolated and you are looking for a specific kind of sentence structure problem. However, in your own writing this major problem may be hidden within your ideas and may be overlooked. If you seem to be having a problem identifying run-ons, comma splices, or fragments, read backwards through your paper—doing this will help you concentrate on the structure of your sentences rather than on the ideas.

WRITING ASSIGNMENT

Using the steps of the writing process that you are familiar with, draft an essay explaining what a person must consider before undertaking one of the following actions:
1. Moving out on one's own
2. Moving back in with parents
3. Moving back with a mate or roommate
4. Becoming a college student
5. Participating in extracurricular activities in school
6. Playing sports in school

Or, draft an essay discussing the advantages or disadvantages of one of the following:

7. Jobs on campus
8. Minimum wage
9. A hobby
10. Breakfast

After you draft your essay, revise for content and edit for mechanics.

Content

> *Essay*

> > Check to see that the thesis sentence states a clear direction or previews the points to be covered in the paper.

> > Check to see that the voice is appropriate for your purpose and audience.

> *Paragraphs*

> > Revise so each has a clear topic sentence that develops an idea suggested by or previewed in the thesis sentence.

> > Include four to six supporting sentences.

> > Include a closing sentence.

Mechanics

> Check for subject-verb agreement.

> Check for consistent verbs.

> Check for a consistent point of view.

> Check for fragments, run-on sentences, and comma splices.

Unit Five

Writing with More Depth and Variety

PART 1 — Parts to Whole: Writing with Examples

OBJECTIVES

....

- Understand the purpose of an example.
- Recognize sources of examples.
- Generate examples through freewriting or brainstorming.
- Recognize and write both extended and short, interrelated examples.
- Use only relevant examples.
- Determine number of examples needed to clarify topic idea.

In composition writing, an example is a specific reference to an experience or experiences that you have had, have witnessed, have read about, or have seen in a movie or on television. Such a reference helps you clarify or illustrate a point, fact, or opinion you wish to make in your paper.

The Purpose of Examples

Just as your paragraphs need specific details for good, solid support, they also can be more fully developed through relevant, well-selected examples. Examples are based on life experiences that can be used to support your thesis, and by presenting them, you add more credibility to your writing. Think of examples as "defence for your case" as you stated it in your thesis. Using examples allows you to win your reader over and to present your essay in a trustworthy and believable way.

As you learned in Unit 2 on topic sentences and paragraphs, the following sentences would not be sufficient for a paragraph.

Even though collies are beautiful dogs, they are also known to be pro-tectors. They seldom harm other animals and often turn guardian of their charges.

These two sentences express the main idea, but you still need more information:

Even though collies are beautiful dogs, they are also known to be pro-tectors. They seldom harm other animals and often turn guardian of their charges. **They have been known to protect small children and other pets and can keep them from being harmed. When someone tries to commit a crime against the owners, collies come to the rescue.**

Notice that the two sentences added (in bold type) give support to the paragraph, but you might want to "show" how this is true through *specific examples* that clarify the point being made. What is needed is one or more detailed examples—*incidents* or *pictures*—to show the topic idea. Now read the following revised paragraph. Two specific **examples** have been added.

Even though collies are beautiful dogs, they are also known to be pro-tectors. They seldom harm other animals and often turn guardian of their charges. They have been known to protect small children and other pets and can keep them from being harmed. When someone tries to commit a crime against the owners, collies come to the rescue. For example, when Charlie was a child, he had a collie that often helped catch loose rabbits when they got out of their cages. One evening she barked at the back door until someone came. She had found a baby rabbit who had fallen out of the wire cage, had picked it up gently in her mouth, and had brought it to the house unharmed. Another time, when a strange man tried to break into the house, she positioned herself between the family members and the stranger. Baring her teeth and growling deeply, she stopped him. The family always felt everything was under control as long as they had their "best friend" close by.

This paragraph shows the reader "in what way" collies are protectors by stating that "they seldom harm other animals and often turn guardian of their charges." This statement is explained and then clarified by two supporting examples. One is the experience in which the collie brought the baby rabbit to the owners, and the other is when the collie protected the family from the strange man. In your writing you, too, can relate specific examples that help the reader understand your main idea.

Sources of Examples

Finding appropriate examples for your writing involves discovering sources through freewriting, brainstorming, or other prewriting activities.

Sources That Provide Examples

personal experiences

personal observations of other people

short stories, novels, television, or movies

facts, statistics, or reports from authoritative sources

Personal Experiences

A personal experience can add convincing information to support your thesis. Frequently, personal experiences that you can recall in detail can help you clarify the main point for the reader. The more specific the example is, the clearer the topic idea becomes to the reader. Freewriting and brainstorming can help you remember details of events in your life. If these events are important enough for you to remember, then perhaps your reader will also be able to relate to these examples. Suppose your topic idea for a paragraph is the following:

Topic: Taking a child shopping can be embarrassing.

Perhaps during freewriting or brainstorming, you remember the following incident:

> When I took my four-year-old child shopping at The West Edmonton Mall, he decided to "check out" the mannequin with a beautiful black slinky dress, and somehow he managed to knock it over with a thud. Instantly a salesperson appeared to see if my child was hurt. He wasn't hurt, but he was scared. People began to gather from all directions. I wasn't sure what to do, so we quietly slipped away.

Notice that the above incident "shows" the reader "in what way" taking a child shopping can be embarrassing. This *incident* or *picture* that you have created for the reader is a strong, *specific example.*

Realistic examples make the topic idea clearer to the reader. Made-up stories often have a fake sound that do little or nothing to add credibility to your writing. It is much easier to remember the time your child knocked over the mannequin than it is to make up an example that never happened. In the earlier paragraph, it would be very difficult to make up a story about a collie that picked up a newborn rabbit and brought it safely to the owner. Therefore, by recalling real events that have happened to you, you can "show" what it is you want to prove. "Showing" makes writing stronger and more interesting than "telling about" an idea.

Observations of Other People

Observations that you have made of other people can illustrate the topic you are discussing and add more credibility to your paragraphs. Perhaps you are writing about fatherhood, but you are not a father. Maybe your brother, husband, or neighbour is a father, and you have observed him with his children. After freewriting or brainstorming, you might have decided to begin with this topic idea:

Topic: Many Canadian fathers are becoming involved in all aspects of their children's lives.

During additional freewriting or brainstorming, you may remember when you saw a father becoming involved in his children's lives:

Last summer I always knew it was 5:30 p.m. when I saw Hugh Dobson and his son, equipped with a bat, gloves, and a baseball, emerge from their front door. Sometimes they would practise catching, sometimes pitching, and other times batting.

Even though these are not your personal experiences, they are events that you have witnessed. They will sound more convincing to your reader than a made-up incident.

Short Stories, Novels, Television, or Movies

Examples that come from short stories, novels, television, or movies can also support or "show" topic ideas. This extensive source for examples can include characters and events that you have read about or seen.

If you are writing an essay about how the meaning of life can change for a person, you might use an incident from Orwell's *1984* as an example. The change Winston feels regarding sex could be an example of your topic idea. You could summarize the incident and use it to support your topic idea:

Winston's sexual encounter with a prostitute is very degrading to him. The prostitute is repulsive, and he feels that the sexual act itself has been lowered to only a mechanical act. Winston feels no love as he performs a loveless, almost disgusting act. (This would be considered one example.)

Or if you are writing an essay about the realistic depiction of the Vietnam War, you might draw from a movie like *Platoon*. The topic idea might be that young men would do anything to get home from the war, and you might use specific examples as follows:

One of the soldiers stabbed himself in the knee so he could go home. Another soldier put a solution on the bottoms of his feet so that they would be severely cracked and look as if he couldn't walk.
(This would be considered two examples.)

Or if you are writing a paper about humorous events in family life, you could use a current television program for appropriate examples.

Facts, Statistics, or Reports from Authoritative Sources

Research studies, verifiable facts, or current news stories can provide examples to support your thesis. To use these kinds of examples, you may have to read material in the library or talk to someone who is an expert on your topic. If you want to write a paper about aquariums but do not have one, you can still write about them if you take the time to read books or articles about aquariums or if you go to a fish store and talk to someone who is knowledgeable in the field. You would want to know if this "authority in the field" is or has been a breeder and/or has been working with fish for a long time. You need this background to decide if you can trust the source of your information, whether it comes from a book or from a personal interview.

Once you have read about or talked to someone about your topic, your freewriting or brainstorming may give you a topic idea for one paragraph in your essay:

Topic: When an aquarium is set up correctly, a natural balance results.

Your conversation at a fish store with an expert has given you a specific example of a natural balance. You could use the information like this:

According to the owner of the Lighthouse fish store, catfish clean up the waste from the bottom of the fish tank. In this way, the catfish help to create a natural balance.

The catfish would be only one specific example for your paragraph. Your reading and your conversation with the store owner would give you other specific examples for your paragraph.

In a different essay, you might be working on one paragraph to support the topic idea that a person can make a profit by investing in a home. You could recall some factual information you have read, or you could go to the library to do research. As a result of your reading in the June 1989 issue of *Reader's Digest*, you find an article by Sonny Bloch and Grace Lichtenstein about affording homes. This article has a great example you might decide to use. You could write something like this in your paragraph:

In the June 1989 issue of *Reader's Digest*, an article titled "Afford a Home of Your Own" includes the story of a young American couple who bought an old home for $61,000. They did a lot of work fixing it up, and in less than three years they sold the home for $127,500.

This specific example could be used in your paragraph; however, as you can see, you do need to let the reader know where you got the information. This is one kind of authoritative example that can give credibility to your writing.

In each of the previous writing situations, you would also need other examples in each paragraph to support the topic idea. These examples could come from your personal experience or from observations of other people you know. As you have already learned, one of your goals in each paragraph is to support the topic sentence with enough specific information to convince your reader.

Generating Examples Through Freewriting and Brainstorming

As you have already learned, freewriting and brainstorming are important steps in the writing process that you can use at different times. You can freewrite or brainstorm to get started in a writing situation. You can also use these strategies to help you think of or "discover" more or better examples needed to support your thesis sentence and/or topic sentences.

Suppose you have developed the following thesis sentence:

> Returning to school has been a rewarding experience because I have found that I have abilities I never knew I had before, have changed the way I dress, and have met new friends.

In looking over the freewriting or brainstorming you have already done, you probably realize that you may not have enough specific information to write strong paragraphs. Using each topic idea previewed in the thesis sentence, then, do more freewriting and/or brainstorming to find the examples you need. For instance, freewriting and brainstorming on "I have found that I have abilities I never knew I had before" might produce the following ideas. (Remember that in freewriting or brainstorming you do not stop to correct errors!)

Freewriting for Examples

Going to school can be rewarding. I need to come up with some examples of times when I found I had new abilities I didn't know I had before. There are many times that I have found that I could things that I didn't think I could do before. I haven't been to school in ten years and I thought that the kids just out of high school would do circles around me or make me feel inferior. I still think it is hard. But I am really not in that bad of shape. I am doing <u>pretty good in my English class and in my computer class</u>. I hope that my average is an A. I am more concerned about learning though. I studied for my grammar test. It came out pretty good too. <u>I made 95 percent on that test. It was on consistent point of view</u>. Most of the kids made around 70 percent, so that really made me feel like I could do alright. No one has made fun of me yet. Some of the younger kids think I am an old lady, but that is ok. Jim didn't seem to think I was so dumb when <u>the teacher asked me to help him with the topic sentence. He began to get it too</u>. I felt real proud when I could show him how to write one. You know, it made it easier for me too. I guess showing someone else how to do things is good for me. It made me feel better, and now I think I'll make it. Maybe I'll even decide to be a teacher. I had a little trouble when I wrote my first essay. The next time I wrote one <u>the teacher told me I had an effective thesis sentence and that my support was good</u>. That really made me feel good. I wasn't sure I could do all that when I came back to school.

When you reread the freewriting, you can see three distinct examples of the way you are doing well in your English class. By using these examples, you can *show* "in what way" you discovered abilities that you didn't know you had. These three examples would help you write a strong support paragraph for this part of your essay.

Study the following list to see how the ideas underlined in the previous freewriting have been rewritten as specific examples that support the topic sentence "I have abilities I never knew I had before." The topic sentence, in turn, clearly relates to the main idea in your thesis sentence.

> *Thesis sentence:* Returning to school has been a rewarding experience because I have found that I have abilities I never knew I had before, have changed the way I dress, and have met new friends.
>
> *Topic sentence:* I have found that I have abilities I never knew I had before.
>
> *Linking sentence:* I did well in my English class.
>
> *Specific example 1:* When I wrote my second essay using my job as the topic, my instructor told me that my thesis sentence was well written and that I had followed through well on my paragraphs.
>
> *Specific example 2:* My English instructor asked me to help a student who was having trouble with the topic sentence, and as I helped him, I felt good because he understood what I was saying.
>
> *Specific example 3:* I took my first grammar test and scored ninety-five percent on it.

Notice that a linking sentence, "I did well in my English class," has been put in. Sometimes in the freewriting you can also find a suitable sentence to link the examples to the topic sentence. Also notice that a lot of unnecessary or "warm-up" information has been left out.

Brainstorming for Examples

> *Topic sentence:* I have abilities I never knew I had before.
> did well on grammar test: 95 percent
> helped other student with topic sentence
> wrote good essay
> did well in English class

Sometimes it is easier to freewrite before you brainstorm and then pull the ideas from the freewriting. Other times it is easier just to brainstorm in order to generate ideas.

The other two support paragraphs can also be developed through freewriting or brainstorming. The choice is yours.

How Finding Examples Fits into the Writing Process

At this point, you might find it helpful to review the writing process. Study the following review of the writing process for a longer paper—from selecting a topic to finding examples.

Steps in the Writing Process to Generate Ideas for a Paper

selecting a topic

freewriting/brainstorming for direction

identifying direction

freewriting/brainstorming and grouping for thesis sentence

writing the thesis sentence

freewriting/brainstorming again to recall specific examples

Suppose you have selected "driving on ice" as the topic for your longer paper, and you decide to use brainstorming to help you find a direction and develop a thesis sentence. Now follow this process from selecting the topic of "driving on ice" to writing one of the support paragraphs in a longer paper.

Choose a topic: driving on ice

Brainstorm for direction: hazardous

dangerous

could get hurt

Identify direction: hazards of driving on ice

Brainstorm and group for thesis sentence:

black ice is scary	braking
nothing can be done to prevent it	weather condition
causes skidding	driving too fast
shiny, clear, invisible	drive slower
freezes at zero degrees Celsius	chains
learn from experienced driver	warnings
salt on road	

Next, group similar ideas, rewrite them, and give each group a "label."

learning to control the car

   realize that braking causes the skid

   know how to bring the car out of a skid

    turn in the direction of a skid

   drive with someone who is used to driving in icy weather

understanding dangerous conditions

   shiny, clear, invisible

   occurs at zero degrees Celsius

following safety precautions

   using chains

   driving only on roads that have been salted

   obeying warnings

   listening to weather reports

   driving at slower speeds

Write the thesis sentence: Driving safely on ice involves learning to control the car, understanding dangerous conditions, and following safety precautions.

At this point in the process, you know that you need more specific examples to write strong paragraphs, so you may either freewrite or brainstorm to find these examples.

Freewrite to recall specific example(s):

   I need to remember examples that show driving on ice safely involves learning to control the car. I am a pretty good driver but ice still scares me. I guess it scares me because of the time that time I almost hit another car because I put on the brakes and went into a skid. That was really scary. I remember that I was near my house and since I thought I was a pretty good driver in winter weather, I wasn't paying too much attention to how fast I was going. It is a good thing I did know how to bring the car out of a skid. I remembered Mr. Belanger, but that really didn't have anything to do with controlling the car. That was more because he didn't have time to bring his car out of a skid.

Brainstorm to recall specific example(s):

   Mr. Belanger, who was fatally injured

   the time I almost got into a wreck

Either of these two incidents, whether generated through freewriting or brainstorming, could provide convincing details. You may choose one or both of them to support your topic idea. Each incident you select would be one *detailed example* that helps you develop the topic idea that learning to control the car is important when driving on ice. You might write the paragraph this way:

   Being able to control the car is important when I drive on dangerous ice. Being a native of Montreal, I am comfortable with my ability to drive in the winter months, but each year I get shocked into reality. This winter was no different. A week after the worst snow storm, I thought things were getting better because the snow was beginning to melt. Suddenly, without warning, a cold night froze the melting snow at a busy intersection close to my house. As I came to the stop sign, I applied the brakes as usual, but my Bronco seemed to accelerate into the flow of traffic. I quickly took my foot off the brake and concentrated on turning into the skid. Thanks to my guardian angel, I barely missed an innocent motorist. Next year I hope I can remember this near-miss as vividly as I do now and can avoid an ice accident.

The following exercise will give you practice in generating examples to support a topic idea. Either freewrite or brainstorm to find these ideas.

EXERCISE 1

Using the following topic ideas, write a personal example, a personal observation of someone else, a fictionalized example, and a fact, statistic, or incident from an authoritative source. (In order to obtain an authoritative example, you may need to go to the library or talk to an expert on your topic.)

1. Pets comfort their owners.

_____

(personal example)

_____

_____

(personal observation of someone else)

_____

_____

(example from a short story, novel, television show, or movie)

_____

_____

(fact, statistic, or incident from an authoritative source)

_____

_____

_____

2. Learning a new skill brings satisfaction.

_____

(personal example)

_____

_____

_____

(personal observation of someone else)

_____

_____

_____

(example from a short story, novel, television show, or movie)

_____

_____

_____

(fact, statistic, or incident from an authoritative source)

_____

_____

_____

3. Big cities offer many attractions.

_____

(personal example)

_____

_____

_____

(personal observation of someone else)

_____

_____

(example from a short story, novel, television show, or movie)

_____

_____

(fact, statistic, or incident from an authoritative source)

_____

_____

Extended Examples and Shorter, Interrelated Examples

Examples can appear in two basic forms:

1. extended examples
2. series of shorter, detailed, interrelated examples

Extended Examples

An extended example illustrates one person, one experience, or one significant incident developed fully so that the reader has not only a clear picture of the example but also its relationship to the topic idea. An extended example appears in the following paragraph.

> **Driving on black ice can be dangerous because it is invisible and can catch motorists unaware.** Mr. Belanger was one of these unsuspecting motorists. As a UPS inspector, he had to take his turn on the graveyard shift. When he drove to work in the early evening, the roads were fine, but when he left at 2:00 in the morning, black ice had formed. Because he was anxious to get home to his warm bed and no traffic slowed him down, he came upon an unexpectedly busy intersection too rapidly. As he applied the brakes, his tires slid on the ice, and his car slammed into a big diesel. Mr. Belanger, who never knew what had hit him, died unnecessarily.

The preceding paragraph uses an **extended example** to support the topic sentence in bold type. The second sentence—"Mr. Belanger was one of these unsuspecting motorists"—is the link between the topic idea and the extended example of Mr. Belanger's accident.

You do not need to relate everything that you know about Mr. Lopez, only the information that supports the topic sentence. Your reader does not need to know if Mr. Belanger was single or married, if he was rich or poor, if he liked to fish or play football. That information is irrelevant to the topic sentence. Remember the pattern:

topic sentence

linking sentence

extended example

The following exercise will help you write extended examples and their linking sentences.

EXERCISE 2

For each topic sentence given, write a sentence that links the topic idea to an appropriate extended example. Then write an extended example that clarifies the topic sentence. (You may find it easier to write the example first and then think of an appropriate linking sentence.)

1. *Topic sentence:* Motherhood can be a frustrating experience.

_____

(linking sentence)

_____

_____

(extended example)

_____

_____

_____

2. *Topic sentence:* A provincial park provides exciting activities for a family.

_____

(linking sentence)

_____

_____

(extended example)

_____

_____

_____

3. *Topic sentence:* Student-athletes or working students must organize their time carefully.

(linking sentence)

_____

_____

(extended example)

_____

_____

_____

4. *Topic sentence:* Looking at a family photo album brings back memories.

(linking sentence)

_____

_____

(extended example)

_____

_____

_____

5. *Topic sentence:* A large city offers exciting activities for tourists.

(linking sentence)

_____

(extended example)

After you have recalled the extended example by freewriting/brainstorming, you need to decide how much of the freewriting/brainstorming you actually need to use in the paragraph. Sometimes in freewriting, you may get carried away and put in details that are not related to the topic sentence. You may remember many more details than you need to use. Just keep in mind the requirements for a good paragraph: topic sentence, related support sentences, and a related concluding sentence.

The following exercise will help you sort out unrelated details in an extended example.

EXERCISE 3

Read the following paragraphs and decide if there is any extra information that is not needed to support the topic idea. First, underline the topic sentence and the linking sentence. Then strike out the sentences in each extended example that do not support the topic sentence.

Paragraph 1

When a child first learns to read, short-term rewards can often be more important than the actual ability to read. My child was an example of this theory. He wanted to be a good reader, but when he realized he needed to work hard and practise, he wasn't sure reading was as important as watching "Mr. Wizzard's World" to obtain his knowledge about the scientific world. However, he was willing to sit down and plan a strategy. Because he also wanted to set up an aquarium that had been unused for many years, together we decided that for every fifty pages he read aloud to me, he could either buy a fish or have two dollars of in-store credit. He had two other pets. With this agreed upon, he assembled the aquarium, filled it with water, and went to the fish store. As soon as we got home and he walked through the door, he said, "Let's read." And read we did. Even though the first book was below his grade level, it took him four days to finish fifty pages. However, it only took twenty minutes to get the first inhabitant for his tank. That one fish looked lonely, and the only solution was to read another fifty pages. Soon he had earned another fish and another fish. The fish cost me anywhere from eight-nine cents to two dollars. Moving up to grade-level books brought a little resistance because there were NO pictures. But soon these books, too, seemed easier and easier until he was able to select books way above grade level. Now he was enjoying reading for the sake of reading, and he began to read extra books on his own. Of all the books he read, he enjoyed the one about a kid who ended up with jars and jars of goldfish with no place to put them. As he earned fish, he began to love reading for the sake of knowledge, but he had seldom found reading a chore because every page had brought him closer to a new fish.

Paragraph 2

Being hospitalized for an illness can cause a person in the United States to suffer a financial setback. The extensive bills can mount up. My uncle in Florida suffered a severe financial setback when he spent several weeks in the hospital. The seven days in intensive care and four additional weeks in the hospital resulted in astronomical costs. Even though he had insurance, he had to pay a $100 deductible and 20 percent of the bill. Because the hospital bill alone was over $14,000, his responsibilities were $2,800. Also, his wife went on a shopping spree for new clothes. On top of this, he had to purchase several hundred dollars worth of medicine. He also had to purchase medical supplies that were not covered by insurance. Because my uncle was unable to work, he was eligible for disability, but this amount was much less than his regular salary. Before his illness, he smoked only one carton of cigarettes a week, but because of the stress during and after his illness, he smoked two cartons. In just a few weeks, he found himself owing $6,000 in medical expenses. It is scary to think how fast medical bills can accumulate when an extended illness occurs.

Shorter, Detailed, Interrelated Examples

In addition to one extended example to develop a whole paragraph, your brainstorming may give you a series of shorter, detailed, interrelated examples that can be used in your support paragraphs. Here is an example:

> When an aquarium is set up correctly, a natural balance results. Choosing the correct plant and animal life provides an opportunity for these two forces to live harmoniously. Not only do plants put oxygen into the water, but they also provide a place for baby fish to hide so they won't be eaten. Selection of animal life is just as important to the owner of the aquarium. Catfish are scavengers that clean up the waste from the bottom and sides of the fish tank. Plecostomus, which are a type of catfish, even clean plants that have become slimy from algae. Snails can be seen removing the algae and slime or eating fish that have died and settled on the bottom of the tank. At the same time, all of these fish return carbon dioxide to the water. If proper thought is put into starting an aquarium, a harmonious balance can be achieved.

The above paragraph has a clear topic sentence and a linking sentence to introduce the short, interrelated examples. Four separate examples support the topic sentence: (1) plants, (2) catfish, (3) plecostomus, and (4) snails.

The following exercise will give you practice in generating short, interrelated examples and the appropriate linking sentences.

EXERCISE 4

Using each topic sentence given, write a sentence that links the topic idea to appropriate short, interrelated examples. You may use the same linking sentences that you wrote in Exercise 2. Then write the short interrelated examples that clarify the topic sentence. If it is easier for you, write the series of short examples first; then write a sentence to link them to the topic sentence.

1. *Topic sentence:* Motherhood can be a frustrating experience.

_____

(linking sentence)

_____

_____

(short, interrelated examples)

_____

_____

_____

2. *Topic sentence:* A provincial park provides exciting activities for a family.

_____

(linking sentence)

_____

_____

(short, interrelated examples)

_____

_____

_____

3. *Topic sentence:* Student athletes or working students must organize their time carefully.

_____

(linking sentence)

_____

_____

(short, interrelated examples)

_____

_____

_____

4. *Topic sentence:* Looking at a family photo album brings back memories.

_____

(linking sentence)

_____

(short, interrelated examples)

_____

_____

_____

5. *Topic sentence*: A large city offers exciting experiences for tourists.

(linking sentence) _____

_____

(short, interrelated examples)

_____

_____

_____

Stressing Relevance in Short, Interrelated Examples

You have already learned that a strong paragraph is unified, with all its sentences relating to the topic sentence. Whenever you use examples to develop your paragraph, be sure that every example is related to the topic idea.

In the previous paragraph about setting up a balanced aquarium, all of the sentences support one topic idea. Suppose, in further reading, you find that "Dojos are Chinese fish that change colour with the weather" and that "African frogs are nocturnal aquatic creatures that come out to play at night when the fish are sleeping." This information sounds so interesting that you decide to include it. Here is your new paragraph:

When an aquarium is set up correctly, a natural balance results. Choosing the correct plant and animal life provides an opportunity for these two forces to live harmoniously. Not only do plants put oxygen into the water, but they also provide a place for baby fish to hide so they won't be eaten. Selection of animal life is just as important to the owner of the aquarium. Catfish are scavengers that clean up the waste from the bottom and sides of the fish tank. Plecostomus, which are a type of catfish, even clean plants that have become slimy from algae. Snails can be seen removing the algae and slime or eating fish that have died and settled on the bottom of the tank. At the same time, all of these fish return carbon dioxide to the water. **Dojos are Chinese weather fish that change colour with the weather, and African frogs are nocturnal aquatic creatures that come out to play at night when the fish are sleeping.** If proper thought is put into starting an aquarium, a harmonious balance can be achieved.

Even though these two new examples are appealing, you cannot add them to the paragraph because they do not support the topic idea of a balanced aquarium. When you are drafting or revising a paragraph, you have time to think through how well your examples support the topic sentence. Do not hesitate to cut examples that are interesting but are not directly related to the topic idea. The following exercise will give you practice in finding such examples.

EXERCISE 5

Read the following paragraphs, and in each paragraph decide which examples are relevant to the topic sentence and which examples are not. Then cross out the examples that do not support the topic idea.

Paragraph 1

Early Canadians had to rely on their own ingenuity to make life comfortable or even to survive. They turned survival skills into a type of art that was passed down from generation to generation. Some of these art forms, which may no longer be practical in today's society, were a part of living for our great-grandparents. In the West, sturdy houses could be made from brick, but first the brick had to be made from mud and straw. Making clothes was also an art of the past that few people could accomplish today. Even buying material for clothes was a luxury few knew. The process of making a new dress or shirt or pants involved shearing sheep, carding wool, spinning yarn, and weaving cloth. Sometimes the clothing maker dyed the yarn different colours, using natural materials like walnut shells. The women enjoyed growing flowers to make the home look more attractive. Tatting—making lace by hand—became an art form that was used to decorate collars or to bring beauty to something as necessary as pillowcases. People loved to get together in the evenings and have dances. Since there were no refrigerators, families found making beef jerky was a way of preserving meat that provided a year-round supply. And if they wanted to take a bath, they needed soap, but making soap at home, an art almost unheard of today, was required before that bath could take place. When the supply of candles, the source of night light, became low, there was one solution—making more from melted lard. Sometimes the men and women would work from sunup to sundown so they could take a day off for celebration. Today, we talk of "the good old days" when life was simple, but maybe we should say when families were resourceful and used art in order to survive.

Paragraph 2

Many farmers and gardeners have tried creative methods to eliminate garden pests organically and safely, without the use of insecticides. Some Canadian gardeners are said to harvest pesky tomato worms, put them into a blender, and then spray the mixture onto the healthy plants. The tomato bugs smell death and depart as quickly as they arrived. Farmers in some parts of Canada depend on irrigation for good crops. In China, farmers build little hibernation huts to encourage spiders to build webs in their rice fields, so when the spiders "wake up" or hatch, they are ready to harvest the bugs that are so damaging to the rice crops. Most American farmers also rotate crops. One season they might plant alfalfa to replenish the soil, and the next season they will plant a different crop like cotton. Cotton farmers in the southwestern parts of the United States are said to have dumped millions of wooly worms into the cotton fields to eat the boll weevils before they could destroy the cotton crop. After a fine feast, the wooly worms marched off, and the cotton crops were saved. All of these solutions to insect problems did not use any lethal sprays that could be passed on to humans.

Deciding How Many Short Examples to Use

Usually after you have drafted your paragraph, you need to decide how many short, interrelated examples are needed to clarify the topic sentence.

This is something you have to think through logically. You want to provide as many different types of examples as you can. You do not, however, want to refer to the same types of examples over and over again. Read again the sample paragraph about the balanced aquarium:

> When an aquarium is set up correctly, a natural balance results. Choosing the correct plant and animal life provides an opportunity for these two forces to live harmoniously. Not only do plants put oxygen into the water, but they also provide a place for baby fish to hide so they won't be eaten. Selection of animal life is just as important to the owner of the aquarium. Catfish are scavengers that clean up the waste from the bottom and sides of the fish tank. Plecostomus, which are a type of catfish, even clean plants that have become slimy from algae. Snails can be seen removing the algae and slime or eating fish that have died and settled on the bottom of the tank. At the same time, all of these fish return carbon dioxide to the water. If proper thought is put into starting an aquarium, a harmonious balance can be achieved.

Catfish are chosen as an example because they clean up the wastes. Plecostomus are added because they do one additional thing—they clean the algae slime from the plants. There are many more varieties of algae eaters, but they are not needed to make the point that an aquarium that is set up properly can result in a natural balance between plants and animals. The four examples clearly and forcefully support the topic idea. All four add something *different* to the supporting details.

Look at the following paragraph on special-interest classes offered by a community college.

> Special-interest classes are offered by many community colleges to meet the needs of all members of a society. The classes are often varied in scope and content depending on the population living around the college. "Remodelling Your Own Kitchen" offers an opportunity for people to become equipped with information before investing thousands of dollars on a remodelling job. "Quilting for Fun" can enable men and women to learn an art that is no longer passed down from generation to generation. "Making Animals from Balloons" is a course offered to children and should provide hours of creative enjoyment. "Living with an Elderly Parent or

Handicapped Child" could ease the responsibility felt by adults in charge. These courses are as varied as the community itself and are intended to provide community enrichment for the public.

Four *different types* of courses are included. More examples could have been added. You would not, however, add an example like "Remodelling Your Bathroom" or "Simple Needlecraft" because these types of examples have already been used. You might, though, use a different type of example, such as "Camping Made Easy."'

Deciding how many examples to use is up to you. Three or four is usually a good number to put into each paragraph. Remember, though, that each one should add something different to support the topic sentence. Each one should show in a different way "how the topic sentence is true."

The following exercise will give you practice in finding duplicate examples in a paragraph that is developed with a series of short, interrelated examples.

EXERCISE 6

Read the following paragraphs carefully. Then decide which examples duplicate a type of example already used and which examples show different ways in which the topic idea is true. Strike out any example that duplicates a type already used. Be prepared to explain how it duplicates another example.

Paragraph 1

Today in Canada, medical researchers are realizing the many ways pets are helping physically handicapped adults. These pets are an extension of these adults, as they perform tasks that are often impossible for the handicapped adult to do alone. Seeing Eye dogs are being used to guide visually handicapped people so these individuals can experience the freedom their blindness has taken from them. Trained monkeys are being used to perform simple manual tasks like turning light switches on and off or holding the telephone receiver for adults with limited or no use of their hands and arms. Parrots are being used to bring companionship to handicapped adults who are confined to their homes. The parrot and master can sing songs together and can even talk to one another. Cats are also being used for companionship so the handicapped adult doesn't feel so lonely. All of these pets and their owners become great friends as they lean on each other for support.

Paragraph 2

Retirement can be one of the most enjoyable times in life for many couples. This wonderful time often gives two people the opportunity to accomplish the things in life that they have had to put off for many years. Bernie and Christina always dreamed of travelling extensively, but they could not take the time off until they retired. They talked to others about travel and checked into all of their options, but it wasn't until they retired that they were able to benefit from the rewards of going on many well-planned tours throughout the world. Joe and Charlotte enjoyed working in the yard but never had enough time to have more than a small garden. Retirement, though, gave them the opportunity to turn their token garden into an elaborate, artistic wonderland. Another couple, Kamil and Mary, lived in the city because that was where their jobs were, but whenever they had the opportunity, they went to the mountains to relax in their cabin. After they retired, they found much pleasure in selling their home in the city and moving to the mountains full-time. Ray and Sara also enjoyed their retirement by taking extended vacations since their children were grown and living on their own. All of these couples found enrichment by using retirement as a means of fulfilling their lifelong dreams.

When adding examples to your writing, use your own judgment to decide whether you want one longer, extended example or many shorter examples. Remember, both types of development are effective because they contain specific details that provide strong support for a topic idea.

EXERCISE 7

Read the following paragraphs and decide whether each one is developed by using several short, interrelated examples or one longer, extended example. Identify the kind of example that is used by writing "SIE" (short, interrelated example) or "Ext" (extended) in the margin to the left of the paragraph.

Paragraph 1

Having car trouble on a vacation can make things rough. However, when my car broke down and my son and I had to wait to get it fixed, a pleasant, courteous group of people made things more pleasant. When we first broke down, a young couple stopped to see what was wrong. They offered to send a tow truck when they reached the next town twenty kilometres away and left us with two cold cans of Pepsi. After my car was towed into town, I needed money to pay the tow charge and the repair bills on my car. The policy of the gas station was not to take out-of-town cheques, but the owner of the station cheerfully offered to take me to the bank and did not mind at all when I stopped next door to the bank to buy a set of clown figurines that were half-price. When my son expressed interest in swimming, she drove out of her way to show us the public swimming pool. Although we did not know if we would have to spend the night in town or if we would be able to go on that night, the people at the Holiday Inn across the street made us feel welcome to sit in the cool lobby rather than hang around at the hot gas station. The mechanic had a tough time locating one of the parts we needed, but when it arrived, he worked past his regular hours without charging anything extra or making us stay another day. Though our vacation was delayed, the positive attitude of the people helped us get through this rough beginning.

Paragraph 2

The saying "You can't judge a book by its cover" rings true many times. Very often when we meet people for the first time, we make quick judgments that are not really true. Later, when we really get to know people, we find that they are very different from what we initially think. The first time I met Brenda Burgess, my husband's boss's wife, she was distant and quiet. I interpreted her aloofness to mean she was self-righteous and egotistical. Later, Brenda called to welcome me to my new home. Once when we went shopping, a disabled person looked as though she needed help. Brenda went over to her without hesitation and helped her find the correct size for a blouse that the lady was unable to find. Throughout the next few weeks, Brenda offered me companionship and support. She demonstrated qualities of friends I missed in my last home. I again experienced the truth of the proverb and learned not to judge too soon.

Paragraph 3

Many times students feel teachers are callous and don't care when the students have problems. Teachers may not be callous or uncaring. They simply may have been taken in by one too many sob stories. For example, a student came in after missing a test plus two other days of class. He said he had had some personal problems—his mother had died. The teacher began to worry about him, and the next day she called to see if there was anything she could do. His mother answered the phone. Another time a student left a message telling his teacher that he was too sick to come to class. Later that afternoon when the teacher was working out at the fitness centre, she saw the student working out there, too. When she asked him how he was feeling, he looked embarrassed. Another time a student came in to say that he hadn't been to class the week before because it was raining too hard for him to catch the bus. The teacher thought he might have some special type of problem and asked why he couldn't ride the bus when she had seen other students getting off the same bus. These teachers are not callous, but rather they do not want to be unfair to the rest of their students by giving a special privilege to an irresponsible student.

Paragraph 4

Gabriel Garcia Marquez's characters in his novel, *Love in the Time of the Cholera*, dedicate their entire lives to fulfilling their commitments. The reader can imagine what it would be like to be able to live this kind of life or to sacrifice a lifetime for a value or purpose. Florentino Ariza is just such a character. Florentino loves Fermina Daza for fifty-one years. He first sees her when he is a delivery boy and is asked to take a telegram to her father. She is inaccessible because of a watchful aunt, yet he knows her route to church, and as he pretends to read a book, he watches her pass every Sunday. He courts her briefly but so does an affluent doctor's son. She feels something for Florentino but chooses money over love. He watches her marry the doctor's son and remains single, waiting for the death of her husband. He thinks of her obsessively. To ease his pain, he fantasizes the smallest details of intimate encounters. Suddenly, Fermina's husband dies, and Florentino now has his long-awaited opportunity. Of course, these events may seem unrealistic, but the reader is swept away and can experience, at least in the reading of the novel, a true undaunted love.

EXERCISE 8

Carefully consider each of the following thesis sentences. Then develop a topic sentence for each point in the thesis sentence. Brainstorm on a separate sheet of paper to generate examples. Decide whether an extended example or several shorter examples would be most effective for the development of each paragraph. Then write each paragraph, using one extended example or several short, interrelated examples.

1. *Thesis sentence:* Throughout my years as a college student, I have experienced many enjoyable times by meeting new people, participating in student activities, and acquiring knowledge.

Paragraph 1

_____

(topic sentence)

_____

_____

(extended example or several shorter examples)

_____

_____

_____

_____

Paragraph 2

_____

(topic sentence)

_____

_____

(extended example or several shorter examples)

_____

_____

_____

_____

Paragraph 3

_____

(topic sentence)

_____

_____

(extended example or several shorter examples)

_____

_____

_____

_____

2. *Thesis sentence*: I have often wondered how birds survive in the middle of a large city because there is danger all around them, little food, and no regular water supply.

Paragraph 1

_____

(topic sentence)

_____

_____

(extended example or several shorter examples)

_____

_____

_____

_____

Paragraph 2

_____

(topic sentence)

_____

_____

(extended example or several shorter examples)

_____

_____

_____

_____

Paragraph 3

_____

(topic sentence)

_____

_____

(extended example or several shorter examples)

_____

_____

_____

_____

3. *Thesis sentence:* I have experienced satisfaction at work because of my new skills, my supportive boss, and my friendly coworkers.

Paragraph 1

(topic sentence)

_____

(extended example or several shorter examples)

_____

_____

_____

_____

Paragraph 2

(topic sentence)

_____

(extended example or several shorter examples)

_____

_____

_____

_____

Paragraph 3

_____

(topic sentence)

_____

_____

(extended example or several shorter examples)

_____

_____

_____

_____

_____

P A R T 2 | # Something to Think About, Something to Write About

....

Would You Know a Computer If You Met One?

Adapted from the original by **Alicia Ottenberg**, *professor of computer information systems, Glendale Community College*

1   If someone were to ask you if you have ever used a computer before, you might answer "No", or, perhaps, "only in school." You may not realize just how many computers you use directly on a regular basis and how many more you use indirectly.

2   Before the computers you have probably used are identified, it might be useful to describe just what a computer is. In his book, *Introduction to Computers and Information Systems*, Robert Szymanski defines a computer as "a device that accepts data, performs certain functions on that data, and presents the results of those operations." Accepting data means that there has to be a way to get the data into the computer. The input device used might be a keyboard or a floppy-disk drive, or perhaps a light pen! There are many ways to get data into a computer.

3   Performing certain functions on that data is accomplished within the computer itself. The functions may include anything from calculating your average to determining when to fire a booster rocket on the Space Shuttle. A set of instructions, called a program, is used to tell the computer just what functions are to be performed.

4   Finally, there must be a way to present the results of the operations. Common output devices include monitors and printers, but there are also many others. All of the input and processing that is done would not be useful unless there were a way to use the results.

5   Some computers that you have used are more obviously identifiable than others, usually because there is a keyboard, a monitor, and often, a box that has slots for disks. When you registered for school, you probably recognized that the registrar used a keyboard to enter the information regarding your chosen classes. He or she may have been able to tell you if the classes were closed by looking at the results of the inquiry on the monitor. If everything was in order, a registration slip was printed on a special form. Think about what happened: Your personal and course data were entered into the computer; your tuition and fees were calculated according to the instructions in the program; and these results were printed on a special registration form.

6   You need to do a little shopping, but you're short on cash and the bank is already closed. This is no longer a problem. Many banks have automatic teller machines, or ATMs, that are "open" twenty-four hours a day, seven days a week. The ATM is another computer that you may have recognized. There are really two input devices here: a specialized one to read your bank card and a keyboard for you to type in your individual identification number and dollar amounts. There are also two output devices: the monitor that displays instructions and informa-

tion, and a mechanical device that distributes money if appropriate. "Banker's hours" are definitely not the obstacle they used to be!

7   Now that you have money to spend, go to the supermarket. Many stores now use computers to help keep track of prices and inventory. They use a bar code that represents each item's unique identification number that can be input using a light pen or a laser device like those found in grocery stores. Once the unique number is read, the program matches it with price and inventory information already stored in the computer. The price is then output onto the cash register and the tape, and the inventory count for that item is adjusted. Thus many stores now no longer have a sticker price on each item; price changes are simply input into the computer instead of being redone on all of the items. This process lowers labour costs and it is hoped, your final total.

8   Before you leave the grocery store, put a quarter in the video game. Your quarter starts a program running on this very specialized computer. You recognize the screen as being an output device, but where's the keyboard? There is none; instead, you input data by pushing buttons and moving the joystick. Each of your actions is processed by the program, and the results are shown on the screen as graphic movements of the video characters. Unfortunately for many inexperienced players, the computer does exactly what you tell it to do; so, often, the games are very short!

9   As you step out into the parking lot, you may not realize that you are probably surrounded by many computers. Late-model cards have not one, but multiple computers controlling various functions. Mechanical gauges provide the input that enables the computers to adjust fuel intake, display warning signals, and do many other jobs. You may have been surprised the first time you heard a car say, "Please fasten your seat belt." The voice was produced from a special output device when the input from the seat-belt sensor revealed that the seat belt was not fastened. Computers operate not only in the car itself, but the engineers who planned the car used computers to design and test it for efficiency and safety. It's less expensive to see how a computer model will perform under normal and adverse conditions than to build an actual car. And, as you can imagine, alterations to improve the design are made more easily on a computer model than on a real car!

10   Look around town. There is a movie theatre across the street; many visual and audio sequences would not be possible without the use of computers. Computer-generated graphics and audio have become so sophisticated that many viewers cannot tell that the spaceship battles they are watching wasn't photographed with actual models or that the sound of the helicopter approaching was never made by a real whirlybird! The newspaper available at the corner stand was created and printed using computers. The hospital down the street uses computers to monitor patients, to perform specialized tests, to aid in diagnosis, and of course, to calculate the bill!

11   Look up. The jet flying overhead has computers controlling every aspect of the flight. The train you hear in the distance is on a computer-controlled route. The ingredients to make the candy bar in your pocket were measured by a computer, and the finished product was packaged and shipped with the aid of more computers. How about a glass of milk with that candy bar? The milk was produced by dairy cows whose amount and type of feed were controlled by a computer and was processed and packaged with equipment monitored by computers.

Virtually everything available for purchase has probably been "touched" by a computer in some way.

12   Go home and put away the groceries. Hungry? Why don't you pop a frozen dinner in the microwave? As you press the numbers on the touch-pad, you realize that you are using another input device to give information to this specialized computer. The performance of the appliance is the output, although you might think the output is your dinner!

13   Many aspects of your home are smoothly controlled by computers without your having to think about it. The letter you put in the mail today had a good chance of reaching its destination because computers help route the millions of pieces properly. The electricity, gas, and water you used in your home this morning were there because computers made them possible. The phone call you need to make could not be accomplished without computers to direct it. Think about how many homes across the nation are enjoying these same benefits, benefits we would simply not have without the aid of computers.

14   At this time, many people are working with computers on your behalf, hoping to improve the quality of life through medical research, product testing, scientific exploration, and education. In most instances, these accomplishments can only be attained because of computers, those marvelous tools.

15   Now, if someone asks you if you have ever used a computer, you can smile and answer, "Of course, every day! Doesn't everybody?"

Something to Write About

Using one of the topics below, develop a strong thesis statement. Then draft your essay.
1. How has technology (any use of machines) made your life different from your grandparents lives?
2. How has television changed people's lifestyles?
3. How have home computers made life easier for people?
4. Give reasons people do not need computers.
5. How have computers helped people with disabilities?
6. Why do people resist change?
7. How have video games affected you?
8. How is playing Nintendo beneficial or harmful?

After you draft your essay, revise for content and edit for mechanics.

Content
    Revise it so that it has a clear thesis sentence.
    Be sure each support paragraph has a strong topic sentence and ample supporting examples.
    Check for unit and a smooth flow of ideas.

Mechanics
    Check for subject–verb agreement.
    Check for consistent verbs.
    Check for consistent point of view.
    Check for fragments, run-ons, and comma splices.

PART 3 | Paragraphs and Essays for Discussion and Analysis

Cigarette, Anyone?

Adapted from the original by **JoAnn Baugh**, *student*

1   Every year hundreds of people light up their first cigarette, and every year hundreds of people die from the effects of smoking cigarettes. The risks outweigh the benefits of smoking, and yet the cigarette industry flourishes. However, a trend has begun to reverse the attractiveness of smoking. Cigarette advertisements have been banned from television, and more statistics are showing the hazards of smoking. Society has become more health conscious, and over the last few years, people have become more aware of the reasons why they should not smoke. The facts that cigarette smoking is expensive, causes addiction, and is harmful to a person's health are just a few incentives to keep them from smoking.

2   Cigarette smoking is not cheap. The cost of a small pack of cigarettes is about $2.50. If the average smoker goes through two packs a day, then spending over $150 a month is easy. Also, since a smoker often marries another person who smokes, the cost of supplying their habits doubles. Sometimes, costly furniture can be left with cigarette burns that cannot be repaired. The expenses also escalate when falling cigarette ashes burn holes in favourite clothes. This cigarette money can put a pinch on any budget, especially when people consider that this money is going "up in smoke."

3   It is a known fact that cigarette smoking causes addiction. Smoking the first cigarette may be a simple act. It probably makes people feel that they are fitting into the crowd, or perhaps it is calming to them. They are unaware at this time of the path of dependency ahead of them if they continue to smoke. Their lives will revolve around cigarettes. They will be in situations in which they are not allowed to smoke, and that urge of dependency will no longer be a calming influence to them but will become a burden. People would probably never take that first cigarette if they could travel ahead in time and see what this addiction could do to their lives.

4   Health factors are the main reason why a person should not smoke. Every pack of cigarettes sold has a warning label about the hazards of smoking cigarettes. But people seem to overlook this warning. Unfortunately, it is not easy to overlook hundreds of people dying from lung cancer each year. Smokers can also develop many other high-risk conditions such as emphysema, high blood pressure, or heart disease. The people suffering from the ill-effects of smoking would have a stronger, more effective warning to share with those people about to take up smoking.

5   The trend has begun to help people recognize the reasons they should not smoke. Although it is unlikely that this trend will bring about the extinction of cigarettes, the number of people who smoke has decreased. If this trend continues and more people are educated about the risks, then it is safe to say that

people suffering from the ill-effects of cigarette smoking are doing so by their own foolishness.

Questions on Content

1. What reasons are given to convince readers not to smoke?
2. What is the main reason?
3. What does the author call the dependence on smoking?

Questions on Form

1. How many examples are given to support the idea that smoking is not cheap?
2. What do you think is the strongest paragraph?
3. Identify the supporting examples in paragraph four.

Responsibility

Adapted from the original by **Charles Marchbanks**, *student*

1   Recently, I spent four years living with my uncle. I was a little apprehensive about living with him because I had not met him, and I had heard that he was very mean and nasty. My first encounter with him proved no different. I was sleeping, and a rude voice came bellowing down the hallway. "Wake up! Get up!" I had a feeling that I was about to come face to face with my uncle for the first time. He walked into my room screaming, "You better get out of that bunk before I drop you." I was so startled that I didn't know what to think. Meanwhile, he continued to yell and scream, and I was wishing that I could transform into a speck of dust and blow away. The first impression I received of my uncle was not very good; however, I later found him to be very fair and giving. My uncle has altered my life in a positive way. He has done this by instilling in me discipline, self-pride, and responsibility.

2   While staying with my uncle, I received a fair amount of what he called justice and I called punishment. When I graduated from high school, I thought that I was ready for the world; I thought incorrectly. I had had a fair amount of discipline while growing up, but I totally lacked self-discipline. Well, my uncle filled in the void. If I got into trouble, I was disciplined, and the discipline was strictly enforced. Staying with my uncle, I found there was no room for slack. For instance, I accidentally called my uncle "Dude." He didn't like that; consequently, I was outside for fourteen days painting curbs, trimming bushes, and sweeping rocks. The discipline was effective, to say the least.

3   Self-esteem is also a quality that I did not possess before living with my uncle. It was something that I had to work on, and my uncle helped me a great deal. He helped me by rewarding and praising me for doing a good job. I remember the first time that he ever praised me. It was when I had stayed late at work while all my coworkers had gone home. I had done this because there was a piece of equipment that was broken, and it needed to be fixed as soon as possible. Well, I stayed there until I had repaired it. My uncle was very pleased, and he praised me for my work. Through his encouragement and positive reinforcement on this and other occasions, I was able to build confidence and pride.

4   Responsibility is one of the major attributes that were implanted in me. I was fortunate to have an uncle who was more than happy to force responsibility on me. He always gave me a job that was a challenge, and he would see how well I could perform the task. If I didn't perform to his satisfaction, he did not give me any responsibilities for a long time. I can see now why he tried so hard to make me more responsible. He knew that if I was irresponsible in the future I could not make it in the job market. Now I accept responsibility with the greatest of ease. Being with my uncle has given me a chance to accept responsibilities that might not have come my way. I find that being a responsible person can make a job or even my life a lot easier to handle.

5   In summary, these three attributes—discipline, pride, and responsibility—are qualities that will make my life flow a little more smoothly. I now feel that my decision to live with my uncle was one of the wisest that I have made, and if I had the choice, I would do it all over again.

Questions on Content

1. What was the author's first impression of his uncle?
2. What did he learn from his uncle?
3. Why did his uncle stress responsibility?

Questions on Form

1. Identify the topic sentence in paragraph 2.
2. Which paragraph, in your opinion, has the strongest support?
3. Do the support paragraphs contain short, interrelated examples or an extended example?

Cooking

Adapted from the original by **Maria Palomino,** *student*

1   When I think of ways to entertain and get acquainted with someone, my thoughts turn to cooking. There are many reasons why people like to cook. For some, it is a hobby; for others, it is a way to relieve stress; and, I think, for most people, cooking is a way to express love and appreciation for family or friends.

2   Cooking as a hobby can be fun, rewarding, and creative. I viewed cooking as a hobby when I took a natural-foods cooking class. I would attend once a week and experiment with new recipes. I found it to be fun, and at the same time it developed my creativity. For example, one day I decided to follow a recipe for bran muffins. The recipe sounded flat to me because all it called for was bran, oil, water, and honey. I decided to experiment with other ingredients, so I added what I thought would improve the taste of the muffins. I added two ripe bananas, molasses, vanilla, eggs, and some sunflower seeds. I was so pleased when they were done. They came out delicious. The muffins were a great success because of their good taste and my fun in creating the new version.

3   I also find that, for me, cooking relieves stress because there are days when I need to take the focus off the demands and pressures of the week. That is when

I decide to cook something. Depending on how ambitious I'm feeling, I might decide to try a new recipe. For instance, one day I came home from a hard day at school. I had taken a long and difficult test. I was still feeling wound up and stressed out, so I decided to tackle a new cheesecake recipe. Well, fifteen minutes into the recipe, I was so immersed in what I was doing that I forgot about all the pressures of the day. The aroma of the cheesecake baking was overwhelming. After having a piece of cheesecake, I had a new and refreshing outlook on my problems. They did not seem so pressing.

4   Finally, one of the most wonderful reasons to cook is to express love and appreciation for someone. Preparing a meal for someone is a special way of showing that I care for and value that person. I am giving a part of myself in a non-threatening manner. When I cook for people and serve them, I am nurturing and providing them pleasure. I don't believe I have to prepare an elaborate meal for them to know how much I care. The "tender loving care" I put into the cooking will be a clear indication of my love. For example, one day my daughter and I had a disagreement. Her feelings were hurt, and she and I didn't have a chance to resolve the problem. I decided to invite her over for dinner. She was reluctant to come until I told her I was preparing her favourite meal. When she arrived for dinner, I could tell that she enjoyed the aroma when she said, "It sure smells good." That seemed to break the ice. She sat down to dinner, and I served her, telling her that we needed to talk. Well, the evening ended with us laughing and enjoying each other's company. She knew that cooking the meal for her was a way to let her know I loved her and wanted to nurture and provide pleasure with her favourite dish.

5   I'm glad God made food for us to eat and cook because cooking provides not only a creative hobby but also therapy for relieving stress and anxiety. One of the most important reasons for cooking, for me, is to show love and appreciation for another person.

Questions on Content
1. In the author's opinion, why do people like to cook?
2. How can cooking be creative?
3. For what special reason did the author cook her daughter's favourite meal?

Questions on Form
1. In each support paragraph, does the author use short, interrelated examples or an extended example?
2. Point out effective details in the examples used.
3. Why does the author discuss the "love and appreciation" reason last?

Wandering through Winter

Adapted from an excerpt from *Summer in January* by **Edwin Way Teale**

In the folklore of the country, numerous superstitions relate to winter weather. Back-country farmers examine their corn husks—the thicker the husk, the colder the winter. They watch the acorn crop—the more acorns, the more severe the season. They observe where white-faced hornets place their paper nests—the higher they are, the deeper will be the snow. They examine the size and shape and colour of the spleens of butchered hogs for clues to the severity of the seasons. They keep track of the blooming of dogwood in the spring—the more abundant the blooms, the more bitter the cold in January. When chipmunks carry their tails high and squirrels have heavier fur and mice come into country houses early in the fall, the superstitious gird themselves for a long, hard winter. Without any scientific basis, a wider-than-usual black band on a wooly-bear cater-pillar is accepted as a sign that winter will arrive early and stay late. Even the way a cat sits beside the stove carries its message to the credulous. According to a belief once widely held in the Rockies, a cat sitting with its tail to the fire indicates very cold weather is on the way.

Questions on Content
1. What does the author call the ideas that farmers and country people have about judging a coming winter?
2. What kind of "basis" or proof is lacking for these ideas?
3. In what part of Canada was there a belief about cats sitting close to the fire?

Questions on Form
1. What makes the paragraph well developed?
2. Identify the kinds of examples used.

PART 4 | The Writer's Tools: Sentence Variety—Forming and Punctuating Compound Sentences

OBJECTIVES

- Combine simple sentences using coordinate conjunctions.
- Combine simple sentences using conjunctive adverbs.
- Combine simple sentences using a semicolon.

One of the first steps of good revision is to change short, choppy sentences into compound sentences. You may already write good compound sentences, but may not be aware of them. On the other hand, perhaps you can strengthen your writing by learning the various ways in which you can revise short, choppy sentences into effective compound sentences. In this way, you will achieve some sentence variety. Additional types of sentence patterns will be covered in Unit 6.

A **compound sentence** is two or more simple sentences combined in a variety of ways. They may be joined by a comma and a coordinate conjunction, a semicolon followed by a conjunctive adverb and a comma, or just a semicolon.

Using a Comma and a Coordinate Conjunction

Coordinate conjunctions join two sentences that are of equal value or are "coordinate" with each other. The coordinate conjunctions you choose depend upon the meaning you want to achieve in your writing.

Coordinate Conjunctions

for	but
and	or
nor	yet
	so

Note Remembering the words "fan boys" can help you memorize the list of coordinate conjunctions. Here are some examples of the use of coordinate conjunctions to join two simple sentences.

and (adds)

Mike enjoys his job.

He performs well.

Mike enjoys his job, **and** he performs well.

but (contrasts)

Mike enjoys his job.

He has a long drive each day.

Mike enjoys his job, **but** he has a long drive each day.

for (gives a reason)

Mike enjoys his job.

It offers a challenge.

Mike enjoys his job, **for** it offers a challenge.

nor (adds another negative idea)

Mike does not enjoy his job.

He does not perform well.

Mike does not enjoy his job, **nor** does he perform well.

or (gives a choice)

Mike can choose to work four ten-hour days.

He can work five eight-hour days.

Mike can choose to work four ten-hour days, **or** he can work five eight-hour days.

so (shows result)

Mike enjoys his job.

He works hard.

Mike enjoys his job, **so** he works hard.

yet (shows change or contrast)

Mike works hard.

He also enjoys life.

Mike works hard, **yet** he also enjoys life.

Combine the two simple sentences into one compound sentence by adding a comma and a coordinate conjunction. Make the revisions above the sentences.

Example:

refreshing, so we
The day was cool and ~~refreshing~~. We went on a picnic.

1. Rose is an outstanding nurse. She anticipates patients' problems.

2. We lived in Germany for six years. My wife was in the armed forces.

3. I did not enjoy the food. I did not care for the entertainment either.

4. Robert exercises regularly. He has trouble losing weight.

5. We jogged ten kilometres. We swam three kilometres.

6. Jeremy finished repairing the car. He filled it with gas.

Using a Conjunctive Adverb

You can combine two simple sentences by placing a conjunctive adverb between them. Place a semicolon at the end of the first sentence to separate the two sentences, and then put a comma after the conjunctive adverb.

> The clerk offended the customer; **consequently,** the customer did not shop at that store again.

When you put a conjunctive adverb *within* a sentence rather than between two simple sentences, put a comma *before and after* the conjunctive adverb.

> The clerk offended the customer. The customer, **consequently,** did not shop at that store again.

> Helen hates the heat; she, **however,** is going to Jamaica in July.

Note In the second example, which is a compound sentence, a semicolon still separates the two complete sentences.

Conjunctive Adverbs

consequently	nevertheless
furthermore	otherwise
however	therefore
moreover	thus

Just as you choose a coordinate conjunction to express a particular meaning you want in your writing, so you must pay close attention to the conjunctive adverb you select. Here are some examples of conjunctive adverbs in compound sentences.

consequently (shows a result)
Mike does not enjoy his job; **consequently,** he does not work very hard.

furthermore (shows an additional idea)
Mike plans to quit his job; **furthermore,** he plans to change his career.

however (shows a contrast)
Mike likes his job; **however,** he plans to find a better one

moreover (adds an equally important idea)
Mike likes his job; **moreover,** he likes his coworkers.

nevertheless (shows a contrast)
Mike enjoys his job; **nevertheless,** he finds time for other things.

otherwise (indicates a result if the first idea did not occur)
Mike enjoys his job; **otherwise,** he would look for a new job.

therefore (shows a result)
Mike wants more money; **therefore,** he will ask his boss for a raise.

thus (shows a result)
Mike has saved money from his job; **thus,** he will be able to go to school.

EXERCISE 2

Combine each of the following pairs of simple sentences into one compound sentence by adding a semicolon, a conjunctive adverb, and a comma. Make the revisions above the sentences.

Example:

salty; however, we
The stew was too ~~salty. We~~ **ate it anyway**

1. Danny graduated from college. He got a job working for Motorola.

2. Her favourite program is "60 Minutes." She watches it every Sunday evening.

3. Many people give to charity. The food bank needs more canned goods.

4. Jordan asked for a raise in pay every three months. He did not receive one.

5. Chris read the entire book. She would not have known the answers.

6. The milk was left out of the refrigerator. It was sour in the morning.

Using a Semicolon

Two simple sentences can also be connected by using a semicolon. However, when they are joined by a semicolon, the second sentence does *not* begin with a capital letter.

The clerk offended the customer.

The customer did not shop at that store again.

The clerk offended the customer; the customer did not shop at that store again.

EXERCISE 3

Combine the two simple sentences into one compound sentence by adding a semicolon. Remember to begin the second sentence with a lowercase letter. Make the revisions above the sentences.

Example:

females; two

Five of the puppies were ~~females. Two~~ were males.

1. We laughed. We cried. We shared memories.

2. They stocked the shelves. They cleaned up the aisles.

3. We dug for worms. Then we set out for fun.

4. The boy was hungry. He ate a hamburger and fries.

5. The dog barked loudly. Soon it stopped.

6. Seventy percent of the work was done. Only thirty percent was left to complete.

EXERCISE 4

For each of the following items, combine the two simple sentences into one compound sentence as indicated. Punctuate correctly.

Example:

Sara trains dogs well. She is always busy.

Sara trains dogs well, so she is always busy.

(coordinate conjunction)

Sara trains dogs well; she is always busy.
(semicolon)

Sara trains dogs well; consequently, she is always busy.
(conjunctive adverb)

1. Pete does excellent carpentry work. He receives many jobs.

_____

(coordinate conjunction)

_____

(semicolon)

_____

(conjunctive adverb)

2. Susan picked two kilograms of blackberries. She made blackberry jam.

_____

(coordinate conjunction)

_____

(semicolon)

_____

(conjunctive adverb)

3. Brenda is an excellent administrative assistant. She works well with people.

_____

(coordinate conjunction)

_____

(semicolon)

_____

(conjunctive adverb)

4. Randi has an extensive doll collection. She attends many doll shows.

_____

(coordinate conjunction)

_____

(semicolon)

_____

(conjunctive adverb)

5. The child got out the peanut butter and jelly. He made a sandwich.

_____

(coordinate conjunction)

_____

(semicolon)

_____

(conjunctive adverb)

6. The lawyer worked hard on the divorce case. He won it.

_____

(coordinate conjunction)

_____

(semicolon)

_____

(conjunctive adverb)

7. The man was working hard all morning. He went swimming.

_____

(coordinate conjunction)

_____

(semicolon)

_____

(conjunctive adverb)

8. The package was well sealed. Nothing fell out.

_____

(coordinate conjunction)

_____

(semicolon)

_____

(conjunctive adverb)

9. They live near the ocean. They spend many hours sailing.

_____

(coordinate conjunction)

_____

(semicolon)

_____

(conjunctive adverb)

10. Angelina works full-time. She goes to school.

_____

(coordinate conjunction)

_____

(semicolon)

_____

(conjunctive adverb)

EXERCISE 5

Revise the following paragraphs by changing the short choppy sentences into compound sentences. Use a variety of ways to combine the sentences.

Paragraph 1

Canadian people do not want to eat less. They want to consume fewer calories. Food companies know this. They are coming out with reduced- or low-calorie food products. Powdered "butter" substitutions boast of having the same taste as real butter with a fraction of the calories. Ice cream is appearing in "light" form also. Producers use fat substitutes and sugar substitutes that add up to fewer calories but have "the same great taste" for the consumer. Even potato chips come with the "light" option. Not only single items but many prepackaged microwave meals specialize in meals with under three hundred calories. The meal can be topped off with a variety of pastries with "less than half the calories of other baked goods." Food producers keep churning out new alternatives. Consumers keep "eating them up."

Paragraph 2

Dyslexia is a learning disability that may be overcome through compensation. Many times people with dyslexia are extraordinarily intelligent. They show no outward signs of this disability. They often have difficulty performing certain tasks such as learning to read. They become frustrated when they attempt these tasks that are simple to other people. For example, Dr. Marie Xavier is a dyslexic. She learned to cope with her learning disability. She was a rebellious teen. She did not take an interest in school. Later she was inspired. She excelled. She overcame her reading problem by using a patch over one eye and special reading glasses. Her study time was always at least double that of her classmates. She went on to medical school. She graduated with honours. She could more keenly relate to those who were suffering. She became a doctor and an advocate for dyslexics. She proved that dyslexia can be overcome. In this way, she set an example for students everywhere.

Paragraph 3

Today more than ever, people are realizing the need to conserve our resources, especially water. This effort can be effective. Every Canadian must be willing to make adjustments. These adjustments will save this essential resource. Anne is one person who has done her part to help in this effort. Inside her house, she always fills her dishwasher. Then she runs it. She always washes a full load of clothes. She has also placed a water saver in her toilet tank. Each flush takes less water. She never leaves the water running while she brushes her teeth. Outside, she has installed a drip-water system to keep her plants wet. This way she does not lose water to evaporation. She has also landscaped her yard with plants that require little water. She never uses the hose to wash off the sidewalk or driveway. If every Canadian will try to follow this example, millions of litres of water will be saved every day.

WRITING ASSIGNMENT

Using the steps of the writing process that you are familiar with, draft an essay on one of the following topics.

1. Qualities that make a perfect mate
2. Reasons people buy clothes
3. Issues facing your municipal government, provincial government, or federal government
4. Reasons cars are important to people
5. Reasons a particular vacation was exciting or boring
6. Information people can learn by reading a newspaper
7. Reasons children or adults find television appealing
8. Reasons music appeals to people
9. Reasons people ride bicycles rather than drive cars
10. Reasons people drive cars rather than ride bicycles
11. Characteristics of memorable birthday celebrations

After you draft your essay, revise for content and edit for mechanics.

Content

> *Essay*
>
>> Check to see that the paper has a strong thesis sentence.
>>
>> Check to see that the voice is appropriate for purpose and audience.
>
> *Paragraphs*
>
>> Revise so that each has a clear topic sentence that develops an idea suggested in the thesis sentence.
>>
>> Include four to six supporting sentences that are developed using short interrelated examples or an extended example.
>>
>> Include a closing sentence in each paragraph.

Mechanics

> Check for subject-verb agreement.
>
> Check for consistent verbs.
>
> Check for a consistent point of view.
>
> Check for fragments, run-on sentences, and comma splices.
>
> Check punctuation of compound sentences.

Sentence variety

> Revise short sentences into compound sentences.

Unit Six

Reaching an Audience by Creating Interest

PART 1 | **Parts to Whole: Introductory and Concluding Paragraphs**

OBJECTIVES

....

- Understand the purpose of introductions.
- Recognize the parts of an introductory paragraph.
- Understand the types of hooks used in introductory paragraphs.
- Be aware of audience and purpose in relation to hook.
- Write an introductory paragraph that has a hook, a transition, and a thesis sentence.
- Understand the purpose of conclusions.
- Recognize and revise a weak conclusion.
- Recognize and write a strong conclusion

   After you are able to write both a thesis sentence and the support paragraphs necessary for the longer paper, you need to add an effective introductory paragraph. Because you already know how to write a thesis sentence, you only need to add a hook and a smooth transition to that thesis sentence.

Parts of an Introductory Paragraph

hook

transition

thesis sentence

The Purpose of Introductory Paragraphs

The purpose of an introductory paragraph is to get the reader's attention and to let the reader know what will be covered in the essay. Very often, it sets the tone for the entire essay. While reading your introduction, your audience might think, "This paper really sounds good," or "I can't figure out what this person is talking about." The first response is what you want from your reader. The introduction gives you a chance to "hook" your audience right away.

Developing Introductory Paragraphs

Writing an introductory paragraph can be simplified if you follow a step-by-step process.

Compose the thesis sentence.

Decide on the type of hook that is most effective.

Write the hook.

Write the transition.

Draft these three parts into an introductory paragraph.

Composing the Thesis Sentence

Although the same process does not always work for everyone, the part of the introductory paragraph that you write first is the thesis sentence. As you recall, the thesis sentence consists of either the topic and a clear direction, or a topic, a clear direction, and a preview of the points to be covered in the paper. Because the thesis sentence keeps you on track, it is composed first; however, it will be the *last* sentence in the introductory paragraph.

Developing the Hook

After you have composed your thesis sentence, you need to write a strong hook. Even though the hook is usually the second part you write, it comes first in the actual introductory paragraph; consequently, it should be strong and should make the reader keep on reading. There are several ways to get the reader's attention, and your job is to be creative in finding the best way for each specific essay that you write. An effective introduction may contain one or more of the following hooks.

Types of Hooks

1. personal examples

2. quotations

3. facts or statistics

4. rhetorical questions

5. current events

6. contrast to the thesis sentence

Using Personal Examples Examples can be either a personal experience or an experience that you witnessed happening to someone else.

Personal experience usually provides strong, maybe even dramatic incidents to use. Writing about personal experiences may be difficult for some people, but if you are honest in expressing your thoughts and feelings, you will establish a real connection with your reader. Sharing with the reader can create interest and form a healthy bond that will last throughout the paper. The reader will want to read further because you are sharing a part of yourself, and that is what communication is all about. This personal experience should have really happened to you. If you make up the experience and the reader discovers you are pretending, you have lost your credibility as a writer, and you have lost your reader as an audience.

Another type of hook can come from **personal observation** of an experience that you saw happening to someone else. It must be something that really impressed you when you saw it, or it will not impress anyone else. For example, if you see a terrible accident, recalling facts or observations from this experience may be appropriate to grab the reader's attention for a paper you are writing.

The following introductory paragraphs effectively use personal examples to hook the reader. In each paragraph the hook is in bold print and the thesis sentence is underlined. First, read this example that uses a personal experience as a hook.

> **On February 19, 1992, life changed for an eighteen-year-old young man. He became very ill from a bacterial infection. His body could not fight the infection. Why? After a week of tests and examinations by several specialists, the diagnosis was made. He had leukemia, a cancer in the bone marrow. I am that young man.** When a person finds out that he has cancer, just as I did, his whole world changes. <u>A cancer patient is affected physically, psychologically, and socially by the impact of cancer.</u>

This paragraph captures the reader's attention immediately. Credibility is established when the author states the exact date, February 19, 1992, and when he notes that the specific type of infection was bacterial. The audience is taken by surprise to read "I am that young man." Probably every reader would be affected by this dramatic statement and would identify with the writer.

Anytime someone is told about a serious, life-threatening illness, the situation is emotional. Telling this incident in a straightforward way, however, makes the information all the more moving. Readers of all ages are able to identify with the young man and will listen to his ideas. The reader knows from this introduction that the experiences and ideas in the paper are real and believable.

Now read the following example showing a personal observation of someone else's experience used as a hook.

One morning my friend had her seven-month-old son in his stroller under the peach tree near our family swimming pool. She walked to my kitchen to get a knife so she could peel a peach for him. Approximately five seconds later I heard her scream. I ran outside to find her administering artificial respiration to her son. We were both very scared. If she had been gone any longer, he might have become one of the statistics that plague our country every year when many children die needlessly in water-related accidents. These child drownings could, however, be greatly reduced if parents never left their children unattended around water, if pools were properly fenced, and if other safety devices were installed in or by the pool.

This example is also very moving because the writer saw and remembered the scene vividly. It helps the reader recognize the fear that comes with a near-tragedy and identify with the memory of an unforgettable trauma. This example brings home the reality of the dangers of a swimming pool. The incident is very appropriate to get the reader interested in ways to keep children from drowning or from becoming permanently disabled in family swimming-pool accidents.

You may think that you do not have experiences as dramatic and emotionally appealing as these, but you do. Be detailed and thorough when you think about ways to get your audience caught up in your topic, and you will discover effective experiences.

The following exercise will help you use a personal experience to create a hook for an introductory paragraph.

EXERCISE 1

Using the thesis sentences that follow the blanks given, write a personal example that you feel would get the reader's attention. You may use either a personal experience or a personal observation.

1. _____

   _____

   _____

   Attending college allows students to learn new information, make lifetime friends, and prepare for a career.

2. _____

   _____

   _____

   Helping a son or daughter plan a wedding can create family unity, leave pleasant memories, yet create unexpected expenses.

3. _____

_____

_____

_____

Spectators enjoy football games because of the excitement of the game, the opportunity to socialize, and the chance to support their favourite team.

Using Quotations Another way to get your reader's attention is to quote an effective line or two from someone famous (or even someone not so famous). Just as the personal examples were dramatic or surprising, the content of the quotation should also be dramatic or in some way emotionally appealing, surprising, or humorous. You might choose a humorous quotation from Stephen Leacock, like "Angling is the name given to fishing by people who can't fish." Or perhaps you might choose a line of poetry, like "Come live with me and be my love,/and we will all the pleasures prove. . . ." Another might be a phrase like "My Canada includes Quebec." If the quotation is relevant to the thesis sentence and the connection between the quotation and the thesis sentence is established, the reader will be not only willing but eager to continue.

Look at another sample introductory paragraph. This time the student writer began with the topic "facing life." After freewriting/brainstorming, the following thesis sentence was composed: "We can control the way we face life through our attitude, determination, and ability." The student then wanted to use a quotation to get the attention of the reader and found one in a book of famous quotations. The student writer knew she wanted to stress how a person's mental outlook can bring success or failure, so she looked up "mind" in the book of quotations. She found a sentence with a "ring" to it. Notice how the student then put the introductory paragraph together, starting with the quotation.

"The mind is its own place, and in itself can make a heaven of hell, a hell of heaven." This thought by John Milton was recorded over four hundred years ago, but it is still timely for us today. He seems to be saying that we are the ones to control our lives. We can be miserable when things are going well, just as we can be happy when things are going wrong. <u>With this thought in mind, we can control the way we face life through our attitude, our determination, and our ability.</u>

The quotation is effective because it is thought-provoking. Although it was said many years ago, it is still applicable to most people today. Also, the writer is quoting a famous man, John Milton, a great English poet. We always seem to pay attention to intelligent, profound comments made by famous people.

Sometimes a quotation used with a personal example can make both more effective. To see how this can be so, first look at the use of a personal example without a quotation as the hook in a paragraph.

> **I am the parent of a child with learning disabilities. I have often felt unprepared to help my son with his handicap and frustrated with attempts to seek the proper placement for him in the public-school system since I have been his advocate through his elementary-school years.** The experience of school can be overwhelming to any child who has trouble learning. <u>The learning-disabled student in the public educational system must deal with academic, social, and emotional problems.</u>

The previous paragraph uses only a personal example for the hook, but the following paragraph is stronger because it combines a quotation with a personal example.

> **"I am stupid. I am never going back to school." These are the words spoken by my learning-disabled child when he was in the first grade. He cried as he slowly walked down the hall shredding his schoolwork into small pieces. Then we both cried. This was the first of many times when I would feel frustrated because there was nothing I could do to help him. I have often felt frustrated with my attempts to seek the proper placement for him in the public-school system since I have been his advocate through his elementary-school years.** The experience of school can be overwhelming to any child who has trouble learning. <u>The learning-disabled student in the public educational system must deal with academic, social, and emotional problems.</u>

This quotation will attract anyone who has had to cope with a disability of any type or anyone who has had a family member with a disability. It will also help arouse sensitivity in a person who has had no direct experience with a disability. The quotation makes the personal example even more effective.

EXERCISE 2

Using the thesis sentences given, write a direct quotation that you think would get the reader's attention. You may use either a quotation that you can remember hearing or a quotation that you looked up in a book of quotations. If you wish, you can combine it with a personal example.

1. _____

_____

_____

_____

_____

A teenager's sexual behaviour can be altered by movies, a fear of AIDS, and peer pressure.

2. _____

_____

_____

_____

_____

People in Canada become homeless because of mental illness, inadequate job skills, and alcoholism.

3. _____

_____

_____

_____

_____

Smoking is detrimental because it costs money, creates pollution, and results in medical problems.

Using Facts or Statistics To generate interest, you may also use a fact or a statistic as your hook. To be effective, the fact or statistic must be startling or unusual. You do, however, need to be sure that it really is a fact and that it comes from a credible source. When you are reading the newspaper or reading for your other classes, be alert for information that catches your attention. If you are keeping a journal, jot these facts down to use in future writing.

The following introductory paragraphs begin with a fact or statistic to hook the reader. The first hook contains a fact that is probably not known to most Canadians and arouses curiosity. This paragraph is from an article by Kevin Cox of *The Globe and Mail*.

At least 300 times a year, a vehicle hits a moose, sometimes killing the moose and often severely damaging the vehicle or injuring its occupants. As many as three people are killed every year in such accidents.

On the Trans-Canada Highway, signs with large white moose silhouettes warn motorists to watch out for the animals. But because the animals don't seem alarmed by cars, biologists with the provincial Department of Tourism and Culture and the National Parks Service hope that a whiff of wolf will keep the moose away from the road.

The second hook quotes statistics of interest combined with a personal experience.

> According to Statistics Canada, a break-in occurs in Canada every two minutes. A representative from my local Neighbourhood Watch suggests that "Although homeowners may eventually recover some of their valuables, they never fully recover their sense of security." I can vouch for this personally because one Sunday afternoon last August, I returned home to find the upstairs of my home totally vandalized. Fortunately, nothing of value was stolen, but the incident made me realize that I needed to make my home more secure. After some research, I learned that the risk of a robbery is greatly reduced if a homeowner uses timers for lights, double bolts on doors and an alarm system.

The writer has experienced firsthand what it feels like to have been robbed. In addition, the writer has taken time to check out the facts from a very reliable source, the representative of a Neighbourhood Watch Program.

EXERCISE 3

Using the thesis sentences given, write a fact or statistic intended to get the reader's attention. You may use either something that you recently heard or something that you took time to look up in a book or periodical. If you wish, you can combine it with a personal example.

1. _____

_____

_____

_____

Women who enter politics are usually socially conscious, extraordinarily bright, and self-directed.

2. _____

_____

_____

_____

Small businesses usually succeed when the owners are adventuresome, creative, and well organized.

3. _____

_____

_____

_____

_____

Buying a new car can bring pride, responsibility, and independence.

Using Rhetorical Questions Rhetorical questions are asked for effect or for emphasis because no answer is actually expected. However, you can present the answer in the thesis statement. The purpose of these rhetorical questions is to generate thought about an idea before it is presented. In the following introductory paragraph, the student writer effectively uses several questions to hook the reader.

> **When I think ahead to the year 3000, many different questions come to mind. What new inventions will be in use in the common household? How much will the world of transportation be advanced? What type of weaponry will have been invented? In what type of environment will people be living?** All of these questions lead me to feel that <u>in the year 3000 there will be major differences in science, in transportation, and in people's lifestyles.</u>

In the hook, the author asks rhetorical questions and provokes curiosity about possible changes made by the year 3000. These questions have inspired the reader to think about how different life might be in 1000 years. The thesis then connects these questions with major ideas to be presented in the paper.

EXERCISE 4

Using the thesis sentences given, write one or more rhetorical questions that you think will get the reader's attention.

1. _____

_____

_____

_____

Heavy flooding can drive people from their homes, destroy crops, and interrupt business activities.

2. _____

_____

_____

_____

_____

Getting enough sleep can make a person healthy, alert, and productive.

3. _____

_____

_____

_____

_____

Canada's war on guns has been strengthened by education, the media, and the government.

Using Current Events A current event is a recent, important incident or a series of incidents made public by newspapers, magazines, television, or radio, and with which most people would be familiar because of the publicity. Your job is to use this occurrence to lead into the thesis sentence.

In the following introductory paragraph, the student writer effectively uses two current events to hook the reader.

> **This morning I picked up the newspaper and read about a man who had shot his twenty-three-year-old girlfriend and her nine-month-old child because he believed his girlfriend had transmitted AIDS to him. Not long ago, a documentary on AIDS discussed three brothers from Florida who had been barred from school because they were hemophiliacs and had been exposed to the AIDS virus. Their home had been bombed by "good" parents who did not want these boys to attend school with their children.** Though these incidents seem bizarre in a twentieth-century civilized country, <u>many people fear AIDS because of the consequences of the disease, the misinformation concerning the disease, and the increasing number of cases of the disease</u>.

The hook in the preceding introductory paragraph contains two different examples related to AIDS, a current topic that is prevalent in the news today. The examples startle the reader because they show how fear makes people behave illogically and violently. Because the reader becomes involved emotionally, the hook works effectively.

If you wish, you may use only one example related to a current event. But keep in mind that you might need more than one brief example to reach your audience immediately, especially if you have access to several examples that do not duplicate one another. You will need to rely on your own judgment to decide how many examples would be effective.

EXERCISE 5

Using the thesis sentences given, briefly describe a current event that you think would get the reader involved right away. If you wish, this current event can be combined with one of the other hooks explained previously.

1. _____

   _____

   _____

   _____

   _____

   Irresponsible and illegal activities of athletic role models usually involve illicit drugs, illegal gambling, and socially unacceptable lifestyles.

2. _____

   _____

   _____

   _____

   _____

   Having a family member in a nursing home can be stressful, expensive, and frightening.

3. _____

   _____

   _____

   _____

   _____

   Coming to a decision about the abortion issue includes legal, physical, and mental considerations.

Using Contrast to the Thesis Sentence Sometimes the thesis sentence contains an idea that might be surprising to the reader or might be different from what is expected. An introduction can be effective when the hook contains information that is in direct **contrast to the main idea in the thesis sentence.**

In the following introductory paragraph, the student writer uses contrast to hook the reader.

> **Since the middle of the 1940s, the female Cannabis sativa plant, commonly known as marijuana, has been classified by the government as a Schedule I drug. This classification recognizes marijuana as a dangerous narcotic, similar in potency to heroin and possessing no redeeming medicinal qualities.** Research in the last few years, however, has brought many new discoveries in medicine relating to the possible uses of marijuana to treat many different illnesses, including glaucoma, cancer, asthma, and phantom limb pain suffered by paraplegics and amputees.

The hook in the previous paragraph reaffirms the reader's opinion because most people think of marijuana as an illegal drug that causes problems. The general public often identifies marijuana use with negative results. Because the main idea in the paper is that this drug may be useful in treating certain health problems, the hook directly contrasts with what the reader expects.

EXERCISE 6

Using the thesis sentences given, write a contrasting idea for a hook that you think will get the attention of the reader. If you wish, you can combine it with one of the other types of hooks.

1. _____

_____

_____

_____

_____

Having guests from abroad can be enjoyable because of the excitement of planning for their arrival, the opportunity for catching up on each other's lives, and the fun of breaking the normal routine.

2. _____

_____

_____

_____

_____

Men's fashions are usually conservative, inexpensive, and restrictive.

3. _____

_____

_____

_____

_____

Buying an old car can reduce the purchase price, provide a chance for restoration, and increase the resale value.

As you have seen in this unit, an effective introduction may contain one type of hook or may contain a combination of hooks. Use the hook that will be most appealing to your audience and most appropriate to help you meet your purpose.

Creating Transition to the Thesis Sentence

Regardless of what you use, the hook must be clearly connected to the thesis sentence in your essay. Nothing jars a reader more than a disjointed introduction—one with no connection between the hook and the thesis sentence. The hook will seem mechanical and artificial if it is not clearly related to the thesis sentence.

Transition is the clear connection between the hook and the thesis sentence and is the part of the introduction that you write last. The transition may be a word, a phrase, or a sentence or sentences between the hook and the thesis sentence that clearly shows the relationship of the hook to the broader thesis so that the reader understands the connection.

For instance, if you use a specific quotation as your hook, you will need to take the reader from that specific quotation to a more general thesis sentence. Look at the following introductory paragraph. The specific quotation is about one person, whereas the thesis statement is about a larger group of people.

"Why try? The white kids get all the jobs!" That is what my best friend Ken used to say whenever I tried to find a job.

After much research, I found that black unemployment is a result of racial discrimination, economic conditions, and the educational system.

Remember, the thesis sentence was written first and the hook second. Now a logical transition is needed to bridge the gap from the quotation, "Why try? The white kids get all the jobs!" to the broader thesis sentence about black unemployment. The sentences in bold type in the following paragraph show how one student bridged this gap.

"Why try? The white kids get all the jobs!" That is what my best friend Ken used to say whenever I tried to find a job. **It seemed that the jobs were out there, but only the white teenagers, not the black teenagers, got those jobs. I realized that this problem could not be something that developed overnight but rather evolved over many years.** After much research, I found that black unemployment is a result of racial discrimination, economic conditions, and a failure in our educational system.

Each of the introductory paragraphs presented earlier has a logical transition that shows the relationship between the thesis sentence and the hook. Note the transitions in the following introductory paragraphs to see how those transitions tie the paragraphs together. The transitions are highlighted in bold type.

Transition from Personal Example to Thesis Sentence

On February 19, 1982, life changed for an eighteen-year-old young man. He became very ill from a bacterial infection. His body could not fight the infection. Why? After a week of tests and examinations by several specialists, the diagnosis was made. He had leukemia, a cancer in the bone marrow. I am that young man. **When a person finds out that he has cancer, just as I did, his whole world changes.** A cancer patient is affected physically, psychologically, and socially by the impact of cancer.

In one simple sentence, this transition transfers the reader from one specific personal example of a young man who discovers he has cancer to all cancer patients.

Transition from Quotation to Thesis Sentence

"The mind is its own place, and in itself can make a heaven of hell, a hell of heaven." **<u>This thought</u> by John Milton was recorded over four hundred years ago, but it is still timely for us today. He seems to be saying that we are the ones to control our lives. We can be miserable when things are going well, just as we can be happy when things are going wrong.** With this thought in mind, we can control the way we face life through our attitude, our determination, and our ability.

The transition in the previous paragraph contains the author's explanation of the meaning of the quotation and its relationship to the thesis sentence. The author also bridges the gap between today and four hundred years ago. The transition between a quotation and the thesis almost always begins with a phrase like "this quotation" or "this thought" (as underlined above).

EXERCISE 7

The following introductory paragraphs lack a transition from the hook to the thesis sentence. Try to bridge the gap logically so that your reader understands the connection between the hook and the thesis sentence.

Paragraph 1

Last year I lost my driver's licence. I planned to get another one the next day. However, a week later, when I got a ticket for speeding, I realized that I had not yet gotten another driver's licence. Instead of just one ticket for speeding, I got two tickets, one for speeding and one for driving without a driver's licence. Instead of paying $45 for one ticket, I had to pay $95 for two tickets.

_____

_____

_____

Putting responsibilities off can be expensive, inconvenient, and embarrassing.

Paragraph 2

In this morning's mail, I received a brown envelope with the following message written in large type: "R. E. Benson, you have won $50,000 if you subscribe to this magazine and mail in your money within 20 minutes!"

_____

_____

_____

Misleading mail advertisements play on people's emotions, have hidden loopholes, and cheat individuals out of thousands of dollars.

Paragraph 3

"Mom, Dad, will you please play a game of Risk with us?"

_____

_____

_____

Playing board games with your family can create a challenge, encourage family unity, and bring excitement.

EXERCISE 8

In the following introductory paragraphs, underline the hook, circle the transition, and underline the thesis sentence.

Paragraph 1

After seventeen years of marriage, I had given up. I felt my marriage was hopeless and irreparable. I had my husband move out for six months until I decided on whether I wanted to try again. However, instead of giving up, we worked on our communication skills, our built-up anger, and our spirituality. I realized what was going to be lost through a divorce and agreed to try again. I now believe I have a great marriage, yet statistics show that I am the exception. Happy marriages, though, should not be the exception; they should be the norm. After this personal experience, I realized that more couples should seek counselling when problems arise, not give up so easily, and spend time alone together.

Paragraph 2

Why are some people self-directed, confident, and personable? Why do some people have high standards and honourable values? Why are some people optimists and others are pessimists? The answers to these questions are complex. Home environment, socioeconomic level, and genetic background are some of the factors that make people what they are. However, one constant in all of these influences is parents. Parents affect children's self-confidence, attitude toward others, and general outlook toward life.

Paragraph 3

"Reading is to the mind, what exercise is to the body," Sir Richard Steele wisely stated. Steele's quotation draws an analogy between the importance of exercise to tone the body and reading to stimulate the mind. If people do not exercise, they become fat, sluggish, unhealthy, and weak, and this condition is readily visible. When people do not exercise their minds, they become mentally unhealthy and weak, yet this situation is even more dangerous because it is not noticeable. This theory is especially true for children in their formative years when habits are developing. Reading can make the difference between a strong or weak mind. Reading improves children's vocabulary, expands their understanding, and increases their creativity.

EXERCISE 9

Using the topics listed below, write introductory paragraphs that include a hook, a logical transition, and a thesis sentence. You may use several types of hook in your beginning. Develop the thesis sentence first, the hook second, and the transition third.

> *food*
> *music*
> *insects*
> *shopping*
> *self-defence*

Paragraph 1

_____

_____

_____

_____

_____

_____

_____

Paragraph 2

_____

_____

_____

_____

_____

_____

_____

Paragraph 3

_____

_____

_____

_____

_____

_____

_____

Here is one final piece of advice: For successful introductory paragraphs, **do not**

repeat the wording the instructor has used for the assignment

apologize for your paper

claim a disinterest in the topic

use an inappropriate tone

write "In this essay, I will. . . ."

The Purpose of Concluding Paragraphs

The last part of your essay is the concluding paragraph. This final paragraph gives you a chance to reemphasize the thesis you have supported throughout the paper. The conclusion should be thorough, not just cut off prematurely. At the end of the paper, the reader should not ask "Where is the rest of the paper?" or "What did the author mean?" Rather, the reader should say, "Now I see how nicely everything fits together and how it applies to me."

The purpose of the introduction is to get the attention of the reader; the purpose of the support paragraphs is to focus on the thesis and develop that main idea thoroughly. The purpose of the conclusion is unique. Its task is to bring all of the thesis points together in a reflective way. In your concluding paragraph, you don't have to worry about building up lots of support. For this reason, conclusions are fun to write because most of the work has been done. Your only concerns are blending together the main points, providing a feeling of closure, and reinforcing your main points. If your reader has drifted away at any time during the paper or lost his or her concentration, you can recap the main points.

Recognizing Weak Conclusions

After you have finished writing the support paragraphs in your paper, it is not time to ease up. It is time to be forceful in order to keep the reader with you. Sometimes you may feel rushed when you get to the end of your paper and might be tempted to finish it in a hurry so you can turn it in. This is like constructing a beautiful house and then deciding that you do not have time to put on a roof because you want to move in "right now." Following through with a strong conclusion is like finishing off your house—it makes good sense!

The following essay includes an introductory paragraph and three support paragraphs but no conclusion. Read the essay and then read the conclusions that follow. All four illustrate weaknesses to avoid.

Family Weekend Vacations

1   "More than 2.1 million children from ages 5 to 13 have no adult supervision after school, and many are alone at other times of the day and night," according to a recent newspaper article. These children come from families in which both parents work or there is only one parent, and that one parent must work full-time. Even though these children must come home alone after school each day, the parents are often home on the weekends. If everyone is willing to cooperate and get the work done during the week, these weekends can be filled with short vacations that can help family members come together whether the household is headed by two parents or one parent. These weekend vacations can provide many rewarding activities for family members, including family togetherness, knowledge, and exercise.

2   Family togetherness is strengthened when the members participate in weekend vacations. Before families go away for the weekend, they often spend time planning what they are going to be doing for the next two days. When a weekend trip includes sight-seeing, family members have time to communicate with one another as they go from place to place. When camping, families often hike together, exploring rivers or streams as they share their thoughts with one another. When visiting relatives, families experience a broader sense of togetherness as time is shared "catching up" with cousins, grandparents, and other relatives, or finding out what mom and dad did when they were young. When it is time for dinner, everyone sits down together and discusses the comedies or tragedies of the day. Whether they have been camping, sight-seeing, or seeing relatives, they become a stronger unit.

3   While family members are sharing themselves, they often find themselves sharing knowledge that is obtained on these treasured weekend vacations. Combing the beach in the early morning as the light slowly appears, children and adults alike realize that shells that are washed onto the shore are more than treasures to be taken home. They bring food to the many sea gulls and other birds that live there. In addition, visiting Native Canadian ruins can teach how the early inhabitants lived on the land that we now enjoy. Visiting Mennonite villages can help each member of the family see what Canada was like before it became so technologically oriented. There is no end to the educational opportunities offered by simple weekend vacations.

4   An additional benefit that cannot be overlooked is the exercise obtained during these weekend vacations. Many occasions require more physical activity than just spending time at home being a couch potato. Amusement parks like Canada's Wonderland are large and keep everyone walking from one attraction to another. Jet skiing or waterskiing seem to work every muscle of the body. Surfing in the ocean or simply swimming in the salt water provides an extensive workout. Some of the beaches are equipped with gymnastic apparatuses that let adults and children test muscles as they fly through the air. Even shopping at resorts or quaint towns requires a lot of walking, if no more than simply window shopping or sightseeing. The best part of all is that all of these activities can be shared by all members of the family.

Following, you will find several weak conclusions that add little to the effectiveness of the essay.

These weekend vacations can provide many rewarding activities for family members, including family togetherness, knowledge, and exercise.

Notice how this conclusion does not do anything for the essay. It simply repeats the thesis sentence and leaves the reader hanging.

These weekend vacations can provide many rewarding activities for family members, including family togetherness, knowledge, and exercise. First, family togetherness is strengthened. Second, family members learn a lot on these trips. And last of all, these same family members get a lot of exercise.

This conclusion shows no creativity. It simply copies the thesis sentence and mechanically repeats what has already been said in the essay. It appears artificial and redundant.

So guys, let's put our heads together and chat about ways to spend the weekends. Well, you only live once, so why not forget the dishes and floors. The dirt won't go away. Just party long and hard. The weekends will be so much fun that you may never want to come back home or back to the drudgery of work and school.

This conclusion has thrown the reader off because instead of ending on a serious note that was consistent throughout the essay, it attempts to be humorous and flippant. The point that should be stressed in the conclusion is lost. Consequently, the unity of the entire essay has been destroyed. If you are ironical throughout an essay, you might want to make the most biting statement in the conclusion. If you are humorous, end on a humorous note. For best effect, do not change to a different tone of voice in the concluding paragraph.

Time is a precious commodity, and certainly mom and dad can find other tasks to do instead of taking the family out for a weekend trip.

However, these weekend trips are important for unifying the family, educating the family, and keeping the family physically active. If families spend weekends together, they can avoid many problems, like juvenile delinquency and divorce. Consequently, this time is worth it.

This conclusion also throws the reader off. It does reiterate the main points of the essay; however, it then goes off on a tangent about major problems like delinquency and divorce. You can mention these issues in the conclusion only if you have mentioned and discussed them in the introduction and in the paper. Also, this type of ending leaves the reader with the feeling that the writer is not clear about the point to be made. A strong conclusion does not suddenly introduce a new idea.

The Conclusion Should *Not*

repeat the thesis sentence exactly as it appeared in the introduction

repeat the thesis sentence and mechanically repeat the topic sentences

change the tone of the essay

introduce a new idea in the conclusion

Recognizing and Writing Strong Conclusions

Just as a weak conclusion can leave the reader confused and cheated, a strong conclusion can leave the reader informed and emotionally gratified. You have flexibility in writing a conclusion because many choices are available.

The Conclusion *Should*

summarize main points made in the paper and creatively restate the ideas in the thesis sentence

end with an obvious closure that leaves the essay with a sense of completeness

Read the following concluding paragraph, which includes both a summary and an obvious closure.

Spending precious days together on weekend vacations can invigorate the mind, the body, and the soul of a family unit. Teenagers, small children, and adults have quality time together as they share the many opportunities offered simply by being alive and enjoying each other's company doing little things. While these family members are strengthening the bond they feel for one another, they are also gaining valuable knowledge and healthy exercise. Weekend vacations provide this for them.

This concluding paragraph shows creativity. The writer has addressed the family as if it is a living being when she identifies the family as having a mind, body, and soul. Family members are identified in "Teenagers, small children, and adults." The thesis idea is repeated but is not redundant because the author has chosen different words. This conclusion links to the introduction as well as to the support paragraphs. It is not rushed and does not cut off abruptly. The writer shows sincerity and maintains a consistent tone.

However, you can use additional strategies to add to or enhance a conclusion.

Strong Conclusions

refer to an example, fact, or statistic made in the introduction

end with a question that leaves the reader thinking about what was said

comment about the future

- **For added emphasis, recall an example, fact, or statistic mentioned in the introduction.**

> Spending precious days together on weekend vacations can invigorate the mind, the body, and the soul of a family unit. Teenagers, small children, and adults have quality time together as they share the many opportunities offered simply by being alive and enjoying each other's company doing little things. While these family members are strengthening the bond they feel for one another, they are also gaining valuable knowledge and healthy exercise. **Even though nothing can be done about the fact that so many children from ages five to thirteen are getting home from school before their parents, something can be done about the weekend that will leave lasting memories for these children.** Weekend vacations can provide these memories for them.

The idea in bold type adds to the effectiveness of this conclusion because it goes back to and enforces the emotional appeal in the introductory paragraph. The statistic that "children from ages five to thirteen are getting home from school before their parents" is smoothly linked to the thesis sentence that "these weekend vacations can provide many rewarding activities..." Without introducing any new ideas, the conclusion is uplifting and optimistic because it reassures the reader that something can be done about the future.

- **Use an appropriate question to leave the reader thinking.**

> Spending precious days together on weekend vacations can invigorate the mind, the body, and the soul of a family unit. Teenagers, small children, and adults have quality time together as they share the many opportunities offered simply by being alive and enjoying each other's company doing little things. While these family members are strengthening the bond they feel for one another, they are also gaining valuable knowledge and healthy exercise. Even though nothing can be done about the fact that so many children from ages five to thirteen are getting home from school before their parents, something can be done about the weekend that will leave lasting memories for these children. **What kind of memories are these parents leaving for their children?**

The preceding paragraph ends with a different kind of emotional reaction. It causes the reader to search her/his conscience. This emotional strategy might cause some parents to stop and think and, as a result, begin spending time with their children.

- **Comment about the future.**

    Spending precious days together on weekend vacations can invigorate the mind, the body, and the soul of a family unit. Teenagers, small children, and adults have quality time together as they share the many opportunities offered simply by being alive and enjoying each other's company doing little things. While these family members are strengthening the bond they feel for one another, they are also gaining valuable knowledge and healthy exercise. Even though nothing can be done about the fact that so many children from ages five to thirteen are getting home from school before their parents, something can be done about the weekend that will leave lasting memories for these children. What kind of memories are these parents leaving for their children? Instead of checking out the TV schedule this weekend, maybe more families should be checking out the adventurous opportunities waiting to be taken.

This concluding paragraph ends with a recommendation for the future. It calls upon parents to make a change in their lives. Instead of being vague, this conclusion gives the reader a definite action to take.

EXERCISE 10

Each introduction below is followed by a weak conclusion. Revise each conclusion. Use a combination of strategies.

1. **Introduction**

    When I think ahead to the year 3000, many different questions come to mind. What new inventions will be in use in the common household? How much will the world of transportation be advanced? What type of weaponry will have been invented? In what type of environment will people be living? All of these questions lead me to feel that in the year 3000 there will be major differences in science, in transportation, and in people's lifestyles.

Conclusion

    The future is important to all of us, and in some small way, we all mould the future. There will be lots of differences in science, in transportation, and in people's lifestyles. I suppose there will be differences in clothing, too.

———————————————————————————————————

———————————————————————————————————

———————————————————————————————————

———————————————————————————————————

———————————————————————————————————

2. Introduction

This morning I picked up the newspaper and read about a man who had shot his twenty-three-year-old girlfriend and her nine-month-old child because he believed his girlfriend had transmitted AIDS to him. Not long ago I viewed a documentary on AIDS in which three brothers had been barred from school because they were hemophiliacs and had been exposed to the AIDS virus. Their home was bombed by "good" parents who did not want these boys to attend school with their children. Though these incidents seem bizarre in a twentieth-century civilized country, many people fear AIDS because of the consequences of the disease, the misinformation concerning the disease, and the increasing number of cases of the disease.

Conclusion

AIDS is the tragedy of the century. It is sweeping the country and killing thousands of innocent victims. The most tragic of all are the small children that are coming into this world already affected by the AIDS virus. Hospitals need to require their health-care workers, including doctors, to be screened for the HIV virus.

———————————————————————————————————

———————————————————————————————————

———————————————————————————————————

———————————————————————————————————

———————————————————————————————————

———————————————————————————————————

3. Introduction

"Why try? The white kids get all the jobs!" That is what my best friend Ken used to say whenever I tried to find a job. It seemed that the jobs were out there, but only the white teenagers, not the black teenagers, got those jobs. I realized that this problem could not be something that developed overnight but rather evolved over many years. After much research, I found that black unemployment is a result of racial discrimination, economic conditions, and the educational system.

Conclusion

In conclusion, black unemployment is an obviously bad condition. The first reason is all the racial discrimination in our society. Another reason is the economic conditions that blacks are subjected to. The third reason is our educational system. All these reasons together result in black unemployment.

_____

_____

_____

_____

_____

EXERCISE 11

Write an effective conclusion for each of the following introductions. Use a combination of strategies.

1. **Introduction**

After seventeen years of marriage, I had given up. I felt my marriage was hopeless and irreparable. I had my husband move out for six months until I decided on whether I wanted to try again. However, instead of giving up we worked on our communication skills, our built-up anger, and our spirituality. I realized what was going to be lost through a divorce and agreed to try again. I now believe I have a great marriage, yet statistics show that I am the exception. Happy marriages, though, should not be the exception; they should be the norm. After this personal experience, I realized that more couples should seek counselling when problems arise, should not give up so easily, and should spend time alone together.

Concluding paragraph

_____

_____

_____

_____

_____

2. **Introduction**

Why are some people self-directed, confident, and personable? Why do some people have high standards and honourable values? Why are some people optimists and others are pessimists? The answers to these questions are complex. Home environment, socioeconomic level, and genetic background are some of the factors that make people what they are. However, one constant in all of these influences is parents. Parents affect children's self-confidence, attitude toward others, and general outlook toward life.

Concluding paragraph

_____

_____

_____

_____

_____

_____

3. **Introduction**

"Reading is to the mind, what exercise is to the body," Sir Richard Steele wisely stated. Steele's quotation draws an analogy between the importance of exercise to tone the body and reading to stimulate the mind. If people do not exercise, they become fat, sluggish, unhealthy, and weak, and this condition is readily visible. When people do not exercise their minds, they become mentally unhealthy and weak, yet this situation is even more dangerous because it is not noticeable. This theory is especially true for children in their formative years when habits are developing. Reading can make the difference between a strong or weak mind. Reading improves children's vocabulary, expands their understanding, and increases their creativity.

Concluding paragraph

_____

_____

_____

_____

_____

_____

PART 2   Something to Think About, Something to Write About

Sudbury's Sense of Place Will Always Be Grounded in the Canadian Shield

by Michael Whitehouse, *a writer living in Sudbury*

1   Among the many constants of my meagre existence in my Sudbury apartment is the first morning view out my picture window of the giant 381-metre Inco Superstack. And, although I can't put my finger on why, there is something reassuring about this stack. Somehow it seems to define this place; it serves as a constant reminder of who we are and grounds us physically and psychologically in the rock here.

2   Physically, the stack is to Sudbury what the CN Tower is to Toronto, the single most obvious structure imaginable, visible from everywhere. Symbolically, though, it is the reverse. While the CN Tower represents progress, chutzpah and an eye to the future. Sudbury's Superstack represents only an old, outmoded economic order, reluctant environmental concern and thoroughly unambitious pragmatism; ideals that to a large degree represent these cities.

3   Indeed, there are many landmarks in both Toronto and Sudbury that represent their respective ideals. But there are now in Sudbury some expectations. The past 25 years have seen the addition of a number of remarkable (and many not so remarkable) public buildings. The juxtaposition of the old and emerging has formed an eclectic mishmash of two different landscapes: a modern city grafted onto an old frontier town.

4   Old Sudbury remains a ramshackle collection of dilapidated retailers, box houses and storefront offices. It is made up of miners with blackened faces and a narrow band of services. New Sudbury still has these things, plus a horde of middle-aged provincial and federal bureaucrats who surge through sturdy malls, palatial homes and gleaming office towers.

5   Old Sudburians continue to frequent the beer halls, the Mine Mill and Steel Worker halls, their various ethnic clubs and Sudbury Wolves games. They live in small clapboard or stuccoed houses in older, run-down parts of town and park their cars in back lanes.

6   New Sudburians frequent the elegant Theatre Centre, attend shows and concerts at the refurbished Grand Theatre, live in burgeoning new curvilinear, cookie-cutter subdivisions and park in their two- or three-car garages with living quarters attached to the back.

7   Old Sudburians walk to the many locally owned mon-and-pop confectioneries, while New Sudburians drive to the nearest franchised convenience store. Old Sudbury was continually flooded with Maritimers from "down east" to toil in the mines, while New Sudbury is inundated with Torontontians "coming up" to beehive in the new government office buildings.

8   In short, Sudbury has been inundated with all the commercial trappings that make every Canadian city look like a Toronto suburb.

9   Sudbury is not alone in this transformation. The growing primacy of Toronto in the constellation of Canadian cities has led to some interesting problems for each. Far from continuing as mere providers of certain resources, all cities seem to want what Toronto has: thoroughly diversified economies featuring high-tech, information technologies.

10   But Sudbury is different in that much of this change has been deliberate. It has demonstrated the ability to remake itself, to stop on a dime, reverse position and move in a new and better direction. Painful? Perhaps. But necessary and, ultimately, quite profitable. Compare Sudbury and its new prosperity to, say, Winnipeg, which has been locked in a protracted death spiral since the Great Depression, and you can see clearly how important it is that a community organize itself so that it can change itself tomorrow.

11   The result of this new binary appearance is that Sudbury no longer exists in any single time or place. It has one foot in the past and one in the present, one foot in the Canadian Shield and one in Toronto, one foot in the hinterland and one in the heartland. And this, I believe, makes Sudbury the typical Canadian community. As Canada gradually becomes known as Toronto-and-its-environs, any community that can firmly plant one foot in each is setting a new standard.

12   But this same ability of the city to transform itself so suddenly and successfully has lulled Sudburians into believing that the transformation is absolute. Just like a caterpillar-turned-butterfly, we believe that we have turned from something ugly and earthbound to something beautiful and airborne, and that we bear absolutely no resemblance to our previous form.

13   The problem with this view, and the disturbing element of the juxtaposition, is that is almost completely abandons our geography. The Canadian Shield is both the cause and effect of our existence. The wealth that it offers is why we are here in the first place, our raison-d'être. It profoundly conditions the way we live, our activities, and our expectations. We might move away from the cause of our existence—mining—but we will never escape its effect.

14   Civic boosters, however, want both but in Toronto, with mining relegated to the status of a hangover from yesterday's party, tolerated if necessary but ignored if possible. But it will never be that easy. It is important to know where your roots lie, and why they lie there. Sometimes they are so ugly that you don't want to see them. Sometimes you look down the road, see something that you like better, and try to emulate it. But to not understand or arbitrarily ignore your roots—or worse, embrace something alien in their place—is to abandon your present and lose control of your future.

15   Are there lessons for other Canadian hinterland communities—fishing villages, farming hamlets, logging towns? No other country in the world has so many variant geographical streams. They are, arguably, our greatest asset. Traditional local economies might falter, local psyches might be infiltrated and homogenized by large ones, but the natural and built landscapes will always serve as a constant grounded reminder of where you are and why you are there, and thus provide the strength to move forward with confidence.

Something to Write About

Using one of the ideas or questions below, develop either a thesis sentence that states a clear direction or a thesis sentence that previews the points to be covered in the paper. Then draft your essay.

1. Write about a landmark in your hometown.
2. Write about a landmark in a town or city in which you live.
3. How has the city you once lived in changed since you left?
4. What lessons have you learned from the Canadian community you live(d) in?
5. What aspects of a city are important to you? (buildings, services, etc.)
6. Why is it "important to know where your roots lie"?
7. Describe the ideal place to live.

After you draft your essay, do each of the following:

Revise it so that it has an effective introduction that includes a hook, a transition, and a thesis sentence.

Be sure that each support paragraph has a strong topic sentence and ample supporting examples.

Check for unity and a smooth flow of ideas.

Revise to include a strong concluding paragraph.

Check for subject-verb agreement.

Check for consistent verb.

Check for consistent point of view.

Check for fragments, run-ons, and comma splices.

Check punctuation of compound sentences.

PART 3 | Essays for Discussion and Analysis

Dancer

Adapted from the original by **Nancy Chandler,** *student*

1   "She is the fool who ruined our recital" are the words that rang in my ears as I looked up to see the whole dressing room looking at my nakedness as Margaruite Swartz pointed her finger at me. At nine years old, I felt that I was never going to dance again in a group. But twenty years later, that's exactly what I was doing professionally. In fact, I was not only dancing but creating dances and leading a troupe. Leading, choreographing, and dancing in a troupe were rewarding for me emotionally, physically, and personally.

2   The emotional stimulation of creating, teaching, and performing dance numbers was the most uplifting experience in my life. I especially enjoyed choreographing the dance routines that our troupe performed because of the recognition I got from my fellow dancers and the management. I remember one time in particular when this was true. The manager of the club in which we performed had given me a song, a favourite of his, to create a dance number with. When I performed this number for him and the dancers so it could be critiqued, they gave me a standing ovation. They also said that if we chose this particular number in a competition we were considering entering, we would surely win. The feeling of accomplishment and respect I got from my colleagues is one of my most cherished memories.

3   The physical benefits of performing regularly in a dance troupe were an outstanding plus for my physical being. I do not think I have ever been in such top shape as when I was dancing professionally. The troupe not only performed on Friday and Saturday nights, we also practised Monday through Friday for about five hours. I never needed to worry about dieting in my days of dance. Even teaching aerobics, as I had in the past, did not sculpture my body in quite the manner that dancing did. Performing regularly in a troupe was definitely the most physically demanding and physically beneficial job I have ever been involved in.

4   Not only was my physical body in shape, but my personal life was also becoming more satisfying as a direct result of being involved in the troupe. The troupe itself had become more like a family to me than anything else. They were a support system for me because I was going through a hard time in my marriage. I remember an especially memorable time when one of my dancers came to my rescue on a particular evening when I was in need of a hero. I had had a bad fight with my husband, and he had thrown me out of the house into the rain. I did not know what to do, so I called Raynard, one of the dancers, and he was there in a flash. Raynard was so understanding and diplomatic when it came to getting my daughter out of the house that my husband let me back into the house and apologized. I never knew what the conversation was between the two men, but my husband was much more civil to me for quite a while afterward. There are many benefits I got as a result of being involved with the dance troupe, such as courage, self-respect, and self-assurance, but most of all it was the friendships that I cherished.

5   Dancing in a troupe was definitely my favourite job, but it did not seem like a job at all to me. Dancing was an outlet for my inner emotions and my physical expression, and a social activity for me. When I was nine years old and red-faced with embarrassment, I would have never guessed that I would end up becoming a dancer and falling so much in love with dancing as I did.

Questions on Content
1. How many hours a day did the author practise dance?
2. What happened when she performed a special number?
3. What was the most physically demanding thing she had ever done?

Questions on Form
1. What makes the introduction so effective?
2. What is effective about the conclusion?

A Good Manager

Adapted from the original by **Marlene Reed,** *student*

1   What qualities make a good manager? Should a manager be a "good buddy" or be stern and strict? Should a manager have a combination of these traits? Because the majority of the population is working-class, many may work under the authority of a manager. They certainly hope to work under managers who know their jobs and know how to work with people. Paul Eweres, a manager at Loblaws, is an excellent manager because he is disciplined, intelligent, and fair.

2   There is a special, admirable quality in Mr. Eweres: his self-discipline. Mr. Eweres is one of the most disciplined people that anyone could work for. Loblaws managers must work with district managers, the constant threat of losing their jobs, and very long hours. Many managers with pressures such as these lose their cool—not Mr. Eweres. He can take all that the job dishes out, get the work done, and not once blame his problems on someone else, much less take these problems out on the employees. This is a sign of considerable maturity, and more managers should have self-discipline such as this.

3   Of equal importance, a manager needs to be intelligent. Without knowing his I.Q., one can tell that Mr. Eweres is very bright. The ease with which he solves complex problems is noteworthy. For example, when his store received new scanner registers, Mr. Eweres had no problems adjusting to the new system, as most managers might. Any problem that came up he knew instantly how to fix. In addition, Mr. Eweres knows how to make a schedule that works well. Scheduling has proven to be a problem for many managers because it takes considerable savvy to know when help is needed and to keep hours within the amount allotted. Managers most often do not schedule enough help at the right times, or they schedule too much help when it is not needed, yet this task has never been a problem for Mr. Eweres. His schedules are accurate, and his store runs smoothly because he has the needed intelligence.

4   Above all else, Mr. Eweres is fair. He does not let his personal preferences guide his decisions, and he always tries to work with his employees. Managers sometimes use intimidation to get work done. Though the use of intimidation might get the job done, it only breeds contempt and ill feelings. When people are treated like animals, they grow to hate their jobs and begin to call in sick. Paul Eweres doesn't use intimidation because he doesn't have to. His employees respect him; therefore, they not only do their jobs, but they do their best. He makes employees feel important to the store, not like cogs in a machine.

5   It is the opinion of this writer that without these three qualities—discipline, intelligence and fairness—this manager at Loblaws would be just a manager, no one special. Yet, because he possesses these qualities, he is so much more effective. No, Paul Eweres is not just a manager; he is the best manager Loblaws has.

Questions on Content
1. What does Mr. Eweres manage?
2. What does Mr. Eweres do that illustrates his intelligence?
3. Why does he not have to rely on intimidation to get employees to work?

Questions on Form
1. What is the hook used in the introduction?
2. Comment on the force of the conclusion. Is it consistent with the rest of the essay?
3. Has the student used any specific examples to support her opinion of Mr. Eweres's character? If so, what are they?

The Car of Tomorrow

Adapted from the original by **Terry M. Donaldson**, *student*

1   With the frenzied pace of rapidly advancing technology, the possibilities of the future seem limitless. Even the vague concept of perfection may someday be a part of daily routine. With a vivid (and moderately warped) imagination, anyone can envision some wild and futuristic example of technological advancements making something perfect. One example could be a perfect car. The idea may strike terror into the hearts of automotive engineers now, but future technologies may prove that the perfect car is simply a combination of versatility, performance, and economy.

2   Versatility is an important feature of the perfect car. Why should a driveway be cluttered with two cars, a truck, and a boat when one car can do it all? Impossible, some people say, but that is nonsense! The same technology that gave the Concord SST jetliner a pivoting cockpit and retractable wings has led to the expandable car! The next time a little leaguer volunteers to give his whole baseball team a ride home from practice, it will be no problem. In just a few minutes, the new two-passenger coupe will stretch into a multipassenger bus with the flip of a switch. With the flip of another switch, the sporty little coupe converts into a motorboat for those times that a person "really would rather be skiing." New lighter materials can even make it possible for new cars to fly. Is that versatility or

what? The new Vertical Take Off & Landing (V.T.O.L.) option can be an accessory with the new car. Traffic jams will be no problem. A simple flip of a switch and the driver can fly off, leaving the traffic behind. Of course, this option is NOT recommended for use in tunnels or on covered bridges. It surely is exciting to imagine so much versatility wrapped in one perfect little package! The driver must, however, be sure to watch the control panel carefully! Inadvertently flipping the wrong switch could convert the bus back into a two passenger coupe and put twenty screaming ten-year-olds into the driver's lap, and if the person happens to be out on the lake...Let me put it this way. How long can a person tread water?

3   Performance is another feature of the perfect car. New discoveries in nuclear fusion have made the hazardous nuclear-fission-based atomic generators and gas-guzzling performance engines of the past obsolete. The advent of this technology, electricity, has replaced gasoline as the fuel of choice for maximum performance from the family car. These new nuclear-fission-based reactors are powerful, safe, compact, and do not produce the hazardous atomic wastes now polluting the country, so an owner need not learn thermonuclear physics just to own and operate a powerful new car. The compact design and light weight of these new reactors make them very conducive to the popular aerodynamically superior sportscar styling people know and love. In common layperson's terms, people DO NOT have to ride around in cars that look like giant potatoes on wheels! Every high-performance automobile should look as powerful as it is, and improving the aerodynamics of a car also improves its high-speed performance and handling. Manoeuvrability and speed are absolute necessities for a truly perfect car, so they are included at no extra charge. The high energy output of technology's newest generators translates into plenty of power for those last minute "banzai" runs downtown. Just how fast will it go? With the V.T.O.L. option, air speeds in excess of Mach 2 are easy. To satisfy a person's curiosity about that speed reference, Mach 2 is twice the speed of sound. A few sharp turns and dives should be a blast at that speed. That kind of performance may sound impossible now, but walking on the moon was impossible once.

4   An additional attraction of the perfect car is economy. The same feature that gives the power, styling, and versatility also make this car extremely economical to operate. Because the perfect car has so few moving parts, the only maintenance it should ever need is a routine lubrication and radiation detoxification. Expensive automobile breakdowns and repairs are things of the past. Just like the dinosaurs, auto repair bills were BIG and DUMB! The atomic power plants used in new cars are eradicating the monstrous repair bills, and they also have an exciting added feature. They will convert any organic material into a radioactive fuel supply that will last for months. Filling up is never a problem. Any plant or stray debris will give a needed refill. Once the stuff is in the tank, the car is ready to go. This innovation could be a very useful way of dealing with a neighbour's garbage that ends up in the wrong place. Operating an automobile has never been more economical!

5   Everyone has a version of perfection, so my idea of a perfect car may differ slightly from someone else's. A car that can grow into a bus and then sink to the bottom of the lake sounds incredibly versatile to me. Performing like a jet and economically feeding on carefully chosen plants could have a beneficial effect on the environment. Think about it. The possibilities really do seem limitless. What kind of car would you call perfect?

Questions on Content

1. What will the car of the future be able to do?
2. What will the car of the future not look like?
3. What could provide fuel for the car?

Questions on Form

1. What does the author do in the introduction to lead to the thesis sentence?
2. What is the thesis sentence?
3. How does the author conclude his essay?

....

The Old Farm and the New Frame

Stephen Leacock

1   When I left the old farm of my childhood which I described in talking about my remarkable uncle, I never saw it again for years and years. I don't think I wanted to. Most people who come off farms never go back. They talk about it, cry about it—but they don't really go. They know better.

2   If they did go back, they would find, as I did, the old place all changed, the old world all gone, in fact no "farms" any more, no cross-road stores, no villages—nothing in the old sense. A new world has replaced it all.

3   I went back the other day in a motor car to have a look round the locality that I hadn't seen since I left it by means of a horse and buggy more than half a century before. I came to do this because I happened to have been looking at one of those typical "motor ads" that you see in the coloured illustrations, motors glistening to an impossible effulgence, a gravelled drive impossibly neat, beside wide lawns of inconceivable grass and unachievable flower beds. In and beside the motor car were super-world beings as impossible as the grass and flowers around them—youths as square in the shoulders as Greek gods, girls as golden as guineas, and even old age, in the persons of the senior generation, smoothed and beautiful to a pink and white as immaculate as youth itself. And as I looked at the picture of this transformed world not yet achieved but at least exciting, in the creative mind of the artist, I fell to thinking of all the actual transformation that new invention has brought to our lives.

4   I thought particularly of how it has changed the aspect of what we used to call the country—the country of the horse and buggy days that I so easily recall. So I went back.

5   Our farm was up in a lost corner of Ontario, but the locality doesn't particularly matter. They're all the same from Ontario to Ohio.

6   We lived four and half miles from the "village." To get to it from our farm you went down a lane—heavy going—up to the hubs in bad weather, then on to a road and up a hill, the same hill really you had just come down only on a different angle; then along a splendid "spin" of at least three hundred yards where you "let the mare out," that is, made her go like blazes (eight miles an hour); then, Whoa! steady! another hill, a mighty steep one, to go down. You had to take it pretty easy. In fact, for the hills you had far better get out and walk, as we generally did; it eased the mare to have us walk up the first hill and it eased the buggy to have us walk down the second.

7   After the second hill, a fine spin of about four hundred yards, good road and "room to pass." You couldn't "let the mare out" all along this, as it might "wind" her; but she could keep going at a pretty smart clip just the same. Then came the "big swamp," about three quarters of a mile or more, in fact. I never knew a road from Maine to the Mississippi that didn't have a swamp in it. A lot of the big swamp was "corduroy" road. The word means cord du roi, or king's rope, but the thing meant logs laid side by side with dirt shoveled over them. In the swamp there was no room to pass except by a feat of engineering in chosen spots.

8   After the swamp you went on over a succession of "spins" and "hills," the mare alternately "eased" and "winded" and "let out"—and at last, there you were, in the village street—yes, sir, right in the village, under an hour, pretty good going, eh? Cover the mare up with a blanket while we go into the tavern or she may get the "heaves"—or the "humps"—or I forget what; anyway it was what a mare got if you stayed too long in the tavern.

9   And the village street, how well I remember it! Romantic, well, I don't know; I suppose it was. But it was just a street—stores on each side with a square sign over each. Trees here and there. Horses hitched to posts asleep; a grist mill at the end where the river hit the village or the village hit the river, I forget which. There were no fancy signs, no fancy stores. The sole place of entertainment was the tavern—beer 5 cents, whiskey 5 cents, mixed drinks (that means beer with whisky or whisky mixed with beer) 5 cents. Food, only at meal times, at a York shilling a meal, later raised to a quarter.

10   Such was the typical farm road and village of fifty years ago—a "social cell" as I believe the sociologists would call us.

11   Now look at the change. I visited it, as I say, the other day in a large smooth-running motor car—this "social cell" from which I emerged fifty years ago. Changed? The word isn't adequate. It just wasn't there anymore. In the first place some one had changed our old farm-house into a "farmstead." You see, you can't live any longer on a farm if you're going to have people coming to see you in motor cars—golden girls. Apollo boys and Joan and Darby elders. You must turn the place into a "farmstead"—with big shingles all over it in all directions—with a "loggia" in front and a "pergola" at the side.

12   And the road? All gone, all changed. A great highway swept by in its course and sheared lane and hills into one broad, flat curve; threw aside the second hill into a mere nothing of a "grade," with a row of white posts; and the swamp, it had passed out of existence to become a broad flat with a boulevard two-way road, set with new shingled bungalows with loggias and pergolas, overgrown with wistaria and perugia, and all trying to live up to the passing motor cars. There's a tea room now where the spring used to be, in the centre of the swamp, the place where we watered the mare to prevent her blowing.

13   But you hardly see all this—the whole transit from farmstead to village by the sweeping, shortened concrete road is just three minutes. You are in the village before you know it.

14   And the village itself! Why, it's another place. What charm is this, what magic this transformation? I hardly know the place; in fact, I don't know it. The whole length of it now is neat with clipped grass and the next-to-impossible flowers copied from the motor car advertisements; there are trim little cedars and box hedges, trees clipped to a Versailles perfection and house fronts all aglow with variegated paint and hanging flowers…And the signs, what a multitude of them;

it's like a mediaeval fair! "Old English Tea Room"! I didn't know this was England! And no, it isn't; see the next sign, "Old Dutch Tea Room," and "Old Colony Rest House"! and "Normandy Post House"! No, it's not England; I don't know where it is.

15   But those signs are only a fraction of the total, each one vying with the last in the art of its decoration or the angle of its suspension. "Joe's Garage"! Look at it—built like a little Tudor house, half-timbered in black and white. Joe's grandfather was the village blacksmith, I remember him well, and his "blacksmith shop" was a crazy sort of wooden shed, out of slope, with no front side in particular and a forge in it. If they had it now they would label it "Ye Olde Forge" and make it an out-of-town eating place.

16   But these new signs mean that, for the people who ride from the city, in the motor cars, the village and its little river has become a "fishing resort." You see, it's only fifty-six miles from the city; you run out in an hour or so. You can rent a punt for $1 and a man to go with you and row for another $1—or he'll fish for you, if you like. Bait only costs about 50 cents and you can get a fine chicken dinner, wine and all, from about $2. In short, you have a wonderful time and only spend $10; yet when I was young if you had $10 in the village no one could change it, and $10 would board you for a month.

17   And the people too! A new kind of people seem to have come into—or, no, grown up in—the village. I find, on examination, that they're really the grandsons and granddaughters of the people who were there. But the new world has taken hold of them and turned them into a new and different sort of people—into super people, as it were.

18   Joe Hayes for example—you remember his grandfather, the blacksmith—has turned into a "garage man," handy, efficient, knowing more than a science college, a friend in distress. What the horse-and-buggy doctor of the countryside was to the sick of fifty years ago, such is now the garage man to the disabled motor car and its occupants towed into his orbit. People talk now of their mimic roadside adventures and tell how there "wasn't a garage man within five miles" as people used to tell of having to fetch the doctor at night over five miles of mud and corduroy.

19   And Joe's brothers and cousins have somehow turned into motor-men of all sorts, taxi-men, and even that higher race, the truckmen. What the "draymen" of Old London were, admired for their bulk and strength even by the fairest of the ladies, so today are the "truckmen" who have stepped into their place in evolution...

20   Nor is it one sex only that the motor has transformed. People who live in a village where motors come and go must needs take thought for their appearance. See that sign BEAUTY PARLOR! You'd hardly think that that means Phoebe Crawford, whose great-aunt was the village seamstress. Or that sign, GEORGETTE: LINGERIE, that's Mary Ann Crowder. Her grandfather was Old Man Crowder up the river.

21   Changed, isn't it? Wonderfully changed, into a sort of prettier and brighter world. And if a little "social cell" has changed like this, it's only part of the transformation that has redecorated all our world.

22   The only trouble is to live up to it—to be as neat and beautiful as a beauty parlor girl, as friendly as a garage man, as bold and brave as a truck driver and as fit a guest to sit down to a frogs' legs dinner in an Old MIll chophouse.

23   Alas! This happy world that might have been, that seemed about to be! The transformation from the grim and sombre country-side to all this light and colour, had it only just begun to be overwhelmed and lost in the shadow of War?

24   Perhaps the old farm had something to it after all.

Questions on Content

1. What caused the author to go back to the farm of his childhood?
2. In your own words, describe the trip from his farm to the village of his boyhood.
3. How had the village changed when Leacock returned many years later?
4. How were the people different?
5. What emotions did Leacock convey? Cite some details that suggest these emotions.

Questions on Form

1. What kind of hook does Leacock use? What words in his opening paragraphs engage your interest?
2. What method of development does the author use to clarify his main idea?
3. Comment on the effectiveness of the conclusion.

PART 4 | The Writer's Tools: Sentence Variety— Using Complex Sentences

OBJECTIVES

....

- Combine simple sentences using subordinators.
- Get additional practice revising sentences.

Sometimes writing can become less interesting to the reader if the sentences are too much alike. A series of short, simple sentences are monotonous. Even too many sentences joined with "and" or "but" will bore or frustrate a reader.

The following draft paragraph contains only simple sentences.

All the players in the basketball game played very hard. They ran up and down the court. They frequently jumped and moved around quickly. They dodged back and forth. The guards dribbled the ball all around the court. They also passed the ball hard to other members of their team. Sometimes the players even knocked opposing team members to the floor. They twisted, turned, and bumped into each other. Occasionally, they ran into the referees. All the activity caused the players to exert lots of energy throughout the game.

As you learned earlier, one way to make writing more interesting is to combine simple sentences into compound sentences.

They ran up and down the court, **and** they frequently jumped and moved around quickly.

Too many compound sentences can also sound monotonous, though, and somewhat elementary. When you revise a draft, you may want to use other kinds of connecting words to combine ideas in a paragraph. For instance, if one sentence gives a reason for something, a word like "because" can be used to make one stronger sentence out of two shorter related sentences.

Sometimes the players even knocked opposing team members to the floor **because** they twisted, turned, and bumped into each other.

A sentence of this kind is called a complex sentence. The simple sentence "They twisted, turned, and bumped into each other" has now become an idea that is *dependent* upon the idea in the first part of the sentence. So that you can understand more clearly how to use complex sentences, a simple discussion follows.

Independent and Dependent Clauses

A complex sentence contains two kinds of clauses: one independent clause and one or more dependent clauses.

A **clause** is a group of words with a subject and a complete verb. An **independent clause** can stand by itself and be a sentence because it contains a complete idea. A **dependent clause** cannot stand by itself and cannot be a sentence. Combining two independent clauses with "because" makes one of them dependent on, or *subordinate* to, the other. The word "because" is called a subordinator. Thus, the new sentence formed has become a complex sentence. It now has two clauses—one independent and one dependent. The "because" idea now has become a dependent clause subordinate to the other idea in the sentence. The idea in a subordinate clause receives *less emphasis* than the idea in the independent clause. Consider the same complex sentence again:

> Sometimes the players even knocked opposing team members to the floor **because** they twisted, turned, and bumped into each other.

Now, "because they twisted, turned, and bumped into each other" can no longer stand by itself as a sentence. The word "because" makes this part a dependent clause, and it also clearly shows why players are sometimes knocked down in a basketball game.

Many common words are used to combine ideas into more mature sentences. Most of these connecting words you probably already know and use. These words are called subordinators. Here is a list of subordinators (you may already have studied them in Unit 4, Part 4 concerning fragments).

Subordinators

after	in order that	whether
although	since	which
as	so that	whichever
as if	that	who
as long as	though	whoever
as soon as	till	whom
as though	unless	whomever
because	until	whose
before	what	whosoever
even though	whatever	why
how	when	
if	where	

Using Subordinators to Form Complex Sentences

Even more important, however, is knowing how to use the subordinators to combine simple sentences into stronger, more mature ideas. These stronger, revised sentences clearly show how ideas relate to each other. Consider the following list of uses of subordinators.

after

I will finish this chapter.

I will treat myself to some fudge cake.

***After* I finish this chapter,** I will treat myself to some fudge cake.*

I will treat myself to some fudge cake ***after* I finish this chapter.**

Note When the dependent clause is an introductory expression in the sentence, put a comma after it.

as soon as

Ivan is coming.

I am leaving.

***As soon as* Ivan comes**, I am leaving.

I am leaving ***as soon as* Ivan comes**.

before

Rick needs to study.

He needs to take his test.

Rick needs to study ***before* he takes his test**.

***Before* he takes his test**, Rick needs to study.

when

The river dries out.

The fish will die.

***When* the river dries out**, the fish will die.

The fish will die ***when* the river dries out**.

while

The bride walked with her father.

The groom waited.

***While* the bride walked with her father**, the groom waited

The groom waited ***while* the bride walked with her father**.

where

The students stood there.

There was shade.

---

* You might need to make changes in wording when you build complex sentences.

The students stood ***where* there was shade**.

The students stood ***where* the shade was**.*

as

She took the medicine.

The doctor had prescribed it.

She took the medicine ***as* the doctor had prescribed it**.*

if

We will not have the picnic.

It might rain on Saturday.

We will not have the picnic ***if* it rains on Saturday**.

***If* it rains on Saturday**, we will not have the picnic.

although

The coach had a winning season.

He cut six players.

***Although* the coach had a winning season**, he cut six players.

The coach cut six players ***although* he had a winning season**.

because

We needed the extra money.

Mom decided to get a job.

Mom decided to get a job ***because* we needed the extra money**.

***Because* we needed the extra money**, Mom decided to get a job.

so that

Maria raked the leaves.

Clay could burn them.

Maria raked the leaves ***so that* Clay could burn them**.

***So that* Clay could burn the leaves**, Maria raked them.

as long as

The girls were content.

They had games to play.

The girls were content ***as long as* they had games to play**.

***As long as* the girls had games to play**, they were content.

*Sometimes it does not sound natural to put the dependent clause first.

as well as

Mary Duncan did not run well.

She could have run better.

Mary Duncan did not run **_as well as_ she could have**.

EXERCISE 1

Using words from the list, choose a subordinator that will logically connect each pair of the following simple sentences. Then combine each pair of sentences into a complex sentence. More than one subordinator may fit, depending upon the meaning you want to express. Also, you may need to make some changes in wording. Reminder: When the dependent clause is an introductory expression in the sentence, put a comma after it.

Example:

The game was over.

The players went into the locker room to change clothes.

The players went into the locker room to change clothes after the game was over.

After the game was over, the players went into the locker room to change clothes.

1. Henry came over to the house to repair the front door.
   We called him yesterday.

   _____

   _____

2. The cocker spaniel ran home.
   His owner whistled loudly.

   _____

   _____

3. The students went to the library to do some research.
   Their classes were over for the day.

   _____

   _____

4. Harriet bought twenty litres of paint.
   She decided to paint the trim on the outside of her house.

   _____

   _____

5. You will not have difficulty making a good grade on the test.
   You can study very hard and work with a tutor.

   _____

   _____

6. Maria will be going to Australia.
   She wants to learn about its varied culture.

   _____

   _____

Words like "who," "whose," "whom," "which," and "that" are also subordinators and can be used to combine simple sentences into more mature sentence patterns. These more mature sentences are also complex sentences because they have an independent clause and one or more dependent clauses. These connecting words are probably familiar to you.

Cindy saw the herd at the gate.

The gate had been left open.

Cindy saw the herd at the gate *that* **had been left open**.

Jason admires Mr. Winters.

Mr. Winters requires his teams to train hard for their games.

Jason admires Mr. Winters, *who* **requires his teams to train hard for their games**.

The sentences may not always fit end to end. To combine them logically, you may have to put one idea inside the other and make changes in wording. More than one revision may be possible, depending upon the idea you want to emphasize. The important point to remember is that you are revising to make stronger sentences.

The car was stolen from the driveway.

The car belonged to my mother.

The car *that* **belonged to my mother** was stolen from the driveway.

Joseph was the best-qualified candidate.

The company hired him after one interview.

Joseph, ***who was the best-qualified candidate***, was hired after one interview.

Note The commas are required because the "who" clause does not identify Joseph. If the man's name had not been given, no commas would be used, as in this sentence: The man who was the best-qualified candidate was hired after one interview.

Joseph, ***who was hired after one interview***, was the best-qualified candidate.

Joseph, ***whom the company hired after one interview***, was the best candidate.

Note This is a more formal sentence. To learn how to use "whom" appropriately, see the special section later in this unit called "Choosing Who or Whom."

EXERCISE 2

Practise combining simple sentences using "who," "whose," "which," or "that." You may have to make some changes in wording to construct the sentences smoothly and logically.

Example:

The novel was *Moby Dick*.

We all liked that book the best.

The novel that we all liked the best was Moby Dick.

Moby Dick was the novel that we all liked the best.

1. The book was my favourite novel.
   My brother borrowed it yesterday.

   _____

   _____

2. You can count on your neighbour.
   He lives across the street.

   _____

   _____

3. Kana learned to cook chocolate cake.
   His dad liked this cake the best.

   _____

   _____

4. Please return the pen.
   You borrowed it from the student next to you.

   _____

   _____

5. The tools for the job were listed in the memo.
   The supervisor sent the memo yesterday.

   _____

   _____

6. The children are afraid to stay alone in their house.
   The children's parents work.

   _____

   _____

Putting the Dependent Clause First

Once in a while for variety, you may even want to use a sentence in which the dependent clause comes first and actually functions as the subject of the sentence. Try varying your sentence patterns by using this kind of construction. The words that begin these dependent clauses are in the list of subordinators on page 239. Each revised sentence will be stronger than the original sentence. Here are some examples:

You are going on vacation.

Where, depends on you.

Where you go on vacation depends on you.

People watch that program.

It is a mystery to me.

Why people watch that program is a mystery to me.

The committee will vote on the proposal.

It must be reported to the public.

How the committee votes on the proposal must be reported to the public.

EXERCISE 3

Use "who," "why," "how," or "that" to combine each pair of simple sentences into a stronger, complex sentence. To make your revised sentences clear and logical, make any changes in wording you think are necessary. Put the dependent clause at the beginning of the sentence, and eliminate vague words at the same time.

Example:

I want to buy a motorcycle.

It does not thrill my mom.

Why I want to buy a motorcycle does not thrill my mom.

That I want to buy a motorcycle does not thrill my mom.

1. That tree will not grow.
    It is puzzling to me.

    _____

    _____

2. The little girl likes to wear her mom's high heels.
    It is amusing to her parents.

    _____

    _____

3. The young couple can get more income.
    How to is a major problem.

    _____

    _____

4. It is the wrong way to start a business.
    They did not plan.

    _____

    _____

5. It is up to the voters.
   Someone will be elected.

   _____

   _____

6. That decision still bothers me.
   We made the decision to buy the car.

   _____

   _____

Putting the Dependent Clause Last

When revising a paragraph or an essay, you may want to eliminate short, ineffective sentences in other ways. Try putting the dependent clause at the end of the sentence and eliminate vague words at the same time.

The director's employees can solve the problem.

He has learned this.

The director has learned **how his employees can solve the problem**.

We know the answer.

At least, we could find it at the library.

We know **that we could find the answer at the library**.

EXERCISE 4

Use "who," "why," "how," or "that" to combine each pair of simple sentences into a stronger, complex sentence. Again, to make your revised sentences clear and logical, make any changes in wording you think are necessary. Put the dependent clause at the end of the revised sentence, and eliminate vague words at the same time.

Example:

The lawyer recalled the information.

Her client told her the facts.

The lawyer recalled what her client had told her.

The lawyer recalled the information that her client had told her.

1. We know the outcome.
   The issue was decided.

   _____

   _____

2. They saw the results.
   It happened after the game.

   _____

   _____

3. We know the difficulties.
   They can be overcome by hard work.

   _____

   _____

4. The archaeologists discovered the answer.
   Something was missing from the ancient ruins.

   _____

   _____

5. The artist realized the problem.
   Her painting lacked the right colours in the sky.

   _____

   _____

6. The books were shelved in the wrong place.
   The librarian realized the situation.

   _____

   _____

Choosing Who or Whom

Occasionally you may have difficulty knowing whether to use "who" or "whom" in your writing. If the subordinator is used as the subject of your dependent clause and it refers to a person, you should select the subject pronoun "who."

Bob will marry Marsha next June.

Marsha is an airline pilot.

Next June, Bob will marry Marsha, **who is an airline pilot**.

In the previous sentence, "who" refers to a person and acts as the subordinator and the subject of the dependent clause. However, if the dependent clause already has a subject, then the subordinator has to be "whom."

Bob will marry an airline pilot.

He met the airline pilot in Peru.

Bob will marry an airline pilot **whom he met in Peru**.

An easier way that might help you choose between "who" or "whom" is a simple substitution.

- If you can substitute "he" or "she" into the sentence, use "who."
- If you substitute "her" or "him" into the sentence, use "whom."

    Who (he) is coming for lunch?

    Josh, **who** (he) is my good friend, will be here soon.

In these examples, you would not use "whom" because neither "him is coming" nor "him is my good friend" is correct.

    Josh is the person **whom** (him) we selected for the job.

Note At times you may have to rearrange the dependent clause to see how the substitution works. Thus, in the previous example, "whom we selected for the job" becomes "we selected whom for the job"; using "whom" is correct because you would say "we selected *him*," not "we selected he."

You can remember whether to use "who" or "whom" more easily if you remember that the two words that end in "m" substitute for each other:

her/him ⟷ whom

she/he ⟷ who

EXERCISE 5

Revise the following draft paragraphs by combining simple sentences into complex sentences. Try to use a variety of complex sentences.

Paragraph 1

Bodybuilding is a sport that demands discipline. Bodybuilders push themselves until their muscles won't work any more. They build muscle mass. Serious athletes must work out at the gym five to seven hours a day. They feel a burning sensation in their muscles. The muscles are sore the next morning. They know they have had a good workout. Athletes must also have the willpower to adhere to a strict diet. They eat no fatty foods, especially hamburgers and french fries. They need to cut fat. They must stay on an even stricter diet than normal. They also must get plenty of sleep. They are at a party with their friends and everyone else wants to stay late. Dedicated athletes will have enough control to go home early. This dedication, however, will result in a body they can take pride in.

Paragraph 2

Though there are many educational toys in the store today, I didn't have an opportunity to learn from them as a child. However, I did learn from simple items. They were free for the taking. I mastered the fine art of making bows and arrows. I learned the types of tree branches that made strong yet flexible bows. Then I learned by trial and error. I learned how tight the string should be to make the arrow "sing." I needed a fishing pole. I learned which pieces of wood would stay strong against the pull of a hungry fish. I learned to braid bracelets from long strands of grass. I learned to take a simple piece of wood and carve it into a gun. Most educational of all, I learned to paint pictures. I made natural dye from various items. For example, I crushed blackberries to get a deep purple and used natural coal for black. These "toys" gave me amusement, but, more important, they gave me knowledge. I still possess this knowledge today.

Paragraph 3

Maintaining a healthy beehive takes careful planning by a beekeeper. He must set up a hive with wax racks. The bees can store their honey, pollen, and eggs. It is time to "rob the hive." He must be sure to leave enough honey to feed the bees during the long winter months. Sometimes there is insufficient honey or a severe winter. He must provide a sweet nectar for the bees. In the springtime, he must check the inside of the hive for more than one queen bee. In this way, he does not lose a swarm of bees to a young queen. Sometimes the bees do swarm. He must either destroy the queen or have a new, well-equipped hive ready for them to occupy. He manages the hive well. He should have a year-round supply of honey.

WRITING ASSIGNMENT

Using the steps of the writing process that you are familiar with, draft an essay on one of the following topics:

1. The most surprising, pleasant experience that has happened to you
2. The most surprising, negative experience that has happened to you

Explain at least three results that occurred because of this experience. Include an introductory paragraph that creates interest (hook) by briefly setting up the experience you remember. End the introductory paragraph with a thesis sentence that focuses on the results of the experience.

After you draft your essay, revise for content and edit for mechanics.

Content

> *Essay*

>> Check the introductory paragraph for an effective hook.

>> Check for a smooth transition between hook and thesis.

>> Check to see that the thesis sentence states a clear direction and, if you wish, previews the points covered in the paper.

>> Check to see that the voice is appropriate for purpose and audience.

> *Paragraphs*

>> Revise so that each has a clear topic sentence that develops an idea suggested in the thesis sentence.

>> Include four to six supporting sentences that are developed using short interrelated examples or an extended example.

>> Include a closing sentence in each paragraph.

Mechanics

> Check for subject-verb agreement.

> Check for consistent verbs.

> Check for a consistent point of view.

> Check for fragments, run-on sentences, and comma splices.

> Check punctuation of compound sentences.

> Check punctuation of complex sentences.

Sentence variety

> Revise short sentences into compound sentences.

> Revise sentences to include complex sentences.

Unit Seven
Making Ideas Flow Clearly

PART 1 | **Parts to Whole: Coherence**

OBJECTIVES

....

- Realize the importance of transition.
- Realize that repeated key words add coherence.
- Realize that time words and other transitional words add coherence.
- Realize that pronouns can add coherence.
- Revise a given paragraph using appropriate transitional words and phrases.
- Recognize how the divisions in the thesis sentence provide the key words for transition in the topic sentences.
- Given a thesis sentence, write topic sentences containing appropriate key words.
- Add coherence within and among paragraphs in an essay.

Clear and interesting writing has logical connections between sentences and between paragraphs, and these clear connections make the writing flow smoothly. Sometimes the relationship is so obvious to you that you do not think it is necessary to make the connection for the reader; however, it is. Writing that flows smoothly contains specific words that make the connections between ideas so the reader does not have to fill in the gaps. These connections help to clarify meaning.

Creating Coherence within Paragraphs

The following paragraph does not have clear connections between the sentences and is choppy.

> When I was growing up, I had many responsibilities around my house after school and on Saturdays. I took care of my cats. I picked up the fallen sour apples from the front yard. Trimming the juniper bushes in the back was my job. Cleaning my room was something I did once a week. Working around the house is one of my clearest memories of growing up.

Each sentence is *isolated* from the next. The sentences might just as well be in a list:

1. When I was growing up, I had many responsibilities around my house after school and on Saturdays.

2. I took care of my cats.

3. I picked up the fallen sour apples from the front yard.

4. Trimming the juniper bushes in the back was my job.

5. Cleaning my room was something I did once a week.

6. Working around the house is one of my clearest memories of growing up.

What idea ties all of these sentences together? Sentences 2, 3, 4, and 5 are all "responsibilities around my house" referred to in the topic sentence, but the sentences have no obvious connections to each other. If the connections were clearer, the information would be more meaningful to the reader.

Clear connecting words can make these sentences flow more smoothly. A revised paragraph might read as follows:

> When I was growing up, I had several responsibilities around the house. I took care of my cats <u>every day</u>. <u>After school each day in the spring</u>, I had to pick up the fallen sour apples from the front yard. <u>I usually had to do this chore first because my mom wanted the front yard clean</u>. <u>In addition to these jobs</u>, I spent <u>most</u> Saturday mornings trimming the juniper bushes in the back. <u>After finishing the trimming (or any other work I had to do)</u>, I would <u>then</u> clean my room. Working around the house is one of my clearest memories of growing up.

Specific words and phrases have been added to the first draft to make clear *when* the activities occurred in relation to each other to establish a coherent sequence of events.

These additional words and phrases are called **transitions**. When you write, select transitions that make clear, logical connections between sentences.

There are several kinds of words and phrases that can be used to create **coherence** in a paragraph:

1. **repeated key words** that refer to the *topic* idea in the paragraph: "responsibilities," "this chore," "these jobs," "the trimming."

2. special **time words** and other **transitional words** or phrases that add definite meaning to link sentences logically into a coherent whole: "every day," "after school each day in the spring," "in addition," "then."

3. **pronouns,** including possessive pronouns ("my" mom) and **words that point out** ("this" and "that"). Avoid "it," "they," and "this" whenever they do not refer to specific nouns in the paragraph.

The following paragraph lacks coherence.

> **Learning how to drive a car with a stick shift is difficult.** The location of each gear and the best speed to drive in for each gear must be learned. How to push in the clutch and change the gear to obtain the best speed can be tricky until the driver discovers just where the clutch accelerates the gear speed. Bouncing and jerking can occur until this manoeuvre is mastered. This "sweet spot" is different in all cars. Down-shifting has to be learned to allow for turns and slowing. The clutch and gear speed work together again, but the gear is shifted to slow down, not to speed up. When shifting and down-shifting are learned, usually driving is easy.

Now consider the following steps for creating coherence within paragraphs.

Repeating Key Words

Repeating **key words** that refer to the topic idea and direction is the easiest way to create coherence in a paragraph. You may want to list words that come to you or refer to a dictionary or thesaurus for variations of the key words. You do not want to look for more complicated words but simply for other common words that will repeat the topic idea without repeating the same word over and over.

The key words in the topic sentence are "learning how to shift a car" and "difficult." Here are other words that could replace "learning how to shift a car":

shifting

changing

speeds

changing gears

slowing down

procedure

Other words could replace "difficult":

hard

frustrating

demanding

complicated

tiring

bothersome

Look at the paragraph after it was revised by adding new key words:

Learning how to drive a car with a stick shift is difficult. The location of each gear and the best speed to drive in for each gear must be learned. How to push in the clutch and change the gear to obtain the best speed can be ~~tricky until~~ *tricky and frustrating until* the driver discovers just where the clutch accelerates the gear speed. Bouncing and jerking can occur until ~~this manoeuvre~~ *this complicated manoeuvre* is mastered. ~~This~~ *To make matters more challenging, this* "sweet spot" is different in all cars. ~~Down-shifting~~ *Though down-shifting is bothersome, it* has to be learned to allow for turns and slowing. The clutch and gear speed work together again, ~~but the~~ *but the procedure is harder because the* gear is shifted to slow down, not to speed up. When shifting and down-shifting are learned, usually driving is easy.

Using Time Words and Transitional Words

Special **time words** and other **transitional words** or phrases add definite meaning to link sentences logically into a coherent whole. Here are some examples of time words and other transitional words that add coherence to the paragraph:

To add something: also, too, in addition, equally important, furthermore, similarly, again, besides

To show a contrast: but, yet, however, in contrast to, on the other hand, nevertheless

To give an example: for example, for instance, thus, in particular, in other words

To compare or show similarity: similarly, in the same way

To show time sequence: then, next, first, second, later, finally, previously, afterward, after, yesterday, today, the day (or week or year) before, as, now

To emphasize: in fact, indeed, to repeat

To show space relationship: above, beyond, below, near, next to, here, there, to the left, to the right, behind, in front of

To acknowledge a point that may be the opposite of the one you are making: although, though, even though, in spite of, no doubt, of course

To summarize: finally, in conclusion, in summary, consequently, thus, therefore, as a result, on the whole, to conclude

Here is the paragraph after revision using time and transitional words:

Learning how to drive a car with a stick shift is difficult. The location of each gear and the speed to drive in ~~for~~ *before changing* each gear must be ~~learned~~ *learned first*.

How to push in the clutch and change the gear to obtain the best speed can be tricky and frustrating ~~until the~~ *until after the* driver discovers just where the clutch accelerates the gear speed. ~~Bouncing~~ *Furthermore, bouncing* and jerking can occur until this complicated manoeuvre is mastered. To make matters more challenging, this "sweet spot" is different in all cars. ~~Though~~ *In addition,* down-shifting is bothersome, ~~it~~ *but it* has to be learned to allow for turns and slowing. ~~The~~ *In the same way, the* clutch and gear speed work together, but the procedure is harder because the gear is shifted to slow down, not to speed up. When shifting and down-shifting are learned, usually driving is easy.

Using Pronouns and Words That Point Out

Pronouns, including possessive pronouns, **and words that point out** also create coherence. Possessive pronouns are words like "our," "my," "his," or "their." Words that point out are "this," "that," "these," and "those."

Now look again at the fully revised paragraph. (All the words that point out are highlighted in bold italics.) This paragraph is now coherent.

Learning how to drive a car with a stick shift is difficult. The location of each gear and the speed to drive before changing each gear must be learned first. How to push in the clutch and change the gear to obtain the best speed can be tricky and frustrating until after the driver discovers just where the clutch accelerates the gear speed. Furthermore, bouncing and jerking can occur until **this** complicated manoeuvre is mastered. To make matters more challenging, **this** "sweet spot" is different in all cars. In addition, down-shifting is bothersome, but **it** has to be learned to allow for turns and slowing. In the same way, the clutch and gear speed work together, but the procedure is harder because the gear is shifted to slow down, not to speed up. When shifting and down-shifting are learned, usually driving is easy.

EXERCISE 1

Revise the following paragraphs by adding key words derived from the topic idea, time and other transitional words, and pronouns that will make each paragraph a coherent whole.

Paragraph 1

A small lakeside park can be a haven for children. Swings are big and sturdy so children can swing, seemingly to the tops of trees. Ducks swim close to the shore to eat whatever the small visitors bring. Older children canoe through rippling water. Others stand or sit at the edges of the lake and throw out fishing lines complete with worms. The children wait for some hungry fish to bite the hook. Parents of the children relax or nap under the shade of nearby trees. Here the world feels safe as children watch other families enjoying the park.

Paragraph 2

Prepackaged, microwavable dishes are a way of life for people on the go. Prepackaged entrees for babies help working mothers serve nutritional meals for small members of the family. Older children can microwave their own dinners. When mom and dad are unable to prepare lunch, children can heat up such items as spaghetti and meatballs or chicken and rice. Entrees that appeal to the whole family can be stored in the freezer and popped into the microwave while the cook throws together a quick salad and sets the table. Chicken and rice, vegetable lasagna, or pork back ribs are a few of the many varieties available. Evening snacks can include popcorn in minutes or milk shakes that defrost in seconds. People with a microwave oven no longer have a reason for skipping a meal.

Paragraph 3

Making a quilt takes some planning. The most important part of making a quilt is selecting a design for the quilt. It is important to buy materials that look nice together. Adding some materials with different textures makes the quilt more appealing. A place to work that has lots of room helps when putting the quilt pieces together. Planning a quilting pattern that looks good helps. A tight quilting frame makes the job easier. Setting up the frame close to other family members or near the television set makes the quilting seem less boring. A beautiful quilt can be created.

Paragraph 4

Driving a school bus is a very responsible job. The driver may be expected to make all the safety checks to see that the bus is in top shape. Tires all need to be checked for proper inflation. Making sure all the children are safely seated helps prevent falls and tumbles. If seat belts have been installed, all children should be properly secured. The driver needs to be alert at all times to prevent accidents and injuries. Responsible people ensure safety for school children.

Creating Coherence between Paragraphs

Just as the sentences within each paragraph must be connected smoothly, so the paragraphs within an essay must be connected smoothly to each other. Each paragraph must flow logically to the next one. When you write an essay, you can use the three previously explained methods for connecting ideas: **key words** (repeated topic words or ideas), appropriate **time** and **transitional words** and **phrases**, and **pronouns**.

Read the following thesis sentence and topic sentences for an essay on what can be experienced at the beach. Notice the coherence provided by the words in bold type: key words (KW), time (T), other transitional words (TW), and pronouns (P).

Thesis sentence:

My family and I always look forward to going to the beach at Cavendish because of the many smells, sights, and sounds that abound there.

Topic sentence for the first support paragraph:

As soon as **we** walk onto the **beach, we** notice a multitude of both good and bad **smells**.

Topic sentence for the second support paragraph:

In addition to fragrances and **odours, we also** observe unusual **sights**—especially people.

Topic sentence for the third support paragraph:

Our **memories** of the **beach also** include a whole array of **sounds**—from small, insignificant ones to the pounding roar of the waves.

Concluding sentence:

T   T   P

Over the years, whenever we have stayed at Cavendish, we have

TW

come away with memories of our vacation **there**.

EXERCISE 2

Using the thesis sentence given, construct three topic sentences with key words that will provide transition. Then construct an appropriate concluding sentence.

1. Even though visiting a zoo can be educational and relaxing, it can be expensive.

   Topic sentence 1:

   _____

   _____

   _____

   Topic sentence 2:

   _____

   _____

   _____

   Topic sentence 3:

   _____

   _____

   _____

   Concluding sentence to begin the last paragraph:

   _____

   _____

   _____

2. Graduating from college requires intelligence, perseverance, and adequate finances.

Topic sentence 1:

_____

_____

_____

Topic sentence 2:

_____

_____

_____

Topic sentence 3:

_____

_____

_____

Concluding sentence to begin the last paragraph:

_____

_____

_____

3. Winning at board games requires strategy, interest, and luck.

_____

_____

_____

Topic sentence 1:

_____

_____

_____

Topic sentence 2:

_____

_____

_____

Topic sentence 3:

_____

_____

_____

Concluding sentence to begin the last paragraph:

_____

_____

_____

EXERCISE 3

Read the following essays and add coherence in the form of key words, time and other transitional words, and pronouns.

Essay 1

During my morning jog, I stopped and talked to a man who was carefully tending his garden. When I expressed interest in the luscious garden, he replied, "I got over five buckets of strawberries alone this summer." I was taken by surprise because the strawberry patch was somewhat small. His green bean vines that were growing along the fence were loaded with long, healthy beans, and I could only wonder how many of those he had harvested. Seeing his garden made me think of all the benefits that gardening can bring to anyone who is willing to put in the time and effort. Though having a small garden can be hard work, it can result in pleasure and savings.

The benefits of a garden do not come without work. She or he must select a location for the garden. It needs to be dug out and loosened. Sawdust, peat, and fertilizer mixed and added will allow the seeds to grow easily. Growing instructions need to be followed when the seeds are planted. The garden must be watered, weeded, and debugged daily. Watering at the correct time of day is necessary. Keeping the weeds to a minimum makes the garden vegetables stronger. A good gardener prepares a good place and watches the plants as if they were helpless, defenceless creatures.

A garden can bring many pleasures. The sight of small sprigs reaching up through the soil toward the sun gives the feeling of capturing a small part of nature and getting in touch with the earth. What greater satisfaction is there for the gardener than to know that she or he has used the elements to produce food? More than enough is produced, and the gardener can proudly share the crisp flavour of fresh produce with a neighbour. In view of the much-publicized insecticides on commercial produce, the gardener can use natural combatants such as ladybugs or praying mantis or ingenuity, to preserve the vegetables and feel comfortable knowing the products from the garden are healthy. A garden can be the source not only of food and pride, but also of peace of mind.

Having a small garden to bring in fresh vegetables provides a savings. Each year grocery prices slowly creep up unnoticeably on such items as lettuce and tomatoes. Tomatoes that last year cost $2.50 a kilogram, cost $3.00. Lettuce is sold at 99¢ a head instead of 69¢ a head. The gradual price increase makes one wonder if the consumer will ever see the end. A pack of tomato or lettuce seeds costs about 70¢ total, and these seeds can provide enough tomatoes and lettuce for an entire summer. Extra vegetables can be frozen or canned to provide a year-round supply of fresh food. Surplus vegetables can be sold to bring in extra money. Trading produce with other gardeners prevents buying so much at the grocery store. Gardens can add much-needed pocket change and give the feeling of defeating the inflationary war.

One can transform a tiny seed into baskets of delicious, healthy food. By gardening, a person can experience a miracle of nature and can save money at the same time. The only way to find out is to try.

Essay 2

"I would like to take good pictures, but I am not sure if I can learn what is necessary." This statement is frequently made by people who would like to take good pictures. They may want to have family pictures or have a visual record of favourite vacation spots, but they do not feel good about their ability. Confidence can easily be built, however, since learning to use a camera is not hard, especially if the beginning photographer can watch someone explain the fundamentals. To take good photographs, a beginning photographer needs some technical knowledge, a little artistic judgment, and patience with beginning errors.

Learning to be a photographer means that some technical knowledge of basic camera functions is needed. Using a camera is more than just looking through the viewfinder and pressing the shutter. It is important to know how shutter speed and the amount of light going through the lens work together to produce a picture. Different shutter speeds and different amounts of light produce different kinds of pictures. The camera must be focused correctly. The beginning photographer can buy a fully automatic camera and not have to learn about shutter speed, light, or focusing. Letting an automatic camera do its own thing can produce good pictures. Greater satisfaction comes from having the knowledge to choose camera functions rather than letting the camera choose the basics.

Acquiring artistic skill means that the photographer can judge or "see" a picture even before looking through the camera. Looking at the particular way objects or people are placed affects the finished picture. Knowing that the centre of interest should not go right in the middle of the frame will create a more pleasing design. A picture of a cat sitting in a window will look better if the cat is either up or down from centre and left or right of centre. The window can provide a nice frame for the picture. The photographer should be able to see the cat within the window frame even before looking through the viewfinder. Looking beyond the cat at what is in the background will affect the finished product. It takes some creative power of observation to arrange a background that will emphasize the centre of interest rather than detract from it. If the background behind the cat shows a cluttered back porch, the cat will no longer be the main part of the picture. Composing a picture is a skill that can be learned.

Much satisfaction can come to beginning photographers if they are patient with their first errors—pictures that they really do not want to show to anybody. The most common mistakes might be to cut off the top of people's heads, or their legs, or to lop off the beautiful bushy tail of the cat in the window. A beautiful red mountain might reflect the setting sun and create a spectacular scene— only to have the picture spoiled by power lines cutting through the middle. Patience with the first bad pictures will help the inexperienced photographer learn to overcome whatever problems created the poor photographs.

Technical skill and artistic judgment will help a photographer take personally satisfying pictures. Patience will allow the person to acquire these skills gradually. Patience will help the photographer learn from the first mistakes and have confidence in a slowly developing ability. A person can learn enough to take good pictures but must not expect too much too soon. A wish can turn into a reality if someone takes the first step, having faith in the ability to learn the skill needed.

PART 2 | Something to Think About, Something to Write About

"Home on the Prairie with Margaret Laurence"

By **Douglas McArthur,** *Assistant Travel Editor*

1 In 18 childhood years spent in this small prairie town, Jean Margaret (Peggy) Wemyss lost her mother, saw her mother's sister become her step-mother, lost her father and lived in three houses—one of them twice.

2 The woman the world now knows as Margaret Laurence (1926–1987) also stored up enough memories and impressions to recreate Neepawa as the fictional town of Manawaka in five classic works of Canadian literature. Fans who come to seek out the landmarks and ghosts that inhabit the Laurence landscape will not be disappointed.

3 Only about 4,000 arrived last year. Neepawa is a 45-minute detour off the Trans-Canada Highway making it too remote for rush-through tourists. Yet it offers the same sense of connection with a fictional universe that readers discover in Lucy Maud Montgomery's Prince Edward Island, James Joyce's Dublin or Mark Twain's Hannibal, Mo.

4 Visitors to Neepawa can locate the three childhood houses of Peggy Wemyss (pronounced Weems). They can even tour the one she called "The Big House"— her home from age 10 until she left for college in Winnipeg eight years later. Now in a state of transition from a cultural centre to a museum—but not really either—the Margaret Laurence Home is the best starting point for touring this town of 3,400 inhabitants.

5 The road to Neepawa from Winnipeg skirts a series of prairie towns that, from the distance, look "dull, bleak, flat, uninteresting," all the things Margaret Laurence said her town was not. Hers was, "A place of incredible happenings, splendours and revelations, despairs like multitudinous pits of isolated hells. A place of shadow-spookiness, inhabited, by the unknowable dead. A place of jubi-lation and of mourning, horrible and beautiful."

6 The Neepawa that visitors discover today is a solid, middle-class town of big houses, groomed lawns and tree-lined streets. In an age when many small towns are withering or becoming dormitory communities for cities, Neepawa exudes a sense of pride, prosperity and permanence, a carrying-on of the values of the town's Scots and Irish Presbyterian pioneers.

7 The sign the way in calls it "Manitoba's most beautiful town" and it could well be true.

8 The Margaret Laurence Home that is open to the public is a two-storey buff-coloured brick structure, built in 1985. In was owned by the author's maternal grandfather, John Simpson, a "stern, authoritarian old man" to young Peggy. She feared and disliked him when she and her stepmother moved in after her father's death, but later made him a sympathetic character in *A Bird in the House*.

9 After first opening to the public in 1987, the building housed an art gallery, quarters for cultural groups and a room where literary scholars could conduct

research. But as donations expanded the collection of Laurence memorabilia, the gallery was closed and some groups evicted.

10   The volunteers who brought the project this far are strapped for cash and still undecided on how to proceed. In the meantime, visitors will have to put up with a tribute building in transition. Wood panelling from the 1950s has been removed, the woodwork refinished and renovations to the original parlour are under way. Oak pillars and wooden filigree doorway decorations; possibly the work of Grandfather Simpson, a cabinet-maker and undertaker, have been restored and put back into place.

11   Peggy's bedroom, with the attached nook where she and friend Mona drew their own blood to look at through a microscope, can be visited but has not been restored. Items associated with the author—her Remington manual typewriter and the gown she wore to receive honourary degrees—are displayed haphazardly throughout the house.

12   But what the project lacks in funds is more than made up for in enthusiasm and imagination. The opening of the home to the public was celebrated with a release of pigeons (substituted for doves that would have symbolized Laurence's links to the peace movement but might not have survived a prairie winter). The burning of the mortgage two years ago was accomplished by dropping flaming papers from Peggy's old bedroom into a barbeque on the front lawn.

13   People still live in Peggy's other childhood houses, so visitors must make do with driving past and photographing them from the outside. Her favourite was "the Little House" with her "favourite attic room" where she lived as a small child and again after her father's death.

14   The big red-brick Wemysss house, where she lived for 1 1/2 years in between, is now covered in white stucco. "I never liked it much," she wrote later in life. "It was too large, too imposing—our father's house, not really ours."

15   Riverside Cemetery "up on a hill where the tall spruces stand like dark angels," is a mandatory stop on any Margaret Laurence tour. The Stone Angel—which became the symbol for 90-year-old Hagar Shipley in the novel of the same name—is, as Laurence wrote, "doubly blind"—made of stone and with the eye-balls blank. It is actually a memorial to John Davidson, one of Neepawa's founders.

16   The angel is not on the brow of a hill as the novel places it. That location is where the author herself is buried, close to a lilac grove and overlooking the valley below.

17   Other Neepawa landmarks do not relate directly to Laurence, but they confirm her vision of a town with traditions and history stretching over generations, of a small community "set in a sea of land" that prospered in good times, suffered in the Depression and was wounded permanently by the loss of its young men at Dieppe.

18   There is the 1884 courthouse for what was once Beautiful Plains County, Knox Presbyterian Church now entering its second century and the Roxy Theatre, originally opened in 1906 as an opera house.

19   The repository for the town's history is the Beautiful Plains Museum, housed in the former CNR train station designed in 1902. Freight trains still shuttle back and forth on their way to and from the Neepawa grain elevator next door, occasionally cutting off access to the museum and blocking patrons inside.

20   The museum is a tribute to Neepawa residents who have donated family treasures and to a volunteer committee that strives to preserve and display them.

Money is too scarce to create a big-city museum look or to keep all items in pristine condition. But the collection is extensive and the organization of material well-thought out.

21   Housed over three storeys are brittle newspapers and fading photos, pioneer farm tools, hand-made toys, old wedding dresses, medical instruments, church altars and army uniforms, mockups of a log cabin and a one-room school and relics of the town's Ukrainian, Polish and First Nation heritage.

22   Margaret Laurence—like her Manawaka heroines—eventually left the small town and the prairie but kept it forever in her head. Those who stayed behind kept Neepawa alive in the present while preserving its past in the museum.

Something to Write About

Using one of the ideas or questions listed below, develop either a thesis sentence that states a clear direction or, if you wish, a thesis sentence that previews the points to be covered in the paper. Then draft your essay. Include instructions.

1. Describe the house of your childhood.
2. Why do we preserve homes of famous people? (Use an example of a celebrity's home you have visited or would like to see.)
3. What role does a museum play in the life of a city?
4. Describe the road leading into your hometown.
5. How do you feel about the place in which you grew up?
6. When you travel to a new city, what places do you visit?
7. How did the city (town, village) of your youth help shape your view of the world?
8. Describe your impressions of a city or town fictionalized in either the movies, television or books.

After you draft your essay, do each of the following:

Revise it so that it has an effective introduction that includes a hook, a transition, and a thesis sentence.

Be sure that each support paragraph has a strong topic sentence and ample supporting examples.

Check for unity and a smooth flow of ideas.

Revise to include a strong concluding paragraph.

Check for subject-verb agreement.

Check for consistent verbs.

Check for consistent point of view.

Check for fragments, run-ons, and comma splices.

Check punctuation of compound sentences.

Check punctuation of complex sentences.

PART 3 | **Essays for Discussion and Analysis**

Education

Adapted from the original by **Jan-Georg Roesch**, *Student*

1   Only fifteen months ago I was sitting in a typical German classroom day-dreaming through the lecture and hoping for a miracle that my grades would improve. All the help I got came too late because I had already wasted too much time in the first semester. My goal was to finish Abitur and then continue going to a university. The goal just seemed to vanish in thin air, and how was I going to do my master's degree? Fortunately, my father was going to retire soon, and plans were made to make a permanent settlement in Phoenix because my grandmother lived there. Hence, I was given the opportunity to continue my educational goal in America, skip the draft in Germany, and enjoy the warm Arizona climate.

2   In Germany, I would have to complete thirteen years of school and attain the diploma in order to go to a university. I had completed twelve of the thirteen years and didn't have enough points to get into the last year. Furthermore, the conditions I was facing made it more or less impossible for me to repeat the class, and I did not want to take the risk of losing the prediploma. The only solution left was to come to the United States and try to finish my educational goal. Again, I was very fortunate to have friends in Phoenix who made my entrance into Arizona State University very easy. Although I knew that much of what I had learned over the past two years was going to be repeated, I accepted the challenge because I did not really have a choice.

3   Yet, finishing the educational goal was not the only reason for my coming here. At the age of eighteen every male teenager who had completed school was picked for the draft. This meant I had to serve for fifteen months and receive a wage of $70 a month. The alternatives were either to sign up for a longer period, either for four or six years, or do social work for the same period. I was not too crazy about the idea of serving fifteen months; I felt that it was a waste of time because the program does not offer any real educational use. Of course, the service does provide people with good educational service; however, I would have to sign up for a longer time period.

4   Finally, my last criterion for coming to Phoenix was the warm climate. I had spent over eighteen years of my life living in countries where the climate was mild, damp, wet, and sometimes very cold. Having the flu five times a year was nothing uncommon and seemed more or less to be part of daily life. In addition, it would sometimes rain for days nonstop and flood all the rivers, a disaster which normally resulted in flooding the cellar or creating total chaos in the streets. The so-called summer was usually brief. The warm weather might have stayed for two weeks when the next rain clouds were already expected. The winter period was mainly characterized by residents watching tourists streaming out to see warmer places or sitting next to the warm fireplace and sipping hot chocolate.

5   It is close to one year now since I moved, and I do not regret living the eighteen years in countries with colder climates. However, I also feel that moving to Phoenix will bring me new experiences that I could not have encountered if I had

stayed in Germany. I will learn new cultural traits and behaviours that differ from the European heartland. Yet, most important of all, I can finish achieving my educational goal that I once dreamed of fifteen months ago.

<table>
<tr><td>

Questions on Content

1. Why could the author not go to a university in his native country?
2. What were two reasons for his move to Phoenix?
3. How long has he lived in the United States?

</td><td>

Questions on Form

1. What key words from the thesis sentence does the author use for coherence in each topic sentence?
2. What is the transition that links paragraphs 2 and 3?
3. How does the author use time words to provide coherence in paragraph 4?

</td></tr>
</table>

A Bad Experience

Adapted from the original by **Dominique Charpentier,** *student*

1   In January 1966, my eldest brother was hospitalized for a detachment of the retina, and he stayed a long month lying in obscurity, with the fear of remaining with a blind eye. A few months before, he was still a very athletic and hard-working student preparing for his bachelor's degree. On a fall day, as he was playing volleyball, the ball hit his face, causing trauma and the progressive loss of sight. The surgical operation and the hospitalization significantly altered my brother's life, leading to drastic, though temporary, changes in his character, his education, and his relationships.

2   After this stay in the hospital and the obligation to keep quiet at home during two more months, it was easy to notice an obvious change in my brother's character. He knew that in the future he could not continue to practise sports with the same fervour he enjoyed so much, and he became bitter. His sight became weak, and he was afraid of the possibility of injury to the other eye or another injury to his face. What a change for the so active and lively young man he was before! He became worried about his sight, fearing a new operation or new failing vision. He had lost his constant optimism and, in a way, something from his youth.

3   If this operation changed my brother's character and behaviour, it also involved the necessity to choose a different way of education. For him it was the important year of the General Certificate of Education, and, of course, he failed his examination. He then had to stay in this class for a second year, and he understood easily that this additional year in school would keep him from joining the engineering college he yearned for. He had to reexamine his plans and his desires according to the new possibilities offered to him. Finally, one year later, he registered in a college specializing in computers. The college was four hundred kilometres away from home. That was very different from his first ambition, but it was the start of a new direction for him.

4   As a result of this trauma, not only did my brother's character and his education change but his personal relationships gradually changed directions. As he began again in the same class, he had to leave his former classmates, losing sight of his best friends. One year later, the break was still worse between him and his friends. He had to go away from home to a distant college, leaving his family and his friends. There, in a way, a new life was beginning for him. Some months later, of course, he had made new friends. He entered into friendships with very interesting teachers and kept in touch with them for many years. At last, it was the place where he met his intended wife and where he settled down to start a family.

5   Today my brother is an engineer in an important computer firm. He enjoys his work, and he loves his family. From his accident he learned that nothing is determined once and for all. An operation in 1966 forced him to change his way of life. He came out of this turmoil more mature and more open-minded. As he says often, it is no good to feel regret. The best thing to do is to turn over the page.

Questions on Content

1. How did her brother's character change?
2. What year did he undergo surgery?
3. Why did he have to have surgery?

Questions on Form

1. What key words are used in the topic sentences to add coherence?
2. What time words and phrases are used?
3. What other transitional words are used?

PART 4 | The Writer's Tools: Reviewing Punctuation

OBJECTIVES

....

- Review the uses of the comma.
- Learn the proper use of quotation marks.
- Learn the use of the apostrophe.
- Learn the use of underlining.
- Learn the use of parentheses.
- Review ways of marking sentences.

Mastering the art of written communication means being able to use appropriate punctuation. Think of punctuation marks as traffic signals. Traffic signs tell people when to stop or slow down, when to be aware of dangers, when to pause, and when to go on. Without accurate road signs, a person's journey through the city would be dangerous. In writing, if you do not place accurate "traffic signals" because of inappropriate or confusing punctuation, your reader's journey through your sentences and paragraphs will be just as risky.

Using Commas

Using a comma correctly is not a matter of guess work. If you follow some very simple rules and use commas only when you know the rules, you will be able to use commas correctly.

Uses of Commas

items in a series

introductory expressions

clarity

    identifying and nonidentifying expressions

    interrupters

    misunderstandings

addresses and dates

direct address

Items in a Series

- **A comma is used to separate three or more items in a series of words, phrases, or clauses.**

A series uses the same grammatical construction—for example, three or more nouns, verbs, phrases, or dependent clauses.

Series of Words

John had a **hamburger, french fries, and a milk shake** for lunch.

Jerry noticed that the dog was **cold, wet, and hungry**.

Books, pens, and papers must be brought to class.

The **blue, yellow, and green** tablecloth is new.

Series of Phrases

People brought aid **to the elderly, to the homeless, and to the sick**.

Playing blackjack, eating Chinese food, and sleeping late in the morning are all activities that Trent enjoys.

The child was guilty of **kicking the nurse, biting the thermometer, and writing on the wall**.

Series of Dependent Clauses

Because the weather turned bad, because the park became crowded, and because we had no more money, we left Ontario Place.

I know **why you came, who sent you, and when you will leave**.

The quality of a product is judged by **how long it will last, what it is made out of, and who makes it**.

- A comma is *not* used between two words, two phrases, or two dependent clauses that are joined by a coordinating conjunction.

    Randy received a raise in pay and better working hours.

- A comma is not used to separate three or more items in a series if a coordinating conjunction is used to separate these items.

    Randy received a raise in pay and better working hours and more insurance.

EXERCISE 1

Punctuate the following sentences by adding the necessary commas. Look for items in a series. If no punctuation is needed, write "none" beside the sentence.

Example:

The material was written to be read ˄ to be absorbed ˄ and to be understood.

1. The team of Huskies needs to be fed and groomed.

2. The jackpot winner was laughing jumping up and down and clapping his hands.

3. At the party, the guests were eating and drinking and talking.

4. We can record a song if you get here by 7:00 p.m. if you bring your guitar and if the microphone works.

5. Richard fed the dog in the backyard the horse in the south field and the cat by the barn.

6. The small sparkling odd-shaped rock was discovered by the farmer taken to the appraiser and sold for a lucrative price.

EXERCISE 2 ›

Punctuate the following paragraphs by adding commas where necessary. Look for items in a series. Do not remove any commas already in the paragraphs.

Paragraph 1

Grandparents aunts uncles and cousins gathered for the annual picnic at the park. Together they ate the attractive and well-prepared food that smelled delicious tasted great and satisfied everyone. Then the older children took turns playing volleyball tennis and tetherball. Some of the grandparents spread blankets on the green grass for the little ones to take their bottles to nap or just to rest. Sometimes the adults, too, fell asleep. Later they took turns riding on the park's train looking through the model-train exhibits and reading about the history of trains. Soon, however, everyone returned to the picnic tables to munch on leftovers and talk about last year's picnic.

Paragraph 2

The cavy or guinea-pig breeder took excellent care of her animals. Every morning she gave them pellets water carrots and alfalfa. Every day she also checked the hutches for newborn babies for any signs of illness and for any guinea pigs that needed to be put into different cages. Every other day she cleaned each hutch and put in new bedding. Once a week she added vitamin C to their water bottles to make sure there were no pigs with a vitamin C deficiency. Because she did not want young boars to create problems in the hutches, she separated them at four weeks of age from the females from the older boars and from the young babies. Customers who bought pets from her knew that they had purchased guinea pigs that had healthy coats were free from disease and would tame easily.

Introductory Expressions

- Use a comma to set off introductory expressions, which may be single words, phrases, or dependent clauses.

Single Words

Silently, the man walked through the park.

Effortlessly, the figure skaters performed their new routine.

Phrases

In the morning, I will work in the yard.

Running in the yard, the puppy stumbled over her own feet.

Stung by the bee, the child began to cry.

Dependent Clauses

When I get to the lake, I will put up the tent.

After he got to work, he realized he had left the papers at home.

Because I am not hungry, I will not go out to eat.

Note If the expression is placed somewhere else in the sentence, it is not set off by a comma.

The man walked **silently** through the park.

He will work in the yard **in the morning**.

I will put up the tent **when I get to the lake**.

EXERCISE 3

Punctuate the following sentences by adding commas where necessary. Look for introductory expressions. If no comma is needed, write "none" beside the sentence.

Example:

Carefully the father placed the baby in her crib.

1. When Bob finished landscaping his yard he needed a vacation.

2. In June the locusts began their chatter.

3. Absentmindedly the lab technician shelved the glass bottles.

4. In a matter of minutes the teenager ate four hamburgers and two orders of fries.

5. Becky was on a diet because she had gained too many pounds over the summer.

6. Although the weather was cold the children went out to play.

EXERCISE 4

Punctuate the following paragraphs by adding commas where necessary. Look for introductory expressions first, and then look for items in a series. Do not remove any commas already in the paragraph.

Paragraph 1

According to Luigi Ciulla the biggest challenge he faced when he came to Canada in 1961 was to find a job. Because he had trouble filling out an application people would say, "I'm sorry. We don't have a job for you. When you learn to speak English then we can hire you." Just to work on an assembly line employees had to pass required IQ tests. Because the tests were in English and because they were timed it was almost impossible for a person who spoke very little English to pass them. Luigi said that even though some words are learned by studying books some words just cannot be learned without living in a country. He also said that he didn't know anyone, so it was hard to find people to use as references on application forms. Because he had never worked in this country he had no references from previous employers either. One other obstacle in finding a job was lack of any "connections." There was no one who could help him get a "foot in the door." He also had to face the reality that many jobs were far away and transportation to these jobs was hard. He said, "Even if I knew how to drive it was hard to pass the written test for a driver's licence." That was thirty-three years ago, and today he is hiring people to work for him in his own business.

Paragraph 2

Fly-fishing is a combination of luck knowledge and experience. The angler has to have the correct combinations of flies for the correct lake. Sometimes, however, a person can cast out use the right fly yet still not catch any fish. Other times he can be at the wrong lake use the wrong flies and catch fish. A little knowledge about nature, however, helps the angler pick the right night to "pull in that big one." From experience the expert angler knows that windy weather stirs up the lake and makes the water cloudy, and, as a result, the fish do not see the flies and do not bite. This also helps to explain why the fish feed at night when the moon is bright and why these same fish choose to feed during the day if there is very little or no moon to give light during the night. Experience comes in handy when the angler knows the precise second to jerk on the line to hook the fish. No matter how a person looks at it know-how makes a difference in fishing, but a person can't discount other factors.

Commas for Clarity

The need for a clear set of road signs referred to previously really becomes evident when you want to be sure your meaning is clearly understood by the reader. Knowing for sure whether or not to use commas helps you to write exactly what you mean. As a result, your reader is more likely to understand your meaning right away and not stumble and reread your sentences several times.

Identifying and Nonidentifying Expressions

- **If an expression is necessary to identify the noun that comes before it, it is called an identifying expression, and no commas are used to set it off.**

    The dogs **that have had their shots** will be allowed in the mall.

    The chickens **that got out of their pen** laid eggs all over the yard.

    The elephant **with twins** is in the next exhibit.

No commas are used because each expression in bold type identifies the noun before it. The expression could not be left out without creating confusion or changing the meaning entirely.

- **If the noun is already specifically identified, the expression that comes after it is nonidentifying, and commas are used to set it off.**

Using commas means that this nonidentifying expression adds more information to the sentence and could be left out without creating confusion. Names (proper nouns) provide specific identification.

    Lester, **who left town yesterday,** took my fishing rod with him.

    Leroy, **my cousin,** will be in town tomorrow.

However, if you put "cousin" first, *no* comma is used because Leroy identifies which cousin.

    My cousin Leroy will be in town tomorrow.

Interrupters   A comma is used before and after an expression that is not really a part of the sentence structure. If the word or expression is not part of the basic structure, the expression is probably an interrupter. Taking these interrupters out of the sentence would still leave a complete idea. However, these interrupters often serve as transition and can be necessary for clarity and a smooth flow of ideas.

Yes, I finished a long time ago.

I will, **of course,** be on time.

"Yes" and "of course" could be left out, leaving complete sentences, but these interrupters would help these sentences connect more smoothly with others in a paragraph.

Words or Phrases Often Used as Interrupters

as a matter of fact	no
for example	of course
for instance	well
however	yes
nevertheless	

Misunderstandings In some sentences, commas are necessary to prevent confusion and misunderstanding. Without a comma, the exact meaning of the following sentence is not clear.

Besides Mary Lou Anne is the only experienced driver.

Notice how adding a comma not only makes the meaning clear right away, but also changes the meaning in each sentence.

Besides, Mary Lou Anne is the only experienced driver.

Besides Mary, Lou Anne is the only experienced driver.

Besides Mary Lou, Anne is the only experienced driver.

EXERCISE 5

Punctuate the following sentences by adding commas where necessary. Look for nonidentifying expressions, interrupters, and possible misunderstandings. If no comma is needed, write "none" beside the sentence.

Example:

The employee who received the award has a special parking space. *none*

Zebras on the other hand were feisty.

1. The candy for instance that the children ate made them sick.

2. Red Deer, Alberta which I visited last summer is a friendly town.

3. My brother Jim as a matter of fact lives in Banff during the winter months.

4. The girl who is a gymnast is from Thunder Bay.

5. We should nevertheless get everything in top order.

6. Muzafar who always is on time made an A in the course.

7. The book had 175 pages many filled with beautiful photographs.

8. Edmonton for instance is known for its cool summers.

EXERCISE 6

Punctuate the following paragraphs by adding commas where necessary. Look first for interrupters, nonidentifying expressions, and expressions that can only be understood with commas. Then look for items in a series and introductory expressions. Do not remove any commas already in the paragraph.

Paragraph 1

The trend of the eighties to rely heavily on "disposables" has created a throwaway society. Everywhere we look trash that has to be disposed of is piling up. People litter the countryside with plastic aluminum cans and glass bottles. At home disposable plates cups plasticware and of course diapers are filling the plastic bags that must be transported to the local landfill. At hospitals paper gowns disposable thermometers towels used in surgery and miles of plastic tubing cannot be resterilized and reused and as a result are being sent to special landfills for medical wastes. Though it takes many years for the paper products to break down in the landfills scientists predict that the plastics will take several hundred years to break down. Styrofoam especially could take an inordinately long time to degrade. These nonbiodegradable plastics are petroleum-based and keep us importing oil to make them. Making aluminum cans likewise uses up our natural resources. Not only does it use up natural resources to make new plastic products aluminum cans and bottles, but it takes energy to manufacture these products. Reusing aluminum cans and glass bottles saves resources and energy. Recycling helps cities and towns that are filling up their landfills and running out of room to construct more.

Fortunately we as environmentalists are trying to make an effort to reverse the trend and use products more than once before throwing them away.

Paragraph 2

Lewis M. Terman an American psychologist found many interesting facts about gifted people in his thirty-five-year study. He found that the general image most have of the gifted being small in stature physically weak and book wormish "nerds" was not true. His study indicates rather that the gifted were superior intellectually as well as physically socially emotionally and morally. Gifted children walked earlier had fewer physical problems and had better posture. When compared with the general population they had a low incidence of delinquency mental illness or alcoholism. Generally the gifted seemed to be more happily married to have fewer divorces and to have fewer offspring. After studying Terman's classic work one cannot help wondering what causes giftedness.

Addresses and Dates

- A comma is used to set off the name of a city, county, province, and postal code in a sentence. There is, however, *no* comma between the province and postal code.

    His work in **Montreal, Quebec,** was of monumental value to all.

    Jason's home at 2 Colborn Street**, Guelph, Ontario N1G 2M5,** burned to the ground.

- A comma is used to set off the month, day, and year in a sentence. However, when the day is omitted, a comma is not used.

    On **June 4, 1990,** I fell in love.

    I went to Cape Breton in **July of 1993**.

    The company opened for business in **November 1991**.

Direct Address

- Use a comma when you use a name in speaking directly to someone.

    "**Dave,** will you please finish this work?"

    "When**, Theresa,** do you think this work will be done?"

However, do not use a comma when you are speaking *about* someone.

    Sam wants to try out for the elite soccer team.

EXERCISE 7

Punctuate the following sentences by adding commas where necessary. Look for addresses, dates, and direct address. If no punctuation is needed, write "none" beside the sentence.

1. Address the card to 644 Pinewood Road North Bay Ontario P1B 4N6.

2. Sondra when did you visit your cousin in Burnaby British Columbia?

3. Why Katsura did you leave him behind?

4. June 18 1971 is my birthday Jim.

5. An ice storm on December 1 1992 was responsible for hundreds of accidents.

6. The letter sent to 70 Dejong Crescent Winnipeg Manitoba R6T 3K5 was returned to the sender.

7. July 1st is a national holiday.

8. On May 26 1996 I plan to graduate from college.

EXERCISE 8

Punctuate the following paragraphs by adding commas where necessary. Look first for addresses and dates. Then look for items in a series, introductory expressions, interrupters, and nonidentifying expressions. Do not remove any commas already in the paragraphs.

Paragraph 1

On September 1 1939 Germany invaded Poland and started World War II. Beginning in 1940 Hitler invaded Belgium Luxembourg Denmark Norway and France. On April 9 1940 the Germans seized Denmark and invaded Norway. Just one month later on May 10 1940 Germany invaded Belgium. Just a few days later on May 14 1940 the Netherlands surrendered. Because England had treaties with France she made good her commitment, and on September 3 1940 Great Britain and France declared war on Germany. On May 26 1940 the Allied Powers began their heroic evacuation at Dunkirk, a seaport in northern France. By 1940 the entire European continent was at war. Then on June 22 1941 Germany invaded the Soviet Union. On December 7 1941 Japan attacked Pearl Harbor bringing the United States into the war. By now almost all countries in the world were involved in this devastating war.

Paragraph 2

During my childhood I moved many times. On July 2 1968 my family and I moved to Kingston, Ontario where my mother attended the nursing program at the university. When she graduated on June 2 1971 we moved to London, Ontario where she got a job working for the hospital there. However we moved again in March of 1974 because my mom got a better job. We stayed there for a little over two years, and on November 7 1976 we moved to Walmer Road Toronto Ontario. We stayed in that house for a year and a half but moved for what I hoped would be the last time when my mom remarried on May 14 1978. But as fate would have it only a few months later we moved again, and on October 3 1978 we moved to a house in the country.

Using Quotation Marks

- Use quotation marks to enclose the exact words (direct quotation) of a speaker. A comma is used to set the direct quotation off from the rest of the sentence.

  Tom said, **"The house that I like is for sale."**

  "The house that I like," Tom said, **"is for sale."**

  However, if you are summarizing or using the word "that," quotation marks are *not* used.

  Tom said **that we could move in tomorrow**.

  Mom said **that we would be going on vacation soon**.

Other Punctuation with Quotation Marks

- Periods and commas are *always* placed *inside* the quotation marks.

  Margarita said, "I want a hot fudge sundae."

  "I want a hot fudge sundae," Margarita said.

- Semicolons are *always* placed *outside* the quotation marks. *for 2 sent.*

  Janice said, "I believe we will buy that house"; then she left.

- Question marks and exclamation points are placed inside or outside the quotation marks. Place them inside if the direct quotation is the question or exclamation.

  Tom asked, "When can we move into the house?"

Place them outside if the entire sentence is the question or exclamation.

Did Tom say, "We can move in in three weeks"**?**

Quotations within Quotations

- Single quotation marks are used inside the double marks when a quotation exists within another quotation.

"I heard Keith say, '**Be careful**,' before the board fell," said Stan.

Stan said, "Before the board fell, I heard Keith say, '**Be careful**.'"

Words or Phrases That Require Special Attention

- Quotation marks or italics are used to set off words that are referred to as words and are not a part of the basic sentence structure.

When you use the word "**clever**," use it carefully.

Try not to use **very** too often.

- Quotation marks are used to set off words that are slang or that are used ironically.

That was a "**rad**" movie.

Would you like to drive the "**green bomber**"?

Titles Contained Within Larger Works

- Use quotation marks around the title of any selection that has been published within a larger work.

"**Learning to See**" is the title of the second chapter in Eudora Welty's book <u>One Writer's Beginnings</u>.

"**On His Blindness**" is a poem that has been included in many anthologies.

Using Apostrophes

An apostrophe is used to show ownership. An apostrophe is also used in contractions, which are informal.

Possessive Nouns

- Form the possessive of singular nouns by adding an apostrophe and -s.

Put **John's** book on the **car's** fender.

- Plural nouns and proper nouns that end in -s form the possessive by adding just an apostrophe.

The **books**' edges have been torn.

The **students**' assignments were all completed on time.

Charles' eyes are brown.

- Plural and proper nouns that end in any letter other than -s form the possessive form by adding an apostrophe and -s.

  The **worker's** wages were paid by the company.

  The puppy played with the **children's** toys.

Note Do not confuse a possessive noun with a plural noun that ends in -s.

  The **books** (plural noun) have not been torn.

  (The books do not own anything.)

  The **books'** edges (ownership) have not been torn.

  (The edges belong to the books; therefore, an apostrophe is used.)

Possessive Pronouns

- An apostrophe is not used to form the possessive of personal pronouns.

  His book was left on the floor.

  This book is **hers**.

  It's time for us to look at its internal structure.

Note "It's" with an apostrophe is a contraction for "it is." The "its" (without an apostrophe) is a possessive pronoun.

  However, an apostrophe is used to form the possessive form of indefinite pronouns.

  One's work must be done well.

  He is **everybody's** favourite trumpet player.

  The smoke from **somebody's** barbecue drifted through the neighbourhood.

Contractions

- In contractions, an apostrophe indicates that one or more letters have been left out.

  He'll have to get there early to get a parking spot.

  That's a nice place to go on vacation.

Using Underlining

- The title of any piece of writing that has been published by itself should be underlined or put into italics. If it has been published within a larger collection or magazine, use quotation marks.

I read the article "Building Solar Homes" that appeared in the <u>Builders' Guide</u>.

<u>Of Mice and Men</u> is a novel that appeals to many people.

I enjoy reading <u>The Vancouver Sun</u>.

Using Parentheses

- Parentheses are used to enclose expressions or sentences that are separate from the main thought of the writing. If the entire sentence is set off by parentheses, the end punctuation mark is inside the closing parenthesis. If the expression is part of a sentence, the punctuation is outside the closing parenthesis.

(The first part needs to be read carefully.)

Please read all of the first chapter carefully (especially the first part).

EXERCISE 9

Punctuate the following sentences by adding the necessary punctuation. Look for missing quotation marks, for words showing ownership, and for contractions. Add any other punctuation marks that are needed.

1. I hope to go to the lake Rene said.

2. As soon as I get home from work Keith said I need to get my car inspected.

3. Keith said that he needs to get his car inspected as soon as he gets home from work.

4. I was sorry Kristi said that Ron lost my favourite book The Red Pony.

5. The poem The Horses is in the book To Read Literature by Donald Hall.

6. Everybodys favourite dessert is homemade ice cream said Susans mother.

7. Close the window Kim Chuck said or Joes camping gear will get wet.

8. According to the book Sheltie Talk its important to brush the dogs coat well.

EXERCISE 10

Punctuate the following paragraphs. Look first for quotations, words that show ownership, titles, and contractions. Then insert any commas that are needed. Do not remove any punctuation marks already in the paragraphs.

Paragraph 1

Surgeons who operate on patients who are not put to sleep sometimes say things that can upset their patients. They forget that the patients are already anxious about having surgery. When Dr. Madox operated on a patient he tuned in some fast music and jokingly commented There, thats good. It helps me cut faster. When he started sewing up the incision before getting the lab results the patient asked if he had gotten all of the cancer. He replied I hope so. Later on when he was putting in the sutures he stated Oh no the nurse is going to be upset with me when she takes this stitch out. I snipped the ends too close. He then headed for the door and said Ill see you later. The patient asked him if he was coming back, and he just bounced on out the door. Fortunately one of the nurses told the patient that the doctor was going to the lab to get the results. Though the surgery was over the patients return visit to the doctors office to have the stitches removed was dreaded.

Paragraph 2

Growing up on a farm offered me many opportunities to study nature. My family always had a garden, and I had the chance to watch my father supply the needed fertilizer water and care for full growth of the finest vegetables. In addition by reading and applying information found in Organic Gardening a useful magazine I learned more about natural gardening. I learned natures way of helping plants along through the use of earthworms ladybugs and praying mantis. This was a natural wonder. In the spring I had the occasion to observe the birthing of many animals a miracle in itself. Through my fathers guidance on the farm I understood what it meant to be in tune with and dependent on nature.

Punctuating Sentences

To maintain clarity, you must mark your sentences clearly. Though all sentences in a paragraph revolve around one main idea, you must separate ideas into sentences.

Simple Sentences

- All simple sentences must end with an end mark like a period, exclamation point, or question mark.

    We went to the store.

We bought new school clothes.

We bought the best school clothes ever!

Would you like to go shopping with us?

Compound Sentences

- Simple sentences are combined into compound sentences by using a semi-colon, a comma and a coordinate conjunction, or a semi-colon followed by a conjunctive adverb and a comma.

Semicolon

We went to the store; we bought new school clothes.

A Comma and a Coordinate Conjunction

We went to the store, and we bought school clothes.

A Semicolon Followed by a Conjunctive Adverb and a Comma

We went to the store; therefore, we bought new school clothes.

Compound-Complex Sentences

- Complex sentences can also be joined to simple sentences by using a comma and a coordinate conjunction or by using a semicolon followed by a conjunctive adverb and a comma.

A Comma and a Coordinate Conjunction

After we got paid, we went to the store, and we bought school clothes.

A Semicolon Followed by a Conjunctive Adverb and a Comma

After we got paid, we went to the store; consequently, we bought new school clothes.

EXERCISE 11

Using all the punctuating skills covered in this section, punctuate the following paragraphs. Do not remove any punctuation marks already in the paragraphs.

Paragraph 1

Summertime offers many opportunities for children of all ages with extra time on their hands. Kids can spend their days at the Boys or Girls Club where they can swim play supervised sports and even go on field trips. If there is no Boys Club or Girls Club for a small fee they can swim in public pools. There they can join swim teams take swim lessons or just swim for pleasure. Often libraries that are equipped with reading programs are close by. There children can attend story time to hear such storybooks as Bears on Wheels or The Honey Hunt check out videotapes or books or leisurely look through magazines. In the evenings these same children can play little league baseball or watch other children play ball. If they want to earn extra money they can collect aluminum cans glass plastic or paper to recycle. Also a great potential exists for a lawn service that can bring in money for school. Older children can also earn extra money babysitting or working for the city supervising younger children in recreational programs. Opportunities abound for kids everywhere therefore all they need to do is look around.

Paragraph 2

Poetry is an art form that can be enjoyed sometimes because of the meaning sometimes because of the way it is written and other times because of both. Can anyone read Walt Whitmans Leaves of Grass without saying That is nice really nice Lines that seem to stick in the mind are often written with a strong message. For instance the lines from Anne Sextons poem Abortion Somebody who should have been born is gone stay in the mind long after the poem has been read. Whenever the question of abortion arises these lines are recalled in the mind again and again. Thomas Hood wanted to change labour laws in England. In his poem The Song of the Shirt he wrote With fingers weary and worn,/With eyelids heavy and red,/A woman sat, in unwomanly rags,/Plying her needle and thread— John Milton, married but miserable, spent much effort inserting lines about divorce into his poetry in an attempt to change the laws that forbade divorce. Some poets however do not moralize but simply present things the way they are James Dickey a well-known American poet wrote of adultery objectively without making any judgment of its wrongness or rightness. On the other hand Joyce Peseroff expresses her ideas in The Hardness Scale in which she seems to be relating a womans feelings about a man who is not such a perfect man. Diane Wakoski writes of revenge in her poem You, Letting the Trees Stand as My Betrayer In this poem nature will pay back someone who loved her and then left her. The meaning is there in these and many other poems but the way they are written makes the lines occur over and over in the readers mind.

WRITING ASSIGNMENT

Freewrite or brainstorm to generate ideas that can be used to analyze or explain the reasons why you enjoyed one of the following. (Do not retell the story.)

1. A movie
2. A play
3. A book

After you draft your essay, revise for content and edit for mechanics.

Content

Essay

Check introductory paragraph for effective hook.

Check for a smooth transition between hook and thesis.

Check to see that your paper has a strong thesis sentence.

Check to see that the voice is appropriate for purpose and audience.

Paragraphs

Revise so that each has a clear topic sentence that develops an idea suggested in the thesis sentence.

Include four to six supporting sentences that are developed using short interrelated examples or an extended example.

Include a closing sentence in each paragraph.

Mechanics

Check for subject-verb agreement.

Check for consistent verbs.

Check for a consistent point of view.

Check for fragments, run-on sentences, and comma splices.

Check for correct punctuation.

Sentence Variety

Revise short sentences into compound sentences.

Revise sentences to include complex sentences.

Check for coherence between and within paragraphs.

Unit Eight

Composing with Effective Alternate Patterns

PART 1   Parts to Whole: Modes of Development

OBJECTIVES

....

Develop an essay by using:

- Illustration
- Comparison/contrast
- Classification
- Definition
- Cause/effect analysis
- Process
- Argumentation

When you master the multiparagraph essay using examples, you are well on your way to becoming an effective writer. You have learned a basic skill. However, it is vital that you understand the *connection between the precise form of this essay*, as you have practised it, *and the other types of writing* that you will need to do.

Mastering a basic plan for a multiparagraph essay is similar to mastering the art of home building because becoming a good builder requires certain skills, just as becoming an effective writer requires precise skills. The following chart shows how both building a house and writing an essay are similar.

Building a Home	Writing an Essay
Planning	Planning
gather house-plan ideas	prewrite
design home for owner	consider audience and purpose
make drawings	outline

Building

    pour foundation

    erect frame

    put on roof

Writing

    draft a thesis sentence

    draft support paragraphs

    draft an introduction and a conclusion

Finishing touches

    add finishing touches

Finishing touches

    revise and edit

If you want to be able to write an effective essay, then you need to understand each step of the process. You might think of these components of the essay as a building code to be followed. This building code keeps you from doing shoddy work; however, it does not keep you from being creative and adding variety to your writing. If you drove into a town and saw that every house was built exactly alike, you might wonder what was wrong with the people who lived there and whether they possessed any creativity at all. Likewise, if you learned to write a multiparagraph essay using examples and never learned to go beyond that point, you might cause people to wonder whether you, too, lacked creativity. Always remember, though, that *every* completed house has a foundation, a frame, a roof, and finishing touches. It may also have a fireplace, an upper story, picture windows, or whatever the builder wanted to add to make the house more appealing. You, too, will want to have that something extra in your essays, even though *every* essay that you write needs an introduction, support paragraphs, a conclusion, and finishing touches.

Once you have learned to write a thesis sentence and support it with examples, you can learn other methods to organize ideas in an essay. You always begin a paper by planning first, using freewriting or brainstorming to generate ideas. Then the organization, no matter what pattern you select, will include an introduction, support, and a conclusion.

Developing a paper can be done in different ways that are usually called **modes of development**. These modes are ways of developing and organizing the support paragraphs that explain a thesis sentence in an essay. The word "mode" can also mean "method." There are many modes of development; all of the following basic modes are important for writers to learn.

Modes of Development

illustration

comparison/contrast

classification

definition

cause/effect analysis

process analysis

argumentation

Your purpose for writing a paper will determine the mode you select to develop your essay. If your purpose is to show how home builders can create energy-efficient homes, you could **illustrate** the way different houses are built to conserve energy. If you are writing an article for home buyers, your purpose might be to **compare/contrast** two different kinds of homes available so that the reader can then decide which home is better. If your purpose is to inform the population about the types of homes available to them, your job would be to **classify** the types of homes available in a certain area. If you wanted to **define** a home, you might include not just the physical structure but the emotions associated with a home. If you want to explain *why* someone wanted to build a home, your purpose would be to explain the **causes** of that event. If you want to discuss remodelling parts of an existing home rather than buying a new home, your purpose would be to explain *how* to remodel or the **process** of remodeling. If you are a person who sells homes, your purpose might be to use an **argument** that would persuade a first-time home buyer that purchasing a repossessed home in need of repair would be more advantageous than buying a new home.

This unit shows how the general subject "homes" can be developed into different kinds of essays, depending upon the particular purpose of the essay. Using the same topic, homes, each of the seven modes of writing is explained and illustrated.

Illustration

In Unit 5, "Writing with More Depth and Variety," you studied how to use examples to clarify and support topic ideas in paragraphs and essays. This use of examples is a mode of development called **illustration**. Previously, you practised writing paragraphs and essays by supporting a topic sentence or a thesis sentence with clarifying details and examples. These examples were illustrations.

To use illustration well in writing a longer paper, you do not need to learn a new way of generating ideas. The simple writing process you used earlier in this text is appropriate in this part, too.

Freewrite/brainstorm your topic.

Group ideas to find a direction or point of view for your topic.

Freewrite/brainstorm again for more details and examples.

Arrange similar details and examples into groups and compose your thesis sentence

Begin drafting the support paragraphs for your essay.

Draft an introduction and a conclusion.

Revise and edit.

The *purpose* of an illustration paper is to explain or clarify by giving specific examples that show the reader "in what way" the topic idea is true. If you say that "when you build a new home, you can make the home energy-efficient by changing the structure," then you need to follow up with specific examples that illustrate structural changes. The entire paper should contain the examples and illustrations that would show how structural changes make the home more energy-efficient.

The *topic* for an illustration paper can be any subject you can convincingly explain by giving examples or illustrations. It is one of the most frequently used modes of writing.

Basically, the pattern of *organization* for this mode of development looks like this:

1. The introductory paragraph includes a hook, a transition, and a thesis sentence.

2. Each support paragraph includes a topic sentence and examples or illustrations.

3. The conclusion includes a restatement of the main idea that the examples have illustrated.

When you use this pattern for a multiparagraph essay develop each supporting paragraph with examples or illustrations. During drafting, you can choose short, interrelated examples or a single, extended example or illustration.

In this section, you are *not* learning a new mode or pattern of development. You are learning that you can use a process and pattern that you have already practised in many writing assignments. You have just learned a new descriptive phrase for it—*development by illustration.*

Suppose you want to write a paper to explain or illustrate to a homeowner the ways in which a house can be energy-efficient. Through brainstorming/freewriting you have written the following possible thesis sentence:

> A homeowner can have an energy-efficient home by changing certain features in construction, installing energy-efficient devices inside the home, and planning landscaping to control the amount of heat or cold coming into the home.

The following essay shows how you can use illustrations to support this thesis.

A Home for the 1990s

hook   1   Thirty years ago, homeowners believed that there were no limits to the energy needed for them to live a comfortable life. They assumed they had the right to own a home without even thinking about how much energy the house required. For most Canadians today, part of the dream still

transition   includes owning a home complete with modern appliances. This dream, however, can turn into a financial nightmare if careful attention is not given to using energy wisely. Having a home that uses too much energy can be a

thesis sentence   financial drain for the owner and, in the long run, for the country. However, a homeowner can have an energy-efficient home by making certain changes in construction, by installing energy-efficient devices inside the home, and by planning landscaping to control the amount of heat or cold coming into the home.

topic sentence 1	**2**
illustration 1	

When the house is built, the homeowner can have certain features changed or added so that the home will be energy-efficient. For example, in hotter regions the country, the roof overhang should be large enough to keep the high summer sun from shining on most of the walls. In the winter, because of the changing position of the sun, the low winter sun can warm the house by shining on the walls under the overhanging roof. When plans are being made for the house, the owner can consider block or brick construction. Also, good insulation in the walls and attic can save energy in both summer and winter. Although they may cost more money to put in, special double-paned windows and weather stripping will save energy, too. All these structural features add up to long-range energy savings.

illustration 2

illustration 3
illustration 4

concluding sentence

topic sentence 2 3

If saving energy in the 1990s is important, one of the best ways is to install energy-efficient devices inside the house. Even small changes can be made, such as adding an insulating blanket to the hot-water tank. Putting up drapes with a thermal lining will also help save energy. The most energy can be saved, however, by the type of heating-cooling unit installed in the home. Most recently, the "seasonal energy efficiency ratio" (SEER) provides the best guide as to the type of unit to install for heating or air conditioning. These ratios are given in numbers like 9, 10, or 11, and by selecting a unit with a high number, the homeowner can save energy as well as money. A new kind of compressor called a scroll compressor is now available for air-conditioning units. This new unit can provide a SEER as high as 12. This new scroll compressor uses so much less energy than older units that the cooling costs will be cut in half. Installing energy-efficient devices like these can help a homeowner conserve energy.

illustration 1
illustration 2
illustration 3

concluding sentence

topic sentence 3 4

After considering these ways of conserving energy in a home, the owner should also plan the landscaping so that it helps the house become energy efficient. If the house is new, the owner can plant trees and shrubs around the home so that they shade the walls and the roof from the sun. Grass that requires little water can be planted close to the house to absorb heat from the sun. In the wintertime, people who live on the prairies should trim their trees and shrubs to allow the sun to shine on the house. In colder parts of the country, landscaping should be planted to give shade in the summer, but trees and shrubs that lose their leaves in the winter should be chosen so that the sun can shine into the house. Landscaping provides more than an attractive appearance for a home. It becomes one more way for the homeowner to save money in day-to-day operating costs and, at the same time, to save energy for the country.

illustration 1

illustration 2
illustration 3
illustration 4

conclusion

concluding paragraph 5

In the 1960s Canadians used as much energy as they wanted without concern for the future. In the 1990s, though, they have learned that sources for energy are limited and that some kind of conservation is needed if they are going to have enough energy in the future to live in the same kinds of comfortable homes they have always dreamed about. Owning a home today carries the responsibility to reduce the amount of energy required to operate a house and live a comfortable life at the same time. By paying attention to the energy-saving devices now available, homeowners can save money for today and natural resources for tomorrow.

Write an essay developed through illustration. Use one of the following topics. During revision and editing, refer to the checklist in the inside back cover.

1. Problems with transportation in your city
2. Ways to keep a body healthy
3. Factors to consider before buying a puppy
4. Summer projects for the family
5. Reasons people enjoy vacationing in national parks
6. Reasons people dread or look forward to holidays
7. Reasons discipline is important at home or at school

Comparison/Contrast

Another useful way to present information is to explain how two items relate to each other. This kind of essay is called a **comparison/contrast** paper. The *purpose* of a comparison/contrast paper is to show how two things are alike or different. A paper may be primarily a comparison (how two items are alike) or primarily a contrast (how two items are different).

The *subject* for a comparison/contrast paper is two people, objects, or places that have both similarities and differences. Two children, two lakes, or two types of flowers would probably be contrasted because their similarities are obvious. A donkey and a person or a flower and a person would probably be compared because it is not so easy to see how they are alike. There would be no point in contrasting two objects if there was no way that they were alike. Likewise, there would be no point in comparing two objects that had no differences. In your other college classes, you may be asked to explain the similarities or differences between ideas: two opinions, two philosophical theories, two personalities, or two political candidates.

In a true comparison/contrast essay, both sides are treated fairly, with equal amounts of information given for each side. However, one side may appear to have the advantage over the other. If one side does have an advantage, it should be discussed *last*. The side with more disadvantages should be covered *first* or should start the discussion. For instance, if you were to write a paper about prime ministers Clark and Trudeau, you would want to start your essay with Clark because he lacked the glamour and prestige of Trudeau and because Clark's term in office was only a few months.

If the paper is a true comparison/contrast, it will present the same characteristics for both sides. For example, if you talk about Clark's appearance, you must also talk about Trudeau's appearance. If you talk about Clark's family, you must talk about Trudeau's family, also. In this way, the paper is balanced equally between the two sides.

The pattern for multiparagraph essays that you have learned can be modified to satisfy the organization for this comparison or contrast paper. Your freewriting or brainstorming is done in two separate parts. One section should be labelled "comparisons" or "similarities." The other section should be labelled "contrasts" or "differences."

Suppose you were writing an essay comparing and contrasting the costs of buying either a new or a "fix-up" home. In this case, "item 1" under consideration might be "fix-up homes," and "item 2" might be "new homes." Your brainstorming might be done in lists like the ones that follow.

Similarities
Item 1 (fix-up homes) and Item 2 (new homes)

_____

_____

_____

Differences

Item 1 (fix-up homes)   **Item 2 (new homes)**

_____   _____

_____   _____

_____   _____

The next step is to group ideas and decide whether the information you have generated can be explained best in a paper that presents contrasts (differences) between the two items or in a paper that presents comparisons (similarities) between the two items. The clustering of ideas should lead to an outline that includes a thesis sentence and a preview of the main points to be covered in the paper. There is no definite, correct number of similarities or differences, but the more points you have, the more paragraphs you will have and the better your thesis will be supported.

If the paper is a _comparison_, it will focus primarily on _similarities_, but to be realistic and effective, it may begin and end with significant differences. If the paper is a _contrast_, it will focus primarily on _differences_, but, again, to be realistic and effective, it may begin and end with significant similarities.

You now have one more decision to make: how to present your explanation. Choose one of the following patterns:

1. items discussed in alternate paragraphs

2. items discussed in two distinct parts within each paragraph

3. items discussed in alternate sentences within each paragraph

On the following pages are outlines of these patterns; each pattern is then followed by a draft of an essay written according to that pattern.

Items Discussed in Alternate Paragraphs

1. The introductory paragraph previews major differences (with brief reference to a major similarity) *or* previews major similarities (with brief reference to a major difference).

2. Support paragraphs include points of contrast (or comparison) in an alternating pattern.

   First point
   > Paragraph 1: Item 1 (fix-up homes)
   > Paragraph 2: Item 2 (new homes)

   Second point
   > Paragraph 3: Item 1
   > Paragraph 4: Item 2

   Third point
   > Paragraph 5: Item 1
   > Paragraph 6: Item 2

   Fourth point (if needed)
   > Paragraph 7: Item 1
   > Paragraph 8: Item 2

3. The concluding paragraph re-emphasizes major differences (with a brief reference to a major similarity referred to in the introduction) *or* re-emphasizes major similarities (with a brief reference to a major difference referred to in the introduction).

Read this example of an essay with paragraphs that alternate between the items.

Saving Money on a New Home

hook   **1**   Jason and Gabrielle had been married for two years when they decided that they were ready to start a family. But they decided that they should buy a house before they had children. On their combined income of $82,000 a year, they felt they could afford a home of their own. After they had contacted a real estate agent and read articles about home buying, they narrowed their options to buying a new home or a "fix-up" home. The decision would be difficult because both options would result in an investment with a guaranteed return. As many other Canadians have learned, the initial money invested, the continual costs, and the return for the investment would vary according to the option selected.

brief reference to similarity

thesis sentence

first point of contrast   **2**   **Probably the most marked difference between buying a new home and a "fix-up" home is the initial costs involved.** A "fix-up" home does not always have a fixed down payment and sometimes can be purchased at the rate of interest paid by the previous homeowners. The cost of a "fix-up" home is set by the current homeowner, but many times an offer of a few thousand dollars less will be accepted. A "fix-up" home is often sold "as is" with an opportunity for the buyer to check everything out before signing the closing papers. Anything that is defective can be negotiated to be repaired or to lower the cost to the buyer. Anything that breaks

item 1 discussed

after the final papers are signed, though, becomes the responsibility of the new owner. A "fix-up" home often needs landscaping but usually has grass, shrubs, and trees that are already established.

first point of contrast   3

item 2 discussed

On the other hand, a new home has higher initial costs and often requires a 10–20 percent down payment with interest rates set by current bank regulations. The initial cost of a new home is set, and an offer at a few thousand dollars less will be met with rejection or even laughter from the salesperson. A new home is not equipped with all of the appliances that will be needed; for example, a washer and dryer, and purchasing new appliances may also mean paying extra for extended warranties. Another initial cost could be upgrading any standard feature that comes with the home, including carpeting or even paint and roofing materials. A new home may be sold with standard landscaping that includes levelling the yard, seeding the lawn, and planting one or two trees, but the buyers may find that they have to spend additional money in the beginning for landscaping.

second point of contrast   4

item 1 discussed

Once the house is purchased, the costs do not end. There are still payments to be made each month. Buying a "fix-up" house means that payments are less than they would have been had the home been purchased new at the current house prices. In addition to house payments, owners of "fix-up" homes often need to spend money on major renovations, such as restoration of walls or replacement of plumbing lines. Remodelling, however, is done to please the owners, and they can often save money by doing the work themselves or getting several bids to keep costs down. Another cost would be taxes, but they may be lower on a "fix-up" home.

second point of contrast   5

item 2 discussed

In contrast, when a new home is purchased, house payments are generally higher by at least 10–15 percent over house payments for "fix-up" homes, which might amount to several hundred dollars. However, owners of new homes seldom need to spend additional money repairing fixtures or appliances for the first five to six years, nor do they usually spend money altering the structure of the new home. Buyers of brand new homes do spend money decorating their homes; however, the decorating is not so extensive or so expensive as the remodelling that is needed in a "fix-up" home. Owners of new homes also pay taxes, which may be higher than the taxes on a "fix-up" home.

third point of contrast   6

item 1 discussed

Though there are many costs, these homes also represent a return to buyers because they both appreciate in value within a certain time frame and they both bring satisfaction. A "fix-up" house, especially an ugly duckling among swans, can appreciate rapidly following repairs. If the home is bought at half the going price of the surrounding homes, it can equal or surpass the other homes within a year. Owners of "fix-up" homes often need to spend months cleaning up and fixing both the interior and exterior of their new home but are able to give the home a distinct personality that is its own.

third point of contrast   7

item 2 discussed

During the same time frame, a new home will appreciate slowly at the same rate as the other homes in the neighbourhood. The home is bought at the same price as the other homes in the neighbourhood, and its value will not change substantially unless it is abused. Buyers of brand new homes are often pleased with their home when they move in and can enjoy it immediately. They do need to spend time and money, though, getting a lawn started and caring for the outside of the home.

concluding paragraph
brief reference to
similarity

8   Both types of homes are available in a wide range of sizes, styles, and locations that appeal to many people. Some people enjoy spending their spare time working on their homes, whereas others do not. Whether buying a new home or a "fix-up" home, all new homeowners can feel a sense of pride in their investment. And, like Jason and Gabrielle, they have an ideal place to raise a family.

Items Discussed in Two Distinct Parts within Each Paragraph

1. The introductory paragraph previews major differences (with brief reference to a major similarity) or previews major similarities (with brief reference to a major difference).

2. Support paragraphs include points of contrast (or comparison) in an alternating pattern.

   First point
   > Paragraph 1: Item 1 (fix-up homes)
   > > Item 2 (new homes)

   Second point
   > Paragraph 2: Item 1
   > > Item 2

   Third point
   > Paragraph 3: Item 1
   > > Item 2

   Fourth point (if needed)
   > Paragraph 4: Item 1
   > > Item 2

3. The concluding paragraph re-emphasizes major differences (with a brief reference to a major similarity referred to in the introduction) *or* re-emphasizes major similarities (with a brief reference to a major difference referred to in the introduction).

Saving Money on a New Home

hook

1   Jason and Gabrielle had been married for two years when they decided that they were ready to start a family. But they decided that they should buy a house before they had children. On their combined income of $82,000 a year, they felt they could afford a home of their own. After they had contacted a real estate agent and read articles about home buying, they nar-

brief reference to
similarity
thesis sentence

rowed their options to buying a new home or a "fix-up" home. The decision would be difficult because both options would result in an investment with a guaranteed return. As many other Canadians have learned, the initial money invested, the continual costs, and the return for the investment would vary according to the option selected

first point of contrast
item 1 discussed

2   **Probably the most marked difference between buying a new home and a "fix-up" home is the initial costs involved.** A "fix-up"

home does not always have a fixed down payment and sometimes can be purchased at the rate of interest paid by the previous homeowners. The cost of a "fix-up" home is set by the current homeowner, but many times an offer of a few thousand dollars less will be accepted. A "fix-up" home is often sold "as is" with an opportunity for the buyer to check everything out before signing the closing papers. Anything that is defective can be negotiated to be repaired or to lower the cost to the buyer. Anything that breaks after the final papers are signed, though, becomes the responsibility of the new owner. A "fix-up" home often needs landscaping but usually has grass, shrubs, and trees that are already established. **On the other hand**, a new home has higher initial costs and often requires a 10–20 percent down payment with interest rates set by current bank regulations. The initial cost of a new home is set, and an offer at a few thousand dollars less will be met with rejection or even laughter from the salesperson. A new home is not equipped with all of the appliances that will be needed, for example, a washer and dryer, and purchasing new appliances may also mean paying extra for extended warranties. Another initial cost could be upgrading any standard feature that comes with the home, including carpeting or even paint and roofing materials. A new home may be sold with a standard landscaping that includes levelling the yard, seeding the lawn, and planting one or two trees, but the buyers may find that they have to spend additional money in the beginning for landscaping.

Once the house is purchased, the costs do not end. There are still payments to be made each month. Buying a "fix-up" house means that payments are less than they would have been had the home been purchased new at the current house prices. In addition to house payments, owners of "fix-up" homes often need to spend money on major renovations, such as restoration of walls or replacement of plumbing lines. Remodelling, however, is done to please the owners, and they can often save money by doing the work themselves or getting several bids to keep costs down. Another cost would be taxes, but they may be lower on a "fix-up" home. **In contrast**, when a new home is purchased, house payments are generally higher by at least 10–15 percent over house payments for "fix-up" homes, which might amount to several hundred dollars. However, owners of new homes seldom need to spend additional money repairing fixtures or appliances for the first five to six years, nor do they usually spend money altering the structure of the new home. Buyers of brand new homes do spend money decorating their homes; however, the decorating is not so extensive or so expensive as the remodelling that is needed in a "fix-up" home. Owners of new homes also pay taxes, which may be higher than the taxes on a "fix-up" home.

Though there are many costs, these homes also represent a return to buyers because they both appreciate in value within a certain time frame and they both bring satisfaction. A "fix-up" house, especially an ugly duckling among swans, can appreciate rapidly following repairs. If the home is bought at half the going price of the surrounding homes, it can equal or surpass the other homes within a year. Owners of "fix-up" homes often need to spend months cleaning up and fixing both the interior and exterior of their new home but are able to give the home

item 2 discussed

second point of contrast   3
item 1 discussed

item 2 discussed

third point of contrast   4

item 1 discussed

item 2 discussed

a distinct personality that is its own. **During the same time frame**, a new home will appreciate slowly at the same time as the other homes in the neighbourhood. The home is bought at the same price as the other homes in the neighbourhood, and its value will not change substantially unless it is abused. Buyers of brand new homes are often pleased with their home when they move in and can enjoy it immediately. They do need to spend time and money, though, getting a lawn started and caring for the outside of the home.

concluding paragraph   5

brief reference to similarity

Both types of homes are available in a wide range of sizes, styles, and locations that appeal to many people. Some people enjoy spending their spare time working on their homes, whereas others do not. Whether buying a new home or a "fix-up" home, all new homeowners can feel a sense of pride in their investment. And, like Jason and Gabrielle, they have an ideal place to raise a family.

Items Discussed in Alternate Sentences within Each Paragraph

1. The introductory paragraph previews major differences (with brief reference to a major similarity) *or* previews major similarities (with brief reference to a major difference).

2. Support paragraphs include points of contrast (or comparison) in an alternating pattern.

    First point
        Paragraph 1: Item 1 (fix-up homes)
                     Item 2 (new homes)
                     Item 1
                     Item 2

    Second point
        Paragraph 2: Item 1
                     Item 2
                     Item 1
                     Item 2

    Third point
        Paragraph 3: Item 1
                     Item 2
                     Item 1
                     Item 2

    Fourth point (if needed)
        Paragraph 4: Item 1
                     Item 2
                     Item 1
                     Item 2

3. The concluding paragraph re-emphasizes major differences (with a brief reference to a major similarity referred to in the introduction) *or* re-

emphasizes major similarities (with a brief reference to a major difference referred to in the introduction).

Saving Money on a New Home

hook   1   Jason and Gabrielle had been married for two years when they decided that they were ready to start a family. But they decided that they should buy a house before they had children. On their combined income of $82,000 a year, they felt they could afford a home of their own. After they had con-

brief reference to
similarity

tacted a real estate agency and read articles about home buying, they narrowed their options to buying a new home or a "fix-up" home. The decision would be difficult because both options would result in an investment with

thesis sentence

a guaranteed return. As many other Canadians have learned, the initial money invested, the continual costs, and the return for the investment would vary according to the option selected.

first point of contrast   2   **Probably the most marked difference between buying a new**
item 1 discussed   **home and a "fix-up" home is the initial costs involved.** A "fix-up" home does not always have a fixed down payment and sometimes can be

item 2 discussed   purchased at the rate of interest paid by the previous homeowners. A new home has higher initial costs and often requires a 10–20 percent down pay-

item 1 discussed   ment with interest rates set by current bank regulations. The cost of a "fix-up" home is set by the current homeowner, but many times an offer of a

item 2 discussed   few thousand dollars less will be accepted. The initial cost of a new home is set, and an offer at a few thousand dollars less will be met with rejection or

item 1 discussed   even laughter from the salesperson. A "fix-up" home is often sold "as is" with an opportunity for the buyer to check everything out before signing the closing papers. Anything that is defective can be negotiated to be repaired or to lower the cost to the buyer. Anything that breaks after the final papers are signed, though, becomes the responsibility of the new

item 2 discussed   owner. A new home is not equipped with all of the appliances that will be needed, for example, a washer and dryer, and purchasing new appliances may also mean paying extra for extended warranties. Another initial cost could be upgrading any standard feature that comes with the home, including carpeting or even paint or roofing materials. A "fix-up" home often

item 1 discussed   needs landscaping but usually has grass, shrubs, and trees that are already
item 2 discussed   established. A new home may be sold with standard landscaping that includes levelling the yard, seeding the lawn, and planting one or two trees, but the buyers may find that they have to spend additional money in the beginning for landscaping.

second point of contrast   3   **Once the house is purchased, the costs do not end. There are still**
item 1 discussed   **payments to be made each month.** Buying a "fix-up" house means that payments are less than they would have been had the home been pur-

item 2 discussed   chased new at the current house prices. When a new home is purchased, house payments are generally higher by at least 10–15 percent over house payments for "fix-up" homes, which might amount to several hundred dol-

item 1 discussed   lars. In addition to house payments, owners of "fix-up" homes often need to spend money on major renovations, such as restoration of walls or replacement of plumbing lines. Remodelling, however, is done to please the owners, and they can often save money by doing the work themselves or

item 2 discussed   getting several bids to keep costs down. However, owners of new homes seldom need to spend additional money repairing fixtures or appliances for the first five to six years, nor do they usually spend money altering the structure of the new home. Buyers of brand new homes do spend money decorating their homes; however, the decorating is not so extensive or so expensive as the remodelling that is needed in a "fix-up" home. Another cost would be taxes, but they may be lower on a "fix-up" home. Owners of new homes also pay taxes, which may be higher than the taxes on a "fix-up" home.

item 1 discussed

item 2 discussed

third point of contrast   4   **Though there are many costs, these homes also represent a return to buyers because they both appreciate in value within a certain time frame and both bring satisfaction.** A "fix-up" house, especially an ugly duckling among swans, can appreciate rapidly following repairs. If the home is bought at half the going price of the surrounding homes, it can equal or surpass the other homes within a year. A new home will appreciate slowly at the same rate as the other homes in the neighbourhood. The home is bought at the same price as the other homes in the neighbourhood, and its value will not change substantially unless it is abused. Owners of "fix-up" homes often need to spend months cleaning up and fixing both the interior and exterior of their new home but are able to give the home a distinct personality that is its own. Buyers of brand new homes are often pleased with their home when they move in and can enjoy it immediately. They do need to spend time and money, though, getting a lawn started and caring for the outside of the home.

item 1 discussed

item 2 discussed

item 1 discussed

item 2 discussed

concluding paragraph   5   Both types of homes are available in a wide range of sizes, styles, and locations that appeal to many people. Some people enjoy spending their spare time working on their homes, whereas others do not. Whether buying a new home or a "fix-up" home, all new homeowners can feel a sense of pride in their investment. And, like Jason and Gabrielle, they have an ideal place to raise a family.

brief reference to similarity

The previous patterns reflect a paper that is primarily a contrast. A *comparison* paper would also follow one of the same patterns; however, it would begin and end with differences, and the support paragraphs would *focus on similarities.*

WRITING ASSIGNMENT

Write an essay developed through comparison/contrast. Using the list below, decide what two specific items you plan to compare or contrast. During revision and editing, refer to the checklist in the inside back cover.

1. Show how two holidays are alike or different.
2. Show how physical or mental abuse are alike or different.
3. Show how a vacation in the city and a vacation at a national park are alike or different.
4. Show how a living pet and a stuffed animal are alike or different to a child.
5. Show how two children are alike or different.
6. Show how competitive swimming and football are alike or different.
7. Show how owning an old car or owning a new car are alike or different.

Classification

Another method of organizing information is called classification. **Classification** means grouping objects, people, or events on the basis of similarities or characteristics they have in common. Each of the groups formed on this basis would be a *category*.

For example, if you wanted to open a small clothing store, it would be much easier for your customers to find what they wanted to buy if items were first grouped in logical categories. Your customers would understand categories like children's clothing, women's clothing, and men's clothing. If you did not form these categories or groups, your customers would have to hunt for a boy's shirt among dresses, men's shirts, ties, or women's shoes—and go searching on and on for what they needed to buy. One way, then, to *classify* the items in the store would be by the age and/or sex of the people for whom the clothing is appropriate. Other logical categories within each of these groups would be underwear and sportswear. By providing your customers with logical categories or groups of items, they could find their way around and you could manage the store better.

Classification can be a useful way of presenting information clearly, but it is not really new for you. When you learned to group the items in your brainstorming, you were also classifying them into groups that have characteristics in common. Classifying and grouping, then, are two words for the same kind of thinking.

The *purpose* for classifying items in a paragraph or an essay works in two ways. First, classification can help you, as the writer, clarify for yourself and explain in writing what many separate items have in common. Second, your reader can in turn better understand the information you are presenting.

One important point to remember about classification, however, is that it is a way of thinking about *similar* characteristics of objects or people or events. The items within each category should have many characteristics in common if the groups are to be useful in your writing. The categories, however, should not ignore so many differences that the groups become illogical.

The *topic* for a classification paper is any group of things that have characteristics in common and can be put into categories. You can classify people by age, sex, occupation, and interests. You can classify cities by size or location. You can classify schools by size or types of programs.

Here are the distinct parts of a classification paper:

1. The introduction contains the thesis sentence, which includes the categories to be discussed in the essay and establishes the basis for the classification.

2. Each support paragraph discusses a separate category established in the introduction. (Each paragraph explains how the items in each category are alike. Each paragraph may also explain how each category is different from the other categories rather than having the reader figure out what the differences are.)

3. The conclusion reaffirms the categories established in the thesis sentence.

The following essay shows how *classification* has been used to organize the information needed by someone who is going to buy a house for the first time.

Buying a House for the First Time

hook   1   Why in the world do so many people every year want to buy a home? Why do they want to take on the often difficult-to-reach goals of paying for and maintaining their own homes? Well, the answers are related to "being a success" or "having a real part of the Canadian Dream" or "always wanting to own a home of their own." Whatever the reasons are at the beginning, people thinking about buying a home for the first time usually begin to try to find out what kinds are available and how much they cost. If they know very little about real estate, they may soon become overwhelmed by the whole process. If they start with some basic knowledge, however, they **transition** can find the process of buying a home to be fun and educational. The basic **thesis sentence** knowledge that the first-time buyer should have is an understanding of the three main categories of homes available for purchase—townhouses, condominiums, and single-family residences.

support paragraph 1;   2   When a young person or a young couple starts thinking of buying a **discusses category 1** home, the idea of owning a townhouse seems appealing. Townhouses are places of residence where the owner buys not only the building but also the land the building sits on. They are not like houses, though, because there is usually only a very small patio or terrace or courtyard that goes with the building. Some townhouses may have only a small plot of ground for a little flower garden by the front door. If there is a community pool or TV satellite dish, it is usually there when a person purchases the townhouse. Townhouse owners do not have to belong to an association that requires fees and monthly meetings. In size, townhouses can be as small or as large as other medium-sized houses. They can contain a living and/or dining room, one or more bedrooms, a kitchen, and various storage areas like closets and cupboards. In one way, having a townhouse can seem like being in an apartment, but the townhouse buyer owns the property, is responsible for its upkeep, and has a solid, long-term investment.

support paragraph 2;   3   The first-time buyer might also consider currently popular residences **discusses category 2** called condominiums. The condominium owner buys the building walls, floors, and ceilings but, unlike the townhouse buyer, does not own the land the building sits on. In contrast to owning a townhouse, owning a condo, as they are frequently called, means that the owner must belong to an association that requires monthly fees for exterior maintenance and for the support of group recreational facilities, such as a pool or tennis or racquetball courts. If the association does not own a pool or a TV satellite dish, the members must vote on the purchase of these items, which then belong to the association rather than to an individual owner. The owner of the condo does not have any exterior piece of ground for flowers or a small yard. Instead, the condo may be one of several built like apartments in a high rise. Although there is no beautiful yard around their individual home, condo owners may still find that living in a condominium is also a glamorous, carefree life that provides a long-term investment and pride of ownership.

support paragraph 3;   4   The third option a first-time buyer may consider is a single-family resi-
discusses category 3   dence because, in most cases, it provides a feeling of more privacy and space
for the money invested. Buying a single-family residence means buying the
land under and around the house as well as the house itself. Decisions like
putting in a swimming pool or a TV satellite dish are made by the individual homeowner, who would then own them. A single-family residence
includes a living room, a dining room, perhaps a family room, as many bedrooms as the owner needs or can afford, a kitchen, and various storage
areas including either a carport or a garage. The house can be as large as
the owner wishes. The owner of this type of house does not belong to an
association requiring fees for upkeep. Rather s/he is responsible for maintaining the yard as well as any other purchased land surrounding the house.
S/he may have more responsibilities than the owner of a townhouse or condominium, but s/he enjoys more privacy and space.

concluding paragraph   5   When the first-time home buyer finally decides to go house shopping,
knowing the basic kinds of homes available will make the process easier and
less frustrating. Regardless of what the outcome is—townhouse, condominium, or single-family residence—the new owner will have made an
informed decision.

WRITING ASSIGNMENT

Write an essay developed through classification. Classify and explain one of the following. During revision and editing, refer to the checklist in the inside back cover.

1. Types of transportation for the elderly
2. Types of transportation in the city
3. Types of transportation in the country
4. Types of pets
5. Special uses for pets
6. Types of activities to keep children busy
7. Sports activities for children
8. Sports activities for physically challenged adults
9. Sports activities for college students
10. Sports activities for people who work

Definition

Your *purpose* in writing a **definition** paper is to explain what you mean by a certain word or concept that could have more than one meaning. When you establish the definition in the beginning of the paper, the reader under-stands how your definition is different from *other usages*. You want the reader to understand *your* definition, which is based on your own experiences or thoughts.

In your college courses, you will need to write definitions that are pri-marily objective and based on a dictionary meaning. You may also be asked to write definitions that are subjective or based on your own feelings or expe-riences. These two types of definitions, with which you need to be familiar, are *denotation* and *connotation*.

The **denotation** of a word is a *general, objective definition* that might be found in a dictionary or in a science class like biology or chemistry.

A house is a building used as a place to live by one or more people.

An apple is the fruit of any Pyres malus tree.

The **connotation** of a word is a more *subjective, emotional definition* of a word or concept whose meaning may differ among people. To one person, an "educated person" might be someone who has read the *Encyclopaedia Britannica* from A to Z. But, certainly, few people would agree with this definition, and this definition would not exist in the dictionary. Another person might consider an "educated person" to be someone who has a degree from a university, and someone else might consider an "educated person" one who has acquired knowledge through experimentation and experience. It would be your job, as the writer, to let the reader know what your definition of "educated person" is. If you were to write an essay defining "educated person," here is a possible thesis sentence: "An educated person is one who has attained knowledge through study, experimentation, and experience and is able to relate it to other people."

The *subject* for a definition paper, then, is any word or concept that has or can have more than one definition.

Here are the distinct parts of a definition paper:

1. The introduction gives the denotation of a word and your own personal connotation of the word. (This connotation either limits the denotation or extends the denotation.)

2. Support paragraphs contain example(s) that clearly show the difference between the denotation and connotation of the word. (The emphasis is placed on the connotation because this clarifies the writer's definition.)

3. The conclusion reinforces the distinction between the denotation and connotation of the word or concept.

The following essay develops a definition of the word "home." It includes both the denotation and the connotation of the word.

A Home

denotation

connotation

1   When many people think about a home, they think about the physical place where they live. This definition restricts a home to a mere physical setting where people reside. Those who consider a home to be a place filled with possessions used solely to impress other people become "married to their home" and forget that a home should be a place where they can retreat from the pressures in life. A home is more than just a place in which to dwell. Instead, it is a physical place with a psychological feeling that allows a person or people to feel comfortable and safe from the outside world, whether they live in a hogan or in the house next door. This place allows people to enjoy life by themselves or with other members of their family.

examples that emphasize what a home is not

2   All members of a family should feel they belong in a home and are free to do the things they enjoy. A home is not a place where the children are forbidden to go into the living room for fear they will mess things up or where they are unable to play with their toys anywhere except in their own rooms. Nor is it a place where children are always asked to play outside or at a neighbour's home. Rather, it is a place where people are able to do the things that they enjoy doing, whether working on a model airplane or painting on canvas. A home is not a residence with gold-plated bathroom fixtures that no one is allowed to touch. This is not to say that the home cannot be expensive or that it should become a pigpen. Members of a home learn to take care of their sanctuary and treat it with great love and respect.

specific example of a home

3   Some Native Americans living on reservations in the Southwest still live in the most cherished homes of all—hogans. Because the hogan has only one room, all activities centre in this room. Here the family members cook, converse with each other, and enjoy life with one another. They are protected from the outside world and find safety around a warm stove. When evening comes, they spread their thick blankets on the floor and sleep close to one another. There is great love and camaraderie in this one room that is home. Though the physical surroundings are limited, the psychological feeling of spaciousness exists, and the family members experience a harmony with the natural world.

example of an ideal home

4   Sometimes the house right next door is a wonderful home because it is more than just a physical structure. Whenever there are family gatherings, everyone prefers to go to this home. The children are provided with art items and are allowed to cut, paste, and paint to create anything they wish. Their efforts never go unnoticed and are rewarded with praise. When they finish, they clean everything up and then head for the pool table. The smell of food is present as the adults cook, play cards, and share parts of each other's lives. Someone who drives by the home might say that it is an ordinary home in a middle-class neighbourhood, but this home is anything but ordinary. The remarkable part of this home is not the physical boundaries but the psychological freedom that provides the love and concern that seem to be everywhere.

conclusion that reinforces distinction between denotation and connotation

5   A home is not just a physical structure where people reside, but rather it is also a place where people feel comfortable and can enjoy doing "their own thing." Here they experience freedom and security in their own sanctuary.

WRITING ASSIGNMENT

Write an essay developed through definition. Show how your meaning is different from the dictionary meaning for one of the following words. During revision and editing, refer to the checklist in the inside back cover.

1. Discipline
2. Loyalty
3. Religion
4. Friend
5. Creativity
6. Beauty
7. Sincerity

Cause/Effect Analysis

This may be the first time you see or hear the term **cause/effect analysis**; however, you use this type of reasoning every day. You get up in the morning and may ask yourself, "Why does it have to rain today of all days?" If your car doesn't start, you mentally question, "I wonder why it isn't starting?" As you rush through traffic, an unconscious thought may be, "Why do I live in such a busy city?" You may also think about the effects of these events: "What will happen next because it is raining?" "What are the results of my having a stalled car?" "What are the effects of my living in such a busy city?" Almost everyone instinctively analyzes day-to-day problems to find the causes and effects. This type of reasoning is similar to the kind of thinking you will do when you write a cause/effect paper. The *purpose*, then, is to explain causes or effects of something that happens.

The *topic* for a cause/effect analysis is any event or occurrence for which you want to find all the causes or effects. For example, if you want to build a custom home, you might want to examine the underlying reasons. Your examination will show that some causes uncover other causes. At times, reasons can be hidden, so when you are analyzing a complex question, spend time seeking all the reasons. Careful thinking and brainstorming will pay off. If you want to examine the effects of an event, you must also do thorough thinking and brainstorming.

For a causal analysis paper, the *thesis sentence* can start as a question but must be in statement form when you draft your paper. For instance, if you want to write an analysis of the causes for the subject "why to build a custom home," the thesis sentence, to start with, could be "Why would anyone want to build a custom home?"

Next, *gather information* to help you discuss and explain the reasons discovered in your brainstorming. In your paper, you want to provide your reader with examples, statistics if needed, and authoritative verification of the causes. Then, *draft your paper.*

The pattern of *organization* for a cause/effect paper follows:

1. The introductory paragraph summarizes the causes (or effects) of the subject being analyzed.

2. Support paragraphs clearly explain the causes (or effects) of the event or occurrence being analyzed. (Each support paragraph usually explains one cause or one effect.)

3. The concluding paragraph reinforces the main idea.

For the purpose of illustration, only causal analysis will be shown here. For an example of an essay that discusses *effects*, see the model essay "Parenting: Singular" in Unit 8, Part 3.

To Build or Not to Build

hook

1   Building permits, water and sewer taps, architectural drawings, delayed schedules, construction mishaps, and disreputable builders are a few horrors that race through a person's mind when thinking of building a house. Those who have never tried it would probably hesitate or at best think it over for several days. Some people who have dared to build their own homes swear that they would never do it again. So then, why is it that some still choose to enter into this uncelebrated, unfamiliar experience? The reasons vary, but the common ones are that building a home may be a necessity, may have a financial advantage, and can provide personal satisfaction in a unique design.

transition
thesis sentence

necessity

2   In some cases, one major cause, necessity, underlies the decision to build one's own home. Unless people have beautiful property and plenty of money, they purchase a preconstructed home when they are in the market for a house. However, when the housing market does not offer the house they want or need, then potential buyers may be forced to construct the house for themselves. For instance, if one is moving to a small town where land is reasonable and the housing market is poor, building is the only choice. Or if a family has a special need like four baths or a walk-out basement for a business, there is no alternative but to build. If a person wants to move into a certain area where the choice of homes is limited, then construction of a custom home becomes unavoidable.

financial causes

3   Another important reason for building a home may be financial. Building a home keeps an owner from paying a large real-estate commission. Currently, a real estate commission is 5 percent, so if someone buys a ready-made $200,000 home, the buyer will be paying close to $10,000 in real-estate fees. Also, a prospective home builder has some flexible control over the total cost of the construction. "Sweat equity" is a term that means that the homeowner and the home builder enter into a partnership in which the owner can do some of the labour to defray costs. Painting, tiling, landscaping, or any labour the owner chooses can be done on weekends to save dollars. In the same way, if the builders have plenty of time and flexible taste, they can find bargains for lumber, concrete, appliances, carpet, or any other major items. The buyers have no control over most of these items in an already-constructed house. More control over finances can be a significant underlying reason for deciding in favour of building a home instead of purchasing a preconstructed home.

personal/psychological causes

4   Other important reasons for building a home are psychological. The challenge of accomplishing a major project can bring a person satisfaction when the job is completed. Also, the prospective home builders feel as though they are the creators of the home and immediately take on the pride of ownership. Because they have a better idea of the struggle and time that went into the home, they have a deep sense of appreciation. Another emotion that might cause a person to build a home is obtaining a sense of individualism. Because the homeowner-builders have the opportunity to create and change the floor plan, they know that no other home exists that is exactly like their own. To those people who feel strongly about having a unique design, this motive may be a very strong incentive for building. Even though emotional causes may not be very obvious at first, they are usually very strong influencing forces.

conclusion   5   A person's home is an extremely important place. It represents not only shelter but personal tastes and satisfactions. It is also the most valuable item a person ever owns. Deciding to build this valuable possession can be frightening and frustrating. Many people would never choose to take on such a major responsibility and task. However, some people are forced into the decision and find that there are advantages. Financial benefits, an opportunity to exhibit creativity, and a deep enjoyment and satisfaction in having a unique design can cause people to undertake this creative and satisfying project.

WRITING ASSIGNMENT

Write an essay developed through cause/effect analysis on one of the following topics. During revision and editing, refer to the checklist in the inside back cover.

1. Why we have funerals
2. Results of a particular disappointment
3. Reasons for being successful in an activity
4. Results of being successful in an activity
5. Reasons people get a divorce
6. Reasons cities levy taxes
7. Reasons the provincial government or federal government levies taxes
8. Impact (effects) of taxes on citizen
9. Reasons people change jobs
10. Reasons young people move away from parents
11. Effects of moving away from parents

Process Analysis

Many times in your life, both in and out of school, you are going to be asked to explain how something is done or how to do something. How well you handle this request will depend on how clearly you can sort out the steps of a process or procedure and present them in a clear, logical way. Your audience, whether listening to you or reading your explanation, needs to be able to understand your information clearly and, if necessary, follow your directions precisely. The easiest way to practise these skills is to think through and write a **process** essay.

The *purpose* of a process essay is to tell how to do something (give a set of directions) or how something occurs or how something works.

These are important skills in school because your instructors expect you to show how well you understand basic concepts in your classes. Sometimes they want you to demonstrate that you can do something, telling on paper how to go through a particular procedure if that skill is part of your learning in the class. You could be asked to write about a variety of topics. For example, you may be asked in your environmental-geology class to explain the process of topsoil erosion in the West. Your history professor may ask you to explain how a tax bill becomes law in Parliament. Your automotive-technology professor may ask you to explain how to overhaul a carburetor.

These kinds of thinking and writing skills are also important in the world outside of school. In the business world, you could not become a supervisor, a manager, or a director if you could not understand and explain how processes work and be able to explain them to someone else. You might be asked to explain a procedure to a superior or to someone under you. For example, if a vice-president asked you to make a presentation to new employees summarizing how your department works within the entire operation of the company, you would be able to do that if you had practised these kinds of thinking and writing skills beforehand. Or, if you were responsible for training new employees, you would be able to explain clearly and logically what they should do by giving them clear directions to follow. You might even be so good at this that you could become the head of an entire department devoted to training.

Regardless of what the project or assignment is, before you start, be sure you know the parts of the process you are going to explain. You know the process because you have either read about it or you have done the process yourself. Most of the time, there is no substitute for firsthand information, information gained from your own hands-on experience. Being able to explain a process or give directions means that you must first break down the process into steps to be sure you understand all that is involved and to see which steps are most important. Breaking down the process or procedure into steps also helps you to decide the best order to put them in to explain them clearly. Again, you will not be able to explain anything that you do not know thoroughly.

Be prepared to do some careful thinking to get the information in clear, logical order and write a paper that can be understood easily. As for any kind of paper, producing a process paper follows a series of steps. The following discussion pertains to explaining how to do something.

Decide the purpose of the essay.

Brainstorm or list the steps as they occur to you.

Rearrange the list in the order in which the steps must be done.

Draft your paper, using command verbs.

With respect to the essay's purpose, decide what you want the reader to understand clearly. The reader should be able to follow the steps you explain and undertake the project you are giving directions for. The reader should know what to do to get the desired results. If your topic were "remodelling a kitchen," then your reader should learn how to make an efficient, new kitchen with new appliances—carefully and professionally done.

Looking at the rearranged list, begin thinking about drafting support paragraphs for your main idea. Write a *topic sentence* for each major step, and use command verbs to tell the reader clearly what to do at each stage of the process. You will stay on track, and your reader can follow you clearly. Obviously, the number of topic sentences you write will also be the number of support paragraphs for your paper.

Here is the pattern of *organization* for this kind of process paper:

1. The introduction clearly states that this paper will give directions for doing something.

2. Support paragraphs guide the reader step-by-step through the process. (Each paragraph is a separate step.)

3. The concluding paragraph completes the process.

The following essay shows the steps that can be followed to remodel a kitchen.

How To Remodel Your Kitchen

hook   **1**   After several years of living in the same house, people find that remodelling must be done if the house is to be kept in "livable" condition. The one room that many people decide to remodel first is the kitchen. Many times all the appliances go at once: the refrigerator leaks when it defrosts; the dishwasher does not get the dishes clean; the thermostat in the oven **transition** does not work; and the garbage disposal quit years ago. The kitchen sud**thesis sentence** denly seems too small for the family. It is time to remodel. Remodelling to have the kitchen of your dreams can be done without disappointments if you follow some simple steps.

first major step   **2**   Before you do anything else, **gather information from all available** sources. Purchase a book on kitchen remodelling or go to the library to check out a book or gather magazine articles on the subject. Take a class on remodelling a kitchen. One very valuable resource is stores that specialize in custom kitchen cabinets. Talk to the people at the stores' showrooms. Remember, though, you are still gathering information at this time, so do not sign any contracts. Another excellent source for getting ideas is to look at model homes, so look at as many as possible. Also talk to friends who have remodelled their kitchens recently. Ask them for their ideas or biggest regrets. Profiting from other people's mistakes can often be valuable. When you feel you know everything about kitchens, move on to the next step.

second major step   **3**   This next step is to **decide exactly which new appliances to buy**. Usually stoves, refrigerators, and dishwashers are replaced. Decide if you want a built-in stove or a drop-in stove. Also consider a range top built into an island and an oven and microwave built into the wall. Because refrigerators come in many sizes and varieties, choose the size and brand you plan to buy before you go on. Also, consider whether or not you want it built into the wall. After looking at the different kinds of dishwashers available, choose one that will not only clean the dishes well, but is energy-efficient. Get the exact measurements of the stove, refrigerator, and dishwasher you have selected and move on to the next step.

third major step   **4**   Now the fun begins. **Get a visual idea of your new kitchen**. Buy a package of graph paper and draw the dimensions of your kitchen walls to scale. Be accurate because appliances and cabinets need to fit snugly. Then, using the same scale, cut out a paper representation of each appliance, including the sink. Once this is done, rearrange the appliances on the piece of graph paper, mentally adding possible counter spaces as you go. If you plan to include an island, be sure that the dishwasher door or refrigerator door can swing open easily and that the traffic pattern meets your needs. It could be disastrous if you planned the kitchen so the back door opened into the refrigerator or dishwasher. Also, be sure you have ample counter space near the refrigerator and stove. Then keep shuffling the "puzzle" pieces until you are satisfied with the outcome.

fourth major step 5 Possibly, the least enjoyable but most profitable part comes next: getting the bids and choosing the contractor or subcontractors. **Get bids from at least three different sources.** Of course, if you have one company responsible for all of the remodelling, go to at least three different companies and ask for comparable bids on your scale drawing. If possible, do the subcontracting yourself. Hire your own cabinetmaker, carpenter, electrician, and tile person. The price on any specific job can vary greatly. For instance, three licensed electricians may bid on the needed electrical work. They could bid $1,200, $800, and $400. Before you decide on which bid to take, however, ask for and check out references for their previous jobs, and check with the local registrar of contractors. If possible, look at some work that she or he has done. Though this step is time-consuming, you will be glad that you took the effort to do this evaluation.

conclusion 6 The final step is the simplest. **Sign the contract or subcontracts with the most-qualified bidders and relax.** In a matter of weeks, your inadequate kitchen will be transformed into a functional, beautiful kitchen that will be enjoyed by every member of the family. The refrigerator will bring forth ice cubes rather than leak on the floor; the oven will cook without burning; and the dishwasher will get the dishes clean. Ask yourself, "Can I afford to put this off any longer? Is it time to 'go for it'?"

WRITING ASSIGNMENT

Write an essay developed through process analysis. Show how to do one of the following activities successfully. During revision and editing, refer to the checklist in the inside back cover.

1. Eat well.
2. Discipline children.
3. Raise a puppy.
4. Celebrate a holiday.
5. Choose a mate.
6. Put on a play.
7. Keep peace in a family.
8. Prepare for a vacation.
9. Vacation with children.

Argumentation

The purpose of an **argumentative paper** is to persuade the reader to your way of thinking. Your audience is usually the uncommitted reader, the one who is not strongly committed to one side or the other. You probably would not even attempt to convince a leadership campaign manager to move to the other side in an election. You do not want to alienate anyone who is committed to the other side, but you do want to appeal to someone who is willing to listen to what you have to say. You would try hardest, though, to appeal to the many people from the general population who are uncommitted or not strongly affiliated with the other side.

The *topic* for an argumentative paper must be an issue that has two sides. After reading and researching, you must decide what your position will be.

Here are the *distinct parts* of an argumentative paper:

1. The introduction states the writer's position (the opponent's position may be included here or elsewhere in the body of the essay).

2. Support paragraphs include statistics and authorities in the field to support each point in the argument.

3. The conclusion includes a restatement of the writer's position.

The writer's position and the opponent's position may function as the introductory paragraph for the argumentative paper. The important part to remember is that you as the writer need to be fair in presenting both positions.

Some instructors will require you to preview your main arguments when you state your position in your thesis sentence. Others do not require you to do this. Previewing the main points will help you know in your own mind what your arguments are before you begin the paper.

The next part of the argumentative paper is the support paragraphs. These paragraphs need to persuade the reader that what is presented in the introduction is true. In order to be persuasive, you must avoid using your own opinion anywhere except in stating your own position. Because the thesis sentence (position) is your opinion, the support paragraphs establish that this opinion is valid. You can do this by using statistics or direct quotations from authorities in the field. An authority in the field is someone who has studied the field thoroughly, has received recognition for his/her ideas, and has experience working in the field.

After you feel you have supported your thesis idea convincingly, you are ready to end your paper. This last part of the argumentative paper is a simple restatement of your position. You have the opportunity to reinforce your opinion (position) given in the thesis sentence.

The following argumentative paper shows how the author has achieved a specific purpose by using arguments to convince the reader to accept the position (opinion) of the writer.

Computers in Classrooms Do More Dazzling Than Teaching

Andrew Nikiforuk

hook   1   The colonization of Canadian schools by computers has begun in earnest. If the nation's offices are any indication (they are among the most computerized in the world), more and more students will soon be staring blankly or intently into glowing screens, all in the name of learning.

thesis   **2**
authoritative source
support paragraph 1

Although the computer invasion is inevitable, its potential to do good is not guaranteed. As technology critic Neil Postman recently observed, the computerization of classrooms merely offers the illusion of progress without solving education's social or moral problems.

support paragraph 2   **3**

My concerns about computers stem from my own classroom observations, as well as the dismal history of innovations in public schooling. If the administrators of public schools have demonstrated one singular ability in the past three decades, it's their willingness to experiment with gadgetry—regardless of the consequences for pupils, teachers and the public purse.

opponent's position   **4**
argument against

When educators embrace computers as "the children's machine" (and children do love them, in much the same way boys love guns), they rarely ask if flooding a five-year-old's brain with a dazzling array of images and sounds is an appropriate practice. It seems that the depressing lessons of television, a mere 30-year-old technology, have been entirely lost on educators, unless the subject is violence.

support paragraph 3   **5**
fact

Yet the research seems clear enough: Children bombarded with images at an early age fail to develop an imagination. And citizens without imaginations may respond well to sensations, but they generally can't deal with abstractions like democracy or community without getting bored very quickly.

opponent's position   **6**
argument against

My point here is that there is probably a proper age to introduce the children to machines and its addictive world of images, but educators don't know what it is. Although people with more graduate degrees than common sense have equated the intensity of feelings young children have with computers as a sign of the medium's innate goodness, I am not convinced the union is entirely benign.

support paragraph 4   **7**
authoritative source

Bureaucrats intent on mandating a computer for every Canadian student should also consider another issue. William Rees-Mogg, former editor of *The Times* of London, has accurately noted that "technological changes makes it even more costly for the authorities to project power—and ever cheaper for alienated citizens to resist power." Most educators have failed to acknowledge that the computer revolution poses this bold question: Why send your child to school when an on-line classroom and parent can do the job just as well at home?

support paragraph 5   **8**
authoritative source

And then there is the issue of software. Most educators will readily concede that the majority of educational programs for computers are garbage. Jerry Pournelle, who writes a column for *Byte* magazine, recently contrasted the two camps that dominate software development. In the minority stand educators who are interested in what students learn, as opposed to how they feel about things. Mr. Pournelle particularly praised a superintendent for developing a CD-ROM on the Lewis and Clark expedition. It employed print, photos, video and sound

example

recordings to build an account of the journey and integrated history, geography and natural science.

support paragraph 6   **9**
contrast
example

Now, contrast this worthy enterprise with technology's twaddle speakers. Mr. Pournelle particularly cites an educator who doesn't care about test or the "usual definition of literacy," but who is interested "in how well kids do things differently." Mr. Pournelle watched the twaddler show a gosh-wow multimedia presentation that conveyed almost no knowledge.

support paragraph 7   **10**
direct quote

"I used to be in operations research," says Mr. Pournelle, "and I recognize what he's doing: if you can't solve the real problem, change the definition and cri-

restatement of thesis		teria so that you can work on something else. It's called dazzling them with foot-
authoritative source		work."
	11	Mr. Pournelle, who is no technophobe, is dead right: Computer software is doing more dazzling than teaching in schools. Richard Worzel, a Toronto futurist, agrees. He says improperly used computers can lull parents and schools into thinking that they are accomplishing something useful when in fact nothing of value is happening.
conclusion	12	The last issue that schools have failed to seriously ponder is one of cost. There are only two kinds of computers, those on the drawing board and those that are obsolete. Countries that innovate recklessly, such as the United States, have spent
call for action		a lot of money on machines to minimal effect. The lessons here are simple: Buy used and buy according to pedagogical need, not fashion.

WRITING ASSIGNMENT

Write an essay developed through argument. Persuade a particular audience that:

1. Taxes are necessary.
2. Taxes make people poorer.
3. Divorce is harmful to children.
4. Divorce is good for children.
5. Nursing homes meet the needs of the elderly.
6. Nursing homes do not meet the needs of the elderly.
7. Photo radar should be used by police.
8. Photo radar should not be used by police.
9. Marriage should be abolished.
10. Marriage should be discouraged until both people graduate from college.
11. Custody of children should be given to fathers more often than currently occurs.
12. Custody of children should be equally split between parents.

One of the most important skills you need is being able to decide which mode of development is most effective for your topic. The possibilities are as varied as the number of people writing the essays. There is no one correct mode of development. Choose the mode that helps you achieve your purpose and seems the most interesting. Sometimes the assignment specifies the mode; at other times, depending upon your purpose, you will need to think about how the subject can be explained in different ways.

The following list shows how different modes can be used to write about the same subject but with different purposes.

Topic: The Circus

reasons people should not attend a circus: argument

kinds of events at a circus: illustration

types of animals at a circus: classification

types of people at a circus: classification

how to enjoy a circus: process

ways a dog act is different from a tiger act: contrast

WRITING ASSIGNMENT

Using the topics given, decide on a particular mode and then develop an essay. Decide what points you want to express. Then choose the method of development that permits you to do this most effectively.

1. Garbage
2. Recycling
3. Historic buildings
4. Movies
5. Custom cars
6. Dates
7. Jobs
8. Gambling
9. Art
10. Investments

After you draft your essay, revise for content and edit for mechanics. Check to see that method (mode) of development is appropriate for topic, purpose, and audience.

Content

  Essay

   Check the introductory paragraph for an effective hook.

   Check for a smooth transition between the hook and thesis.

   Check to be sure the thesis sentence states a clear direction or previews the points to be covered in the paper.

   Check to see that the voice is appropriate for purpose and audience.

  Paragraphs

   Revise so that each has a clear topic sentence that develops an idea suggested in the thesis sentence.

   Include four to six supporting sentences that are developed using short interrelated examples or an extended example.

   Include a closing sentence in each paragraph.

Mechanics

   Check for subject-verb agreement.

   Check for consistent verbs.

   Check for a consistent point of view.

   Check for fragments, run-on sentences, and comma splices.

   Check for correct punctuation.

Sentence variety

   Revise short sentences into compound sentences.

   Revise sentences to include complex sentences.

   Check for coherence between and within paragraphs.

PART 2 | Something to Think About, Something to Write About

Thunderbayisms or The Idiosyncracies of Place

Joan Skelton *is a novelist and a free-lance writer who lives outside of Thunder Bay.*

1   Do all places have an invisible web of unwritten rules?

2   When my husband and I moved to Thunder Bay a few years ago, we literally fumbled our way through a maze of protocol and codes of behaviour that were unique to this city.

3   After being caught several times, we dubbed these local idiosyncrasies: *thunderbayisms*. We wondered if these mini-traps were like the Cockney rhyming slang, both, it seemed to me, an in-joke or conspiracy against outsiders. Because they were only understood by long-term residents, both *thunderbayisms* and rhyming slang immediately tip off the presence of a stranger. After all, who outside Soho would know that almond rocks are socks, or a holy *friar* is a liar, or *kiss the cross* is the boss?

4   Similarly, in Thunder Bay, inquiry and consternation about the unwritten rules immediately labels the inquirer as STRANGER. Are you likely to get a loan at the bank without a lot of credit checking if you complain about getting a ticket for parking in the quarter of a block space in front of the bank that everybody, except newcomers, *knows* is totally reserved for buses?

5   Don't expect the Harbour Expressway will run along the harbour; it cuts through the centre of the city. Don't expect there will be Ukrainian street names in the Ukrainian end of town; the street names are Scottish. Don't expect to find West Arthur Place on West Arthur Street. In Thunder Bay, that would be much too simple. Instead, West Arthur Place is located at 1265 East Arthur Street!

6   Thunder Bay is a long city strung along the harbour. Originally two port cities, Port Arthur and Fort William, amalgamation took place in 1970. It might be assumed that the long streets that snake through the length of the city would make it easier for strangers finding their way. No. Each main street has many names. Algoma becomes Memorial becomes May. Algonquin becomes Balmoral becomes Waterloo. River becomes Junot becomes Golf Links becomes Edward. Confusing?

7   Houses are known by the name of a previous owner. The house that my husband and I have lived in for twelve years is known as Willie LeDain's house. In other words, you don't live in your house, you live in someone else's house. Maybe after we leave, it will become our house.

8   With the second highest ethnic concentration in Thunder Bay being Italian—the first is British—there are, needless to say, a number of Italian halls with innumerable Sunday spaghetti suppers, with the option of either a sit-down meal or a take-out. You can feel pretty stupid when you arrive to take your place in line with everyone carrying their own pot or container, you empty-handed.

9   "How do ya think you can take-out spaghetti without a container?" I was asked.

10   During out first winter here, my husband notified his secretary that the outside plug-in for his car was not working.

11   "Oh," she replied, "it is only turned on when it is cold."

12   "What do you call twenty-five below?" my husband asked.

13   "That's just *fairly* cold," she replied.

14   We were invited to many large parties to meet endless people, who could always remember our name—we being only two—but whose names we had great difficulty remembering, they being in the hundreds. This, of course, is a problem of newcomers anywhere. The Thunder Bay idiosyncrasy, or thunderbay-ism, involved the protocol at these elegant cocktail-buffets. At the first one we attended, when it became my turn in the rather long line proceeding towards the buffet table spread with white linen and laden with cold meats, roast beef, turkey, condiments, salads, jellied salads, I noticed there was no cutlery, no knives, no forks.

15   "I wonder if we should tell the hostess she has run out of knives and forks," I said to the person standing beside me, a fairly obvious remark as far as I was concerned.

16   "Knives and forks are never put out at these parties," she said.

17   Following the adage about doing as the Romans do, I discretely watched how the other guests coped with the tomatoes and meat and jellied salads without so much as a fork. I thereby learned the protocol.

18   Feeling like Dagwood Bumstead and Hagar the Horrible wrapped into one, I loaded prime ribs and horseradish and tomatoes and jellied salad on, you guessed it, bread. There were few chairs, and there I stood in my Roue gown, fashionably messy hair, and chauvinistic spike-heeled shoes, balancing my plate and wine on the mantel piece, my hands wrapped around a sandwich three times wider than my mouth.

19   (At a later party, sitting on a footstool, my red wine on the white rug beside me, it, of course, mysteriously spilled, the spreading pool of wine like a stain on my suitability as invited guest. Oh boy...)

20   The funniest fumbling moment, and not quite so embarrassing, took place at Candy Mountain, one of the many downhill ski areas just outside Thunder Bay. After a warm day of spring skiing, my husband and I decided to split a hot dog and a beer in the *al fresco* cafeteria restaurant. (We are not cheap; just calorie conscious, and alcohol conscious.) As my husband munched away on his half of the mustardy morsel, I sipping the beer, I asked him what the hot dog was like.

21   "It's not very good. Try your half."

22   I took a bite.

23   "It's terrible. It doesn't taste cooked. I think I'll get some coffee."

24   I went to the counter where the food was served and asked for coffee.

25   "I hope the coffee is better than the hot dog," I asked. "The hot dog tasted raw."

26   "Raw? It was raw. Didn't ya cook it? Didn't ya see the barbecue over there?"

27   Sure enough, over in the corner was a barbecue, where you were supposed to *know* you cooked your own food.

28   It took several years for our indoctrination to be complete. I have heard myself say it is *only* twenty below. I know know when someone gives an address on Golf Links road it really means River and Junot streets *et al*. I now eat before going to a cocktail buffet in order not to appear Dagwoodish with a mile high sandwich. I know when and where to take the containers for take-out.

29   The initiation was worth it. To have an auditorium bringing in world-class entertainment like the Moscow Symphony, and Jon Kimura Parker, to have a professional theatre, and a university with a good library, two Olympic swimming pools, all plumped down beside Lake Superior and dramatic rock cuestas that rear up out of the boreal forest like guardian sentinels, is special. The forests and the water and the snow are appreciated by the people. The woods are alive with paths and trails, the harbour with boats, Thunder Bay very much an outdoor community. Except for the travesty of ignored pollution, the blend of civilization in the ecosystem is about right.

30   We hardly noticed the sign in front of the ski chalet: NO PARKING MEANS NO PARKING. After all, in Thunder Bay, NO PARKING, could mean something else.

Something to Write About

Write an essay on one of the following questions. Before you draft your essay, however, be sure you have your audience and purpose clearly in mind so that you can select an appropriate mode.

1. What "rules" are unique to the city you live in?
2. When you moved to a new city, what did you have to learn?
3. Describe your feelings the first time you ventured out in your new city/neighbourhood.
4. How do you make yourself comfortable in a new place?
5. Describe your most embarrassing moment in a new environment.
6. How (when) do you know when you belong?

After you draft your essay, do each of the following:

Revise it so that it has an effective introduction that includes a hook, a transition, and a thesis sentence.

Be sure that each support paragraph has a strong topic sentence and ample supporting examples.

Check for sentence variety.

Check for unity and a smooth flow of ideas.

Revise to include a strong concluding paragraph.

Check for subject-verb agreement.

Check for consistent verbs.

Check for consistent point of view.

Check for fragments, run-ons, and comma splices.

Check punctuation of compound sentences.

Check punctuation of complex sentences.

PART 3 | Paragraphs and Essays for Discussion and Analysis

Illustration

....

Heroes—"Sung" and "Unsung"
Lorena Acosta, *student*

1   Every nation, every family, every individual has heroes. These people have done something so outstanding that they are admired and respected for their actions. Usually, they have saved a life or lives, or they have done something else that has profoundly affected the beliefs and values of the people who look upon them as heroes. Most of the time these outstanding individuals get wide public recognition for their acts. Sometimes, though, heroic people may not receive any recognition for what they have done. These unrecognized heroes are called the "unsung heroes" of our time. Whether they are publicly acknowledged or not, however, heroes are special people because of their ability to react quickly, calmly, and unselfishly.

2   People who become heroes may have saved someone's life by reacting quickly in circumstances that could lead an ordinary person to freeze or not react in time. Perhaps one of the best illustrations would be a drowning child at the beach or in a swimming pool. The child might be struggling and crying for help or might not be making a sound. A person who can quickly evaluate the situation and dive into the surf or the pool to save the child would certainly be a hero in the eyes of the public. Recently, a five-year-old child jumped into a swimming pool at an apartment complex because he had seen other children doing the same thing. The children at the other end of the pool noticed that he was floating below the surface of the water and quickly pulled him out. The child did not drown or sustain permanent damage because the rescuers were able to see quickly what was happening to the child and, instead of calling out for someone else to help, jumped in and did the job.

3   Sometimes, heroes are those who not only react fast but also calmly under terrifying circumstances. In a 1989 airliner crash landing in Sioux City, Iowa, there were several heroes, one in particular. When the DC-10 crash-landed, it broke apart and caught fire. Although many people died, more than half of the passengers lived. Twenty-five or thirty lived because of one passenger who calmly took charge of one section of the burning plane. Without panic, he helped many people unbuckle their safety belts. He stood calmly and held up out of the way a heavy tangle of cables and wires blocking their way out of the plane. He gave directions to some who could not see because of the smoke, and he had to drop the cables to help some elderly people who fell while trying to get to the opening. After he had them on their feet, he pushed up the cables high enough so the people could get out. Although this hero was one of the "unsung" variety, he certainly deserves the name.

4   The pilot and the crew of the DC–10 described above are prime illustrations of the unselfish hero, who may be the first to deny any heroics. They reacted

quickly, calmly, and—most importantly—unselfishly. They had to fly the large airliner after it had been fatally crippled by a blown engine that had destroyed all the plane's hydraulic systems. While receiving as much help as possible from other experts and from the controllers at the Sioux City airport, the pilot repeatedly asked for instructions to help him keep the plane away from the city itself. Miraculously, having lived through the crash landing, the pilot said several times afterwards that they were not heroes, having done just what they had to do under the circumstances. From the point of view of many, the public and other professional pilots, getting the plane to the end of the runway was a clear example of calm, unselfish heroism.

5   Whether "sung" or "unsung," special heroes save many lives in America every year. Not all heroes become well known, but they are heroes just the same. Their heroic actions display unselfish actions.

Questions on Content
1. What makes heroes special people?
2. What happened to the five-year-old child who jumped into a swimming pool?
3. What did the hero in paragraph 3 do to save lives?

Questions on Form
1. What mode of development is used in this essay?
2. Where is the thesis sentence?
3. Does paragraph 2 have short interrelated examples or one extended example? Paragraph 3? Paragraph 4?

Comparison/Contrast

Rabbit or Parakeet?

Adapted from the original by **Jason Herrington,** *student*

1   There are many people who own either a parakeet or a rabbit (or perhaps both) as a pet, and a new pet owner may wonder which of the two animals makes the better pet. While there are many differences in physical appearance, the care they require, and the rewards an owner would receive from them, both the parakeet and the rabbit make splendid pets.

2   A parakeet and a rabbit show many differences in physical appearance. A parakeet is obviously a bird with wings instead of arms and two spindly legs, each equipped with four long toes used to perch upon a limb. A parakeet has no visible ears and no teeth and must use his beak to crack open seeds. A parakeet is feathered with brightly colored green, red, blue, orange, or purple. In contrast, a rabbit is a mammal with four legs, two short ones in front and two longer ones in back used for hopping. A rabbit has long ears and strong teeth with a double cutting edge on the upper front teeth to cut and grind food. Rabbits are furred in earth-toned colors of white, grey, brown, or black. Because of their physical appearance, it is quite easy to tell the two apart.

3   Because of these physical differences, pet owners should be aware of the differences in care these pets require. Because parakeets are birds, they must be kept in suitable cages with perches and have plenty of room to flutter about. These

birds must have a cuttle bone and beak conditioner available to keep their beaks worn down so they can eat properly. Because a parakeet has feathers, its wings must be clipped to keep it from flying away, and special care must be taken when it moults. Rabbits are diggers by nature and must be kept in a cage that reflects this. Wood must be made available for them to gnaw on and to scratch on to keep their teeth and claws worn down. Because a rabbit has fur, it must be brushed and kept clean. Both require care but care in moderation.

4   Finally, the rewards an owner would receive by owning one of these pets also differ. The sweet song of a parakeet on a sunny afternoon has delighted many a parakeet owner. With a little training, a bird can perform tricks on its perch and learn to talk. Rabbits, while they make few noises, are warm and affectionate, and they love contact. With encouragement, rabbits can be housebroken and will hop to meet the owner when called.

5   It is obvious that many differences occur in physical characteristics, the work involved in taking care of these pets, and the satisfaction a person receives by owning them. Yet these differences seem insignificant compared to the fact that both are small animals that make excellent pets for an owner, and they bring love and enjoyment.

Questions on Content

1. What physical differences are given between a bird and a rabbit?
2. What keeps a parakeet from flying away?
3. How does a parakeet delight its owner?
4. How does a rabbit delight its owner?

Questions on Form

1. What mode of development is used in this essay?
2. Why doesn't the author state whether a parakeet or a rabbit is a better pet?
3. How does the thesis sentence help the author organize his essay?

Classification

Which One Are You?

Adapted from the original by **Kristi Von Aspen,** *student*

1   Midterms! Midterms! Midterms! The mere sound of that word sends chills down most spines. Why? Well, midterms translate into tests and tests require studying—not the most favourable extracurricular activity on a student's agenda. But no matter what the subject may be, a person acquires certain methods of preparation over the years. I have observed these habits and concluded that there are three major types of students: The Perfectionists, the Naturalists, and the Procrastinators.

2   First of all, the Perfectionists are methodical people. They are always calculating and planning ahead for events in the future. One can usually find them making lists of things to do and then carefully arranging those items into well-thought-out time schedules. For example, if a test is to be given in two weeks and there are 140 pages of material to be covered, the Perfectionist immediately

divides the days into the pages. The answer will give him the average number of pages he will need to read each night. There's even a good chance that this person will finish in advance and move on to something else. Perfectionists are high achievers and, on the whole, earn better grades than the other two groups.

3   The second category of students is the carefree spirits I like to call Naturalists. These people possess a casual, happy-go-lucky kind of attitude that reflects in every aspect of their lives. For instance, when it comes to schoolwork, Naturalists study only when it is convenient for them. Their motto is, "If it gets done, it gets done." Don't get me wrong. Most Naturalists do have a conscience; in the back of their minds they know what they have to do, but they do their work in a nonconformist manner. They just refuse to allow academics to dominate their world.

4   Finally, there are the Procrastinators—the obvious choice to discuss last. Waiting until the final hour to study for that big test is one of the main traits of these people. As a result of their postponements, Procrastinators sometimes have to resort to cheating as a means of receiving an acceptable grade. Mothers of these students often have hoarse voices from constantly yelling at their children to do homework. Usually, a person of this nature never learned how to manage time and probably never will. Occasionally, some are able to break out of this rut and begin to lead normal lives.

5   Everyone, at one time or another, has experimented with all three of these studying methods. It's just a matter of discovering what works best for the individual and how to adapt to it. In the meantime, good luck on those midterms!

Questions on Content
1. Who are the methodical people?
2. What characterizes the naturalists?
3. What does "procrastinator" mean?
4. What does a procrastinator sometimes do to pass a test?

Questions on Form
1. What is the basis for the classification, and where is it made clear to the reader?
2. Where does the supporting information come from?
3. Identify a shift in point of view in the conclusion. Does it seem to work in this essay?

Definition

....

Wealth

Andrea Gonzales, *student*

Wealth is quite often defined as a great quantity or store of money or property of value. However, wealth can be a great quantity of many other things acquired, not just material items. There are those who have had the good fortune to have seen many beautiful places throughout their lives. They have acquired many priceless memories. There is the man who is wealthy because he has many friends who are loyal and true, and to acquire friends like these makes a man rich. Perhaps the most wealthy man of all is the man who has a loving family around him. This alone can bring great happiness, which no amount of money can buy.

Wealth is so much more than a great store of money. It can be any possession that is priceless to its owner.

Questions on Content
1. Who is perhaps the wealthiest person of all?
2. What is the denotation of wealth?
3. What is the connotation of wealth?

Questions on Form
1. What did the author do to make the connotation of wealth clear?
2. What makes the end of the paragraph effective?

A Run

Adapted from the original by **Tim Darcy**, *student*

1   "I've decided to go on a run over the holiday weekend." This statement is simple enough and would be understood perfectly by millions of bikers and motorcycle enthusiasts throughout the English-speaking world. Why then, out of no less than thirty-two noun definitions of the word "run" in one dictionary, do none of them apply? Apparently, lexicographers don't have the same kind of fun that bikers have because fun is what runs are all about. For the benefit of the uninitiated, a run is a planned motorcycle trip or destination that is meant to be attended by a group of riders.

2   It is interesting to wonder about how the word "run" came to be used by motorcyclists as it is today. The mere thought of a bunch of bearded, beer-bellied bikers in running shorts and Nikes, huffing and puffing down the road, is enough to rule out the most obvious literal connotation. Parallels could be drawn, if rather facetiously, to several standard uses of the word: "a run of good luck," "a dog run," "a beer run," and probably as many more as the imagination would allow. None of these meanings, however, really fits, so the question of why these events are called runs will just have to remain unanswered.

3   A run, as stated above, can be either a trip or a destination, and motorcycles are the common denominator. There are poker runs, in which riders stop at pre-determined points along the way to pick up a playing card, and at the last stop, the rider with the best poker hand wins a prize. There are memorial runs, which bring people together to remember and honour departed friends. There are benefit and charity runs, in which bikers ride to bring toys, food, clothing, or money to try to help the needy. Finally, there is the classic run, which is really nothing more than an outdoor party. To qualify as a run, though, the party really should be an overnighter, and travel must be involved. Riding to the local tavern and passing out in the alley until morning just doesn't constitute going on a run.

4   So what makes a run different from any other motorcycle ride or trip? First, a run is a planned happening; a spur-of-the-moment ride really couldn't be called a run. Runs are not something that are to be done alone, either. Individuals might ride to a run alone, but there must be a group at the destination. A ride to Newfoundland from Ontario could be a mighty long trip, but unless there is a

purpose that is shared with other riders, it just isn't a run. In short, a run differs from any other type of ride because, large or small, far away or close by, it is a social event.

5   When a motorcycle enthusiast says that he is going on a run, he is not going for the aerobic exercise and he is not in training for a marathon. When he says that the run is five hundred kilometres, it is not a five-hundred-kilometre race. He is going for a ride, very probably with friends, and there is a definite purpose for that ride, even though that purpose may not be obvious to everyone.

<table>
<tr><td>Questions on Content</td><td>Questions on Form</td></tr>
<tr><td>1. What is the author's definition of a run?</td><td>1. Identify the hook in the introduction</td></tr>
<tr><td>2. Where could he not find an appropriate definition?</td><td>2. Describe the voice in this essay</td></tr>
<tr><td>3. Why aren't all motorcycle trips runs?</td><td>3. What transitional phrase links paragraph 3 to paragraph 2?</td></tr>
</table>

Cause and Effect Analysis

Parenting: Singular

Adapted from the original by **Jenefer Radas,** *student*

1   "Single parents" is a term that we are hearing more about every day. Statistically, the number of single-parent families is rising at the same rate as the divorce rate. The percentage of single-parent families may be as high as 50 percent in some areas of our country. The majority of single parents are women, even though in single-parent families, men have recently had to raise their children on their own also. For many reasons, single parents are in this predicament. Alcohol and drug abuse can cause a parent to leave the children. Also, unwed mothers decide not to marry. With all that is known about single parents, however, the number one reason for a parent to raise a family alone is divorce. Regardless of the causes, the effects on both the parents and the children are serious. The effects of single parenthood can be felt financially, physically, and sociologically.

2   As a country, we know about financial instability. Our economy experiences ups and downs, but the financial stability of single parents is even worse. On the average, single parents are in the lower-income group, yet they are willing to work hard for their family's existence. Not all single parents are able to work. Some are home with infants while others simply do not have the educational background for well-paying jobs. Single parents who have high-paying employment may also have serious financial obligations to meet, which create financial tensions. These obligations can be a high house payment or car payment. In the movie Baby Boom , Diane Keaton is a businesswoman with an infant. Her male partner chooses not to help raise the child, leaving Diane alone to support and raise her. Even with Diane's well-paying job, she is almost left bankrupt because of her home repair costs. Eventually, Diane is asked to resign because of her parental responsibilities, leaving her to reevaluate her employment opportuni-

ties. This movie example gives a clear picture of a single parent's loss in financial status. A single parent, like the one played by Diane Keaton, can lose financial security and can become destitute very quickly. The finances of a single-parent family can drop dramatically, within a few weeks of onset. Consequently, because of the financial strains put on single-parent families, many children are poorly fed, poorly dressed, and shunned by those more affluent. Furthermore, many single-parent families must depend on welfare or food programs for their mere existence. Because single parent families make up such a large percentage of families in our country, their needs should be more seriously considered than they are now.

3   The physical effects of being a single parent are another serious issue. To look at many single parents, a person would not know that they were in pain. Chances are those parents are hurting inside. Physical problems in these men and women can be caused by many different factors, but a major problem that exists for many single parents is depression, which leads to physical problems. Doctors found that infants who were refused any physical touch or intimate love became listless and depressed. After a time, the babies refused to eat and became catatonic. Depression in the single parent is brought about in the same manner. These adults that had loving relationships are now without any physical touch or love. This experience has left them in a state of loneliness, which is the cause of the debilitating illness, depression. This physical illness causes a feeling of exhaustion, anxiety, and tension that leaves them feeling listless. Single parents are vulnerable human beings that are more susceptible to all forms of illness. There are other physical effects of single parenthood. Compared to single adults without children, single parents usually contract many more of the childhood illnesses than the single person. They are exposed to these illnesses around the clock. Consequently, single parents put their health needs second to their children. This priority causes the parent to be sick longer and more frequently than a non-single parent. Single parents carry the weight of the world on their backs. With all that weight there is no wonder they are affected physically.

4   Equally important, the sociological effects on the single parent's life can be the hardest to overcome. Our society dictates what it considers a normal family. A normal family under these prejudiced guidelines is a mother and father and 2.5 children. The single-parent family consists of a mother or father and any number of children. On a daily basis, single parents are painfully reminded of this cultural ideal. These unusual families are looked on as different; they are usually excluded from neighbourhood gatherings because of this presumed oddity in their family structure. Single-parent families are what society considers outcasts. Their children are reminded in storybooks and role playing that they are missing a mother or father in their home. Children from two-parent families tell their mommy and daddy stories with proud exuberance. Quietly, one-parent children sit and listen to their stories but feel ashamed to tell their own stories. These feelings of inadequacy and humility in the single-parent family are brought about by society. Even with this stigma toward single-parent families, society is slowly turning around. Single-parent families are being recognized by many as the strength and hope for the children growing up with only one parent. The strength that a single-parent must possess to raise children alone is far greater than the bellows and complaints of a blinded, backward society.

5   Parenting is not for everyone. It takes a strong person to raise a family alone with the financial, physical, and sociological pressures that exist. The parent may

fall short of perfection but keeps working to make a good life for the children. Regardless of the causes of single-parent families, the impact on the family is serious and should be given more priority. These families are willing to overcome their problems but must be given a chance to do so.

Questions on Content

1. Why is the number of single-parent families increasing?
2. What is the ideal family in our culture?
3. How are children from single-parent families made to feel inferior?

Questions on Form

1. Why are causes given in the introduction even though the paper is about effects?
2. How are the effects organized for the reader?
3. What provides support for each effect?
4. Is the conclusion effective? Why or why not?

Process Analysis

Reducing Fear of a Hospital Stay for a Child

Adapted from the original by **Eric Beach,** *student*

1   Years ago, children were taken to the hospital, strapped down on a stretcher, and told to be good while the nurse slapped a gas mask on and the parent disappeared to another room. Little thought was given to the terrified child who didn't have the slightest idea what was going on. Those terrifying experiences do not have to happen. A caring parent can easily prepare a child for a surgical procedure. Though the process of getting a child ready for a hospital stay for the first time can still be scary for both the adult and the child, the stay can be made easier and much less stressful if some careful planning is done beforehand. Role playing, discussion with honest responses, and access to factual information help the child understand what is going on and, thus, keep her from imagining all sorts of scary experiences.

2   Tension can be reduced when preparation involves role playing. First, the child can pretend to be in the hospital and the adult can pretend to be the nurse or doctor. As a "nurse," the adult can fluff up the pillow, take the child's temperature, and take the child's blood pressure—all with a play doctor's kit. Then the "pretend" nurse can show the child how to ring for help or turn on the television set. The "nurse" can then set up a tray for lunch and say, "This is the way you will be served lunch in the hospital." The "nurse" can be resourceful by finding items around the house that they can pretend with. Then the adult and child might reverse the roles, with the child becoming the nurse and the adult becoming the patient. Then, when it is time for the child to check in at the hospital, she will have some idea of what to expect.

3   The most important part of the process might be to discuss with the child the fact that she will not be left alone in a strange place and forgotten. The child can be encouraged to take a favourite stuffed animal with her or maybe even her spe-

cial blanket. The child needs to know that after she falls asleep for surgery, some-one will be there waiting when she wakes up. The child needs to know that she will not be dropped off in a strange environment with no familiar items or faces. Rather, mom, dad, grandma, sister, or brother will be there as much as possible. Also, this is a good time to let the child know that a nurse will always be there when she needs anything and the stuffed animal can stay right there in bed with her the whole time.

4   Equally important is to allow the child the chance to ask questions. The adults should answer questions as honestly as possible. If the child wants to know if "it" will hurt, the adult should respond by saying, "Yes, it may hurt a little bit, but the nurse or doctor will be as gentle as possible." Then the benefits of the procedure should be explained. If it is the appendix that is being removed, then the adult can say, "But it won't hurt here (touching child's side) as much as it does now." If it is to repair a heart, then the adult might say, "But then you can play more. Remember how tired you get now?" The adult must be honest with the child. If the child asks, "Will I have to have a shot?" the adult should answer by saying, "Yes, and I am sorry." It is important for the child to know that the adult cares.

5   If time allows, the adult and child might visit a library and/or hospital for more specific information. At the library they can read children's books and view simple videos about hospitals. At the hospital, they might pick up a pamphlet that would show the child pictures of what to expect once in the hospital. A book that shows the internal parts of the body can also be useful. If a child is to have ton-sils removed, a picture of the tonsils can be found. If the procedure is to be a com-plicated one, like heart surgery, the adult might show the child what will be fixed. The adult only needs to explain what the child is old enough to understand.

6   Following this process of preparing a child for surgery can have benefits for both the child and the adult. In today's world, it is unforgivable not to give the child information that she can understand and that will reduce anxiety and fear. Hospital stays do not need to be nightmares that are relived over and over again.

Questions on Content
1. What process is being explained?
2. What can the adult do to make this process easier?
3. What are the benefits of planning ahead?
4. What can a child take to the hospital with him or her?

Questions on Form
1. How does the writer organize the process?
2. What point of view is being used?
3. What makes the introduction effective?

Argumentation

Think Twice before Demonizing Cartoons

Kathleen McDonnell *is a Toronto writer*

1   What a relief. We're finally getting a handle on what's at the root of the vio-lence and social breakdown rampant in North American culture. Is it poverty?

Widespread child abuse and neglect? The proliferation of guns? A too-lenient Young Offenders Act? No. The main culprit is—wait for it!—cartoons.

2   A recent study at Quebec's Laval University found that children's cartoon shows had the "highest level of violence of all TV programs." The study's authors didn't draw any conclusions themselves about how watching cartoons influences actual behaviour. But their findings give yet another round of ammunition to crusaders against TV violence, who take as their starting point the belief that children learn violence primarily from TV rather than from the adults in their lives.

3   And apparently the problem isn't with *all* cartoons. One of the researchers who carried out the study speculated that the violence in Bugs Bunny cartoons might not be as bad as the violence on *Teenage Mutant Turtles*. Keith Spicer, chairman of the Canadian Radio-Television and Telecommunications Commission, has said on more than one occasion that he'd exempt old favourites like Bugs and the Road Runner from the new broadcasters' anti-violence code.

4   The targets of the anti-violence campaign, in other words, aren't the cartoons that we adults remember with such nostalgic fondness from our own youth, but the contemporary ones our kids enjoy so much. Yet by any objective measure, such as the violent-acts-per hour index used by the Laval researchers, the slapstick mayhem of Bugs blowing up Yoesmite Sam with a stick of dynamite is every bit as "violent" as—if not more so than—The Ninja Turtles' martial-arts moves.

5   But in a sense Mr. Spicer is right. Common sense tells him that growing up on a steady diet of Bugs Bunny didn't turn him and his contemporaries into serial killers. But he's not willing to extend the same trust or tolerance to the young audiences of today. It's amazing to me how seldom the experts deign to actually talk (and even more important, *listen*) to children themselves about these issues. They might find they'd have to alter some of their fixed notions about how kids take in pop-culture messages.

6   We still don't know all that much about how the images and stories of popular culture influence behaviour. As one wag pointed out recently, television is full of comedy, so why don't we have comedy in the streets? And the violent-acts-per-hour yardstick currently in favour is simply too crude a measure to yield a meaningful picture of TV violence, particularly where cartoons are concerned. It takes no account of context or genre, and treats Plucky Duck dropping an anvil on another Tiny Toons characters as the equivalent of a cop beating a suspect to pulp on *NYPD Blue*.

7   The latter is meant to be a realistic simulation of reality, but cartoons have no such pretensions: They are patently unreal pictures of characters and events. Slapstick violence has been a major comic element in cartoons since their earliest days, as it was in older traditions such as the Punch-and-Judy puppet shows. The popular animated sitcom *The Simpsons* mercilessly satirizes this cartoon stock-in-trade in its often hilarious "Itchy and Scratchy" segments.

8   I think we're doing parents and kids a real disservice by whipping up this frenzy about cartoons, painting them as a near-demonic force in modern life. The problem of media violence is a real one, but over the whole span of popular culture, adult–oriented entertainment is a far greater source of violent imagery than kids' shows. And having spent the past couple of years researching these questions, I've become convinced that the TV violence issue is serving as a smokescreen, deflecting our attention from some of the deeper causes of violence that are much more difficult to address.

9   It's a lot easier to point the finger at cartoons than to take responsibility for the fact that, as a society, we are failing our children. Violent shows and video games clearly serve as outlets for kids' aggressive impulses. But that doesn't mean they are the *source* of those impulses.

10   One thing we know about violent crime is that most of it is committed by people whose childhoods were marked by varying degrees of abuse, poverty, and profound neglect. We're barking up the wrong tree if we harp on fantasy violence in cartoons while ignoring the real-life roots of violent behaviour.

Questions on Content

1. What is the author's opinion of the cartoons of her youth?
2. What distinction does she make between "Tiny Toons" and "NYPD Blue"?
3. What types of support does McDonnell use?

Questions on Form

1. Comment on the effectiveness of the first paragraph as an attention-getter.
2. Where is the author's position stated?
3. Find at least two examples where the author confronts and refutes the opposition to her position.

Unit Nine

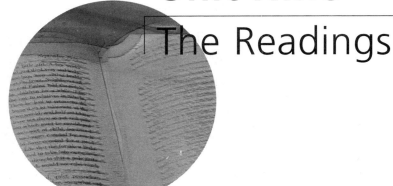

The Readings

Notes about the Authors

(in order of appearance)

Val Sears (1928): Born in Vancouver, Val Sears is a journalist and writer who "pursues the perfect anecdote with relish." Sears joined *The Toronto Telegram* in the 1950s and in 1960 moved to *The Toronto Star* where he became political editor. His book *Hello Sweetheart...Give Me Rewrite* (Key Porter, Fall, 1988) is an anecdotal account of "the last great newspaper war" between the *Telegram* and the *Star* during the late 1950s. Sears now lives and writes in Ottawa, Ontario.

Erika Ritter: Ritter was born in Regina, Saskatchewan. She is a humourist, writer, broadcaster, and columnist who has won an ACTRA Award and Chalmers Play Award, among others.

Michele McAlpine (1963): McAlpine was born and educated in Toronto, Ontario. She is currently a part-time student working towards a degree in English from the University of Toronto. This essay is her first published piece.

Mordecai Richler (1931): Novelist, story writer, playwright, and essayist, Richler was born in Montreal. He has claimed that he views his literary vocation as the challenge to bear accurate witness to his time and place, to "get it right."

Margaret Laurence (1926–1987): Born in Neepawa, Manitoba, Laurence wrote novels, essays, short fiction and children's books. Much of her work is based on her travels, especially in Africa, and her life in the small Canadian prairie town in which she was born.

Cary Fagan (1957): Fagan was born in Toronto and educated at the University of Toronto. He has edited a collection of short fiction about Toronto, *Streets of Attitude* (Yonge and Bloor Publishing, 1990), and a collection of stories and novellas, *History Lessons* (Hounslow Press) among others. His most recent novel is *Animals' Waltz*, published in October, 1994.

Stuart Ross (1959): Ross has been involved in a variety of literary pursuits. He is a founder of The Toronto Small Press Book Fair; he has sold poems on the street. A member of PEN International, Ross is one of the founders of "Meet the Presses," an event designed to bring Toronto writers, publishers, and readers into close contact. His writing often aims for a balance between the real and the surreal.

Stephen Leacock (1869–1944): A famous Canadian humourist, Leacock was born in England, but grew up near Lake Simcoe, Ontario. He spent most of his summers in Orillia, Ontario, the small town that is the setting for many of his literary pieces. A much coveted award for Canadian humour writing bears his name.

Daniel David Moses (1952): Moses was born at Obsweken, Ontario, and grew up on a farm on the Six Nations land near Brantford, Ontario. He has a degree in creative writing from the University of British Columbia. His work includes *Delicate Bodies* (blewointment press, 1980), *The White Line: Poems* (Fifth House, 1991), and *Coyote City* (Williams-Wallace publishers, 1991).

P A R T   1 | Non-fiction

Spring Fancies

By **Val Sears**

1   I come from that part of the country where spring is rare as reason. We switch from the furnace to the air conditioner with hardly a pause here in Ottawa, in fact throughout Eastern Ontario. But now and then, in this cruelest of climates, there are a precious few days, perhaps even a week, when it is truly spring—soft and green and so captivating that we stop to sit in the park, on our steps, or on the curb and turn our faces toward the sun, opening up like flowers. We venture into Ottawa's backyard, the Gatineau Hills, to walk among the luminous trilliums, listen to brooks babbling their way and hold mittened hands with our loved one. The best thing about spring around here is that it comes when it's needed most.

2   My favourite springtime spot is up in those hills, near an old mill and a country cemetery where Prime Minister Lester Pearson, his wife Marion and some of their friends are buried. It's a cheerful place with a view of the green valley and a rolling meadow down among some trees where, with a bottle of wine and book, one can laugh out loud, chew a blade of new grass and think about nothing at all.

3   Across Canada, spring has a thousand faces—a mood for every fancy. In Vancouver, where I grew up, spring comes so soon the Christmas tree is hardly out of the house. Once (not now I suppose) the daffodils grew like weeds beside the ditches and you could gather an armload for the living-room along with bunches of blue lupines (we call them snake tails) which were less appreciated. We waited anxiously for the red berries on mountain ash trees because they made fine ammunition for slingshots, to bounce off an enemy's head.

4   Out on the prairies, where I lived for a while near Regina, spring's beautiful emptiness fills your heart. As soon as the roads are dry enough to drive on, it is an aesthetic adventure—on an April day—to catch a golden column of sunshine hitting the wheat stubble or splitting into a million colours when it strikes a new pond.

5   In Quebec, on a May day, I drove down a road east of Montreal to a ferry that splashed its way to Butternut Island. A bare few minutes after arriving at an inn, a family I had met on the boat called and insisted I come to dinner. I sat on the back porch with my elderly hostess as she gutted small fish from a pail and threw them, sparkling in the sun, to the pan destined for the oven. That evening, with a little French, and a little English and grinning, we ate the fish, drank home-made dandelion wine and sang songs in the moonlight.

6   Another spring I vividly recall found me on a political campaign, airborne in a helicopter convoy bound for a remote Newfoundland harbour. On the return trip, in the blaring, late-afternoon sun, the choppers swooped and whirled around icebergs, glittering and fanciful as the Emerald City of Oz.

7   It is a fact of spring that there can be no planning. Plan for a picnic and it snows; wax the skis and there are rocks and bushes springing from every slope. So you have to be ready to jump when Mother Nature shouts—and you have to take risks.

8   One spring of my youth, a rich uncle gave me $400 and told me to go to New York City and spend it all in one weekend. Every young man should have a magic weekend in New York, never mind Paris, he said. It was late in April, warm as a bagel. At the Edison Hotel, I paid in advance and went out to the cab rank. I gave the first taxi driver there—an old man $200 cash and asked him to look after me for my weekend. It was a wonderful game which he loved as much as I. We went everywhere that was important: Empire State Building, Rockettes at Radio City Music Hall, a caleche in Central Park, dinner at Toots Shore, jazz until dawn in the Village. On Sunday he insisted we drive to Wall Street. I must walk down the empty streets because, he said, it was like being on the bottom of the Grand Canyon. It was, only with a taxi crawling along behind me. Then the Staten Island ferry, lunch in Brooklyn and the airport. We said goodbye and I gave him what was left of my money—it would have been bad luck to take any home. I've been to New York many times since, but never alone and never so heady. I guess in spring, if you don't believe in miracles, you're not a realist.

9   A final fact about spring, never mind geography, is that it is the season of promise. The first boat trip, the golf game at par, that big fish at the bottom of the pool, an invigorating tennis game outdoors.

10   But the calendar is unreliable; you have to find your way of knowing that spring is here. If you are a child of the city, as I was, growing up in a top floor apartment on a busy street, it's the first fly. Suddenly there's a buzzing and that soft banging on the window. A kind of robin's song. The first fly of spring. I suppose there are birds and groundhogs and buds bursting in other places , moss on the antlers of the deer up north, the Americans crossing our southern border.

11   In Ottawa, curiously, the first sign of spring is a sound—a shattering sound. Somebody responsible for rivers, I suppose, plants dynamite charges in the ice of the slumbering Rideau and blows it to pieces so the water can flow freely again. A winter doze cannot survive such a blast.

12   Then, hey nonny, nonny, we are alive again, we can survive again. There are poems to be written, songs to be sung. Pity the poor people who live in the tropics and can only read about spring. This is Canada's season, everybody's favourite.

13   Except me. I like autumn better.

Questions for Discussion and Analysis
1. What comment does this essay make about the Canadian climate?
2. Which of the author's springs appeals to you the most and why?
3. Why does Sears call spring "the season of promise"? (paragraph 9)
4. What does the author reveal about himself in this essay?
5. What do you think about the last line of the essay?
6. Describe your favourite Canadian spring.

Bicycles

By Erika Ritter

1   It wasn't always like this. There was a time in the life of the world when adults were adults, having firmly put away childish things and thrown away the key.

2   Not any more. The change must have come about innocently enough, I imagine. Modern Man learning to play nicely in the sandbox with the grown-ups. Very low-tension stuff.

3   Now, in every direction you look, your gaze is met by the risible spectacle of adults postponing adolescence well into senility by means of adults toys: running shoes, baseball bats, roller skates, and—bicycles!

4   But the attitude is no longer the fun-loving approach of a bunch of superannuated kids, and I'm sure you can envision how the evolution occurred. Jogging progressed from a casual encounter with the fresh air to an intensive relationships, attended by sixty-dollar jogging shoes and a designer sweatband. Playing baseball stopped being fun unless you had a Lacoste (as opposed to low-cost) tee-shirt in which to impress your teammates. And where was the thrill in running around a squash court unless it was with a potential important client?

5   As for bicycles—well, let's not even talk about bicycles. On the other hand, maybe we *should* talk about them, because there's something particularly poignant about how it all went wrong for the bicycle, by what declension this once proud and carefree vehicle sank into the role of beast of burden, to bear the weight of sobersided grown-ups at their supposed sport.

6   First, there was the earliest domestication of the North American bicycle (*cyclus pedalis americanus*) in the late Hippie Scene Era of the 1960s. This was the age of the no-nuke whole-grain cyclist, who saw in the bicycle the possibility of Making a Statement while he rode. A statement about pollution, about materialism, about imperialism, about militarism, about—enough already. You get the picture: two wheels good, four wheels bad.

7   Thus it was that the basic bicycle gradually evolved into a chunky three-speed number from China, bowed down under a plastic kiddie carrier, army surplus knapsacks, and a faded fender-sticker advising Make Tofu, Not War. And a rider clad in a red plaid lumber-jacket, Birkenstock sandals, and an expression of urgent concern for all living things.

8   Once the very act of bicycle riding had become an act of high moral purpose, it was an easy step to the next phase of the bicycle's journey along the path of post-Neanderthal seriousness.

9   I'm speaking of the era of the high-strung thoroughbred bicycle, whose rider had also made advances, from pedalling peacenik to a hunched and humorless habitué of the velodrome, clad in leather-seated shorts, white crash helmets, and fingerless gloves, whizzing soundlessly, and with no hint of joy, down city streets and along the shoulders of super-highways, aboard a vehicle sculpted in wisps of silver chrome. A vehicle so overbred, in its final evolutionary stages, that it began to resemble the mere exoskeleton of a conventional cycle, its flesh picked away by birds of carrion.

10   Having been stripped of any connection with its innocent and leisurely origins, the bicycle had no longer bore the slightest resemblance to the happy crea-

ture it once had been. And in the mid-Plastic Scene Era, another crippling blow was struck by the upscale name-brand cyclist, who came along to finish what the fanatical velodromist had refined. Namely, the complete transformation of an ambling and unhurried mode of transit into a fast, nerve-wracking, expensive, and utterly competitive display of high speed, high technology, and high status.

11   The Upscale Cyclist was looking for a twelve-speed Bottecchia that matches his eyes, something that he'd look trendy upon the seat of, when riding to the office (the office!), and he was ready to pay in four figures for it.

12   Not only that, was also prepared to shell out some heavy bread for those status accessories to complete the picture: the backpack designed by the engineers at NASA, the insulated water-bottle to keep his Perrier chilled just right, the sixteen-track Walkman that would virtually assure him the envy of all his friends.

13   So much for the cyclist. What of his poor debased mount?

14   Not surprisingly, amongst the breed of bicycle, morale is currently low, and personal pride all but a thing of the past. And yet…and yet, there are those who say that *cyclus pedalis americanus* is an indomitable creature, and that it is the bicycle, not its rider, who will make the last evolution of the wheel.

15   In fact, some theorize that the present high incidence of bicycle thievery, far from being evidence of crime, is actually an indication that the modern bicycle has had enough of oppressive exploitation and man's joyless ways, and is in the process of reverting to the wild in greater and greater numbers.

16   There have always remained a few aboriginal undomesticated bicycles—or so the theory goes—and now it is these free-spirited mavericks, down from the hills at night, who visit urban bikeracks, garages, and back porches to lure tame bicycles away with them.

17   Costly Kryptonite locks are wrenched asunder, expensive accouterments are shrugged off, intricate gear systems are torn away, and lo—look what is revealed! Unadorned, undefiled *cyclus* in all his pristine glory, unfettered and unencumbered once more, and free to roam.

18   A wistful fantasy, you might say? The maundering illusions of someone who's been riding her bicycle too long without a crash helmet? I wonder.

19   Just the other day, there was that piece of paper about a bicycle that went berserk in a shopping centre, smashing two display windows before it was subdued. And did you hear about the recent sighting of a whole herd of riderless bicycles, all rolling soundlessly across a park in the night?

20   It all kind of gets you to thinking. I mean, do *you* know where your ten-speed is tonight?

Questions for Discussion and Analysis
1.   In the first three paragraphs, what is Ritter's attitude towards adults?
2.   Why does she document the history of the bicycle?
3.   How does this evolution reinforce her description of the cyclist?
4.   What other types of bicycles can you add to her list?
5.   What is the author's tone throughout the essay? What details in the essay help you determine its tone?
6.   Explain three of Ritter's allusions. Suggest how these contribute to the essay.

Together at the Death of a Stranger

By Michele McAlpine

1   My father died when I was a child. Like anyone who has lost a loved one, I will never forget the day as long as I live. He died in a restaurant. His car had broken down and he had gone in to buy a cup of coffee and wait for a tow truck. Precisely 10 minutes after he hung up the phone from calling my mother to say he would be late arriving home, he was dead. How could we have known at 11:10 a.m. that day that our lives had changed forever? No trumpets blared, no bands played, no balloons were released to mark the moment. He was just gone.

2   Fifteen years after I still recall the most intricate moments of the days that followed. The growing collection of tinfoil-clad foodstuffs from neighbours, the endless chorus of "yes, he was a fine man…," the long nights laying awake and wondering if this loss was really happening. I kept waiting for my father to come home so I could tell him about this wonderful man who had passed on so unexpectedly. But he never came home.

3   As the days turned into months, the healing began and now, all these years later, I remember him with a smile. If anything from the past still haunts me it is only that I wasn't there when he died. I didn't get to try to help him. In my mind, he died in a restaurant by himself, undoubtedly surrounded by veritable strangers, and I've never known if anyone came to his aid.

4   Until now. Something happened this week that gave me my answer.

5   As I was leaving a restaurant with a friend, an elderly man collapsed in our path. Before I realized what had happened, my friend Kevin had knelt down by the man, whispering encouragement and covering him with his coat to keep him warm. Within minutes, there was a group of passers-by who had all stopped to ask how they could help.

6   When I returned from calling an ambulance, the man's condition had deteriorated and life-saving measures were being taken. Even though we had our suspicions, we learned only later that, at that point, the man was dead. Not that anyone in the crowd acknowledged this, mind you, because collectively we had a mission. We were determined that this man would pull through, and a small group of us worked like a well-oiled machine to ensure it. (The fact that he was already dead was a mere inconvenience.)

7   We ran into the street to flag the ambulance, we made sure his eyeglasses, which had fallen from his face when he collapsed, were safely back in his pocket, we kept laying more coats over him to ensure his ultimate comfort and, most important, we kept is heart beating with our very hands. And when the ambulance whisked him off, we felt let down that we had not been allowed to climb in with him and see our challenge through. Some of us were openly emotional while others, their heads hung low, shook hands in a show of what we had shared. We never saw the man again. He was just gone.

8   Kevin and I got into our car and drove away from the scene, but never really left it behind. Days later we found ourselves, checking the local newspaper for an obituary we were sure would appear. It did. The man's name was Nigel Anderson; he was 87 and predeceased by his wife, Eleanor, but this "much cherished" man was survived by his daughter, Ruth. (Some of the names in this story have been changed.)

9   I felt compassion for Ruth. I knew she would experience all that I had gone through when my father passed away. The growing collection of tinfoil-clad food-stuffs from neighbours, the endless chorus of "yes, he was a fine man…," the long nights lying awake and wondering if the loss was really happening. I knew that for the rest of her life she would wonder just what had happened: Who had been the last person with her father, where exactly did he die and was it as awful as she imagined?

10   And that's why, on the day before Nigel was laid to rest, Kevin and I went to the funeral home to meet Ruth and answer her questions. Our hearts were pounding as we entered the room full of strangers. A rather frail-looking woman glanced up to acknowledge our entrance and hurried towards us. She said that even though she didn't recognize us, she knew who we were. The police had told her that people had come to the aid of her dad and that he had died outside a restaurant—was that true? And so our conversation began.

11   She embraced us and thanked us for our efforts. I told her that her father had died admist a show of concern and she needn't worry that he had died alone. It occurred to me that one of the most private events of this woman's life was being shared by strangers, and while the conversation lasted only 15 minutes, I knew she would never forget it.

12   And likewise, I will never forget Nigel Anderson. Through him I got my own answer to the question that had haunted me for years. I know now that my father did not die alone. Someone was there to call an ambulance; to put his eyeglasses in his pocket; to keep him warm and to keep his heart beating with their hands. My father had been cared for, just as we had cared for Nigel, because apparently that is what strangers do. It was something that, in a split second, needed to be done and we did it.

13   And this is astounding to me. For every day we read in the newspaper that one human being has killed another, that people are boarding New York commuter trains and murdering those in their path. We read of pestilence and disease, of families being broken apart by domestic violence. All these stories tell us exactly the same thing—that the regard for human life is seemingly diminishing before our very eyes.

14   All that considered, it's no wonder that the care and love shown to Nigel astounds me. Maybe it's easier to administer care to a stranger, because there is no emotional attachment and therefore you have nothing to lose. Or maybe it's selfish motives that make us extend ourselves to people in need—a way to boost our own self-worth and confirm that we are capable of reaching out to others. Whatever the case, in a world where violence seems to reign, there are glimmers of compassion and a respect for human dignity. I know, because I witnessed such a glimmer.

15   I'm sure Nigel Anderson—and my father—would agree.

Questions for Discussion and Analysis

1. What details does the author remember about the day her father died?
2. How did the strangers react when Nigel Anderson collapsed?
3. Why does the author feel compassion for the dead man's daughter?
4. Why was the strangers' behaviour so remarkable?
5. This essay documents a true story. What qualities in the writing make it so authentic?
6. Why does the author place her thesis in paragraph 14?

Main Street

By Mordecai Richler

1   If the Main was a poor man's street, it was also a dividing line. Below, the French Canadians. Above, some distance above, the dreaded WASPS. On the Main itself there were some Italians, Yugoslavs and Ukrainians, but they did not count as true Gentiles. Even the French Canadians, who were our enemies, were not entirely unloved. Like us, they were poor and coarse with large families and spoke English badly.

2   Looking back, it's easy to see that the real trouble was there was no dialogue between us and the French Canadians, each elbowing the other, striving for WASP acceptance. We fought the French Canadians stereotype for stereotype. If many of them believed that the St. Urbain Street Jews were secretly rich, manipulating the black market, then my typical French Canadian was a moronic gum-chewer. He wore his greasy black hair parted down the middle and also affected an eye-brow moustache. His zoot trousers were belted just under the breastbone and ended in a peg hugging his ankles. He was the dolt who held up your uncle endlessly at the liquor commission while he tried unsuccessfully to add three figures or, if he was employed at the customs office, never knew which form to give you. Furthermore, he only held his liquor commission or customs or any other government job because he was the second cousin of a backwoods notary who had delivered the village vote to the Union Nationale for a generation. Other French Canadians were speed cops, and if any of these every stopped you on the highway you made sure to hand him a folded two dollar bill with your licence.

3   Actually, it was only the WASPS who were truly hated and feared. "Among them," I heard it said, "with those porridge faces, who can tell what they're thinking?" It was, we felt, their country, and given sufficient liquor who knew when they would make trouble?

4   We were a rude, aggressive bunch round the Main. Cocky too. But bring down the most insignificant, pinched WASP fire insurance inspector and even the most arrogant merchant on the street would dip into the drawer for a ten spot or a bottle and bow and say, "Sir."

5   After school we used to race down to the Main to play snooker at the Rachel or the Mount Royal. Other days, when we chose to avoid school altogether, we would take the No. 55 streetcar as far as St. Catharines Street, where there was a variety of amusements offered. We could play the pinball machines and watch archaic strip-tease movies for a nickel at the Silver Gameland. At the Midway or the Crystal Palace we could see a double feature and a girlie show for as little as thirty-five cents. The Main, at this juncture, was thick with drifters, panhandlers, and whores. Available on both sides of the street were "Tourists Rooms by Day and Night," and everywhere there was the smell of french fried potatoes cooking in stale oil. Tough, unshaven men in checked shirts stood in knots outside the taverns and cheap cafés. There was the promise of violence.

6   As I recall it, we were always being warned about the Main. Our grandparents and parents had come there by steerage from Rumania or by cattleboat from Poland by way of Liverpool. No sooner had they unpacked their bundles and cardboard suitcases than they were planning a better, brighter life for us, the

Canadian-born children. The Main, good enough for them, was not to be for us, and that they told us again and again was what the struggle was for. The Main was for *bummers*, drinkers, and (heaven forbid) failures.

Questions for Discussion and Analysis

1. Characterize the people who lived on the Main.
2. How does Richler describe the typical French Canadian? the typical St. Urbain Street Jew? the typical WASP?
3. What motivates people to stereotype others?
4. Why were the WASPs "dreaded"?
5. How does Richler's language reflect the vitality of the street?
6. Account for the shift in paragraph 6.

Where the World Began

By Margaret Laurence

1   A strange place it was, that place where the world began. A place of incredible happenings, splendours and revelations, despairs like multitudinous pits of isolated hells. A place of shadow-spookiness, inhabited by the unknowable dead. A place of jubilation and of mourning, horrible and beautiful.

2   It was, in fact, a small prairie town.

3   Because that settlement and that land were my first and for many years my only real knowledge of this planet, in some profound way they remain my world, my way of viewing. My eyes were formed there. Towns like ours, set in a sea of land, have been described thousands of times as dull, bleak, flat, uninteresting. I have had it said to me that the railway trip across Canada is spectacular, except for the prairies, when it would be desirable to go to sleep for several days, until the ordeal is over. I am always unable to argue this point effectively. All I can say is—well, you really have to live there to know that country. The town of my childhood could be called bizarre, agonizing repressive or cruel at times, and the land in which it grew could be called harsh in the violence of its seasonal changes. But never merely flat or uninteresting. Never dull.

4   In winter, we used to hitch rides on the back of the milk sleigh, our moccasins squeaking and slithering on the hard rutted snow of the roads, our hands in ice-bubbled mitts hanging onto the box edge of the sleigh for dear life, while Bert grinned at us through his great frosted moustache and shouted the horse into speed, daring us to stay put. Those mornings, rising, there would be the perpetual fascination of the frost feathers on windows, the ferns and flowers and eerie faces traced there during the night by unseen artists of the wind. Evenings, come back from skating, the sky would be black but not dark, for you could see a cold glitter of stars from one side of the earth's rim to the other. And then the sometime astonishment when you saw the Northern Lights flaring across the sky, like the scrawled signature of God. After a blizzard, when the snowploughs hadn't yet got through, school would be closed for the day, the assumption being that the town's young could not possibly flounder through five feet of snow in the pursuit

of education. We would then gaily don snowshoes and flounder for miles out into the white dazzling deserts, in pursuit of a different kind of knowing. If you came back too close to night, through the woods at the foot of the town hill, the thin black branches of poplar and chokecherry now meringued with frost, sometimes you heard coyotes. Or maybe the banshee wolf-voices were really only inside your head.

5   Summers were scorching, and when no rain came and the wheat became bleached and dried before it headed, the faces of farmers and townsfolk would not smile much, and you took for granted, because it never seemed to have been any different, the frequent knocking at the back door and the young men standing there, mumbling or thrusting defiantly their requests for a drink of water and a sandwich if you could spare it. They were riding the freights, and you never knew where they had come from, or where they might end up, if anywhere. The Drought and Depression were like evil deities which had been there always. You understood and did not understand.

6   Yet the outside world had its continuing marvels. The poplar bluffs and the small river were filled and surrounded with a zillion different grasses, stones, and weed flowers. The meadowlarks sang undaunted from the twanging telephone wires along the gravel highway. Once we found an old flattened scow, and launched her, pulling along the shallow brown waters, mending her with wodges of hastily chewed Spearmint, grounding her among the tangles of yellow marsh marigolds that grew succulently along the banks of the shrunken river, while the sun made our skins smell dusty-warm.

7   My best friend lived in an apartment above some stores on Main Street (its real name was Mountain Avenue, goodness knows why), an elegant apartment with royal-blue velvet curtains. The back roof, scarcely sloping at all, was corrugated tin of a furnace-like warmth on a July afternoon, and we would sit there drinking lemonade and looking across the back lane at the Fire Hall. Sometimes our vigil would be rewarded. Oh joy! Somebody's house burning down! We had an almost-perfect callousness in some ways. Then the wooden tower's bronze bell would clonk and toll like a thousand speeded funerals in a time of plague, and in a few minutes the team of giant black horses would cannon forth, pulling the fire wagon like some scarlet chariot of the Goths, while the firemen clung with one hand, adjusting their helmets as they went.

8   The oddities of the place were endless. An elderly lady used to serve, as her afternoon tea offering to other ladies, soda biscuits spread with peanut butter and topped with a whole marshmallow. Some considered this slightly eccentric, when compared with chopped egg sandwiches, and admittedly talked about her behind her back, but no one ever refused these delicacies or indicated to her that they thought she had slipped a cog. Another lady dyed her hair a bright and cheery orange, by strangers often mistaken at twenty paces for a feather hat. My own beloved stepmother wore a silver fox neckpiece, a whole pelt, *with the embalmed (?) head still on*. My Ontario Irish grandfather said, "sparrow grass," a more interesting term than asparagus. The town dump was known as "the nuisance grounds," a phrase fraught with weird connotations, as though the effluvia of our lives was beneath contempt but at the same time was subtly threatening to the determined and sometimes hysterical propriety of our ways.

9   Some oddities were, as idiom had it, "funny ha ha"; others were "funny peculiar." Some were not so very funny at all. An old man lived, deranged, in a shack in the valley. Perhaps he wasn't even all that old, but to us he seemed a wild

Methuselah figure, shambling along the underbrush and the tall couchgrass, muttering indecipherable curses or blessings, a prophet who had forgotten his prophesies. Everyone in town knew him, but no one knew him. He lived among us as though only occasionally and momentarily visible. The kids called him Andy Gump, and feared him. Some sought to prove their bravery by tormenting him. They were the mediaeval bear baiters, and he the lumbering bewildered bear, half blind, only rarely turning to snarl. Everything is to be found in a town like mine. Belsen, writ small but with the same ink.

10   All of us cast stones in one shape or another. In grade school, among the vulnerable and violet girls we were, the feared and despised were those few older girls from what was charmingly termed "the wrong side of the tracks." Tough in talk and tougher in muscle, they were said to be whores already. And may have been, that being the only profession readily available to them.

11   The dead lived in that place, too. Not only the grandparents who had, in local parlance, "passed on" and who gloomed, bearded or bonneted, from the sepia photographs in old albums, but also the uncles, forever eighteen or nineteen, whose names were carved on the granite family stones in the cemetery, but whose bones lay in France. My own young mother lay in that graveyard, beside other dead of our kin, and when I was ten, my father, too, only forty, left the living town for the dead dwelling on the hill.

12   When I was eighteen, I couldn't wait to get out of that town, away from the prairies. I did not know then that I would carry the land and town all my life within my skull, and they would form the mainspring and source of the writing I was to do, wherever and however far away I might live.

13   This was my territory in the time of my youth, and in a sense my life since then has been an attempt to look at it, to come to terms with it. Stultifying to the mind it certainly could be, and sometimes was, but not to the imagination. It was many things, but it was never dull.

14   The same, I now see, could be said for Canada in general. Why on earth did generations of Canadians pretend to believe this country dull? We knew perfectly well it wasn't. Yet for so long we did not proclaim what we knew. If our upsurge of so-called nationalism seems odd or irrelevant to outsiders, and to some of our own people (*what's all the fuss about?*), they might try to understand that for many years we valued ourselves insufficiently, living as we did under the huge shadows of those two dominating figures, Uncle Sam and Britannia. We have only just begun to value ourselves, our land, our abilities. We have only just begun to recognize our legends and to give shape to our myths.

15   There are, God know, enough aspects to deplore about this country. When I see the killing of our lakes and rivers with industrial wastes, I feel rage and despair. When I see our industries and natural resources increasingly taken over by America, I feel an overwhelming discouragement, especially as I cannot simply say "damn Yankees." It should never be forgotten that it is we ourselves who have sold such a large amount of our birthright for a mess of plastic Progress. When I saw the War Measures Act being invoked in 1970, I lost forever the vestigal remains of the naive wish-belief that repression could not happen here, or would not. And yet, of course, I had known all along in the deepest and often hidden caves of the heart that anything can happen here, for the seeds of both man's freedom and his captivity are found everywhere, even in the microcosm of a prairie town. But in raging against our injustices, our stupidities, I do so *as family*,

as I did, and still do in writing, about those aspects of my town which I hated and which are always in some ways aspects of myself.

16   The land still draws me more than other lands. I have lived in Africa and England, but splendid as both can be, they do not have the power to move in the same way as, for example, that part of southern Ontario where I spent four months last summer in a cedar cabin beside a river. "Scratch a Canadian, and you find a phony pioneer," I used to say to myself in warning. But all the same it is true, I think, that we are not yet totally alienated from physical earth, and let us only pray we do not become so. I once thought that lifelong fear and mistrust of cities made me a kind of old-fashioned freak; now I see it differently.

17   The cabin has a long window across its front western wall, and sitting at the oak table there in the mornings, I used to look out at the river and at the tall trees beyond, green-gold in the early light. The river was bronze; the sun caught it strangely, reflecting upon its surface the near-shore sand ripples underneath. Suddenly, the crescenting of a fish, gone before the eye could clearly give image to it. The old man next door said these leaping fish were carp. Himself, he preferred muskie, for he was a real fisherman and the muskie gave him a fight. The wind most often blew from the south, and the river flowed toward the south, so when the water was wind-riffled, and the current was strong, the river seemed to be flowing both ways. I liked this, and interpreted it as an omen, a natural symbol.

18   A few years ago, when I was back in Winnipeg, I gave a talk at my old college. It was open to the public, and afterward a very old man came up to me and asked me if my maiden name had been Wemyss. I said yes, thinking he might have known my father or my grandfather. But no. "When I was a young lad," he said, "I once worked for your great-grandfather, Robert Wemyss, when he had the sheep ranch at Raeburn." I think that was a moment when I realized all over again something of great importance to me. My long-ago families came from Scotland and Ireland, but in a sense that no longer mattered so much. My true roots were here.

19   I am not very patriotic, in the usual meaning of that word. I cannot say "My country right or wrong" in any political, social or literary context. But one thing is inalterable, for better or worse, for life.

20   This is where my world began. A world which includes the ancestors—both my own and other people's ancestors who became mine. A world which formed me, and continues to do so, even while I fought it in some of its aspects, and continue to do so. A world which gave me my own lifework to do, because it was here that I learned the sight of my own particular eyes.

Questions for Discussion and Analysis
1. What physical characteristics of Laurence's hometown make it memorable? Relate these to the details in Douglas McArthur's article on pages 265–267.
2. What does she remember about the behaviour of some of the people who lived here?
3. What comparison does she make between her prairie town and "Canada in general"?
4. Comment on Laurence's sense of patriotism.
5. What is her thesis and where is it stated?
6. How would your describe the tone (voice) of this essay?
7. Select two or three examples of Laurence's effective use of language. Include why you find these appealing.

| PART 2 | Fiction |

Cartoon

By Cary Fagan

1   One day Fischer, eating lunch at his desk, was startled by a cartoon in the latest issue of a magazine.

2   The cartoonist was one of those notetakers to contemporary manners whom Fischer rarely found amusing, but this cartoon perfectly captured the nature of his affair with D. The failure of this relationship, during which marriage had been seriously discussed, had tormented Fischer for a month now. He suffered not only from the loss, but also because he blamed himself for mishandling a crucial moment. One evening Fischer had deliberately brought things to a head in order to tell D. everything that was wrong and yet at the same time to speak unguardedly of how he felt about her. But these complex feelings had come out as a kind of whine, and he had succeeded only in giving D. a chance to break it off.

3   And here was this cartoon, so astonishingly true to his experience with D., to everything that had been hopeful and absurd about it. He reached for a ruler to tear it from the page. Then he folded the cartoon and slipped it into his wallet.

4   Over the next few days Fischer became possessed by the idea of showing the cartoon to D. While he couldn't phone her or show up at her apartment door or even send it in a letter, he was bound to run into her some time. What he expected of this encounter he wasn't sure, only that the cartoon would make everything he had meant to say clear to her. But he didn't run into D.—not in a week or a month or three months. He relapsed into bachelorhood and slowly learned again how to enjoy the single, uncompromised life.

5   And then of course he saw her. She was standing on Bloor Street, looking confused for a moment, as if she had forgotten where she was going. Fischer said her name aloud before he knew what he was doing. The two exchanged pleasantries for a few moments and then D., glancing at her watch, excused herself. He didn't remember the cartoon until she was halfway across Bloor Street and by then it was too late. He merely watched her turn a corner and the meeting he'd been anticipating for almost a year was over.

6   His own lunch hour was almost up but he couldn't bear the thought of immediately returning, so he ducked into one of those new, sterile chain-cafés that seemed to be taking over the city. He sat down by the window and took the cartoon from his wallet, worn from all those months in his back pocket. Somehow it wasn't quite what he remembered, as if the characters had changed their expressions or the words had rearranged themselves. Had it never had anything to do with his affair with D., or had he forgotten what they had been like together? Looking at it now, he started to weep. An awful, physically painful weeping. Without looking up, Fischer thought: if only D. would walk by and see me. But the only person who noticed him was one of the secretaries from the office. And she thought: good, you bastard, you suffer for a change. Flushed and trembling, she hurried up the street on her high heels. So that a cab driver, stuck at a red light, noticed her and thought of his mother, dead for over twenty years.

Questions for Discussion and Analysis
1. Characterize Fischer.
2. Explain the story's ending.
3. What may be Fagan's view of the world as portrayed in this short story?
4. This short story is very compact. How would it be possible to develop this into a longer story?
5. Have you ever cut something out of the newspaper and kept it for a while? Explain what it was and why it was important.

The Wedding Dress

By Stuart Ross

1   A waiter spills a tureen of soup on the bride during a wedding dinner. As the liquid spread across her wedding dress, the bride's radiant smile turns to a grimace. The father of the bride strikes the waiter, who falls to the floor, where he receives kicks to the abdomen and head from various members of the wedding party, including the priest and the bandleader. That night the groom is unable to perform. He locks himself in the bathroom of the honeymoon suite and weeps. The bride watches television until the last national anthem dissolves to a test pattern. The waiter lies in a hospital bed with tubes up his nose.

2   Ten years later, the husband and wife find themselves unemployed, victims of the arrogant economic policies of an unrepentantly conservative government voted into power by a bullied populace. Soon their cupboards are bare and their child is crying. Both the man and woman are too proud to line up for food packages at the Salvation Army. Crippled by weakness, they are almost unable to move, until the woman remembers her wedding dress, rolled up in a trunk under the bed, where it has been since their night of holy matrimony. She extracts the dress from the trunk and puts it in a pot on the stove, adding copious amounts of water. The dress disintegrates as it cooks, transforming into vermicelli-like strands, floating in a vegetable stock prepared a decade earlier.

3   As the family sits down at the table to eat, there is a knock at the door. It is the waiter. He has been searching for them all these years, and has come at last to apologise for his clumsiness. He wears a mask to hide his disfigured face, and his arms and torso are stiff as he enters the house. Instead of the flurry of blows he had anticipated, he receives an invitation to dinner, and being himself a hungry victim of the government of corporate interests, he accepts.

4   Soon the government falls, and the waiter enters the political arena, rising with unprecedented rapidity to the position of prime minister. In no time, once-abused waiters all over the world have ascended to the top positions of their respective governments. Armament factories are closed down and corporate polluters fined and jailed. No one goes without soup.

Questions for Discussion and Analysis
1. Describe the tone. When do you become aware of this tone (voice)?
2. Why are the characters not named?
3. Where does the story take place?
4. Who or what might the priest, bandleader, and waiter symbolize?
5. Comment on the appropriateness of the length of this story.
6. What may be the author's message?

My Financial Career

By Stephen Leacock

1   When I go into a bank I get rattled. The clerks rattle me; the wickets rattle me, the sight of the money rattles me; everything rattles me.

2   The moment I cross the threshold of a bank and attempt to transact business there, I became an irresponsible idiot.

3   I knew this beforehand, but my salary had been raised to fifty dollars a month and I felt that the bank was the only place for it.

4   So I shambled in and looked timidly round at the clerks. I had an idea that a person about to open an account must needs consult the manager.

5   I went up to a wicket marked "Accountant." The accountant was a tall, cool devil. The very sight of him rattled me. My voice was sepulchral.

6   "Can I see the manager?" I said, and added solemnly, "alone." I don't know why I said "alone."

7   "Certainly," said the accountant, and fetched him.

8   The manager was a grave, calm man. I held my fifty-six dollars clutched in a crumpled ball in my pocket.

9   "Are you the manager?" I said. God knows I didn't doubt it.

10   "Yes," he said.

11   "Can I see you," I asked, "alone?" I didn't want to say "alone" again, but without it the thing seemed self-evident.

12   The manager looked at me in some alarm. He felt that I had an awful secret to reveal.

13   "Come in here," he said, and led the way to a private room. He turned the key in the lock.

14   "We are safe from interruption here," he said. "Sit down."

15   We both sat down and looked at each other. I found no voice to speak.

16   "You are one of Pinkerton's men, I presume," he said.

17   He had gathered from my mysterious manner that I was a detective. I knew what he was thinking, and it made me worse.

18   "No, not from Pinkerton's" I said, seeming to imply that I came from a rival agency.

19   "To tell the truth," I went on, as if I had been prompted to lie about it, "I am not a detective at all. I have come to open an account. I intend to keep all my money in this bank."

20   The manager looked relieved but still serious; he concluded now that I was a son of Baron Rothschild or a young Gould.

21   "A large account, I suppose," he said.

22   "Fairly large," I whispered. "I propose to deposit fifty-six dollars now and fifty dollars a month regularly."

23   The manager got up and opened the door. He called to the accountant.

24   "Mr. Montgomery," he said unkindly loud, "this gentlemen is opening an account, he will deposit fifty-six dollars. Good morning."

25   I rose.

26   A big iron door stood open at the side of the room.

27   "Good morning," I said, and stepped into the safe.

28   "Come out," said the manager coldly, and showed me the other way.

29   I went up to the accountant's wicket and poked the ball of money at him with a quick convulsive movement as if I were doing a conjuring trick.

30   My face was ghastly pale.

31   "Here," I said, "deposit it." The tone of the words seemed to mean, "Let us do this painful thing while the fit is on us."

32   He took the money and gave it to another clerk.

33   He made me write the sum on a slip and sign my name in a book. I no longer knew what I was doing. The bank swam before my eyes.

34   "Is it deposited?" I asked in a hollow, vibrating voice.

35   "It is," said the accountant.

36   "Then I want to draw a cheque."

37   My idea was to draw out six dollars of it for present use. Someone gave me a cheque-book through a wicket and someone else began telling me how to write it out. The people in the bank had the impression that I was an invalid millionaire. I wrote something on the cheque and thrust it in at the clerk. He looked at it.

38   "What! Are you drawing it all out again?" he asked in surprise. Then I realized that I had written fifty-six instead of six. I was too far gone to reason now. I had a feeling that it was impossible to explain the thing. All the clerks had stopped writing to look at me.

39   Reckless with misery, I made a plunge.

40   "Yes, the whole thing."

41   "You withdraw your money from the bank?"

42   "Every cent of it."

43   "Are you not going to deposit any more?" said the clerk, astonished.

44   "Never."

45   An idiot hope struck me that they might think something had insulted me while I was writing the cheque and that I had changed my mind. I made a wretched attempt to look like a man with a fearfully quick temper.

46   The clerk prepared to pay the money.

47   "How will you have it?"

48   "What?"

49   "How will you have it?"

50   "Oh"—I caught his meaning and answered without even trying to think—"in fifties."

51   He gave me a fifty-dollar bill.

52   "And the six?" he asked dryly.

53   "In sixes," I said.

54   He gave it me and I rushed out.

55   As the big door swung behind me I caught the echo of a roar of laughter that

went up to the ceiling of the bank. Since then I bank no more. I keep my money in cash in my trousers pocket and my savings in silver dollars in a sock.

Questions for Discussion and Analysis
1. What is the point of view in this story? Comment on its effectiveness.
2. Characterize the narrator.
3. Show how Leacock develops humour throughout the short story.
4. How does the narrator view the bank employees?
5. How would the narrator feel about today's banking system?

King of the Raft

By Daniel David Moses

1   There was a raft in the river that year, put there, anchored with an anvil, just below a bend, by the one of the fathers who worked away in Buffalo, who could spend only every other weekend, if that, at home. The one of the mothers whose husband worked the land and came in from the fields for every meal muttered as she set the table that the raft was the only way the father who worked in the city was able to pretend he cared about his sons. Her husband, also one of the fathers, who had once when young gone across the border to work and then, unhappy there, returned, could not answer, soaking the dust of soil from his hands.

2   Most of the sons used that raft that was there just that one summer in the usually slow-moving water during the long evenings after supper, after the days of fieldwork of haying and then combining were done. A few of them, the ones whose fathers and mothers practised Christianity, also used it in the afternoons on sunny Sundays after the sitting through church and family luncheons. And the one of the sons who had only a father who came and went following the work— that son appeared whenever his rare duties or lonely freedom became too much for him.

3   The sons would come to the raft in Indian file along a footpath the half mile from the road and change their overalls or jeans for swimsuits among the goldenrod and milkweed on the bank, quickly, to preserve modesty and their blood from the mosquitoes, the only females around. Then one of the sons would run down the clay slope and stumble in with splashing and a cry of shock or joy for the water's current temperature. The other sons would follow, and, by the time they all climbed out on to the raft out in the stream, the rough laughter would become boys again.

4   The boys used that raft in the murky green water to catch the sun or their breaths on or to dive from when they tried to touch the mud bottom. One of the younger ones also used to stand looking across the current to the other side, trying to see through that field of corn there, the last bit of land that belonged to the Reserve. Beyond it the highway ran, a border patrolled by a few cars flashing chrome in the sun or headlights through the evening blue like messages from the city. Every one of the boys used the raft several times that summer to get across

the river and back, the accomplishment proof of their new masculinity. And once the younger one who spent time looking at that other land, crossed and climbed up the bank there and explored the shadows between the rows of corn, the leaves like dry tongues along his naked arms as he came to the field's far edge where the asphalt of that highway stood empty.

5   Toward the cool end of the evenings, any boy left out on the raft in the lapping black water would be too far from the shore to hear the conversations. They went on against a background noise of the fire the boys always built against the river's grey mist and mosquito lust, that they sometimes built for roasting corn, hot dogs, marshmallows. The conversations went on along with or over games of chess. Years later, one of the older boys, watching his own son play the game with a friend in silence, wondered if perhaps that was why their conversations that year of the raft about cars, guitars and girls—especially each other's sisters—about school and beer, always ended up in stalemate or check. Most of the boys ended up winning only their own solitariness from the conversations by the river. But the one who had only a father never even learned the rules of play.

6   One sunny Sunday after church late in the summer, the one who had only a father already sat on the raft in the river as the rest of the boys undressed. He smiled at the boy who had gone across through the corn, who made it into the water first. Then he stood up and the raft made waves as gentle as those in his blue-black hair—I'm the king of the raft, he yelled, challenging the boy who had seen the highway to win that wet wooden square. And a battle was joined, and the day was wet and fair, until the king of the raft, to show his strength to the rest of the boys still on shore, took a hank of the highway boy's straight hair in hand and held the highway boy underwater till the highway boy saw blue fire and almost drowned. The story went around among the mothers and the fathers and soon that son who had only a father found himself unwelcome. Other stories came around, rumours about his getting into fights or failing grades or how his father's latest girlfriend had dyed her Indian hair blond. And the boy who almost had drowned found he both feared the king of the raft and missed the waves in his blue-black hair.

7   One muggy evening when pale thunderheads growled in from the west, the boy who had almost drowned, who had the farthest to go to get home, left the raft and the rest by the river early. On the dark road he met the king, who had something to say. They hid together with a case of beer in a cool culvert under the road. The king of the raft was going away with his father to live in Buffalo in the United States and thought the boy who had almost drowned could use what was left of this beer the king's father would never miss. The boy who had almost drowned sipped from his bottle of sour beer and heard the rain beginning to hiss at the end of the culvert. He crawled and looked out in time to see the blue fire of lightning hit a tree. In the flash he saw again the waves in the king's blue-black hair, the grin that offered another beer. The boy who had almost drowned felt he was going down again, and, muttering some excuse, ran out into the rain. The king yelled after him the old insult boys use about your mother wanting you home.

8   The boy who had almost drowned found he could cross through the rain, anchored by his old running shoes to the ground, though the water came down like another river, cold and clear and wide as the horizon. He made it home and stood on the porch, waiting for the other side of the storm, hearing hail hitting

the roof and water through the eaves filling up the cistern. Later, out of the storm, he could still hear far off a gurgling in the gully and a quiet roar as the distant river tore between its banks. The storm still growled somewhere beyond the eastern horizon.

9   The raft was gone the next evening when the boys came to the bank and the current was still too cold and quick to swim in. No one crossed the river for the rest of the summer. The king of the raft never appeared again anywhere. In the fall, a rumour came around about this going to work in the city and in the winter another one claimed he had died. The boy who had crossed through the rain thought about going down even quicker in winter river water. Then a newspaper confirmed the death. In a traffic accident, the rain boy read. None of the boys had even met that impaired driver, that one of the fathers, surviving and charged without a license. One of the mothers muttered as she set another mother's hair about people not able to care even about their kids. The rain boy let the king of the raft sink into the river, washing him away in his mind and decided he would someday cross over and follow the highway through that land and find the city.

Questions for Discussion and Analysis
1. Recount this story in your own words.
2. What are your expectations from reading the opening sentence of the story?
3. What is the setting? Quote some of the details that pinpoint this locale.
4. What are the literal and figurative meanings of the borders in the story (mentioned or implied)?
5. What may be the theme of this story?
6. How does Moses' formal style reinforce the theme?
7. Explain the irony in the death of the king of the raft.

This appendix is designed to help you clarify and eliminate misunderstood words. These errors may often seem minor to you, but they can distract the reader or change the meaning of a sentence.

Similar Words Misused

Some words are pronounced so similarly to another word or words that they are misspelled. You may want to learn and practise one or two a day or practise only those that are troublesome to you. To learn the slight differences in the pairs of words, study the meanings; then look at the spelling or construction of the word. Finally, by practising the correct use of these words in sentences, you will be ready to use them properly in your writing. If you still have difficulty with a pair of words, write them down and restudy them.

EXERCISE 1

Read the following definitions and examples of confusing words. Work through the following sentences by striking through the word errors. Then write the correct form above the words that are wrong. Write "C" if the sentence contains no errors.

Pair 1

advise: (verb) to give valuable information
Please advise John of the change.

advise: (noun) valuable information given
John followed the advice.

1. John advised Butch not to hike the steep mountain.

2. Take the lifeguard's advise and don't swim while it is raining.

3. I advised her to do her house chores early.

4. Margaret refused to take my advice.

Pair 2

all ready: fully or completely ready
We are all ready for finals.

already: something completed previously
Finals are already over.

1. Are you already?

2. She is all ready at the soccer game.

3. When she got to the party, everyone was already there.

4. I was not at already for the English exam.

Pair 3

accept: receive   **except:** excluding
      I accept your apology for not calling.   Everyone except Jason came home.

1. She accepted my apology and walked away with a frown on her face.

2. Everyone went to the ball accept Cinderella.

3. She accepted the money greedily.

4. When Natalie arrived in class, everyone was present accept Marla.

Pair 4

brake: act of stopping or the device for   **break:** separate into parts
      stopping   I do not want to break the dishes.
      I brake for animals.

1. The bus driver slammed on the break, and the passengers flew forward.

2. How did you break the lamp last night?

3. When the car in front of us stopped, I hit the break with my foot.

4. The karate expert will brake twenty boards in twenty-five seconds.

Pair 5

by: a preposition indicating near, through,   **buy:** to purchase
      during, no later than, or respect to   I want to buy a new car.
      He parked his car by a fire hydrant.

1. Mrs. Smith needed to by detergent for her washing machine.

2. The fishing gear is by the car in the garage.

3. Mick needs to be at church by 8:30 a.m.

4. Who put the *TV Guide* by the lamp?

Pair 6

conscience: (noun) moral value that guides behaviour   **conscious:** (adjective) aware
His conscience bothers him when he lies.   He was conscious of his mistake.

1. The crowd sighed in relief when she became conscious.

2. My conscious forced me to return the lost wallet.

3. I didn't want to study, but my conscience reminded me of the importance of making good grades.

4. My grandmother is always conscience of my birthday.

Pair 7

hear: ability to pick up sounds with   **here:** location
one's ears   We can all gather here for lunch.
She hears what she wants to hear.

1. Didn't you here the car honking?

2. Come here and write your paper.

3. From our kitchen, we could here birds singing.

4. Here is my assignment.

Pair 8

hole: an opening in something   **whole:** entire
I have a hole in my shoe.   He ate the whole pie.

1. Be careful; I think there's a whole around here.

2. The hole house was a mess.

3. Tall yellow weeds covered the hole field.

4. The yard was filled with small groundhog wholes.

Pair 9

know: to understand   **no:** a response in the negative
I know what you are thinking.   There are no raisins in the oatmeal.

1. Don't you no not to stick a fork into the toaster?

2. Know, you cannot play on the computer.

3. I know I shouldn't watch TV when I have homework.

4. Margaret asked her dad for $200, but he said, "No."

Pair 10

knew: understood   **new:** not old
We thought we knew the answers.   The puppy liked his new bed.

1. The meteorologist knew it was going to rain Wednesday.

2. Mary was disappointed because she ripped her knew red dress.

3. I new the test would be difficult.

4. The new peach sweater looked terrific on Olivia.

Pair 11

passed: (verb) completed; handed to;   **past:** time gone by, yesterday
filed by or went by   In the past five years, they moved twice.
She passed the bar exam.

1. My teammate past the ball to me, and I made a touchdown.

2. Susie was dreaming about her passed when she was awakened.

3. Mr. Van passed out the test at 8:00.

4. Karen sprinted past Matt to win the fifty-metre dash.

Pair 12

peace: quiet and calm   **piece:** a section or part
It is hard to keep world peace.   He ate a piece of fudge cake.

1. Pass Julio a peace of cherry pie.

2. The Protestants made piece with the Catholics in Ireland.

3. Roger lost a peace of my science project, but I passed anyway.

4. The piece symbol was part of the sixties generation.

Pair 13

principal: main; head of a school
Money was his principal reason
for quitting the job.
The school principal called
a meeting.

principle: rule, law, or regulation
His answer was based on a
simple principle.

1. Our principle, Ms. Jones, is a sensitive woman.

2. We learned the three semantic principles in English.

3. I called her and explained the new club's principals.

4. As a matter of principle, I defended the child.

Pair 14

lose: (verb) misplace or not win
They managed to lose only the
last game.

loose: (adjective) not bound, free, not tight
The children were turned loose
after school.

1. Mom didn't want to loose Amy in the crowd, so she held her hand tightly.

2. The fashion today is lose clothing.

3. The knot Bob made was too loose to hold the calf.

4. Louise lost the lose ring Friday.

Pair 15

right: correct or opposite of left
Richard gave the right answer
every time.

write: communicate with written words
Please write me a letter.

1. Beatrice started to right her essay but was interrupted by another phone call.

2. Henry turned write into a small bush.

3. My right hand has a cut on it.

4. When I finished my writing, it was time for dinner.

Pair 16

quiet: calm, peaceful
The baby was finally quiet.

quite: very, to a great extent
He was quite sure of himself.

1. Laura is quiet a pretty girl.

2. Grand Lake is always calm and quite.

3. The ex-champions were quiet surprised that they came in second in the gymnastics events.

4. After the children are put to bed, the Wagners' house is quite.

Pair 17

there: location
    He left his papers there.

their: ownership
    Their papers were all turned in on time.
    they're: contraction of "they are"
    They're determined to finish first.

1. They left there book in their car.

2. They're making excellent grades.

3. The puppy is hiding there in the grass.

4. Sam said their going to there favourite spot.

Pair 18

though: (even), (although), however, nevertheless
    He wants to buy a car even though he cannot afford one.

thought: thinking or an idea
    I thought you would never ask.

1. Though Juana was tired, she stayed up and baked bread.

2. The though of cooking another meal depressed the cook.

3. The Oilers lost the game though they played their best.

4. Her thought was to plan a surprise party for Jim.

Pair 19

threw: toss in air (past tense)
    He threw the ball into the net.

through: from one side to the other
    They passed through the city.

1. Sarah climbed threw the tunnel and ran for the slide.

2. The muscular football player through a bullet pass to the receiver.

3. Ann ran threw the woods, jumping over logs and stones.

4. Janice accidentally poked the sharp pencil threw the soft Styrofoam.

Pair 20

to: a preposition that shows direction toward or part of an infinitive (to sing, to act)
Sara wanted to go to the fair.

too: also, more than enough
Sharon wanted to go, too.

two: number two
The two women enjoyed the same types of activities.

1. The final score was three to too.

2. The Fishers love too swim at night in the summer.

3. Nicki finished her paper, to.

4. Two many people were at the party in the small house.

Pair 21

weather: outside temperature and conditions
Canada's weather can be extremely cold.

whether: if, in case of
She wanted to know whether or not she needed to take a sweater.

1. The whether is great in Halifax in the summer.

2. Whether or not you apologize, Tracey's feelings are hurt.

3. The weather for tomorrow is predicted to be beautiful.

4. Tom was sorry weather he could admit it or not.

Pair 22

were: past tense verb
Six flowers were placed in the vase.

where: place
Where can we find a good place to eat?

1. Were were you when I needed help?

2. Fifteen of the students where going on a hike.

3. Tanya went were the other students were playing volleyball.

4. They were moving into a new apartment.

Pair 23

woman: one adult female human
     She was the woman of his dreams.

women: two or more adult female humans
     The women shared their concerns with
     one another.

1. The three woman went through nurse's training together.

2. The women Jason married was his childhood sweetheart.

3. The most prestigious award was given to an outstanding woman student.

4. Of all the woman he dated, that woman stole his heart.

Misunderstood Words

Some errors are made because the construction of certain words is not fully understood; consequently, these words are misused for other words. Much of the confusion centres around the use of the apostrophe in contractions.

In contractions, an apostrophe indicates that a letter or letters have been omitted. To determine whether you have used the correct word, simply say the two words in the sentence. If it doesn't make sense, you know you need the other construction.

Study the following contractions and the two words each contraction stands for. Then read the definition of the similar words.

it's	=	it is, it has
they're	=	they are
you're	=	you are
who's	=	who is, who has

Here are the meanings of the words often confused with these contractions:

its	=	ownership or possession (third person singular)
there	=	shows location unless at the beginning of a sentence or question
their	=	ownership or possession (third person plural)
your	=	ownership or possession (second person singular or plural)
whose	=	relating to possession of an object, frequently in a question

EXERCISE 2

Read the following sentences and look for words that have been misused for other words. If the word has been used correctly, write "C" beside the sentence; if not, mark out the incorrect word and write the correct one above.

1. The high school band members left they're instruments out in the rain.
2. Who's the person that gave those beautiful, red roses?
3. Look over their at the water skier!
4. Your not feeling well, are you?
5. There over there at the Etobicoke Community Centre.
6. The cat loves it's new food.
7. There not in the left-side drawer.
8. The children left their books at home.
9. Is there something you forgot?
10. Who's at the door, Giovanni?
11. Look at there beautiful dog.
12. It's water bowl is empty.
13. They're house is always spotless.
14. I'm sorry, Michelle; your not going to be able to go swimming today.
15. Whose drink is in the refrigerator?

Other Misused Words

"Alot" is not a word in the English language, yet it is repeatedly used. The proper construction for the word is "a lot." You may want to consider alternate words that say the same thing, such as "many," "frequently," "much," or "often."

"Well" used to introduce a sentence adds little meaning to your sentences. It is an expression that should not be used in objective composition papers. It is frequently used in informal speech:

Well, I'm broke.

Well, I guess we could do it.

Well, there you go again.

However, use "well" rather than "good" when you describe how something is done:

Santos hit the ball well.

Kim learned her lesson well.

"Of" after "could," "should," "must," or "might" must be avoided. Instead, "have," is the correct verb form: could have, should have, must have, or might have.

Incorrect: Jake could of gone to work.

Correct: Jake could have gone to work.

Journal writing serves several purposes, none of which should be overlooked. It helps you

work through emotions

make the words flow more freely

communicate with others

remember events in the past

make class notes clearer

Journal writing helps you *work through emotions* so you can back off and then deal objectively with whatever was bothering you.

Someone once said that you can become a journal writer only after you have written about the thing that hurt the most, and as you release your feelings on paper, you also release the tears that have been long overdue. For example, a man in his forties had not spoken to his mother and father for twenty years. He filled two journals in which he communicated with them only on paper. Eventually he wrote his mother and initiated some type of interaction. Though he could not change what had happened in his childhood, he was able to begin a new relationship with his parents.

When Ivan Lacore, a serious journal writer, was asked if journal writing helped him cope with life, he said, "Writing in my journal helps me face the future without the anger of the past."

One bonus to journal writing is that *it makes the words flow more freely*. The more you write, the easier it becomes. This can be compared to walking. If you stayed in bed for six weeks and did not once walk, you would lose that ability to walk and would have to "learn" to walk all over again. Elementary school teachers often remind us that children who do not read over the summer cannot read as well in September as they did in June. Whether walking, reading, or writing, the more you do of it, the better you become at it. As you began this course, it might have been an effort to write one paragraph. However, by the end of the term you may be able to write a multiparagraph essay in the same length of time you once needed for one paragraph.

Journal writing can also help you *communicate with others*. What you write in your journal often involves your feelings about other people. Sometimes you may choose to write a letter to someone. Another time you may want to take parts of your journal to share with another person or with many people. Then editing and reworking the material becomes an important part of the writing. One lady wrote her memories of her childhood and her daughter's childhood. She then typed her journal and presented it to her grandchild. This journal became a treasure that will most likely be passed down from generation to generation.

Journal writing often allows you to *remember events in the past* that you have blocked from your mind, but when you begin writing about these things, details surface and memories are renewed.

Another important purpose of journal writing is to *make class notes clearer*. Sometimes you may want to rework the notes that you took in this class or in another class. This reorganizing helps you understand ideas and concepts that your instructor wants you to grasp. You often take notes so rapidly in class that rewriting and reworking your notes immediately after class can make the concept "stick" in your mind.

Some instructors think that a notebook should be turned in and graded. Others think that these notebooks can be checked without the teacher reading the entries at all. These instructors do not check the entries because they feel that students should be able to write about their most personal feelings without worrying about an audience. For instance, if your instructor were to say that the journal is to be read and graded for grammar, you would be concerned with both form and content. On the other hand, if your instructor were to say that he or she would only flip through the pages without reading the contents, you would feel assured that you could write about anything you wanted to without worrying about form.

The actual journal may be a special composition book your instructor requires you to buy at the book store, a leather-bound book that might cost twenty dollars, or a spiral notebook you bought for twenty-five cents on sale. Whatever you use really does not matter. Unless your instructor requires a special type of writing instrument, you should use anything that feels comfortable. You can use a pencil, a pen, a typewriter, or a computer. You can write in neat lines and will want to if your instructor is going to read your journal. If not, you might find yourself writing from corner to corner, in circles, or whatever feels right. Likewise, you might have a special desk you like to sit at when you are writing, or you might like to sit on the floor. You might like everything quiet, or you might like both the radio and the TV going.

One last thought about journals is that you are not just meeting a requirement to pass a course. You are learning to feel on paper. Though writing how you feel about what is happening in your life may seem strange at first, you may be willing to keep a journal years after this course is finished. This journal can help you improve your writing and thinking skills for many years to come.

WRITING ASSIGNMENT

1. *Try writing in your journal about the most wonderful place you can remember as a child. Close your eyes until you can re-enter this place. Then let the reader enter this place with you. What do you see, feel, touch, taste, smell? What is above you? What is around you? Begin to write when your mind can re-enter this place and continue to write as long as you can.*

2. *Try writing in your journal about the last time you got mad. Describe how you felt. Why did you feel that way? Who made you angry? Why were you angry? (Just continue to write until nothing more comes.)*

3. *In your journal, write a letter that is overdue. Perhaps you can write a letter to someone who might have reason to be upset with you. Or perhaps you can write a letter to someone whom you really dislike or like. (There is no need to mail this letter.)*

4. *In your journal, rework your notes in this class or another class immediately after the class is over.*

5. *In your journal, write about anything that bothers you. This can be prejudice, frustration, homelessness, your classes, or anything else. Try to recall a particular event that bothered you.*

APPENDIX C | Irregular Verbs

Irregular verbs may cause a few problems because they have many different forms. Feel confident, however, that you probably use most of these verbs correctly.

You may find that you do not know some of the forms. Perhaps, in addition to not knowing them, you may say the verb forms correctly but not spell them correctly when you write them. In either case, you may need to refer to the following list.

What makes a verb "irregular"? It is irregular if it forms the past tense in any of the following ways:

By changing the internal sound and/or spelling

I speak now. I spoke yesterday.

I write now. I wrote yesterday.

By changing most of the sound and most of the spelling

I bring my lunch on Mondays.

I brought it yesterday.

By changing to a different word

I go today. I went yesterday.

I am here now. I was here earlier.

You do not need to know these changes by name. Being able to use the verbs is much more important. Do not try to memorize all the forms in the following table; instead, use it as a reference when you are revising your writing.

IRREGULAR VERBS

PRESENT	PAST	PAST PARTICIPLE*	PRESENT PARTICIPLE*
am	was	been	being
become	became	become	becoming
begin	began	begun	beginning
bite	bit	bitten	biting
blow	blew	blown	blowing
break	broke	broken	breaking
bring	brought	brought	bringing
buy	bought	bought	buying
catch	caught	caught	catching
choose	chose	chosen	choosing
come	came	come	coming

*When the past participle or present participle is used as a complete verb, a *helping verb* is always used.

PRESENT	PAST	PAST PARTICIPLE*	PRESENT PARTICIPLE*
dig	dug	dug	digging
draw	drew	drawn	drawing
drink	drank	drunk	drinking
drive	drove	driven	driving
eat	ate	eaten	eating
fall	fell	fallen	falling
fight	fought	fought	fighting
fly	flew	flown	flying
freeze	froze	frozen	freezing
get	got	gotten	getting
give	gave	given	giving
go	went	gone	going
grow	grew	grown	growing
hang	hung	hung	hanging
have	had	had	having
hear	heard	heard	hearing
hide	hid	hidden	hiding
know	knew	known	knowing
lay (set something down)**	laid	laid	laying
lead	led	led	leading
lie (recline)***	lay	lain	lying
lie (tell untruth)	lied	lied	lying
pay	paid	paid	paying
read	read	read	reading
ride	rode	ridden	riding
ring	rang	rung	ringing
rise	rose	risen	rising
run	ran	run	running
see	saw	seen	seeing
set (put something down)	set	set	setting
shine	shone	shone	shining
sing	sang	sung	singing
sit	sat	sat	sitting
speak	spoke	spoken	speaking
sting	stung	stung	stinging
steal	stole	stolen	stealing
swear	swore	sworn	swearing
swim	swam	swum	swimming
take	took	taken	taking
think	thought	thought	thinking
throw	threw	thrown	throwing
wake	woke	woken	waking

*When the past participle or present participle is used as a complete verb, a helping verb is always used.

**Takes a direct object.

***Does not take a direct object.

PRESENT	PAST	PAST PARTICIPLE*	PRESENT PARTICIPLE*
wear	wore	worn	wearing
win	won	won	winning
write	wrote	written	writing

*When the past participle or present participle is used as a complete verb, a helping verb is always used.

UNIT 2/Part 1

EXERCISE 1

1. *Topic:* Enrolling in college
   Direction: can be a surprising experience

3. *Topic:* That movie
   Direction: has a lot of action

5. *Topic:* Planting a tree
   Direction: is hard work

7. *Topic:* Owning a car
   Direction: can be expensive

9. *Topic:* Walking to school in the spring
   Direction: saves money

11. *Topic:* Going out to eat
    Direction: can be a cultural experience

13. *Topic:* Doing cross-stitch pictures
    Direction: some people find relaxing

15. *Topic:* Character
    Direction: can be built through studying karate

17. *Topic:* Figure skaters
    Direction: give graceful performances

19. *Topic:* A remodelled kitchen
    Direction: brings pleasure

EXERCISE 2

Answers will vary.

EXERCISE 3

TS	1. Yard work can be fun.
broad	3. The causes of world hunger are complicated.
broad	5. The historical events that have affected our English language are many.
TS	7. Our spring weather was unusual this year.
broad	9. Pollution causes many environmental problems.
fact	11. Blue Rodeo will appear at 9:00 next Saturday night.
fact	13. Howard drove his Jeep to the garage.

<u> fact </u> 15. Listing the people who have died of AIDS is heartbreaking.

<u>broad</u> 17. Native Canadian cultures are varied.

<u> fact </u> 19. The English computer lab is open twelve hours a day.

EXERCISE 4

1. Many advantages result from owning and operating small cars.

3. Saving money may not be as hard as you think.

5. Telephones have become sophisticated home appliances.

7. Tips for keeping a home cooler in the summer heat are helpful.

9. A good pet owner has several responsibilities to meet.

11. The showroom presented a carefully arranged collection of automobiles.

13. The beautiful public park offers many inexpensive outdoor activities for the city.

EXERCISE 5

Answers will vary.

EXERCISE 6

Answers will vary.

EXERCISE 7

Additional support sentences in each paragraph will vary. In each paragraph, the first sentence is the topic sentence, and the last sentence is the conclusion.

EXERCISE 8

1. <u> 2 </u> Charlie planted the lettuce seed in early spring.

   <u> 1 </u> He spaded his garden carefully and worked in fertilizer.

3. <u> 3 </u> Ruth attended classes.

   <u> 2 </u> Ruth paid her registration fees for two classes in the fall.

   <u> 1 </u> Ruth took a hundred dollars from savings for her fees.

5. <u> 3 </u> Kenita turned in her essay at the beginning of class.

   <u> 2 </u> Kenita wrote her name carefully at the top of the essay.

   <u> 1 </u> Kenita typed her assignment on the computer.

7. <u> 4 </u> Harry deposited his paycheque in the bank.

   <u> 2 </u> Harry walked to the personnel office to pick up his paycheque.

   <u> 1 </u> Harry cleared his desk for the day at 4:30.

   <u> 3 </u> Harry filled out the deposit slip on the way to the bank.

9. __4__ Paula filled out the application for the mechanic's job.

__1__ Paula checked the jobs advertised in the local paper.

__5__ Paula waited patiently to be called for an interview.

__3__ Paula went to Robinson Motor Company the next morning.

__2__ Robinson Motor Company was advertising for a mechanic.

EXERCISE 9

1. __2__ George bought a Ford.

__1__ George admires North American cars.

__3__ He needs a new lawn mower.

3. __2__ The science teacher started a chemistry class for nurses.

__3__ The English department needed computers.

__1__ The school planned new math and science courses.

5. __2__ The librarian ordered fifteen new Canadian novels.

__1__ The library has an extensive collection of Canadian literature.

__3__ The library's art collection is outstanding.

7. __1__ Going to college and having a job may leave little time for recreation.

__3__ Gerald forgot to do his math homework.

__2__ Gerald could not go to the movies last weekend.

9. __2__ The rose quartz was one of the best pieces displayed.

__3__ Kim liked to go rock hunting on weekends.

__1__ The school library had a special rock and gem collection.

11. __1__ Children need a lot of attention.

__2__ Susan loves to be read to before bedtime.

__3__ Susan ate all the ice cream.

13. __2__ The dishes need to be done.

__3__ I finally hired a gardener to do the yard work.

__1__ Housekeeping can be a never-ending job.

EXERCISE 10

Paragraph 1

People from other countries have different reasons for wanting to come to live in Canada. For example, some might want higher-paying jobs than they can get in their own countries. Some want the freedom to change jobs or professions. Some might want the chance to get more education for themselves and their families. <u>Church groups often sponsor people coming to Canada.</u> Perhaps one of the most important reasons would be the desire to own and operate a business. <u>Many people wait a long time for the chance to live in the Canada.</u> Every year, regardless of the reasons, many more people come to live in Canada.

EXERCISE 11

Topic sentences with key words or phrases circled are given. Answers will vary for the rest of each paragraph.

Paragraph 1

Paragraph 3

UNIT 2 / Part 4

EXERCISE 1

1. Jill went home early (because of the rain).

3. (During the winter) we enjoy travelling (to a warmer climate).

5. The peaches (on the table) are ripe.

7. (Beside the lake) is a wonderful place.

9. We floated (down the river) (on an inner tube).

11. I appreciate working (with people) (like her).

13. One (of my favourite sights) is the Vancouver sunset.

15. The child (behind the tree) is looking (for her kitten).

17. They will be back (within an hour or two).

19. The participant (in the Iron Man contest) continued (beyond human limits).

EXERCISE 2

Paragraph 1

A person who wants to earn a living (by crabbing) must learn (about crabs and their varying market value). A Jimmy or male bull crab sells (for the most money). It is large and provides a generous supply (of sweet, white meat). A sook or full-grown female crab is next (in size) (to the Jimmy). She sheds her shell, becomes soft, mates, and rehardens. She then becomes a mature crab. (At this point), she is a fairly large crab, but she cannot compete (with the bull crab) (for equal market value) because she is a bit smaller. A young female crab also lacks the size needed (for the market). Crabbing can be a profitable business if a person learns (about crabs), especially (from a good crabber).

EXERCISE 3

1. There are many <u>jobs</u> left to be completed.
3. <u>Jana</u> was late (for the meeting).
5. The <u>dog</u> and the <u>cat</u> are playing together.
7. The <u>water</u> (in the swimming pool) is clear and blue.
9. Here are the <u>books</u> (for you).
11. The <u>members</u> (of the committee) left (at 6:00) (in the evening).
13. (You) Pick the books up (off the floor) and do your homework.
15. <u>Ting</u> and <u>Li</u> shopped and shopped (for clothes).
17. The <u>wedding</u> took much planning and work.
19. (<u>You</u>) Turn the water off, please.

EXERCISE 4

Paragraph 1

This spring a mother <u>sparrow</u> (with her two young sparrows) ventured (out of their nest) (in search) (of food and water) (for the first time). As the <u>trio</u> bounced along, <u>it</u> was easy to pick out the baby birds (from the mother) because the young <u>sparrows</u> fluttered their wings and opened their beaks. Then the mother <u>sparrow</u> inserted a crumb (of bread) or a little bug (into the tiny gaping beaks). (In her effort) to feed both babies, <u>she</u> quickly hopped (from one) (to the other), attending (to both) (of them). <u>She</u> then slowly drank (from a small rain puddle). The <u>babies</u>, however, had nothing (on their minds) (except food). <u>It</u> was a pleasant sight to see.

EXERCISE 5

1. Mike <u>enjoys</u> putting chrome (on his Jeep).
3. <u>He</u> <u>reminds</u> me (of my brother).
5. The <u>parents</u> (of young children) <u>have</u> many responsibilities.
7. There <u>are</u> many <u>tasks</u> to complete today.
9. The <u>bags</u> (of groceries) <u>need</u> to be put away.
11. The blue <u>book</u> (on the shelf) <u>illustrates</u> many home projects.
13. The <u>telephone</u> <u>rings</u> many times each day.
15. The <u>puppies</u> <u>play</u> (with each other).
17. All <u>phases</u> (of production) <u>are done</u> (by the students).
19. The <u>flowers</u> (in the vase) <u>need</u> water.

EXERCISE 6

        boxes   *weigh*

1. The <u>box</u> (on the top) (of the table) <u>weighs</u> five kilograms.

       deer   *are*

3. The <u>deer</u> (at the zoo) <u>is</u> very tame.

        leaves fall

5. The <u>leaf</u> <u>falls</u> (from the tree) (onto the sidewalk).

       churches need

7. The <u>church</u> <u>needs</u> a new paint job.

      cats like

9. My <u>cat</u> <u>likes</u> to climb (on the roof).

   The pairs   *need*

11. A <u>pair</u> (of scissors) <u>needs</u> to be sharpened.

       doctors work

13. The <u>doctor</u> <u>works</u> (on cars) (in the evening).

     children   *like*

15. The <u>child</u> (on the bicycle) <u>likes</u> to play tag.

   Good theses are

17. A good <u>thesis</u> <u>is</u> important (in writing essays).

   Geese   *live*

19. A <u>goose</u> <u>lives</u> (at the park).

EXERCISE 7

1. <u>All</u> (of the players) <u>know</u> the rules.

3. Neither <u>batter</u> <u>sees</u> the balls.

5. <u>Few</u> (of the fans) <u>realize</u> the pressure the players are under.

7. <u>Nobody</u> <u>likes</u> to lose a ball game.

9. Each <u>one</u> (of the players) <u>tries</u> hard to play well.

11. Each <u>play</u> <u>makes</u> a difference (in the outcome) (of the game).

13. There <u>is</u> something <u>special</u> (about this team).

15. Each <u>person</u> (on the team) <u>is</u> expected to perform well.

17. <u>Some</u> (of the players) actually <u>feel</u> underpaid.

19. <u>Baseball</u> <u>appeals</u> (to a wide range) (of people).

EXERCISE 8

        needs

1. <u>Everybody</u> ~~need~~ to take time to enjoy the little things (in life).

        like

3. <u>Some</u> even ~~likes~~ money more than time (with their children).

5. <u>Some</u> (of the people) ~~finds~~ *find* time (for themselves).

7. Any <u>diversion</u> (from routine activities) ~~are~~ *is* rewarding.

9. <u>Others</u> ~~enjoys~~ *enjoy* playing soccer.

11. <u>Children</u> often ~~enjoys~~ *enjoy* camping.

13. <u>Nobody</u> ~~enjoy~~ *enjoys* working all the time.

15. <u>Everyone</u> ~~want~~ *wants* to be (around friends).

17. <u>Each</u> (of the drivers) ~~need~~ *needs* more practice.

19. Without a doubt, <u>someone</u> ~~think~~ *thinks* (of a good solution).

EXERCISE 9

Paragraph 1

College <u>years</u> ~~is~~ *are* more than just a time when <u>students</u> <u>can achieve</u> knowledge. These <u>years</u> <u>are</u> also a time when <u>students</u> ~~acquires~~ *acquire* lifetime friends <u>that are</u> never <u>forgotten</u>. Years later a <u>person</u> ~~hear~~ *hears* of the new president of a company and ~~say~~ *says*, "<u>I know</u> him. <u>We went</u> to college together." A <u>student</u> ~~have~~ *has* the opportunity to date others on her or his own intellectual level and enjoy the same activities. <u>Students meet</u> friends, and <u>they become</u> professional contacts many years later. <u>They</u> also ~~finds~~ *find* others with the same personal feeling as <u>they</u> ~~moves~~ *move* into the residences or apartments and, subsequently, into an independent lifestyle. In college, as <u>friends</u> <u>share</u> the same political and social beliefs, they ~~comes~~ *come* together and ~~strives~~ *strive* to help humanity. The <u>friendships</u> in college ~~is~~ *are* as important as any other aspect of a student's education.

EXERCISE 10

Paragraph 1

Tense: Past

Our favourite vacation spot was Disneyland. We ~~enjoy~~ *enjoyed* the many sights and activities in this famous park. We ~~look~~ *looked* forward to seeing the Disney characters at the entrance. We ~~know~~ *knew* that we would enjoy the walk down Main Street again. We always ~~see~~ *saw* eager children who ~~ride~~ *rode* in strollers or ~~run~~ *ran* and ~~skip~~ *skipped* beside their parents. As we walked down Main Street, we all probably ~~think~~ *thought* of the first attractions that we ~~want~~ *wanted* to ride. Disneyland never ~~loses~~ *lost* its ability to enchant us.

Paragraph 3

Tense: *Present*

   Senior citizens **receive** many recreational opportunities by living in retirement communities. Retired men and women ~~attended~~ *attend* craft classes that range from needlecraft to wood-work. Community members ~~frequented~~ *frequent* one or more recreational halls that are usually equipped with pool tables and shuffleboard courts. In the evenings, they ~~stayed~~ *stay* busy stay attending dances or parties. They ~~received~~ *receive* exercise in indoor or outdoor swimming pools, depending on the specific region of the country. Fervent golfers ~~teed~~ *tee* off on well-manicured greens or ~~played~~ *play* tennis on clean courts any time of the day. No matter what activity people enjoy, they find many others who ~~enjoyed~~ *enjoy* doing the same type of things.

UNIT 3/Part1

EXERCISE 1

Situation 1

   Topic: broken TV, no TV parts

   Purpose: persuade to get money back

   Audience: president of company that manufactured the television

   Voice: factual, straightforward, sincere

Situation 3

   Topic: death of friend's mother

   Purpose: show sympathy, understanding

   Audience: friend

   Voice: personal, serious, warm, comforting

Situation 5

    Topic: himself

   Purpose: to get a job

 Audience: personnel supervisor

    Voice: sincere, serious, formal, convincing

EXERCISE 2

Words used will vary.

1. a. formal, neutral
   b. positive, praising
   c. a put-down, offensive

3. a. neutral
   b. positive, complimentary
   c. negative, derogatory

5. a. positive, happy, proud
   b. negative, offensive
   c. understanding, formal

7. a. compelling, serious
   b. light, friendly, suggestive
   c. nostalgic, reminiscent
   d. happy, excited
   e. obligatory, commanding
   f. blaming, angry

EXERCISE 3

Answers will vary.

1. a. polite   Please turn on the light.
   b. frightened   Hurry and turn on the light!

3. a. angry   We are making the world into a stench ball.
   b. informal   Don't people realize we have all pitched in to save the environment?

5. a. positive   Shovelling the snow was exhilarating!
   b. informal   Why do I have to shovel the snow?

7. a. angry   The fat neighbourhood bully crushed Lisa's Easter basket.
   b. negative   The Easter bunny hoax is usually realized by age eight.

9. a. angry   The opposing team scowled at the referee and angrily shook the hands of their opponents.
   b. negative   The game was a show of poor sportsmanship, inept coaching, and no game strategy.

EXERCISE 4

Paragraph 1

    Topic: personal conflict about the future

Audience: counsellor, friend, teacher

    Voice: nostalgic, sad

Paragraph 3

    Topic: thanks for visit

Audience: Rick, a subordinate

    Voice: businesslike but warm and gracious

Paragraph 5

    Topic: job recommendation, qualifications of Shawn Stevens

Audience: fire department, employer

    Voice: formal, perceptive, sincere, persuasive

EXERCISE 5

Answers will vary.

UNIT 3/Part4

EXERCISE 1

    He
1. ~~Sam~~ is doing well in calculus this semester.

    She
3. ~~Mary~~ returns to P.E.I. for vacation every summer.

        We
5. ~~Roger, Stephanie, and I~~ watched the Santa Claus Parade, and we enjoyed it.

    They
7. ~~Real friends~~ are always ready to help.

          It
9. ~~Maintaining a consistent point of view~~ is really quite simple.

EXERCISE 2

      You
1. second person: ~~Robert~~ should consider the detrimental consequences as well as the advantages.

        They   their
3. third person: ~~My friend and I~~ have always tried to edit ~~our~~ papers carefully.

5. second person: ~~Mr. Jones is~~ *You are* the most challenging math professor on campus.

7. third person: ~~Henry,~~ *He listens* ~~listen~~ to ~~your~~ *his* conscience when decisions need to be made.

9. second person: ~~Some~~ *You* ~~students~~ have learned excellent time-management skills this semester.

EXERCISE 3
Paragraph 1

Playing golf is a rewarding experience. It can be a time for relaxing and enjoying a beautiful day. Because many golf courses are located throughout the city, finding an available tee time is also easy and convenient. When ~~you~~ *golfers* play eighteen holes, ~~you~~ *they* walk approximately four miles and get ~~your~~ *their* day's exercises. Furthermore, golf is challenging. ~~I used to~~ *Some might* think that golf was an easy game that did not require any ability, but it does require precision, patience, and skill. In addition, unlike other high-endurance sports that only younger players can participate in, golf is a lifelong activity. ~~You~~ *Anyone* can enjoy it at just about any age. Consequently, golf is a sport everybody should consider playing.

Purpose: to explain why playing golf is rewarding.

Voice: informative

Audience: someone thinking of taking up golf

Paragraph 3

The high-tech computer lab at our college is an efficient room. Over one hundred computers are laid out so that maximum room is obtained for traffic flow, comfort, and usability. Students can choose from a variety of hardware, and technicians are available to give help or to answer questions. In addition, ~~you~~ *students* can easily check out the software ~~you~~ *they* desire and sign in on the computer at the entrance to the room. One advantage that ~~I have found in my~~ *students may find in their* experience in the high-tech centre is that *they* can get copies of ~~my~~ *their* work quickly because all

Students

stations are hooked up to printers. ~~You~~ might say that the high-tech centre is a

perfect place for computer business and pleasure.

  Purpose: <u>to express pride in computer facilities</u>
     Voice: <u>positive, informative</u>
Audience: <u>potential users</u>

UNIT 4/Part 1

EXERCISE 1

1. _____c_____ is the most general word or statement.

   ___b,d,e___ are equal to one another.

   _____a_____ is unrelated or part of another group.

3. _____d_____ is the most general word or statement.

   ___a,b,e___ are equal to one another.

   _____c_____ is unrelated or part of another group.

5. _____a_____ is the most general word or statement.

   ___b,c,e___ are equal to one another.

   _____d_____ is unrelated or part of another group.

7. _____b_____ is the most general word or statement.

   ___c,d,e___ are equal to one another.

   _____a_____ is unrelated or part of another group.

9. _____c_____ is the most general word or statement.

   ___b,d,e___ are equal to one another.

   _____a_____ is unrelated or part of another group.

EXERCISE 2

1. *most general idea:* children enjoyed the pictures
   words that are coordinate: large, simple, colourful

3. *most general idea:* having surgery is difficult
   words that are coordinate: expensive, painful, frightening, depressing

5. *most general idea:* important when a consumer buys a home
   words that are coordinate: location, price, size

7. *most general idea:* specialties of the cooking school
   words that are coordinate: appetizers, main courses, salads, desserts

9. *most general idea:* as trees grow, they develop
   words that are coordinate: root systems, thick trunks, full branches

11. *most general idea:* pets aid the elderly
    words that are coordinate: security, companionship, self-esteem

EXERCISE 3

1. a. to write memos, to make phone calls, to file materials
    b. making phone calls, typing materials, filing materials
    c. filed materials, typed materials, made phone calls

3. a. to be happy, to be outgoing, to be helpful
    b. was outgoing, was happy, was helpful
    c. is helpful, is outgoing, is happy

5. a. to practise long hours, to read the directions, to talk to experts
    b. read the directions, practise long hours, talk to experts
    c. talking to experts, practising long hours, reading the directions

7. a. convenience, fairness, variety
    b. to be fair, to be convenient, to be varied
    c. of its variety, of its fairness, of its convenience

9. a. growing wheat, canning wild blackberries, raising chickens
    b. canned wild blackberries, grew wheat, raised chickens
    c. raises chickens, grows wheat, cans wild blackberries

EXERCISE 4

Answers will vary.

1. My summer spent in Muskoka brings pleasant memories of socializing with friends, <u>earning</u> extra money, and buying my first car.

    My summer spent in Muskoka brings pleasant memories of socializing with friends, <u>of earning</u> extra money, and of buying my first car.

3. I enjoy going to that restaurant because the prices are reasonable, the food is excellent, and the <u>service is good</u>.

5. Many homeless people exist in Canada because of mental illness, <u>physical illness</u>, and <u>lack of ambition</u>.

7. For safe driving, one must drive under control, <u>obey</u> the speed limit, and never drive under the influence of alcohol.

9. When you go river rafting, you must know how to pack the gear, to <u>manoeuvre a raft</u>, and to judge the rapids.

11. Before going to college, consider <u>money</u>, time, and attitude.

13. Leaving home was very difficult for me because I <u>had</u> to say goodbye to my family, had to leave my friends, and had to break up with my girlfriend.

EXERCISE 5

Answers will vary.

UNIT 4/Part 4

EXERCISE 1

Answers will vary.

 it
1. Perhaps even gave them a new perspective on life.

 he
3. Suddenly and frantically searched for his girlfriend.

 His talk also
5. ~~Also~~ gave us a new perspective on life.

EXERCISE 2

Answers will vary.

Paragraph 1

Before revision

Richard was looking for something in the refrigerator. Something to fix for lunch. He found luncheon meat and cheese. Mozzarella cheese. Red juicy tomatoes and sweet white onions. He looked further for lettuce. Crisp lettuce. Underneath the lettuce, he found a package. A package of bacon. If he could find the mayonnaise, he could make a sandwich. A "house special" sandwich.

After revision

Richard was looking for something in the refrigerator to fix for lunch. He found luncheon meat, mozzarella cheese, red juicy tomatoes, and sweet white onions. He looked further for crisp lettuce, and underneath it, he found a package of bacon. If he could find the mayonnaise, he could make a "house special" sandwich.

EXERCISE 3

Answers will vary.

1. Jake was playing chess.
    Add a subject and some form of the verb "be."

    Playing chess is a popular hobby.
    Make the fragment the subject and add a main verb. (Add other words if needed.)

    Playing chess, Robin practised thinking skills.
    Add a sentence (subject and a verb) after the fragment.

3. Danny was welcoming his friends.
    Add a subject and some form of the verb "be."

    Welcoming his friends turned out to be easy for Danny.
    Make the fragment the subject and add a main verb. (Add other words if needed.)

Welcoming his friends, Danny seemed at ease.
Add a sentence (subject and a verb) after the fragment.

5. Joe is typing a research paper.
Add a subject and some form of the verb "be."

Typing a research paper is easier on a computer than on a typewriter.
Make the fragment the subject and add a main verb. (Add other words if needed.)

Typing a research paper, Tony spent hours in the lab.
Add a sentence (subject and a verb) after the fragment.

EXERCISE 4

Answers will vary.

1. To say a kind word, Mary made a special trip to her neighbour's house.
Link the fragment to a complete sentence.

He was not reluctant to say a kind word.
Add both a subject and a verb.

To say a kind word is easy.
Make the fragment the subject and add a verb. (Add other words if needed.)

3. To win the lottery, the secretaries bought ten tickets each.
Link the fragment to a complete sentence.

The secretaries wanted to win the lottery.
Add both a subject and a verb. (Add other words if needed.)

To win the lottery seemed hopeless.
Make the fragment the subject and add a verb. (Add other words if needed.)

5. To play hockey, the boys needed protective equipment.
Link the fragment to a complete sentence.

My sons learned to play hockey.
Add both a subject and a verb.

To play hockey requires practice and good equipment.
Make the fragment the subject and add a verb. (Add other words if needed.)

EXERCISE 5

Answers will vary.

1. As soon as I finish my homework, I shall go to the store.

3. Even though his birthday is on Saturday, John will have to work.

5. Before the day is over, I will finish my research paper.

7. If Ranjit will send us the information, we can complete the project.

9. If the price is right, I will buy the used car.

EXERCISE 6

Paragraph 1

Before revision

I found that setting up an aquarium is expensive. After buying the tank, light, filter, and heater. I had other initial expenses. I needed to purchase chemicals. Chemicals to eliminate chlorine and to reduce the acidity. I made the tank attractive. Adding coloured gravel and plants. Adding ceramic figures. Placing a nice background behind the glass. To test the water and to keep the tank water at the right temperature. Adding a variety of fish with beautiful colours. When everything was set up. I had fun. The aquarium can provide a centre of enjoyment.

After revision

I found that setting up an aquarium is expensive. After buying the tank, light, filter, and heater, I had other initial expenses. I needed to purchase chemicals to eliminate chlorine and to reduce the acidity. By adding coloured gravel and plants, adding ceramic figures, and placing a nice background behind the glass, I made the tank attractive. Next I needed to test the water and keep the tank water at the right temperature. Adding a variety of fish with beautiful colors also helped. When everything was set up, I had fun. The aquarium can provide a centre of enjoyment.

EXERCISE 7

1. He wanted to ride his ~~bike she~~ wanted to walk. *(bike. She)*

3. I feel sorry for ~~Claude he~~ had his tonsils out. *(Scott. He)*

5. Michelle sang in the talent ~~show she~~ danced, also. *(show. She)*

7. My cat had ~~kittens we~~ had to find homes for them. *(kittens. We)*

9. Sam came ~~over we~~ played football. *(over. We)*

EXERCISE 8

Answers will vary.

1. Let's applaud ~~him he~~ is a jolly good fellow. *(him, for he)*

3. The men placed third ~~overall the~~ women placed second overall. *(overall, and the)*

5. A frost came in ~~May many~~ flowers didn't blossom. *(May, so many)*

7. Jack walked to the ~~library he~~ forgot his library card.
        library, but he

9. Hank found a lost ~~kitten he~~ wanted to keep it.
        kitten, and he

EXERCISE 9

1. Airplanes are convenient for long-distance ~~travel much~~ time can be saved.
        travel; much

3. Football players have employment ~~benefits their~~ jobs can be very exciting, too.
        benefits; their

5. I got plenty of sleep on the ~~weekend it~~ was nice.
        weekend; it

7. I bought a new ~~computer now~~ I need a printer.
        computer; now

9. The bus arrived on ~~time I~~ was waiting to get on.
        time; I

EXERCISE 10

Answers will vary.

1. Eating well can help keep the body ~~healthy exercising~~ can also help keep the body healthy.
        healthy; moreover, exercising

3. The road was ~~winding it~~ was several lanes wide.
        winding; nevertheless, it

5. Owning a new car can be ~~exciting driving~~ a new car can be expensive.
        exciting; however, driving

7. Keeping rivers clean should be ~~a priority children~~ can get involved.
        a priority; in fact, children

9. Working is good for ~~teenagers they~~ learn responsibility.
        teenagers; in fact, they

EXERCISE 11

Answers will vary.

1. I need to go on a ~~vacation I~~ am tired.
        vacation because I

3. I will be there on ~~time I~~ have a lot of work to do.
        time because I

5. The bananas turned ~~black we~~ had put them in the refrigerator.
        black because we

7. The occupational therapist put in long ~~hours he~~ **hours until he** had seen everyone.

9. Playing chess can improve a person's ~~mind most~~ **mind since most** moves are based on strategy.

EXERCISE 12

Answers will vary.

1. The young lady was hungry after ~~work, she~~ **work. She** stopped at the grocery store.

3. Fishing, kayaking, and rafting require ~~skill, these~~ **skill, yet these** activities can be exciting.

5. Teenagers need a lot of ~~sleep, they~~ **sleep; in addition, they** especially enjoy sleeping in the mornings.

7. Inside the registration building, students made out their schedules for next ~~year, they~~ **year. They** checked the computers to see which classes were open.

9. When we arrived at the beach, we headed for the ~~water, then~~ **water, and then** we took off our shoes and waded in the surf.

11. Harry read the three articles about drug abuse in the ~~newspaper, he~~ **newspaper. He then** took notes for his history paper, yet he had more work to do.

EXERCISE 13

Paragraph 1

Because pizza is so versatile**, it** ~~. it~~ is no wonder that it is one of Canada's favourite foods. Pizza is available frozen at the grocery store or piping hot from a variety of pizza restaurants. It can be bought with thin crust **,** or thick crust, ~~it can be~~ **or** sandwiched between two crusts. Plain pizza crust can be bought frozen **,** ~~or~~ already baked in packages much like bread, or mixed at home. Almost every person's individual taste can be satisfied because of the variety of toppings**,** ~~Toppings~~ spread on the sauce. Pepperoni leads the list of favourites, but jalapeño, anchovies, olives, and sausages are some of the other options, ~~even~~ **Even** sausage comes in different types. For a real "like-home" Italian taste**, the** ~~. The~~ pizza can be topped with garlic bits and a little Parmesan cheese without the sauce. Since pizza can be so varied, almost everyone can be satisfied.

Paragraph 3

Being able to save money is a valuable skill for teenagers to have. If they learn to save money from their jobs. ~~They~~ *, they* may be able to purchase expensive items like stereos, recorders, or cars. ~~Which~~ *, which* their parents cannot afford. Saving money also gives them a big boost*/* *so* they are able to go to college later to prepare for a careèr. Their parents may not be able to pay for their college tuition, books, and spending money while they are in college. Without saving money, the teenagers might have to spend the rest of their lives flipping hamburgers*/* ~~Flipping hamburgers~~ at minimum wage. Having saved for attending college would show maturity *. Young* ~~young~~ people would have learned the valuable skill of putting aside money for something important for their future life

UNIT 5/Part 1

EXERCISE 1

Answers will vary.

EXERCISE 2

Answers will vary.

EXERCISE 3

Paragraph 1

<u>When a child first learns to read, short-term rewards can often be more important than the actual ability to read. My child was an example of this theory.</u> He wanted to be a good reader, but when he realized he needed to work hard and practise, he wasn't sure reading was as important as watching "Mr. Wizard's World" to obtain his knowledge about the scientific world. However, he was willing to sit down and plan a strategy. Because he also wanted to set up an aquarium that had been unused for many years, together we decided that for every fifty pages he read aloud to me, he could either buy a fish or have two dollars of in-store credit. ~~He had two other pets.~~ With this agreed upon, he assembled the aquarium, filled it with water, and went to the fish store. As soon as we got home and he walked through the door, he said, "Let's read." And read we did. Even though the first book was below his grade level, it took him four days to finish fifty pages. However, it only took twenty minutes to get the

first inhabitant for his tank. That one fish looked lonely, and the only solution was to read another fifty pages. Soon he had earned another fish and another fish. ~~The fish cost me anywhere from eighty-nine cents to two dollars.~~ Moving up to grade-level books brought a little resistance because there were NO pictures. But soon these books, too, seemed easier and easier until he was able to select books way above grade level. Now he was enjoying reading for the sake of reading, and he began to read extra books on his own. ~~Of all the books he read, he enjoyed the one about a kid who ended up with jars and jars of goldfish with no place to put them.~~ As he earned fish, he began to love reading for the sake of knowledge, but he had seldom found reading a chore because every page had brought him closer to a new fish.

EXERCISE 4

Answers will vary.

EXERCISE 5

Paragraph 1

Early Canadians had to rely on their own ingenuity to make life comfortable or even to survive. They turned survival skills into a type of art that was passed down from generation to generation. Some of these art forms, which may no longer be practical in today's society, were a part of living for our great-grandparents. In the West, sturdy houses could be made from brick, but first that brick had to be made from mud and straw. Making clothes was also an art of the past that few people could accomplish today. Even buying material for clothes was a luxury few knew. The process of making a new dress or shirt or pants involved shearing sheep, carding wool, spinning yarn, and weaving cloth. Sometimes, the clothing maker dyed the yarn different colors, using natural materials like walnut shells. ~~The women enjoyed growing flowers to make the home look more attractive.~~ Tatting—making lace by hand—became an art form that was used to decorate collars or to bring beauty to something as necessary as pillowcases. ~~People loved to get together in the evenings and have dances.~~ Since there were no refrigerators, families found making beef jerky was a way of preserving meat that provided a year-round supply. And if they wanted to take a bath, they needed soap, but making soap at home, an art almost unheard of today, was required before that bath could take place. When the supply of candles, the source of night light, became low, there was one solution—making more from melted lard. ~~Sometimes the men and women would work from sunup to sundown so they could take a day off for celebration.~~ Today, we talk of "the good old days" when life was simple, but maybe we should say when families were resourceful and used art in order to survive.

EXERCISE 6

Paragraph 1

Today in Canada, medical researchers are realizing the many ways pets are helping physically challenged adults. These pets are an extension of these adults, as they perform tasks that are often impossible for the challenged adult to do alone. Seeing Eye dogs are being used to guide visually challenged people so these individuals can experience the freedom their blindness has taken from them. Trained monkeys are being used to perform simple manual tasks like turning light switches on and off or holding the telephone receiver for adults with limited or no use of their hands and arms. Parrots are being used to bring companionship to challenged adults who are confined to their homes. The parrot and master can sing songs together and can even talk to one another. ~~Cats are also being used for companionship so the challenged adult doesn't feel so lonely.~~ All of these pets and their owners become great friends as they lean on each other for support.

EXERCISE 7

Paragraph 1 SIE

Paragraph 3 SIE

EXERCISE 8

Answers will vary.

UNIT 5/Part 4

EXERCISE 1

Answers will vary.

             nurse, for she
1. Rose is an outstanding ~~nurse. She~~ anticipates patients' problems.

         food, nor did I
3. I did not enjoy the ~~food. I did~~ not care for the entertainment either.

        kilometres, and we
5. We jogged 10 ~~kilometres. We~~ swam 3 kilometres.

EXERCISE 2

Answers may vary.

       college; in addition, he
1. Danny graduated from ~~college. He~~ got a job working for Motorola.

      charity; nevertheless, the
3. Many people give to ~~charity. The~~ food bank needs more canned goods.

      book; otherwise, she
5. Chris read the entire ~~book. She~~ would not have known the answers.

EXERCISE 3

   laughed; we cried; we
1. We ~~laughed. We cried. We~~ shared memories.

3. We dug for ~~worms. Then~~ we set out for fun.

   worms; then (above "worms. Then")

5. The dog barked ~~loudly. Soon~~ it stopped.
   loudly; soon (above "loudly. Soon")

EXERCISE 4

Other conjunctions may be selected.

1. <u>Pete does excellent carpentry work, so he receives many jobs.</u>
   (coordinate conjunction)

   <u>Pete does excellent carpentry work; he receives many jobs.</u>
   (semicolon)

   <u>Pete does excellent carpentry work; therefore, he receives many jobs.</u>
   (conjunctive adverb)

3. <u>Brenda is an excellent administrative assistant, and she works well with people.</u>
   (coordinate conjunction)

   <u>Brenda is an excellent administrative assistant; she works well with people.</u>
   (semicolon)

   <u>Brenda is an excellent administrative assistant; in addition, she works well with people.</u>
   (conjunctive adverb)

5. <u>The child got out the peanut butter and jelly, and he made a sandwich.</u>
   (coordinate conjunction)

   <u>The child got out the peanut butter and jelly; he made a sandwich.</u>
   (semicolon)

   <u>The child got out the peanut butter and jelly; thus, he made a sandwich.</u>
   (conjunctive adverb)

7. <u>The man was working hard all morning, yet he went swimming.</u>
   (coordinate conjunction)

   <u>The man was working hard all morning; he went swimming.</u>
   (semicolon)

   <u>The man was working hard all morning; nevertheless, he went swimming.</u>
   (conjunctive adverb)

9. <u>They live near the ocean, and they spend many hours sailing.</u>
   (coordinate conjunction)

   <u>They live near the ocean; they spend many hours sailing.</u>
   (semicolon)

   <u>They live near the ocean; as a result, they spend many hours sailing.</u>
   (conjunctive adverb)

EXERCISE 5

Answers will vary.

Paragraph 1

less; nevertheless, they
Canadian people do not want to eat ~~less. They~~ want to consume fewer calo-
this, and they
ries. Food companies know ~~this. They~~ are coming out with reduced- or low-calo-

rie food products. Powdered "butter" substitutions boast of having the same

calories; furthermore, ice
taste as real butter with a fraction of the ~~calories.~~ Ice cream is appearing in

"light" form ~~also~~. Producers use fat substitutes and sugar substitutes that add

up to fewer calories but have "the same great taste" for the consumer. Even

potato chips come with the "light" option. Not only single items but many

prepackaged microwave meals specialize in meals with under three hundred

calories, and the
~~calories. The~~ meal can be topped off with a variety of pastries with "less than

half the calories of other baked goods." Food producers keep churning out new

alternatives, so consumers
~~alternatives. Consumers~~ keep "eating them up."

Paragraph 3

Today more than ever, people are realizing the need to conserve our

effective, but every
resources, especially water. This effort can be ~~effective. Every~~ Canadian must be

adjustments, for these
willing to make ~~adjustments. These~~ adjustments will save this essential resource.

Anne is one person who has done her part to help in this effort. Inside her

dishwasher, and then
house, she always fills her ~~dishwasher. Then~~ she runs it. She always washes a full

tank; as a result, each
load of clothes. She has also placed a water saver in her toilet ~~tank. Each~~ flush

takes less water. She never leaves the water running while she brushes her

wet,
teeth. Outside, she has installed a drip water system to keep her plants ~~wet. This~~

so
~~way~~ she does not lose water to evaporation. She has also landscaped her yard

water; moreover, she
with plants that require little ~~water. She~~ never uses the hose to wash off the

sidewalk or driveway. If every Canadian will try to follow this example, millions

of litres of water will be saved every day.

UNIT 6/ Part 1

EXERCISES 1–7

Answers will vary.

EXERCISE 8

Paragraph 1

After seventeen years of marriage, I had given up. I felt my marriage was hopeless and irreparable. I had my husband move out for six months until I decided on whether I wanted to try again. However, instead of giving up we worked on our communication skills, our built-up anger, and our spirituality. I realized what was going to be lost through a divorce and agreed to try again. I now believe I have a great marriage, yet statistics show that I am the exception. Happy marriages, though, should not be the exception; they should be the norm. After this personal experience, I realized that more Canadian couples should seek counselling when problems arise, not give up so easily, and spend time alone together.

Paragraph 3

"Reading is to the mind, what exercise is to the body," Sir Richard Steele wisely stated. Steele's quotation draws an analogy between the importance of exercise to tone the body and reading to stimulate the mind. If people do not exercise, they become fat, sluggish,unhealthy, and weak, and this condition is readily visible. When people do not exercise their minds, they become mentally unhealthy and weak, yet this situation is even more dangerous because it is not noticeable. This theory is especially true for children in their formative years when habits are developing. Reading can make the difference between a strong or weak mind. Reading improves children's vocabulary, expands their understanding, and increases their creativity.

EXERCISES 9–11

Answers will vary.

UNIT 6/Part 4

EXERCISE 1

Answers will vary.

                                                    after we
1. Henry came over to the house to repair the front door. ~~We~~ called him yesterday.

                                                    as soon as their
3. The students will go to the library to do some research. ~~Their~~ classes are over for the day.

5. You will not have difficulty making a good grade on the test. ~~You~~ *if you* study very hard and work with a tutor.

EXERCISE 2

Answers will vary.

1. The book <u>that my brother borrowed yesterday is my favourite novel</u>.

3. Kana learned to cook the chocolate cake <u>that his dad liked</u>.

5. The tools for the job were listed in the memo <u>that the supervisor sent yesterday</u>.

EXERCISE 3

Answers will vary.

1. <u>Why that tree will not grow is puzzling to me</u>.

3. <u>How the young couple can get more income</u> is a major problem.

5. <u>Who will be elected</u> is up to the voters.

EXERCISE 4

Answers will vary.

1. We know <u>how the issue was decided</u>.

3. We know <u>that the difficulties can be overcome by hard work</u>.

5. The artist realized <u>that her painting lacked the right colours in the sky</u>.

EXERCISE 5

Paragraph 1

Bodybuilding is a sport that demands discipline. ~~Bodybuilders push~~ *Bodybuilders who push* themselves until their muscles won't work any more. ~~They~~ build muscle mass. Serious athletes must work out at the gym five to seven hours a ~~day. They~~ *day until they* feel a burning sensation in their muscles. ~~The~~ *If the* muscles are sore the next ~~morning. They~~ *morning, they* know they have had a good workout. Athletes must also have the willpower to adhere to a strict ~~diet. They~~ *diet in which they* eat no fatty foods, especially hamburgers and french fries. ~~They~~ *When they* need to cut ~~fat. They~~ *fat, they* must stay on an even stricter diet than normal. They also must get plenty of sleep. ~~They~~ *When they* are at a party with their friends and everyone else wants to stay ~~late. Dedicated~~ *late, dedicated* athletes will have enough control to go home early. This dedication, however, will result in a body they can take pride in.

Paragraph 3

Maintaining a healthy beehive takes careful planning by a beekeeper. He
must set up a hive with wax ~~racks. The~~ *racks where the* bees can store their honey, pollen, and
eggs. ~~It~~ *When it* is time to "rob the ~~hive." He~~ *hive," he* must be sure to leave enough honey to
feed the bees during the long winter months. ~~Sometimes there~~ *Sometimes if there* is insufficient
honey or a severe ~~winter. He~~ *winter, he* must provide a sweet nectar for the bees. In the

springtime, he must check the inside of the hive for more than one queen ~~bee.~~
~~In this way, he~~ *bee so that he* does not lose a swarm of bees to a young queen. ~~Sometimes~~ *If* the
bees do ~~swarm. He~~ *swarm, he* must either destroy the queen or have a new, well-equipped
hive ready for them to occupy. ~~He~~ *If he* manages the hive ~~well. He~~ *well, he* should have a year-

round supply of honey.

UNIT 7/Part 1

EXERCISE 1

Answers will vary.

Paragraph 1

A small lakeside park can be a haven for children. ~~Swings~~ *The park swings* are big and sturdy
so children can swing, seemingly to the tops of trees. ~~Ducks~~ *Children love to feed the ducks that* swim close to the
shore to eat whatever the small visitors bring. ~~Older~~ *At the same time, older* children canoe through rippling ~~water. Others~~ *water while others* stand or ~~sit at~~ *sit safely at* the edges at of the lake and throw out fishing lines complete with worms. The ~~children wait~~ *children are content to wait* for some hungry fish to bite
the hook. ~~Parents of the children relax or nap~~ *They feel comfortable knowing their parents are relaxing or napping* under the shade of nearby trees.

Here the world feels safe as children watch other families enjoying the park.

Paragraph 3

Making a quilt takes some planning. The most important part of making a
quilt is selecting a design for the quilt. ~~It is~~ *After choosing the design, it is also* important to buy materials that look
nice together. ~~Adding~~ *In addition, adding* some materials with different textures makes the quilt
more appealing. A place to work that has lots of room ~~helps when~~ *helps make the work more pleasant when* putting the
quilt pieces together. Planning a quilting pattern that looks good ~~helps. A~~ *helps, too, just as a* tight

Moreover, setting
quilting frame makes the job easier. ~~Setting~~ up the frame close to other family

When all phases of the project are planned carefully, a
members or near the television set makes the quilting seem less boring. ~~A~~ beau-

tiful quilt can be created.

EXERCISE 2

Answers will vary.

EXERCISE 3

Answers will vary.

Essay 1

During my morning jog, I stopped and talked to a man who was carefully

tending his garden. When I expressed interest in the luscious garden, he replied,

"I got over five buckets of strawberries alone this summer." I was taken by sur-

prise because the strawberry patch was somewhat small. His green-bean vines

that were growing along the fence were loaded with long, healthy beans, and

I could only wonder how many of those he had harvested. Seeing his garden

made me think of all the benefits that gardening can bring to anyone who is

willing to put in the time and effort. Though having a small garden can be hard

work, it can result in pleasure and savings.

garden, however, do   *First, the gardener*
The benefits of a ~~garden do~~ not come without work. ~~S/he~~ must select a loca-
After the plot of ground is selected, it   *Next, sawdust,*
tion for the garden. ~~It~~ needs to be dug out and loosened. ~~Sawdust,~~ peat, and

Just as important, growing
fertilizer mixed and added will allow the seeds to grow easily. ~~Growing~~ instruc-
Finally, the
tions need to be followed when the seeds are planted. ~~The~~ garden must be
sometimes can be difficult but is
watered, weeded, and debugged daily. Watering at the correct time of day ~~is~~
minimum is hard work but makes
necessary. Keeping weeds to a ~~minimum makes~~ the garden vegetables stronger.

A good gardener prepares a good place and watches the plants as if they were

helpless, defenceless creatures.

With a little dirt, water, and sunshine, a
~~A~~ garden can bring many pleasures. The sight of small sprigs reaching up

through the soil toward the sun gives the feeling of capturing a small part of

nature and getting in touch with the earth. What greater satisfaction is there

for the gardener than to know that she or he has used the elements to produce

Usually, more

food? ~~More~~ than enough is produced, and the gardener can proudly share the crisp flavour of fresh produce with a neighbour. In view of the much-publicized insecticides on commercial produce, the gardener can use natural combatants such as ladybugs or praying mantis, or ingenuity, to preserve the vegetables and feel comfortable knowing the products from the garden are healthy. A garden can be the source not only of food and pride, but also of peace of mind.

After the initial work is done, having

~~Having~~ a small garden to bring in fresh vegetables provides a savings. Each year grocery prices slowly creep up unnoticeably on such items as lettuce and

For example, tomatoes   *kilogram, now cost*   *Likewise, lettuce*

tomatoes. ~~Tomatoes~~ that last year cost $2.50 a ~~kilogram cost~~ $3.00. ~~Lettuce~~ is

These gradual price increases make

sold at 99¢ a head, instead of 69¢. ~~The gradual price increase makes~~ one won-

The savings are easy to see because a

der if the consumer will ever see the end. ~~A~~ pack of tomato or lettuce seeds costs about 70¢ total, and these seeds can provide enough tomatoes and lettuce

Moreover, extra

for an entire summer. ~~Extra~~ vegetables can be frozen or canned to provide a

Additional savings occur when vegetables

year-round supply of fresh food. ~~Surplus vegetables~~ can be sold to bring in extra

The gardener also saves money by trading   *gardeners to prevent*

money. ~~Trading~~ produce with other ~~gardeners prevents~~ buying so much at the grocery store. Gardens can add much-needed pocket change and give the feeling of defeating the inflationary war.

Work, time, and patience

~~One~~ can transform a tiny seed into baskets of delicious, healthy food. By gardening, a person can experience a miracle of nature and can save money at the same time. The only way to find out is to try.

UNIT 7/Part4

EXERCISE 1

1. None

3. None

5. Richard fed the dog in the back yard, the horse in the south field, and the cat by the barn.

EXERCISE 2

Paragraph 1

Grandparents, aunts, uncles, and cousins gathered for the annual picnic at the park. Together they ate the attractive and well-prepared food that smelled delicious, tasted great, and satisfied everyone. Then the older children took turns playing volleyball, tennis, and tetherball. Some of the grandparents spread blankets on the green grass for the little ones to take their bottles, to nap, or just to rest. Sometimes the adults, too, fell asleep. Later, they took turns riding on the park's train, looking through the model-train exhibits, and reading about the history of trains. Soon, however, everyone returned to the picnic tables to munch on leftovers and talk about last year's picnic.

EXERCISE 3

1. When Bob finished landscaping his yard, he needed a vacation.

3. Absentmindedly, the lab technician shelved the glass bottles.

5. None

EXERCISE 4

Paragraph 1

According to Luigi Ciulla, the biggest challenge he faced when he came to Canada in 1961 was to find a job. Because he had trouble filling out an application, people would say, "I'm sorry. We don't have a job for you. When you learn to speak English, then we can hire you." Just to work on an assembly line, employees had to pass required IQ tests. Because the tests were in English and because they were timed, it was almost impossible for a person who spoke very little English to pass them. Luigi said that even though some words are learned by studying books, some words just cannot be learned without living in a country. He also said that he didn't know anyone, so it was hard to find people to use as references on application forms. Because he had never worked in this country, he had no references from previous employers either. One other obstacle in finding a job was lack of any "connections." There was no one who could help him get a "foot in the door." He also had to face the reality that many jobs were far away and transportation to these jobs was hard. He said, "Even if I knew how to drive, it was hard to pass the written test for a driver's licence." That was thirty-three years ago, and today he is hiring people to work for him in his own business.

EXERCISE 5

1. The candy, for instance, that the children ate made them sick.

3. My brother Jim, as a matter of fact, lives in Banff during the winter months.

5. We should, nevertheless, get everything in top order.

7. The book had 175 pages, many filled with beautiful photographs.

EXERCISE 6

Paragraph 1

The trend of the eighties to rely heavily on "disposables" has created a throwaway society. Everywhere we look, trash that has to be disposed of is piling up. People litter the countryside with plastic, aluminum cans, and glass bottles. At home, disposable plates, cups, plasticware, and, of course, diapers are filling the plastic bags that must be transported to the local landfill. At hospitals, paper gowns, disposable thermometers, towels used in surgery, and miles of plastic tubing cannot be resterilized and reused and, as a result, are being sent to special landfills for medical wastes. Though it takes many years for the paper products to break down in the landfills, scientists predict that the plastics will take several hundred years to break down. Styrofoam, especially, could take an inordinately long time to degrade. These nonbiodegradable plastics are petroleum-based and keep us importing oil to make them. Making aluminum cans, likewise, uses up our natural resources. Not only does it use up natural resources to make new plastic products, aluminum cans, and bottles, but it takes energy to manufacture these products. Reusing aluminum cans and glass bottles saves resources and energy. Recycling helps cities and towns that are filling up their landfills and running out of room to construct more. Fortunately, we, as environmentalists, are trying to make an effort to reverse the trend and use products more than once before throwing them away.

EXERCISE 7

1. Address the card to 644 Pinewood Road, North Bay, Ontario P1B 4N6.

3. Why, Katsura, did you leave him behind?

5. An ice storm on December 11, 1992, was responsible for hundreds of accidents.

7. None

EXERCISE 8

Paragraph 1

On September 1, 1939, Germany invaded Poland and started World War II. Beginning in 1940, Hitler invaded Belgium, Luxembourg, Denmark, Norway, and France. On April 9, 1940, the Germans seized Denmark and invaded Norway. Just one month later, on May 10, 1940, Germany invaded Belgium. Just a few days later, on May 14, 1940, the Netherlands surrendered. Because England had treaties with France, she made good her commitment, and on September 3, 1940, Great Britain and France declared war on Germany. On May 26, 1940, the Allied Powers began their heroic evacuation at Dunkirk, a seaport in northern France. By 1940, the entire European continent was at war. Then, on June 22, 1941, Germany invaded the Soviet Union. On December 7, 1941, Japan attacked Pearl Harbor, bringing the United States into the war. By now, almost all countries in the world were involved in this devastating war.

EXERCISE 9

1. "I hope to go to the lake," Rene said.

3. (No punctuation is needed.)

5. The poem "The Horses" is in the book *To Read Literature* by Donald Hall.

7. "Close the window, Kim," Chuck said, "or Joe's camping gear will get wet."

EXERCISE 10

Paragraph 1

Surgeons who operate on patients who are not put to sleep sometimes say things that can upset their patients. They forget that the patients are already anxious about having surgery. When Dr. Madox operated on a patient, he tuned in some fast music and jokingly commented, "There, that's good. It helps me cut faster." When he started sewing up the incision before getting the lab results, the patient asked if he had gotten all of the cancer. He replied, "I hope so." Later on, when he was putting in the sutures, he stated, "Oh, no, the nurse is going to be upset with me when she takes this stitch out. I snipped the ends too close." He then headed for the door and said, "I'll see you later." The patient asked him if he was coming back, and he just bounced on out the door. Fortunately, one of the nurses told the patient that the doctor was going to the lab to get the results. Though the surgery was over, the patient's return visit to the doctor's office to have the stitches removed was dreaded.

EXERCISE 11

Paragraph 1

Summertime offers many opportunities for children of all ages with extra time on their hands. Kids can spend their days at the Boys' or Girls' Club where they can swim, play supervised sports, and even go on field trips. If there is no Boys' Club or Girls' Club, for a small fee, they can swim in public pools. There they can join swim teams, take swim lessons, or just swim for pleasure. Often libraries that are equipped with reading programs are close by. There children can attend story time to hear such storybooks as <u>Bears on Wheels</u> or <u>The Honey Hunt</u>, check out videotapes or books, or leisurely look through magazines. In the evenings, these same children can play little league baseball or watch other children play ball. If they want to earn extra money, they can collect aluminum cans, glass, plastic, or paper to recycle. Also, a great potential exists for a lawn service that can bring in money for school. Older children can also earn extra money babysitting or working for the city supervising younger children in recreational programs. Opportunities abound for kids everywhere; therefore, all they need to do is look around.

APPENDIX A

EXERCISE 1

Pair 1

1. C

2. Take the lifeguard's ~~advise~~ *advice* and don't swim while it is raining.

3. I ~~adviced~~ *advised* her to do her house chores early.

4. Margaret refused to take my ~~advise~~ *advice*.

Pair 2

1. Are you ~~already~~? *all ready*

2. She is ~~all ready~~ at the soccer game. *already*

3. C

4. I was not at ~~already~~ for the English exam. *all ready*

Pair 3

1. C

2. Everyone went to the ball ~~accept~~ Cinderella. *except*

3. C

4. When Natalie arrived in class, everyone was present ~~accept~~ Maria. *except*

Pair 4

1. The bus driver slammed on the ~~break~~, and the passengers flew forward. *brake*

2. C

3. When the car in front of us stopped, I hit the ~~break~~ with my foot. *brake*

4. The karate expert will ~~brake~~ twenty boards in twenty-five seconds. *break*

Pair 5

1. Mrs. Smith needed to ~~by~~ detergent for her washing machine. *buy*

2. C

3. C

4. C

Pair 6

1. C

2. My ~~conscious~~ forced me to return the lost wallet. *conscience*

3. C

4. My grandmother is always ~~conscience~~ of my birthday. *conscious*

Pair 7

                  hear
1. Didn't you ~~here~~ the car honking?

2. C

                                   hear
3. From our kitchen, we could ~~here~~ birds singing.

4. C

Pair 8

                            hole
1. Be careful; I think there's a ~~whole~~ around here.

      whole
2. The ~~hole~~ house was a mess.

                           whole
3. Tall yellow weeds covered the ~~hole~~ field.

                                    holes
4. The yard was filled with small groundhog ~~wholes~~.

Pair 9

        know
1. Don't you ~~no~~ not to stick a fork into the toaster?

    No
2. ~~Know,~~ you cannot play on the computer.

3. C

4. C

Pair 10

1. C

                                             new
2. Mary was disappointed because she ripped her ~~knew~~ red dress.

3. C

4. C

Pair 11

                 passed
1. My teammate ~~past~~ the ball to me, and I made a touchdown.

                          past
2. Susie was dreaming about her ~~passed~~ when she was awakened.

3. C

4. C

Pair 12

1. Pass Julio a ~~peace~~ *piece* of cherry pie.

2. The Protestants made ~~piece~~ *peace* with the Catholics in Ireland.

3. Roger lost a ~~peace~~ *piece* of my science project, but I passed anyway.

4. The ~~piece~~ *peace* symbol was part of the sixties generation.

Pair 13

1. Our ~~principle~~ *principal*, Ms. Jones, is a sensitive woman.

2. C

3. I called her and explained the new club's ~~principals~~ *principles*.

4. C

Pair 14

1. Mom didn't want to ~~loose~~ *lose* Amy in the crowd, so she held her hand tightly.

2. The fashion today is ~~lose~~ *loose* clothing.

3. C

4. Louise lost the ~~lose~~ *loose* ring Friday.

Pair 15

1. Beatrice started to ~~right~~ *write* her essay but was interrupted by another phone call.

2. Henry turned ~~write~~ *right* into a small bush.

3. C

4. C

Pair 16

1. Laura is ~~quiet~~ *quite* a pretty girl.

2. Grand Lake is always calm and ~~quite~~ *quiet*.

3. The ex-champions were ~~quiet~~ *quite* surprised that they came in second in the gymnastics events.

4. After the children are put to bed, the Wagners' house is ~~quite~~ *quiet*.

Pair 17

1. They left ~~there~~ *their* book in their car.

2. C

3. C

4. Sam said ~~their~~ *they're* going to ~~there~~ *their* favourite spot.

Pair 18

1. C

2. The ~~though~~ *thought* of cooking another meal depressed the cook.

3. C

4. C

Pair 19

1. Sarah climbed ~~threw~~ *through* the tunnel and ran for the slide.

2. The muscular football player ~~through~~ *threw* a bullet pass to the receiver.

3. Ann ran ~~threw~~ *through* the woods, jumping over logs and stones.

4. Janice accidentally poked the sharp pencil ~~threw~~ *through* the soft Styrofoam.

Pair 20

1. The final score was three to ~~too~~ *two*.

2. The Fishers love ~~too~~ *to* swim at night in the summer.

3. Nicki finished her paper, ~~to~~ *too*.

4. ~~Two~~ *Two* many people were at the party in the small house.

Pair 21

weather
1. The ~~whether~~ is great in Halifax in the summer.

2. C

3. C

whether
4. Tom was sorry ~~weather~~ he could admit it or not.

Pair 22

Where
1. ~~Were~~ were you when I needed help?

were
2. Fifteen of the students ~~where~~ going on a hike.

where
3. Tanya went ~~were~~ the other students were playing volleyball.

4. C

Pair 23

women
1. The three ~~woman~~ went through nurse's training together.

woman
2. The ~~women~~ Jason married was his childhood sweetheart.

3. C

women
4. Of all the ~~woman~~ he dated, that woman stole his heart.

EXERCISE 2

their
1. The high school band members left ~~they're~~ instruments out in the rain.

2. C

there
3. Look over ~~their~~ at the water skier!

You're
4. ~~Your~~ not feeling well, are you?

They're
5. ~~There~~ over there at the Etobicoke Community Centre.

its
6. The cat loves ~~it's~~ new food.

They're
7. ~~There~~ not in the left-side drawer.

8. C

9. C

10. C

11. Look at ~~there~~ their beautiful dog.

12. ~~It's~~ Its water bowl is empty.

13. ~~They're~~ Their house is always spotless.

14. I'm sorry, Michelle, ~~your~~ you're not going to be able to go swimming today.

15. C

Copyright Acknowledgments

Index